HISTORICAL ATLAS OF CALIFORNIA

HISTORICAL ATLAS OF CALIFORNIA

HISTORICAL ATLAS OF CALIFORNIA

by
Warren A. Beck
and
Ynez D. Haase

UNIVERSITY OF OKLAHOMA PRESS · NORMAN

By Warren A. Beck and Ynez D. Haase

Historical Atlas of New Mexico (Norman, 1969)
Historical Atlas of California (Norman, 1974)

Library of Congress Cataloging in Publication Data

Beck, Warren A.
    Historical atlas of California.

    Includes bibliographical references.
    1. California—Historical geography—Maps.
2. California—History. I. Haase, Ynez D., joint
author. II. Title.
G1526.S1B4 1974   911'.794   74–5952
ISBN 0–8061–1211–5 (cloth)
ISBN 0–8061–1212–3 (paper)

PREFACE

MANY PERSONS HAVE offered valuable advice, but in developing this *Historical Atlas of California* the authors have had to, in the end, rely on their own judgment. There are so many exciting possibilities for maps covering the history and geography of the Golden State that some had to be omitted, and we know that our final choices will not satisfy all. Some of our maps cover subjects which, although essential to our atlas, have been adequately treated elsewhere. Many, however, have never been properly researched and presented in map form before: for example, readily available sources do not include the location of the Hispanic land grants. In addition, our maps of the Spanish and Mexican expeditions, those of the great Anglo ranchos, and those of the World War II military installations are examples of the many areas in which the authors have had to do primary research and plow new ground. We hope that specialists in isolated areas of California will forgive any unintentional slighting of their interests; the authors had to produce an atlas for the student, the scholar, and those with a general interest in California.

A book of this kind must depend on the efforts and expert knowledge of many institutions and persons. This is particularly true when the subject is relatively new and different. Foremost of those to whom we are indebted are the untold number of scholars who have labored in Clio's vineyard for years to produce the many monographs which have been utilized in the preparation of this work. Individuals to whom a special note of appreciation is due include Mr. Granville L. Rogers, Mr. Donald Duke, Mr. Leslie Walker, Professor George P. Hammond, Professor Sherburne F. Cook, Professor John Leighly, Professor Rodney Steiner, Professor Charles A. Bell, and Professor Imre Sutton.

Libraries which have assisted the authors over the past five years of work on this book are the University of California, Santa Barbara (Map Room), California State University, Fullerton (Special Collections), University of California, Los Angeles (Special Collections), Henry E. Huntington Library, Southwest Museum, Santa Barbara Franciscan Mission Archives, Museum of Vertebrate Zoology of the University of California, Berkeley, Bancroft Library of the University of California, Berkeley, California Historical Society (Jay Williar), La Casa de Rancho Los Cerritos, Kern County Historical Society, Santa Barbara Botanical Garden Library, Wells Fargo Bank History Room, Title Insurance and Trust Company Library, and California State Library.

Public and private agencies who answered our many questions either by mail or phone include California State Division of Forestry, California Agency-Bureau of Indian Affairs, California State Land Division, California Department of Water Resources, City of Los Angeles Department of Water and Power, United States Geological Survey, United States Bureau of Land Management, United States Fish and Wildlife Service, United States National Park Service, United States Bureau of Indian Affairs, United States Forest Service-headquarters, San Francisco, Angeles National Forest, Klamath National Forest, Tahoe National Forest, San Bernardino National Forest, Cleveland National Forest, Los Padres National Forest, Stanislaus National Forest, Pacific Southwest Forest and Range Experiment Station of the United States Forest Service (Berkeley and Riverside Offices), Engineering Department, County of Monterey, Orange County Road Department, San Joaquin Valley Information Service, Western Engineers, Miller & Lux inc., Heggbade-Marguleas-Tenneco, Inc., Tejon Ranch Co., and Sunical Division, Hearst Corporation.

A special word of thanks is due to Mr. Grady Overstreet, who gave of his time to help draft some of the final plates, and to Mr. Edward H. Parker, who made valuable suggestions to improve both maps and manuscript.

WARREN A. BECK
YNEZ D. HAASE

CONTENTS

HISTORICAL ATLAS OF CALIFORNIA

A GOODLY ILANDE

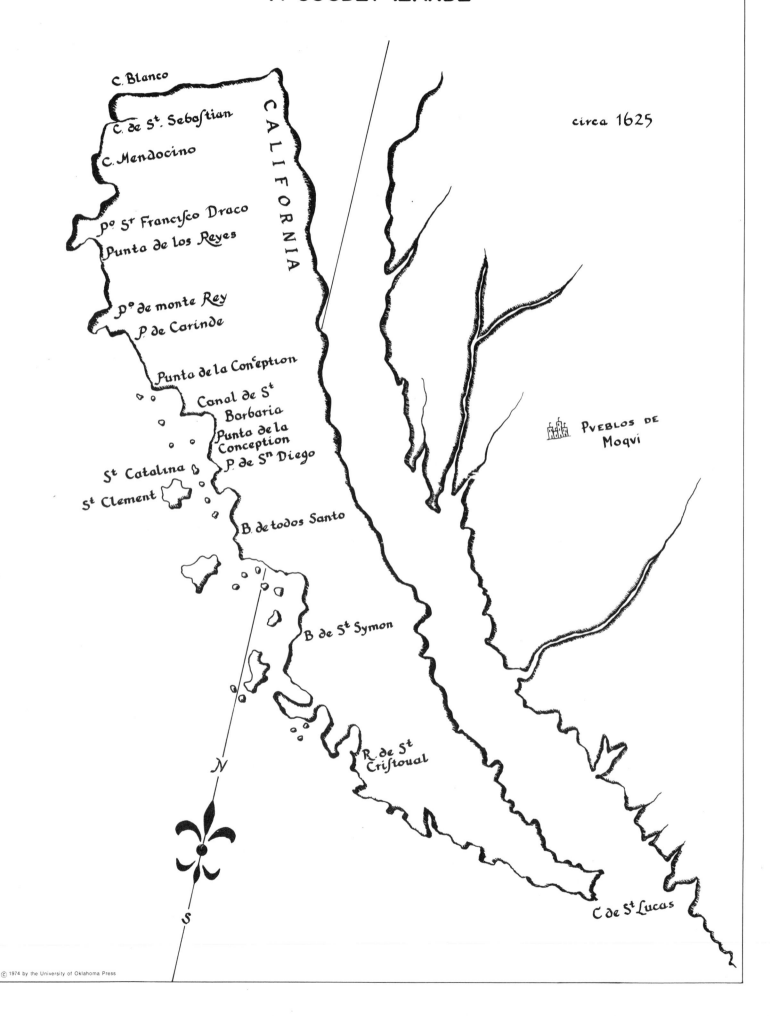

C. Blanco

C. de S^t. Sebastian

C. Mendocino

P^o. Sr Francisco Draco

Punta de los Reyes

P^o de monte Rey

P. de Carinde

Punta de la Conception

Canal de St Barbaria

Punta de la Conception

P. de S^n Diego

St Catalina

St Clement

B. de todos Santo

B de St Symon

R. de St Cristoual

C de St Lucas

CALIFORNIA

circa 1625

PVEBLOS DE MOQVI

N

S

1. A GOODLY ILANDE

THE NAME CALIFORNIA initially designated what we know today as Baja California. It was first used by Cortes in the 1530's and is found in the journal of Juan Rodríguez Cabrillo in 1542, where it was used in a manner which indicated it was a name already well known. The name, as well as the idea that there was an island called California, appeared first in a romantic novel by the Spaniard García Ordóñez de Montalvo titled *Las sergas de Esplandian* (*The Deeds of Esplandian*). The legendary land was described in the words, "Know ye that on the right hand of the Indies there is an island called California, . . . very close to the Terrestrial Paradise." The expedition of Francisco de Ulloa in 1539–40 proved that Baja California was a peninsula and not an island. However, myth was more powerful than fact, and the belief that California was an island lived on until a Jesuit mission leader and explorer, Friar Eusebio Kino, near the end of the seventeenth century again established proof that California was not an island.

This Dutch map copied from the fruit of Spanish explorations portrays the concept of California in many European minds. It also depicts the state of geographical knowledge in that era. Alta California (the name used by the Spanish to designate the present state of California) and the peninsula of Baja California are joined to form the mythical island: Spaniards often used the designation "the Californias" to refer to both areas. The map also indicated the belief that the Indian pueblos of Arizona were only a short distance from California, despite the Coronado expedition proving that they were far removed.

The remote location of California helped perpetuate many of the legends which circulated. For the Golden State was on the periphery of Spain's colonial empire, with the Pacific Ocean being any-thing but peaceful for the ships of that day. Just to reach Alta California from ports such as San Blas in New Spain took as much as three months, with scurvy taking a frightful toll of the crew. The land approach was even more formidable, for many miles of desert wasteland had to be traversed en route to California. It is little wonder that it was 250 years from the initial discovery before the area was settled! But even after colonization began, the land was so difficult to reach that few Spaniards were tempted to migrate there.

Despite the isolation of California (or because of it) it was truly "a goodly islande" in the minds of many. For one of the most persistent themes of the Judaeo-Christian heritage of the Western World was the existence of an earthly paradise such as the one described by the Spanish novelist. In this Utopia beautiful women, gold, silver, and pearls were abundant, and the fruits of nature were easily plucked by all. When Columbus discovered America, with its exotic flora and fauna, and gold from Mexico and Peru enriched Spain, it was assumed that the ancient prophecies were being fulfilled, and that paradise had truly been found. The quest for the seven cities of Cíbola, the legend of El Dorado where gold had been gathered for years, and even the belief of Ponce de León that there existed a fountain capable of restoring youth are all part of the European dream that America was the promised land. To many migrants who made their difficult and hazardous way to California in the nineteenth century, California was the land of abundance which man had sought for centuries. Even in the twentieth century, with all of its problems, the new arrival to California sees the land as truly "a goodly islande" and not as the figment of the Dutch map maker's imagination.

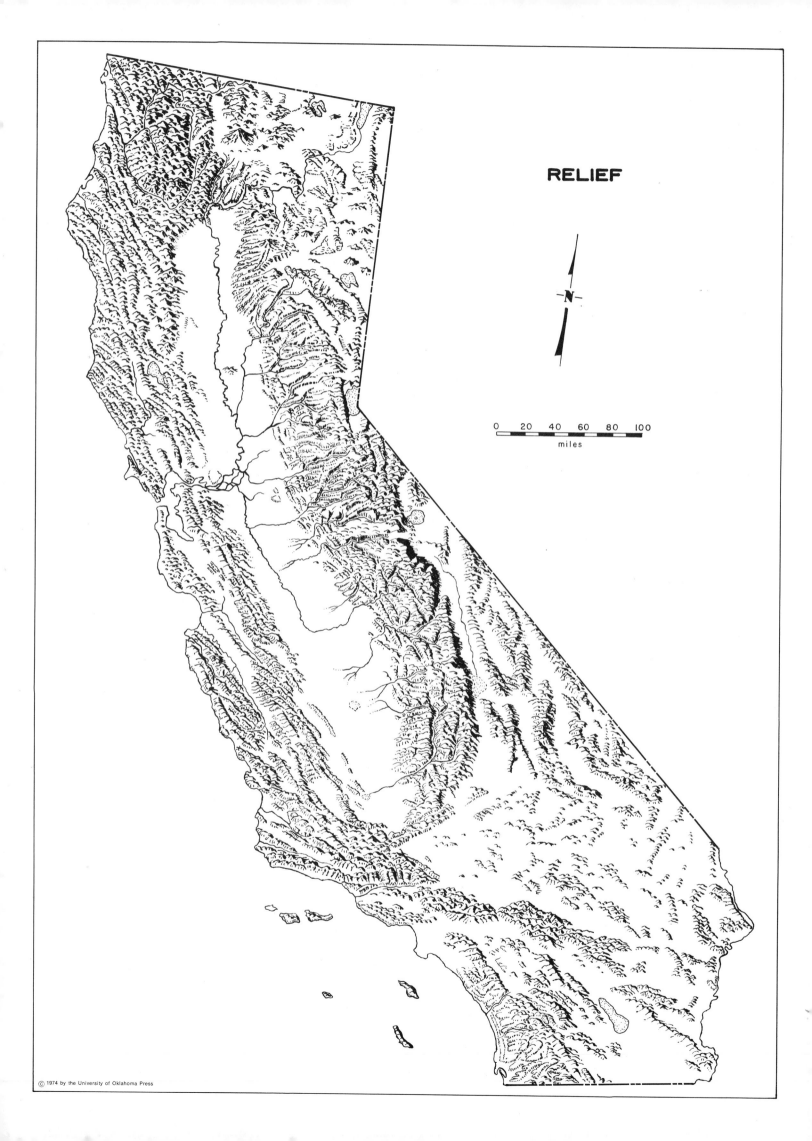

RELIEF

0 20 40 60 80 100
miles

2. RELIEF

THE MOST STRIKING characteristic of California's topography is its great diversity. The state contains 41 peaks more than 10,000 feet in height. The tallest, Mt. Whitney (14,496), is the second loftiest in the United States. Only 60 miles from Mt. Whitney lies Death Valley, 282 feet below sea level, the lowest point in the country. By taking the aerial tramway near Palm Springs, a person moves from the desert floor to above the timber line. This sharpest ascent in the nation brings in review many of the life and crop zones and accents the great variation in relief.

The general pattern of California landforms is dominated by mountains, chief of which is the Sierra Nevada. Stretching for some 400 miles along the eastern edge of the state and some 80 miles wide, it is one of the most impressive ranges in the world.

The Cascades in the northeastern corner of the state are a separate mountain range, although on relief maps they may appear to be an extension of the Sierra Nevada. Mt. Lassen (10,457), only recently an active volcano, and Mt. Shasta (14,162) dominate the area. In the extreme northeast corner of the state, the Modoc Plateau, with an average altitude of some 5,000 feet, gives way to the Warner Mountains, with peaks towering nearly a mile above the plateau.

In the northwest corner of the state are the rugged Klamath Mountains. The highest peaks are Eddy and Thompson at about 9,000 feet. The principal rivers—Klamath and Trinity—have cut deep, twisting gorges. The Coast Ranges continue southward from the Klamaths for some 600 miles. Of non-volcanic origin, they roughly parallel the coast and have a series of valleys of such rivers as the Eel, Mad, Russian, Salinas, and others, which separate ridges of 2,000 to 7,500 feet in height. At the southern end of the Central Valley the Coast Ranges curve east and northeast to connect with the Sierra Nevada. This extension, encompassing the Tehachapis, or Transverse Ranges, forms a natural boundary between the northern and southern regions of the state. Farther south the coastal lowlands are bounded by the Santa Ana and San Jacinto Ranges which extend into Mexico. The southern California ranges are marked by lofty peaks of more than 10,000 feet—San Bernardino, San Jacinto, and San Antonio.

The southeastern corner of the state is a great expanse of desert terrain interspersed with short rugged mountain ranges, large sandy valleys, and dried lake bottoms. This area is the Mojave Desert, but the extreme southern part is referred to as the Colorado Desert. Valleys such as Coachella and Imperial, when irrigated, are very productive. The region east of the Sierras is also essentially desert and includes areas such as Owens Valley and Death Valley.

The central part of the state is dominated by the Central Valley of Sacramento and San Joaquin rivers. Some 430 miles in length and 50 miles wide, it is the state's premium agricultural area. There are numerous valleys of all sizes nestling in the coastal range. Each has its distinctive climate, and, frequently, its distinctive agricultural complex. Most of these valleys are longitudinal; none extend for any distance; some open to the sea. The most important valleys are: the Napa-Livermore; the Santa Clara–Santa Rosa, which fronts on the San Francisco Bay; the Salinas; the San Luis; the Santa Maria; the Santa Ynez; and the Santa Clara of the south. The Los Angeles lowland, the largest lowland area in California which directly fronts on the sea, actually contains several valleys. They include the San Fernando, the San Gabriel, and the San Bernardino.

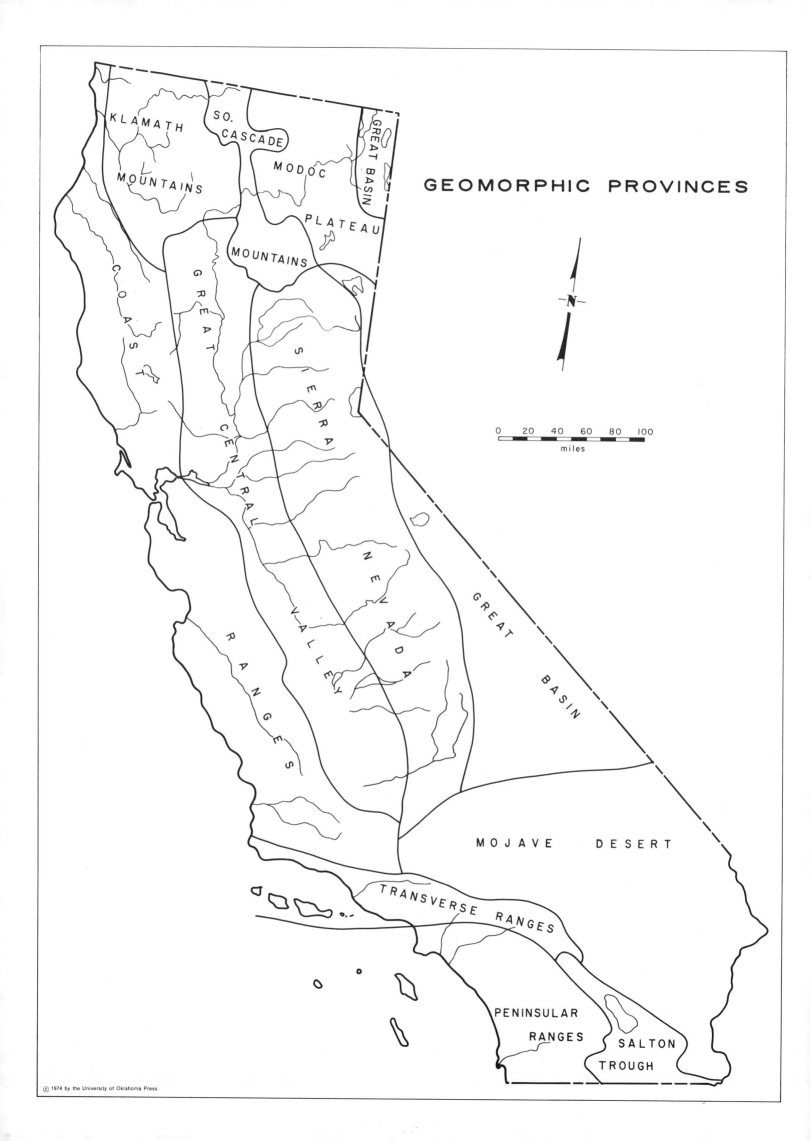

GEOMORPHIC PROVINCES

KLAMATH MOUNTAINS

SO. CASCADE

MODOC PLATEAU

MOUNTAINS

GREAT BASIN

COAST

GREAT CENTRAL VALLEY

SIERRA NEVADA

RANGES

GREAT BASIN

MOJAVE DESERT

TRANSVERSE RANGES

PENINSULAR RANGES

SALTON TROUGH

N

0 20 40 60 80 100
miles

3. GEOMORPHIC PROVINCES

CALIFORNIA LANDFORMS determine climate, drainage, soils, and natural vegetation. They also influence where man lives, what he does with the land, and what kind of communication and transportation he has. The diversity of the state landforms is reflected in the geomorphic provinces. Most important of these are the two mountain systems, the Sierra Nevada and the Coast Ranges, and the Great Central Valley lying between them.

The Coast Ranges extend from north of Cape Mendocino some 500 miles to Point Conception. On the north they merge with the foothills of the Klamath Mountains, on the south with the Transverse Ranges, and to the east they descend to the Central Valley. Running in a northwest-southeast direction, they are usually 2,000 to 4,000 feet in elevation. These ranges constitute a formidable barrier to man and also influence atmospheric conditions. Only at San Francisco is there any real break in the Coast Ranges. They are of sedimentary origin but have been metamorphosed, sometimes more than once. The ranges usually extend to the ocean, with narrow beaches the rule rather than the exception. Many valleys opening on the ocean are formed between the ridges.

The Coast Ranges terminate on the south in ranges which have an east-west trend and are known as the Transverse Ranges. With peaks as high as 10,000 feet, these mountains have effectively separated northern from southern California. To the south of this barrier the Los Angeles basin is the largest lowland area fronting on the ocean. This has made possible a profitable agricultural endeavor and the greatest population concentration in the state.

The Peninsular Ranges extend southward into Lower California and include the Santa Ana, San Jacinto, and Santa Rosa ranges. Usually of higher elevation than the Coastal Ranges they are more difficult for man to transverse and have caused the "desert" condition of the Salton Trough. At the opposite end of the state are the Klamath Mountains, which include several smaller ranges such as the Siskiyou, the Salmon, and the Trinity mountains. With many peaks of 9,000 feet, they are the most rugged of the Coastal Ranges.

The Sierra Nevadas are the most impressive mountain range in California, containing many peaks over 13,000 feet. They are some 400 miles long and 70 miles wide. Mainly of igneus origin, they have been both uplifted and tilted. The Sierra Nevadas gradually slope on their western side but drop off abruptly to the east. The Southern Cascades, the northern edge of the Sierra Nevadas, and the Modoc Plateau are of volcanic origin.

The Great Central Valley lies between the Coastal Ranges and the Sierra Nevada. It is 450 miles long and some 50 miles wide. Of alluvial origin it is the most important agricultural region of California. The Salton Trough is a continuation of the great trough in which the Gulf of California lies. Until recently, in geological time, an arm of the sea, it was closed by alluvium deposited by the Colorado River as it entered the Gulf of California. With irrigation, the Coachella and Imperial valleys have flourished agriculturally. The Mojave Desert is of economic importance because of its mineral wealth. The Great Basin has some 8,500 square miles within California.

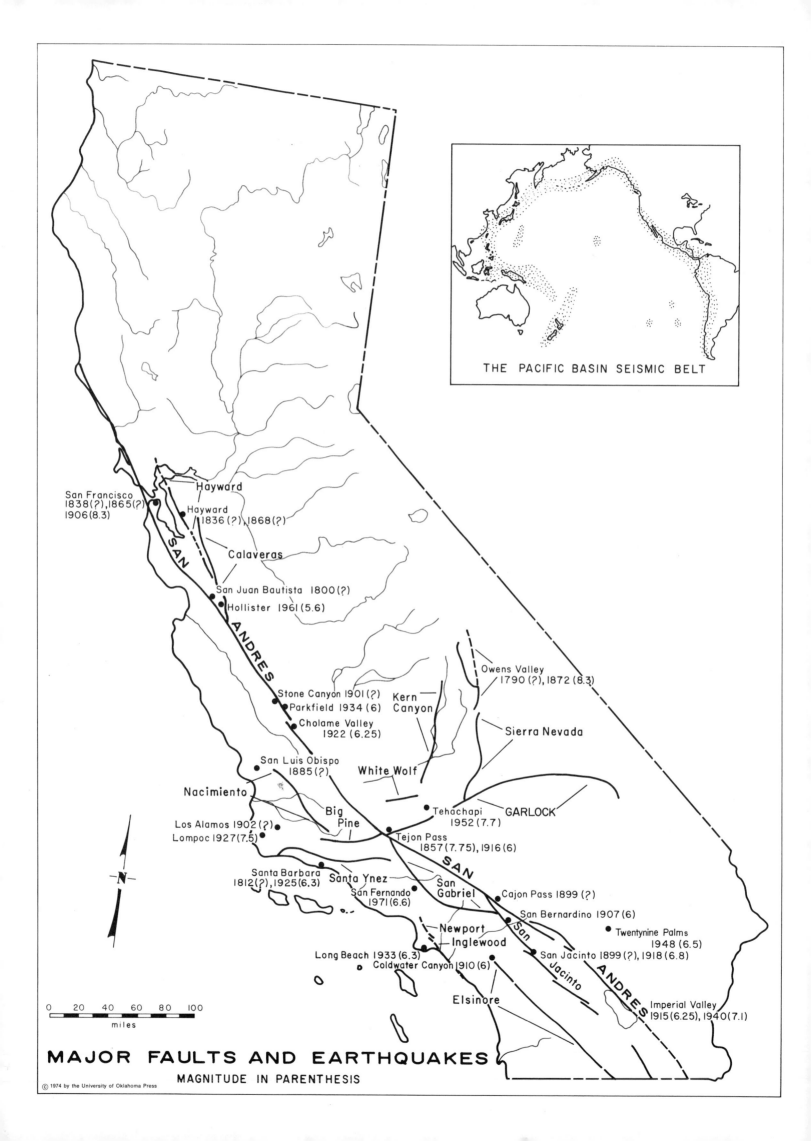

THE PACIFIC BASIN SEISMIC BELT

San Francisco
1838(?),1865(?)
1906(8.3)

Hayward

Hayward
1836(?),1868(?)

Calaveras

SAN

San Juan Bautista 1800(?)

Hollister 1961 (5.6)

ANDRES

Owens Valley
1790(?),1872 (8.3)

Stone Canyon 1901(?)

Kern
Canyon

Parkfield 1934 (6)

Cholame Valley
1922 (6.25)

Sierra Nevada

San Luis Obispo
1885(?)

White Wolf

Nacimiento

GARLOCK

Big
Pine

Tehachapi
1952 (7.7)

Los Alamos 1902 (?)

Lompoc 1927 (7.5)

Tejon Pass
1857 (7.75), 1916 (6)

N

SAN

Santa Barbara
1812(?),1925(6.3)

Santa Ynez

San
Gabriel

Cajon Pass 1899 (?)

San Fernando
1971(6.6)

San Bernardino 1907 (6)

Newport
Inglewood

Twentynine Palms
1948 (6.5)

Long Beach 1933 (6.3)

San

San Jacinto 1899 (?), 1918 (6.8)

Coldwater Canyon 1910 (6)

Jacinto

ANDRES

Elsinore

Imperial Valley
1915(6.25), 1940(7.1)

0   20   40   60   80   100
miles

MAJOR FAULTS AND EARTHQUAKES
MAGNITUDE IN PARENTHESIS

4. MAJOR FAULTS AND EARTHQUAKES

WHEN THE EXPLORATORY party led by Gaspar de Portolá paused by the Santa Ana River on July 28, 1769, they were frightened by "a horrifying earthquake which was repeated four times during the day." This prompted Friar Juan Crespi to name the stream "the River of the Sweet Name of Jesus of the Earthquakes." Since that date the recurrence of earthquakes has complicated man's adaptation to California and, as his technology has become increasingly more complex, the impact of such earth tremors has become more destructive of life and property.

California has experienced only three "great" earthquakes in recorded history: in 1857 at Tejon Pass in southern California, in Owens Valley in 1872, and San Francisco in 1906. However, there have been scores of "lesser" quakes, one of which killed a hundred persons and caused damage in excess of forty million dollars at Long Beach in 1933. The most recent, at San Fernando, 1971, took sixty-four lives, destroyed homes and buildings (many supposedly quake-proof), and toppled twenty freeway overpasses, to create damages which will ultimately total several hundred million dollars.

As a part of the Pacific Basin seismic belt, which has 80 per cent of the world's earthquakes, the Golden State records more earth tremors than any other state in the Union except Alaska. The accompanying map locates the state's most important faults and the areas of recorded earthquakes. The most important fault, or crustal fracture of the earth, is the San Andreas. This huge fissure has been studied extensively because it caused the San Francisco earthquake of 1906, and perhaps most of those of the state. Extending for some 650 miles through southern California and along the coast in central California, it is not a single break in the earth's surface, but is made up of several roughly parallel lines of activity. Numerous minor faults branch off from the main San Andreas. The location of the San Andreas has prompted several fantasists to predict that the area west of the fault will some day break off and fall into the ocean. The Garlock Fault, on the other hand, runs in an east-west direction, and also has many interwoven branches. Actually, it is impossible to record all of the faults in California, because the state is literally honeycombed with fissures. No part of the state is free of the threat of an earthquake.

The magnitude of earthquakes is measured by the Richter Scale expressed in whole numbers and decimals, usually between three and eight. The numbers represent recordings on a seismograph 62 miles from the epicenter. On the Richter Scale an increase of a whole number represents a tenfold increase in the size of the earthquake. Hence, an earthquake of the magnitude of 8.3 (San Francisco, in 1906) is not twice that of 4.3 but is 10,000 times as great. The extent of damage from a tremor also depends on the distance from the epicenter. Fortunately, many of California's earthquakes have occurred in isolated areas, but as population grows so also do the chances of a devastating quake costing hundreds of thousands of lives.

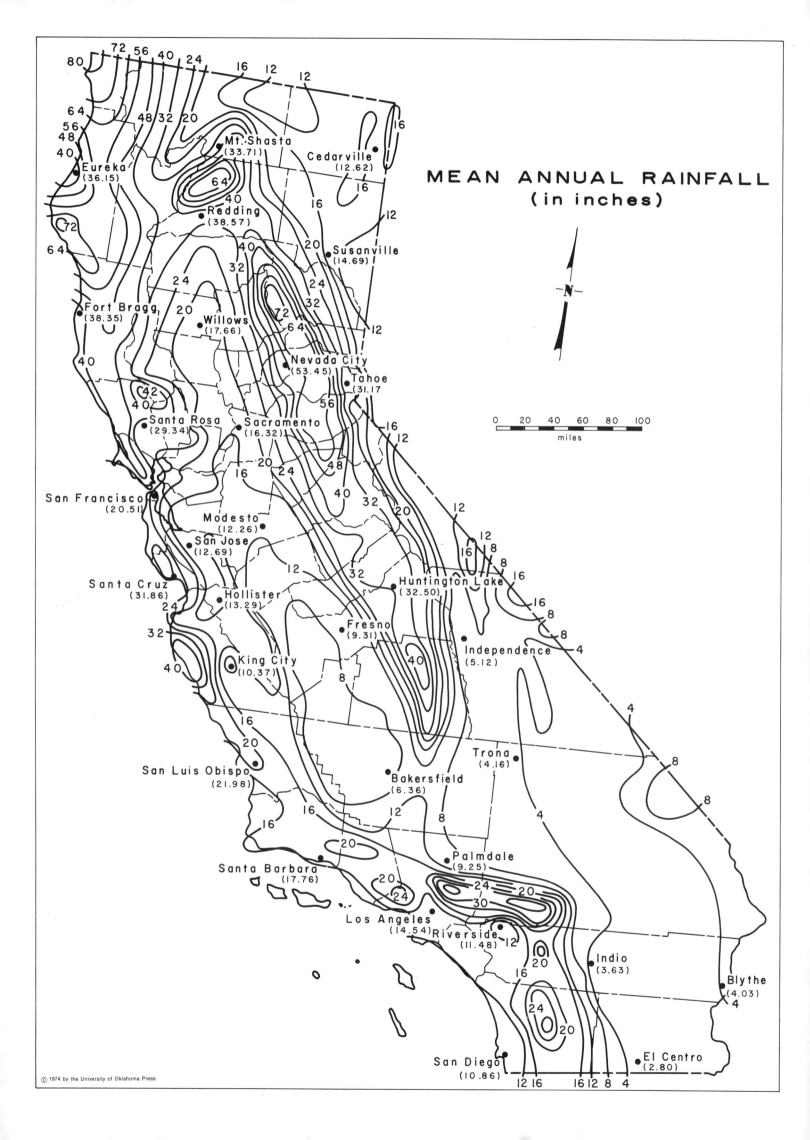

MEAN ANNUAL RAINFALL
(in inches)

80 72 56 40 24 16 12 12

64
48 32 20 16

56
48
40
16

Mt. Shasta
(33.71)

Cedarville
(12.62)

72
16

64

Eureka
(36.15)

64
40

Redding
(38.57)

16

12

40 20

Susanville
(14.69)

32

24

Fort Bragg
(38.35)

24

32

20

Willows
(17.66)

72
64

12

40

Nevada City
(53.45)

Tahoe
31.17

42
40

56

Santa Rosa
(29.34)

Sacramento
(16.32)

16

12

20 24 48

San Francisco
(20.51)

16

40

32

20

Modesto
(12.26)

12

12

San Jose
(12.69)

16

12
8
8
16

Santa Cruz
(31.86)

Hollister
(13.29)

32

Huntington Lake
(32.50)

16

24

Fresno
(9.31)

16
8
8
4

King City
(10.37)

40

Independence
(5.12)

32

8

4

16

20

Trona
(4.16)

8

San Luis Obispo
(21.98)

Bakersfield
(6.36)

4

16

12

16

8

16

20

Palmdale
(9.25)

Santa Barbara
(17.76)

20

20
24

24 20

30

Los Angeles
(14.54)

Riverside
(11.48)

12

20

Indio
(3.63)

16

Blythe
(4.03)
4

24
20

San Diego
(10.86)

El Centro
(2.80)

12 16   16 12 8 4

0 20 40 60 80 100
miles

N

5. MEAN ANNUAL RAINFALL

UNLIKE MOST OF the United States, which has four seasons, California basically has but two seasons, the wet and the dry. Rain falls mainly from October to March, with most of it concentrated in December, January, and February. Except for occasional local desert storms, rain is virtually unknown during the summer months. The wet and dry seasons result from the presence of a continental high pressure area from late spring to early fall which sends hot, drying winds westward toward the coast. These deflect the cool, moisture-laden breezes moving southeastward and, hence, onshore from the North Pacific. When winter approaches, the high pressure area breaks down.

Rainfall in California is also distinguished by great diversity. Annual averages can be 80 inches in the northwest corner of the state while less than 3 inches is recorded in the southeast. Such great diversity is caused by latitude, the distance from the ocean, elevation, and location in relation to the mountains; the windward side naturally receiving greater rainfall than the leeward. One windward station records 50 inches annually, while a leeward station of similar altitude and latitude receives 9 inches. Even on the windward side of the Sierra, precipitation increases with elevation at approximately the rate of one inch per 100 feet until the maximum is reached at the 6,500 feet level. Where the wind strikes the low hills near San Francisco precipitation is 22.7 inches, while it is more than 50 inches on the upper slopes of the Sierras in the same latitude.

Unreliability is another feature of the state's rainfall. During some years several times the average amount of precipitation will be recorded, resulting in extensive flooding. In other years a fraction of the annual average rainfall will fall, causing disastrous drouth. Even when the average is recorded, difficulties can result when most of the rainfall is concentrated in a few days instead of being portioned throughout the rainy season. The largest annual precipitation was 153.54 inches at Monumental, Del Norte County, in 1909. The greatest monthly amount was 71.54 inches at Helen Mine, Lake County, in January, 1909. The heaviest precipitation within 24 hours was 16.71 inches on January 16–17, 1916, at Squirrel Inn, San Bernardino County. On the other hand, no measurable rain fell at Bagdad, San Bernardino County, from October 3, 1912, to November 8, 1914. At numerous stations in Death Valley and Imperial Valley there have been many annual periods in which less than an inch of rain has been recorded.

Another unfortunate aspect of the rainfall pattern is that most of it falls in the area of least population. Heavy rainfall in the northwest has helped create the majestic redwoods, perhaps the heaviest stand of timber on the earth, but precipitation would be more valuable to man if it fell on his cropland. The basic objective of the California Water Plan is to redistribute surplus water from wet northern areas with few people to the dry southern areas with a rainfall deficiency and most of the state's population. One of the more important resources of the Sierra is its snow cover, from which the run-off provides city water and irrigation. Tamarack, Alpine County, recorded 844 inches of snow during the winter of 1906–1907, the heaviest ever recorded in the United States in a single season.

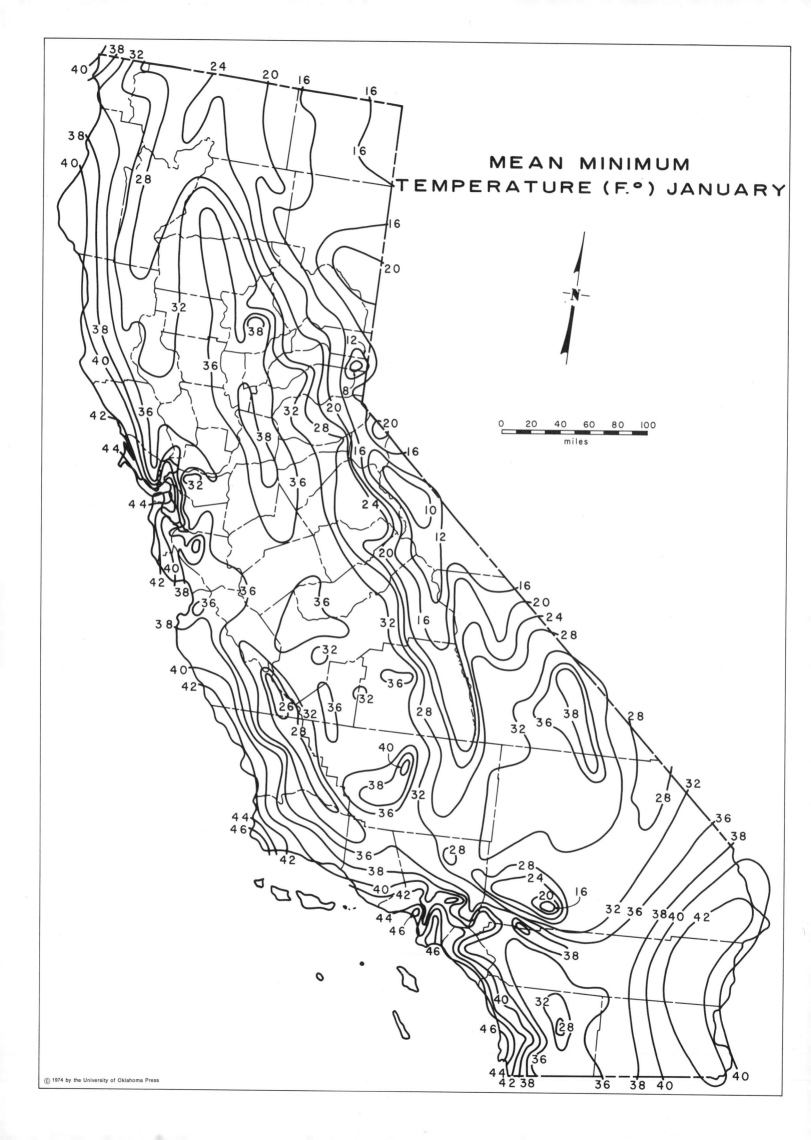

MEAN MINIMUM
TEMPERATURE (F.°) JANUARY

miles

6. MEAN MINIMUM TEMPERATURE (F.°), JANUARY

CALIFORNIA'S MEAN minimum temperature in January is as diverse as the total climatic scene. There is no such thing as a distinct "California climate." There is not just one, but many climates. This is partially the result of the vastness of the state. For Northern California is on the same latitude as Chicago, while the southern edge is on the same latitude as Savannah, Georgia. Other factors determining climate are distance from the ocean, altitude, and location in relation to mountains. As the isothermic lines showing the mean minimum January temperature illustrate, the contours of the mountain ranges are the primary influence. Temperature usually changes one degree for every 330 feet of elevation, but the sheltering influence of nearby mountains, the location of mountain passes and foothills are also important. In California, isotherms generally run north and south instead of in the more common east to west direction. With so many determinants influencing climate, it is common to have much variation within a small area. It is possible to go skiing within sight of roses in bloom, or see snow-capped peaks while surfing in the ocean.

Temperatures along the coast vary little. The mean minimum at the northwest corner is 40°, while it is only 42° at San Diego, and reaches a maximum of only 46° and a low of 38°. In fact, the climate in the San Diego area is the most equable in the United States. Because of the prevailing westerly winds along the coast, the moderating effect of the marine influence extends inland.

Winter temperatures inland are colder as a result of elevation and because land heats and cools more rapidly than water. However, the Sierra Nevada–Cascade barrier range protects the area to the west from the cold air masses of the continental interior. A low temperature of 45° F. below zero occurred at Boca, Nevada County, at an elevation of 5,532 feet on January 20, 1937. At the top of Mount Lassen in the winter of 1932–33 it fell to 56° F. below zero. At the higher elevations sub-zero weather is common in winter. Although the January mean minimum is high enough in much of the state to permit a year-round growing season, danger from killing frost is always present, and man has had to devise costly ways in which to protect agriculture.

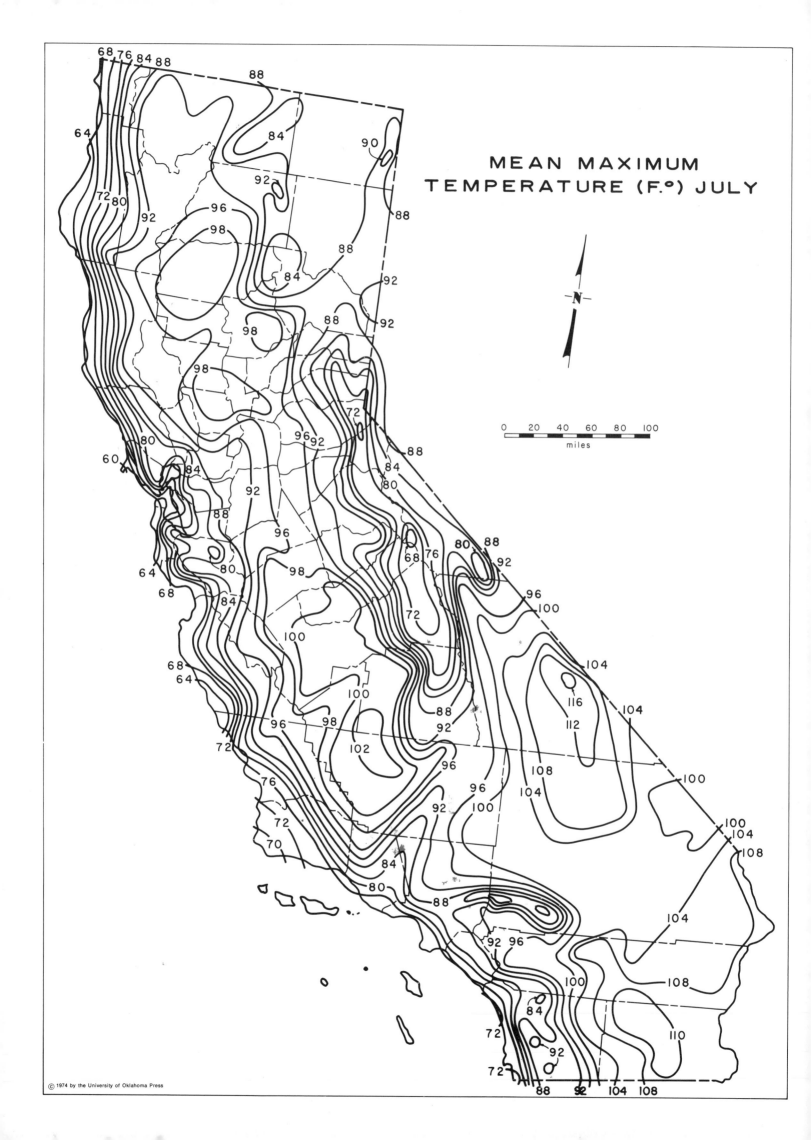

MEAN MAXIMUM
TEMPERATURE (F.°) JULY

–N–

0   20   40   60   80   100
miles

© 1974 by the University of Oklahoma Press

7. MEAN MAXIMUM TEMPERATURE (F.°), JULY

CALIFORNIA'S JULY maximum is just as varied as the January minimum. Along the lengthy Pacific coast the temperature ranges from 60° to only 72°. However, only a few miles inland it is very hot, and, in some areas of California, summers have recorded the highest temperatures anywhere in the world. On July 10, 1913, it reached 134° in Death Valley. The prime determinant in the July maximum temperature is the ease with which sea air and continental air can move to any given locality.

During the summer months the Pacific High moves northward to a point between 30° and 40° N. latitude, causing strong onshore winds. The extent to which they reach the interior depends on the geographic barriers. In the San Francisco area the Golden Gate acts as a funnel to bring oceanic air masses in through the breach in the Coast Range. At the same time, inland areas of the Central Valley receive more heat from the sun in July than does the equator. The hot air rises, causing an inrush of ocean air. The incoming cool, heavy sea air mingles with the hot, drying air, causing a lowering of temperatures. In a matter of days the whole process is repeated. Distance from the ocean and situation in a valley determine the temperature effect of this conflict between cool sea and hot continental air. Marin County residents may shiver in 50° weather while 10 miles eastward in San Rafael it is a comfortable 70°. Another 40 miles east it may be 100°, or a temperature change of 50° in 50 miles. The high temperature isotherms on the leeward side of the Coast Ranges graphically illustrate this point.

All river valleys open to the sea allow air to move inland, but its penetration usually depends on the nature of the valley. The Santa Clara River area (Ventura County) is subjected to full marine influence, but its valley narrows to a width of only a mile some 15 miles upstream, causing very little cool, heavy ocean air to reach inland, and so its influence on hot, dry continental air is minimal. This is true of the many small valleys along the coast. Western San Fernando Valley is only a third as far from the ocean as the upper Santa Ana River Basin, but the San Fernando Valley is open to marine influence only through the Glendale Narrows, while the Santa Ana Basin receives sea air on a broad front. Thus, temperatures are more moderate in the latter area.

The high July maximum temperature in the Great Valley, the Coachella and Imperial valleys, and the numerous smaller valleys, when combined with irrigation water, has made California the nation's richest agricultural state.

Temperatures in excess of 100° are uncomfortable for man, but the low relative humidity makes them more tolerable than in the more humid areas of the country. The relative accessibility of the cooler coastal or mountain regions have also aided man in his adaptation to California in July.

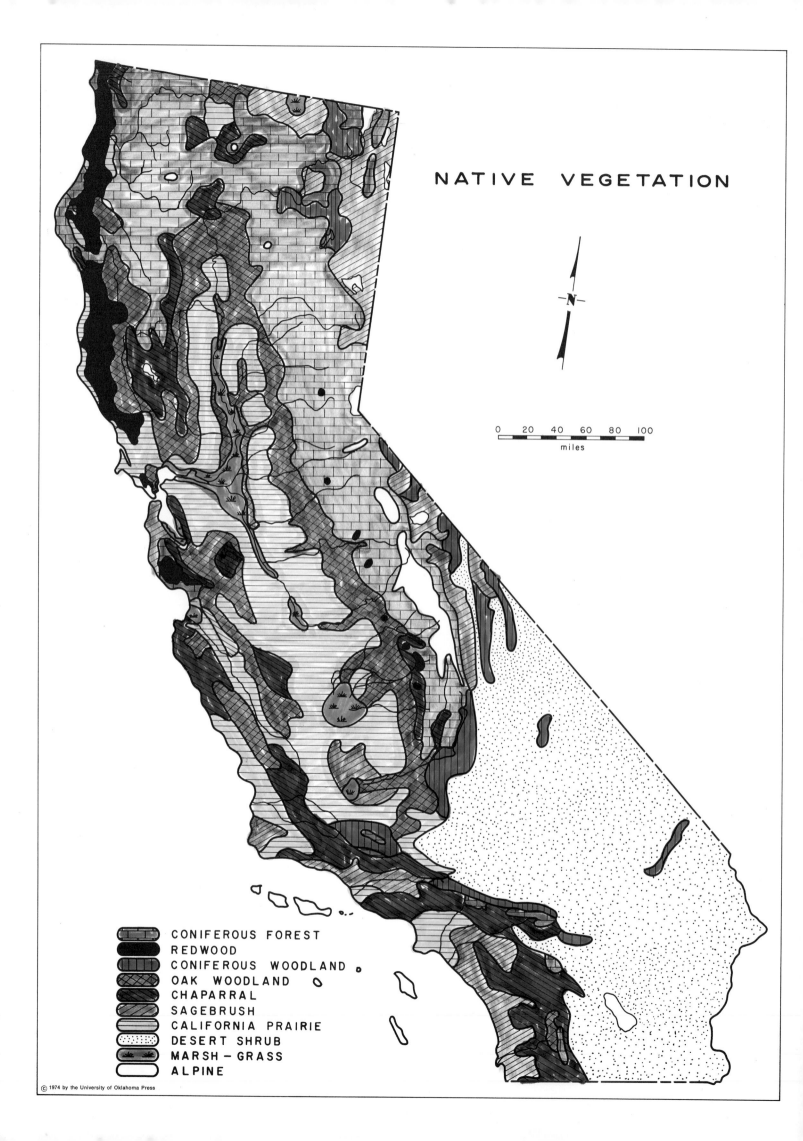

NATIVE VEGETATION

0 20 40 60 80 100
miles

CONIFEROUS FOREST
REDWOOD
CONIFEROUS WOODLAND
OAK WOODLAND
CHAPARRAL
SAGEBRUSH
CALIFORNIA PRAIRIE
DESERT SHRUB
MARSH-GRASS
ALPINE

8. NATIVE VEGETATION

NATIVE VEGETATION reflects the diverse topography, many types of soil, and differences in rainfall of the Golden State. The coniferous forest covers some 21 million acres and includes several distinct forest communities. The ponderosa pine forest is the most extensive in California and includes ponderosa pine, sugar pine, Douglas fir, white fir and incense-cedar. It is located in the Sierra Nevada between 3,000 and 6,500 feet. In Southern California it is found at elevations from 5,000 to 8,000 feet. Ponderosa pine is dominant where it is more arid, but white fir takes over in humid areas. The Douglas fir, which occurs in almost pure stands, is found west of the summit of the Cascade Range and south through the Klamath Mountains and Coast Ranges. The red fir forest is located above the ponderosa pine forest; above the red fir is located the lodge pole pine.

The redwood is the most famed of all California trees because of its great size. The redwood forest is found on the seaward slopes of the Coast Ranges at elevations from sea level to 3,000 feet from Oregon to Monterey County in a strip some 35 miles wide, and in scattered stands in the Sierra Nevada.

The coniferous woodland is mainly the "piñon-juniper" area and is found in the Basin-Range province, in the mountains of the Mojave Desert, and on the north side of the Transverse Ranges. In the north its elevation is 4,000 to 7,000 feet, and in the south, 5,000 to 8,000 feet. It covers about 3.5 million acres.

The oak woodland sub-region, the foothill woodland, is located along the valley borders and lower slopes of the Coast Ranges, Klamath Mountains, Sierra Nevada, and southward into Southern California below 2,500 feet elevation. A possible 10 mil-lion acres were included originally. The valley woodland of the oak woodland was on the alluvial fans and floodplains of the Central Valley. These great oak groves provided excellent game forage, as well as the acorns many Indians processed for food.

Chaparral is found throughout the state on slopes and ridges west of the Sierra Nevadas and the Mojave Desert, usually at elevations from 1,000 to 4,000 feet. Sagebrush of the Great Basin variety is found between 4,000 and 7,500 feet in the Modoc Plateau, and on the western edge of the Mojave Desert and the eastern portions of the Peninsular ranges southward into San Diego County. Coastal sagebrush is found along the coast from San Francisco southward, usually below 3,000 feet. It is normally found below chaparral, but there is also considerable mingling of the two.

The California prairie is dominated by the Central Valley grassland. It is essentially a treeless grassland, but numerous valley oaks are the exception. The north coastal prairie is scattered along the coast as far south as the Marin Peninsula. It has cooler temperatures and more rainfall than the Central Valley and is found from sea level to 4,000 feet. The desert shrub area covers some 24.2 million acres, or about one-fourth of the state. It includes the Mojave and Colorado deserts as well as Owens and Death valleys. Its forage potential is very limited. Marsh-grass or "tule lands" are located mainly in the Central Valley, but with a few other scattered locales near Monterey and Klamath Lake. It may have occupied an original area of 500,000 acres. The Alpine area is above the timber line. It is important as a snow storage area and is also used for summer grazing and recreation.

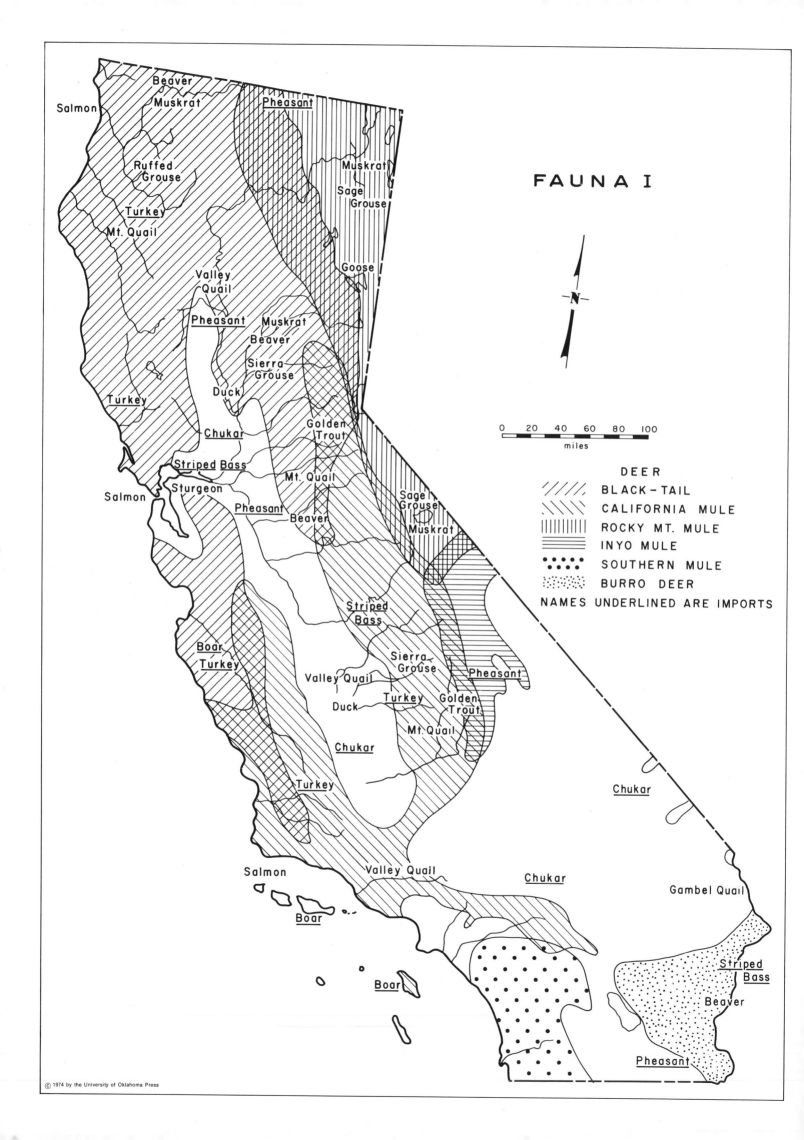

FAUNA I

Salmon
Beaver
Muskrat
Pheasant
Ruffed Grouse
Turkey
Mt. Quail
Muskrat
Sage Grouse
Goose
Valley Quail
Pheasant
Muskrat
Beaver
Sierra Grouse
Duck
Turkey
Golden Trout
Chukar
Striped Bass
Salmon
Sturgeon
Mt. Quail
Pheasant
Sage Grouse
Beaver
Muskrat
Striped Bass
Boar
Turkey
Sierra Grouse
Valley Quail
Pheasant
Duck
Turkey
Golden Trout
Chukar
Mt. Quail
Turkey
Chukar
Salmon
Valley Quail
Chukar
Gambel Quail
Boar
Boar
Striped Bass
Beaver
Pheasant

N

0 20 40 60 80 100
miles

DEER

/// BLACK-TAIL
\\\ CALIFORNIA MULE
||| ROCKY MT. MULE
≡ INYO MULE
⋯ SOUTHERN MULE
░ BURRO DEER

NAMES UNDERLINED ARE IMPORTS

© 1974 by the University of Oklahoma Press

THE FAUNA OF California is as diverse as its climate and topography. In addition, the state's animal life is often distinctive and sometimes unique. This has possibly resulted from the relative isolation from the rest of the continent. While species have migrated from Oregon on the north and from Mexico on the south, few species have been able to cross the desert from the east and scale the Sierra.

Today, deer are the most abundant and most popular of the state's big game animals. It is possible that deer were also numerous when the Spanish first arrived, since several explorers mention seeing them from San Diego to the Bay Area; in 1792 Longinos Martínez reported deer as "the most abundant animals." The Spanish settlers may have been few in number and restricted in the area they occupied, but their large numbers of livestock destroyed essential vegetation and thus reduced the number of deer. The arrival of the Anglo in force after 1849 caused a rapid decline in deer population. Hunting for hides and meat was the main reason, but overgrazing by cattle and sheep and a series of extremely severe winters were equally important. By 1900, deer were so few that it was feared they would soon be extinct. However, they have increased in number, so that today they may be more numerous than in primitive days. The most important reason for this increase has been the ability of the deer to live close to human beings. Man has destroyed most of the deer's natural enemies and has provided better forage.

The beaver, the largest member of the rodent family in North America and the only wild animal capable of altering its environment to suit its needs, provided the lure which first brought the Anglo overland to California. For it was the profitable beaver fur traffic which brought the mountain men to explore the state and prepare the way for the invasion of American settlers. A semi-aquatic animal, the beaver was once found wherever an annual supply of water was available. Except in the Colorado River Valley their numbers were few in Southern California. However, Hudson's Bay Company trappers found beaver as far south as Buena Vista Lake in Kern County. The beaver were nearly extinct by 1900, and legislative action prohibited hunting of them for thirty-five years (except in certain agricultural areas). The Department of Fish and Game introduced Idaho and Oregon beaver and transplanted many native species. Hence, they have increased rapidly in numbers and rank second in importance in the California fur trade. The muskrat, a similar rodent, is first in importance.

Most of the state's game birds are associated with upland areas that supply the required food, cover, and living space. Foremost of these are quail, which are found throughout the state; most numerous are mountain quail. The pheasant, Indian Chukar, and turkey are not native but have been successfully introduced into California.

A different type of import is the European wild pig or boar. Originally brought from Europe to North Carolina in 1910, the animal was released in Monterey County in 1925 or 1926. They have spread in the mountain terrain southward to San Luis Obispo County and are also found on Santa Catalina, Santa Cruz, and San Clemente islands. They have also mixed with domestic pigs gone wild. They root for bulbs, mushrooms, insects, and grass roots, and eat acorns and other nuts. Unfortunately, they also damage ground crops extensively. They are one of the most dangerous game animals when wounded, cornered, or encountered with young.

The icy lakes and streams of the Sierra abound with many species of native and introduced trout. Sturgeon were once plentiful in California's streams but are today limited to only a few areas. Striped bass, one of the most successful imports, are found in the San Francisco Bay region or in the lower Sacramento or San Joaquin Rivers and annually increase in value of the catch. Salmon, migrating from the ocean to their upstream spawning beds, are found in the coastal rivers from San Francisco Bay northward.

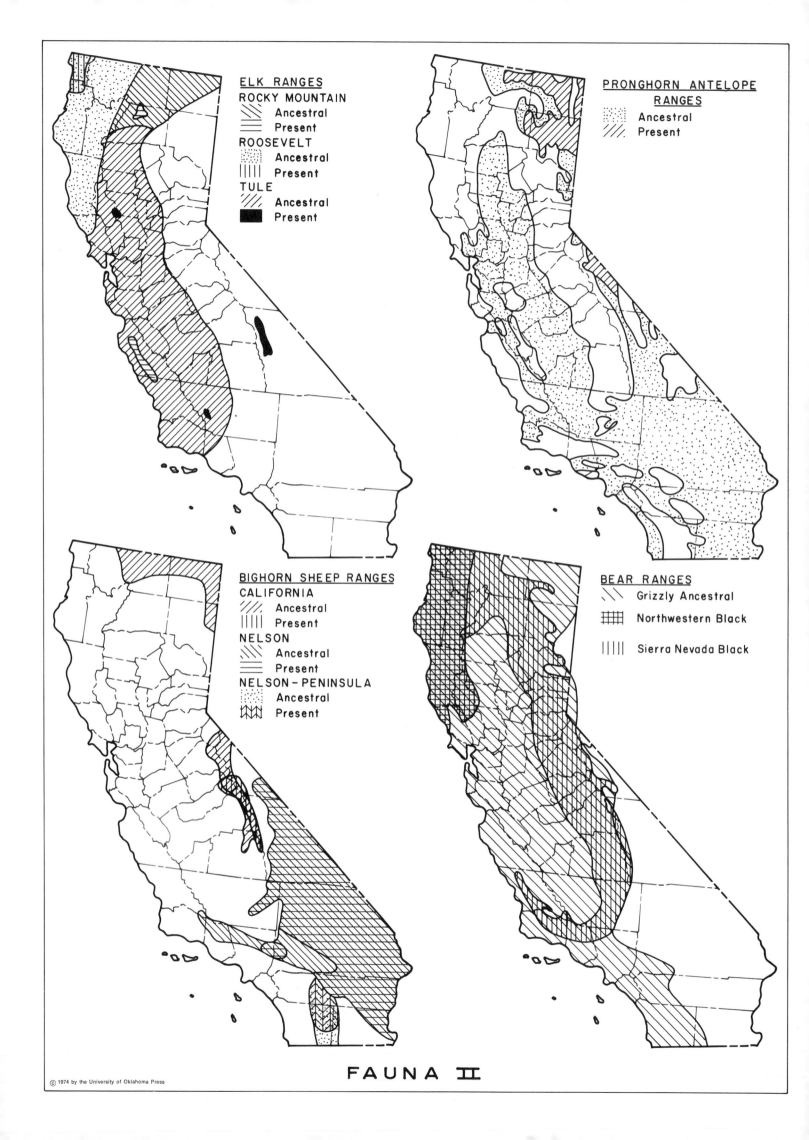

ELK RANGES
ROCKY MOUNTAIN
≡ Ancestral
≣ Present
ROOSEVELT
Ancestral
||||| Present
TULE
/// Ancestral
█ Present

PRONGHORN ANTELOPE
RANGES
Ancestral
/// Present

BIGHORN SHEEP RANGES
CALIFORNIA
/// Ancestral
||||| Present
NELSON
\\\ Ancestral
≡ Present
NELSON–PENINSULA
Ancestral
Present

BEAR RANGES
/// Grizzly Ancestral
⊞ Northwestern Black
||||| Sierra Nevada Black

FAUNA Ⅱ

THE LARGE SIZE and stately appearance of elk influenced early explorers and emigrants to record their appearance whenever they were encountered. As a result the impression is created that elk were more numerous than deer in primitive times. This was probably not true, although Tule elk were plentiful around San Francisco Bay and individual herds of some two thousand were reported in the San Joaquin Valley in 1846. Roosevelt elk are the largest species found in the state and are mainly inhabitants of the coastal area of the Pacific Northwest, from whence they drifted south into California. Rocky Mountain elk are next in size, and although they are the most common species on the North American Continent they may not have been native to California. The Tule (also Dwarf or Valley) elk is the smallest American elk and is usually identified with California. Abundant in the foothills and valleys, they were threatened with extinction as settlers moved in during the second half of the nineteenth century. Henry Miller, a large landowner, protected a few Tule elk. This herd grew to four hundred by 1914 and was used to stock other ranges. The Kern County Tule Elk Refuge was established in 1934. Animals were moved from Yosemite in 1933, and these elk became the nucleus of herds in the Owens Valley. The Cache Creek herd in Colusa and Lake counties were transplanted from Del Monte State Park in 1922.

The ancestral home of the pronghorn antelope covered most of the valleys of California as well as the more fertile areas of the desert terrain. Their abundance was mentioned by Spanish as well as early American explorers. As land settlement began in earnest in the past century, the antelope suffered the same fate as other wildlife. On the verge of extinction in the 1920's, they have slowly increased in numbers. Airplane censuses, begun in 1953, indicate that their numbers have increased from less than two thousand to almost three thousand. Their principal range today is in Modoc and Lassen counties, with a small number in Mono County.

Bighorn sheep were largely confined to mountain areas or the adjacent lowlands. Ability to go long periods without water enables them to inhabit desert terrain. In California are found three types: the California, the Nelson, and Nelson-Peninsula, the latter a hybrid between the Nelson bighorn and the Peninsula bighorn. These sheep were probably never numerous but were virtually eliminated by the Anglo influx, despite total protection since 1873. Bighorn sheep, unlike deer, are intolerant of human disturbances. They rapidly declined in number because of overgrazing of their range by domestic sheep, transference of infectious diseases and parasites from domestic livestock, elimination or fencing of water holes, and poaching.

The Northwestern and the Sierra Nevada are the two species of black bear found in California. Largely vegetarian in habit, the black bear seldom kills domestic livestock and but very rarely has been known to attack man. The black bear is still found in timber and brush areas. It was the grizzly that gave California bears their evil reputation. Notoriously fierce and intractable, and one of the largest of American carnivores, the grizzly cannot tolerate the presence of man. Reports of Indians being killed by grizzlies are numerous. Native Californians so feared these bears that in their legends they accorded the bear the role of a deity, and grizzly bear medicine men were the most feared practitioners of their art. Spaniards and Mexicans used them in their "sport" of bear and bull hunting. These bears are now extinct in California. The last recorded kill of a grizzly occurred in Tulare County in 1922, but the symbol of his strength has been preserved as a part of the state's flag.

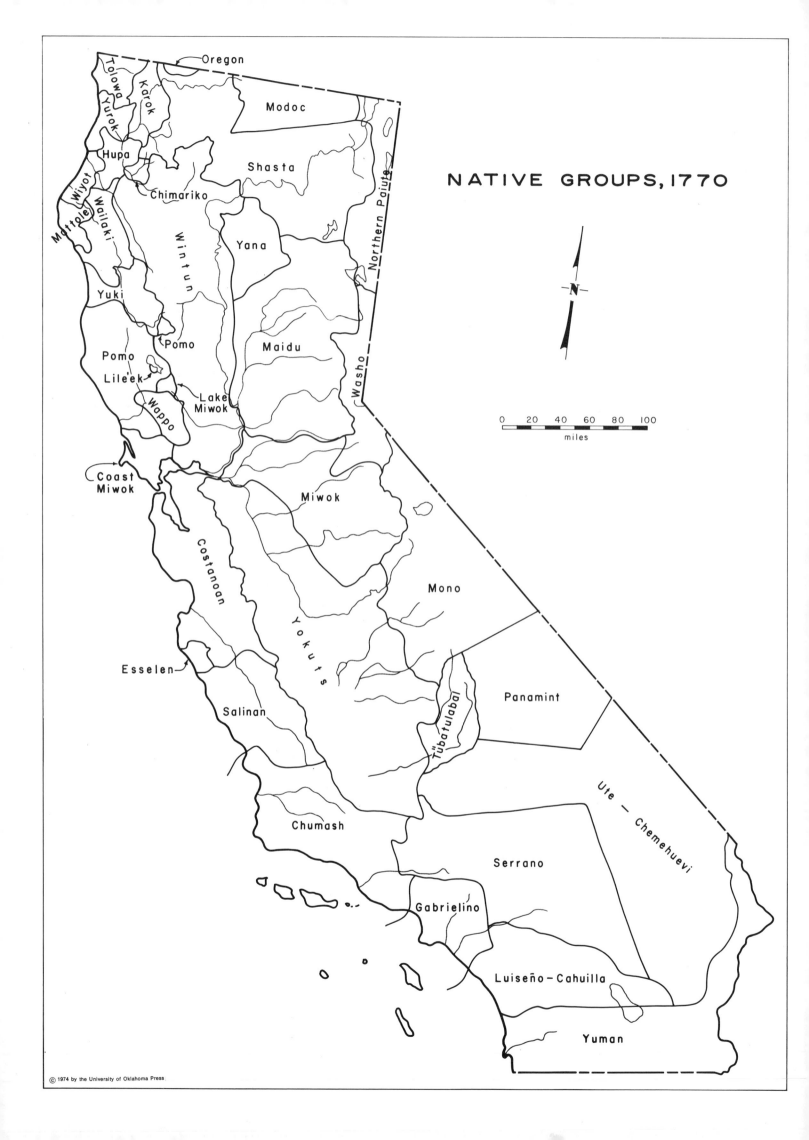

NATIVE GROUPS, 1770

Oregon

Tolowa
Yurok
Karok
Modoc
Hupa
Shasta
Wiyot
Chimariko
Mattole
Wailaki
Wintun
Yana
Northern Paiute
Yuki
Pomo
Pomo
Maidu
Lile'ek
Wappo
Lake Miwok
Washo
Coast Miwok
Miwok
Costanoan
Mono
Yokuts
Esselen
Salinan
Tübatulabal
Panamint
Chumash
Ute - Chemehuevi
Serrano
Gabrielino
Luiseño - Cahuilla
Yuman

0 20 40 60 80 100
miles

11. NATIVE GROUPS, 1770

WHEN THE SPANIARDS arrived in California, the area supported a relatively large number of Indians. Some enthusiastic authorities have estimated the total as high as 700,000. However, Alfred L. Kroeber, the dean of the state's anthropologists, has set the figure as low as 133,000, while contemporary scholars estimate that there were 275,000 within the present boundaries of California in 1769. Some 135 different Indian languages were spoken, which included 21 or 22 different linguistic families. Most natives lived in villages (or rancherias) seldom exceeding 1,000 in population. The majority were food-gatherers, with acorns as the basic staple. In their processing of food, much ingenuity was displayed. Some fishing and small game hunting supplemented the acorn. Only the Yuman Indians of the Colorado River Valley engaged in agriculture similar to the corn-growers of Arizona and New Mexico. The Indians in the northwest corner of the state were similar to the tribes of the Pacific Northwest in that they were primarily hunters and fishers.

The largest of the speech groupings were the Penutians, estimated at 57,000. Included in this family were the Wintun, on the west side of the Sacramento River; east of the same river were the Maidu. To the south in the Sierra foothills from the Cosumnes to the Merced lived the Miwok (except for the Lake Miwoks and Coast Miwoks). The Yokuts occupied most of the San Joaquin Valley. South of San Francisco Bay dwelled the Costanoan.

The Hokans were the second largest linguistic family, with an estimated 37,500. Their tribal groups approximately encircled the Penutians. The Pomos, famed for exceedingly fine basketwork, were found in modern Sonoma, Lake, and Mendocino counties. In the northern part of the state were the Chimariko, Karok, Shasta, and Yana. The Washo inhabited the eastern Sierra from Lake Tahoe northward. The Esselen, Salinan, and Chumash dwelled in the southern Coast Ranges and the Yumans in the southeastern edge of the state and along the Colorado River.

The Shoshoneans, whom Kroeber described as an "un-California people," possibly totaled 23,500. The Paiutes, in the northeast corner of the state, were members of this speech group, as were also the Monos in the valley of the same name. The Tübatulabal of the Kern River area were a small part of this family. The basic concentration was in Southern California and included the Panamint, Ute-Chemehuevi, Serrano, Gabrielino, and Luiseño-Cahuilla.

The remaining groups of California Indians were much smaller in numbers and were found in the northern part of the state. Largest of these were the Athabascans, with perhaps 7,000 members. In this linguistic family were found the Tolowa, Hupo, Mattoe, and Wailaki. The Yuki, some 4,000 in number, had a speech and physical appearance unlike that of any other California (or North American for that matter) Indians and were more warlike than other tribes. Perhaps 1,000 strong, the Wappos, a Yuki tribe, received their unaboriginal name from the Spanish "guapo" meaning brave. A mountain people, they resisted Spanish efforts to dislodge them from their mountains, mainly in Napa County. The Lile'ek are a Wappo group on the shores of Clear Lake. The Yuroks and Wiyot, perhaps 3,500 in all, are a distant outpost of the very large Algonquin family of central and eastern North America. The Modocs, members of the Lutuami family of Oregon, possibly had a population of 500 in the northeastern part of the state.

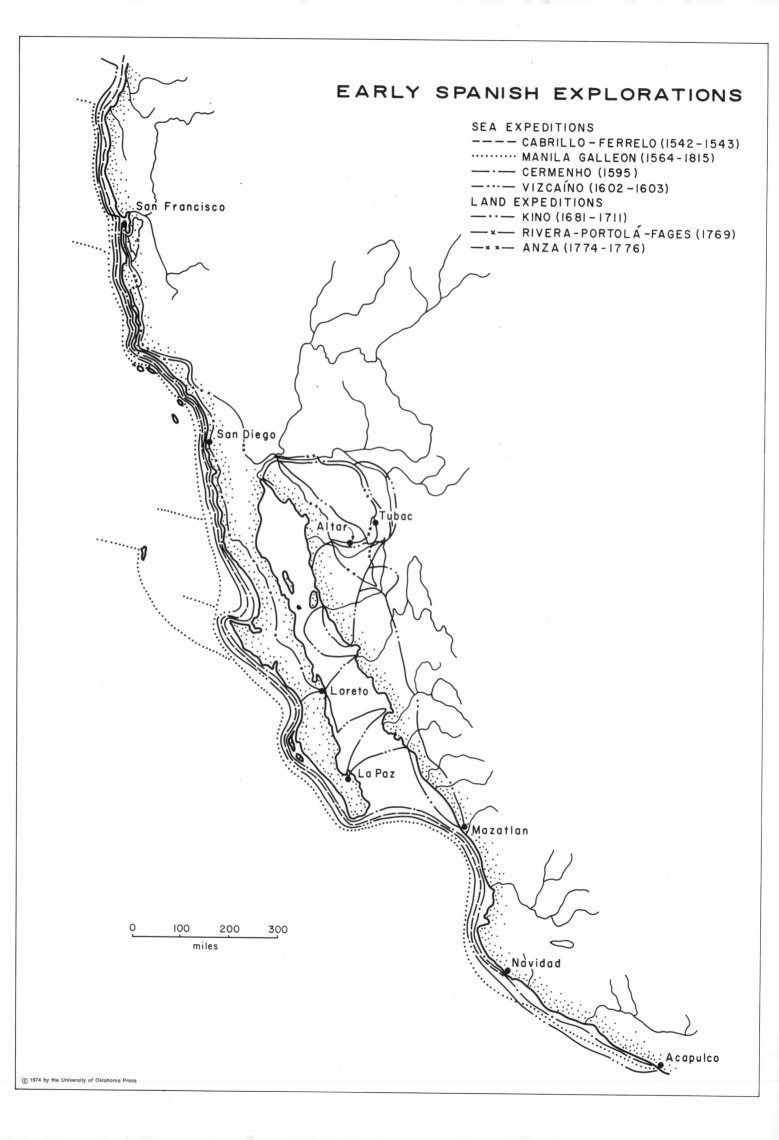

EARLY SPANISH EXPLORATIONS

SEA EXPEDITIONS
– – – CABRILLO–FERRELO (1542–1543)
· · · · · · MANILA GALLEON (1564–1815)
— · — CERMENHO (1595)
— · · — VIZCAÍNO (1602–1603)
LAND EXPEDITIONS
— · · — KINO (1681–1711)
— x — RIVERA–PORTOLÁ–FAGES (1769)
— x x — ANZA (1774–1776)

San Francisco

San Diego

Tubac

Altar

Loreto

La Paz

Mazatlan

0   100   200   300
miles

Navidad

Acapulco

© 1974 by the University of Oklahoma Press

12. EARLY SPANISH EXPLORATIONS

FROM THE NUCLEUS of settlement in the highlands of Mexico, Spain sent out numerous exploring expeditions whose discoveries were essential to the ultimate colonization and settlement of Alta California. Less than half a century after Columbus' discovery of America, Spanish conquistadores had made their way by sea along the coast of what is today the state of California in their search for treasure. Acapulco was the main point of origin for these expeditions and also the point of departure for the Manila galleons. In addition, Navidad and Mazatlan were used as bases from which to equip and outfit the ships. La Paz never lived up to its promise of great treasure from the pearl fisheries, but it was frequently visited by Spanish ships and was the site of a mission.

One of the more important means of advancing the Spanish frontier was the mission. This institution was originally developed as a training station in which missionaries could Christianize the Indians and teach them how to function as members of the Spanish society of the day. It was initially assumed that these difficult tasks could be accomplished in ten years, but in actual practice the clergy retained control of their native charges for life. The religious function of the missions undoubtedly remained most important, but through the years they gradually took on the responsibility of being a significant and relatively inexpensive means of expanding Spanish civilization in New Spain. A few friars could erect mission installations and control potentially dangerous natives at far less cost than could the military.

First in importance among the missionaries were the Jesuits. (The Franciscans took over much of their work after 1767 and brought the gospel to the Indians of Alta California). From 1591 to 1767 they labored under the most difficult and hazardous conditions to carry the frontier forward from central Mexico until California was but one step away. Their work furnished the base from which ultimate exploration and colonization took place. The chain of missions the Jesuits founded along the western face of the Sierra Madre Occidental up the "west coast corridor" through the modern Mexican states of Sinaloa and Sonora into Arizona merged with those established in Baja California to provide "the long road to California."

In 1591 the first Jesuits began work at the Villa de San Felipe north of Mazatlan at a time when civil authorities were ready to abandon the area to rebellious Indians. From that time, the Jesuit mission frontier expanded northward in orderly fashion from one river valley to another: the Sinaloa, Fuerte, Mayo, Yaqui, and Sonora. Greatest of the talented Jesuits was Friar Eusebio Francisco Kino, who arrived on the northwestern frontier in 1687. As mission administrator, Kino founded more than a score of missions and was constantly exploring for new sites. In this capacity he was truly the "pathfinder" of the region, charting the way others were to follow. He made half a dozen journeys to the Gila, usually by different routes, and two trips to the Yumas on the Colorado. On these journeys Kino proved conclusively that California was a peninsula and not an island. Key missions he founded on the northwestern frontier were Altar and Tubac, which became way stations from which other missions could be established, or were the starting point for further exploration. Until his death in 1711, Kino was a vigorous supporter of extending the Jesuit mission chain into California, and his work certainly provided the base from which final colonization came.

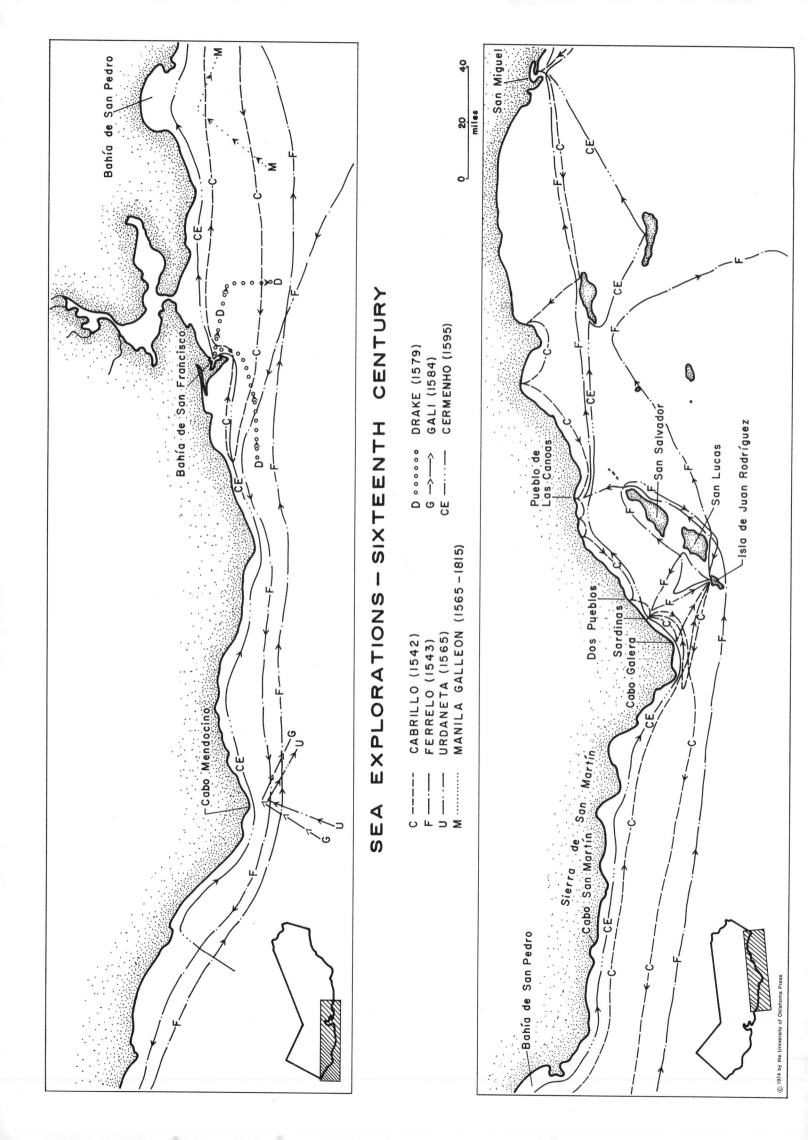

SEA EXPLORATIONS—SIXTEENTH CENTURY

C ——— CABRILLO (1542)
F ——— FERRELO (1543)
U —··— URDANETA (1565)
M ········ MANILA GALLEON (1565–1815)

D ∘∘∘∘∘∘ DRAKE (1579)
G —>— GALI (1584)
CE —·—·— CERMEÑHO (1595)

Left map labels:
Bahía de San Pedro
Bahía de San Francisco
Cabo Mendocino

Right map labels:
San Miguel
0 20 40
miles
Pueblo de Las Canoas
Dos Pueblos
Sardinas
Cabo Galera
San Salvador
San Lucas
Isla de Juan Rodríguez
Sierra de San Martín
Cabo San Martín
Bahía de San Pedro

13. SEA EXPLORATIONS—SIXTEENTH CENTURY

EARLY SPANISH SEA explorations resulted from a desire to find riches like those of the Aztec Empire and to discover a passage through North America to Europe (the legendary Northwest Passage). The most important of these was made by Juan Rodríguez Cabrillo, a Portuguese who had served in New Spain and Guatemala. Cabrillo sailed from La Navidad June 27, 1542, with two small ships. This expedition furnished the first known account of the California coast, for Cabrillo visited most of the prominent coastal sites from San Miguel (San Diego) north to the Oregon border. But a later cartographer renamed most of these points: San Salvador (Santa Cruz), San Lucas (Santa Rosa), Isla de Juan Rodríguez (San Miguel), Puebla de las Canoas (Ventura), Dos Pueblos (Rincon Point), Sardinas (Gaviota), Cape Galera (Point Conception), Cape San Martin, Bahía de San Pedro (Monterey Bay), Bahía de San Francisco (Drake's Bay), and Cape Mendocino. In addition to describing the coastline, the expedition reported in some detail on the civilization of the Channel Indians. On January 3, 1543, Cabrillo died as a result of injuries, and Bartolomé Ferrelo succeeded him as commander of this first exploration of California's coast.

Interest in a California settlement continued in the second half of the century as a by-product of the Philippine trade. The Manila galleons first sailed in 1565, and the trade between Mexico and the Philippines continued until 1815. Because this commerce was highly profitable, it was imperative that a port of call be located where inbound ships could pause for the scurvy-ravaged crew to recuperate, to take on fresh food and water, and to overhaul their ships. Such a base could also be used to provide protection against foreign freebooters. The California coast was a logical location for such a port. In 1565, in an effort to establish an eastward crossing of the Pacific, a ship, commanded by Andrés de Urdaneta but captained by Alonso de Arellano, probably reached the California coast at Cape Mendocino en route from the Philippines to New Spain. In 1584, Francisco de Gali, also returning from Manila, came into California waters again near Cape Mendocino. In command of the Manila galleon in 1595, Sebastian Rodríguez Cermenho was ordered to examine the California coast. First reaching the coast near the present city of Eureka, Cermenho sailed southward, surveying the shoreline, taking soundings, and searching for a suitable port of call. He paused at Bahía de San Francisco (Drake's Bay) to refurbish his ship and to obtain much-needed fresh food and water. While the overhaul of his vessel was in progress, Cermenho constructed a launch to be used for inshore exploration. This action was most fortunate, since his cargo ship, the *San Agustin*, was driven ashore and wrecked, with the loss of its valuable cargo from the Orient. The royal inquiry into this disaster recommended that these bulky, heavily-laden Manila galleons not be used for California coastal exploration because the ships were unsuited for such purposes. In addition, it was stressed that the crews were too fatigued after the four- or five-month crossing to perform the exacting duty of coastal exploration.

Spanish interest in a suitable port of call was heightened by the visit of Sir Francis Drake to California in 1579. The English sea captain's entry into the area was a by-product of his audacious attack on the Spanish treasure ships. Madrid authorities had long feared that enemies might use California as a base from which to attack Mexico, or that they might find the elusive Northwest Passage. Drake sailed northward into California waters and stopped to repair his ships and replenish food and water stores. While it was generally assumed he paused at Drake's Bay, there is still speculation over the exact site, and in 1974 a scholarly commission was still wrestling with the problem.

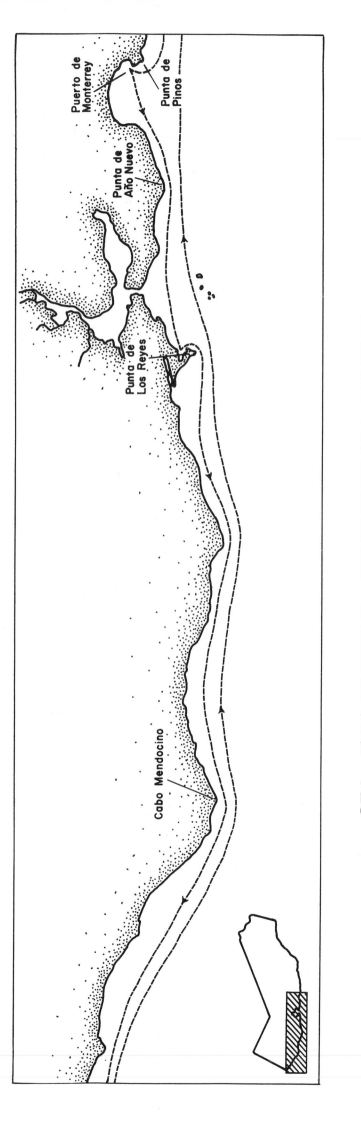

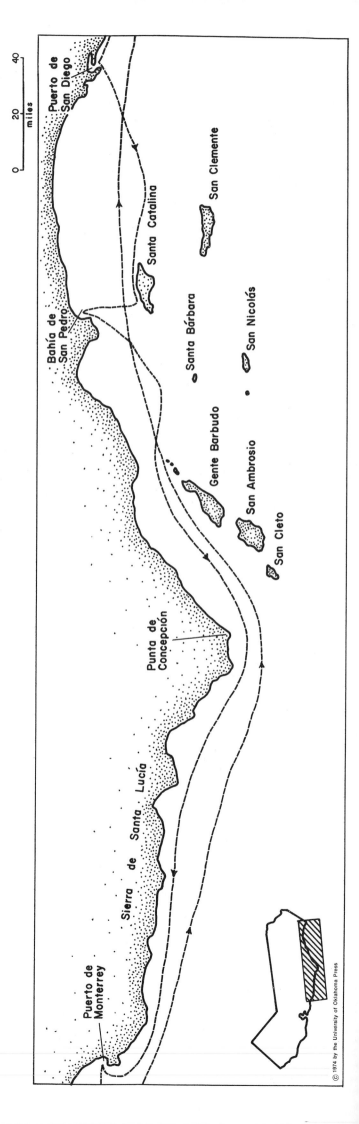

SEA EXPLORATIONS – SEVENTEENTH CENTURY

----- VISCAÍNO (1602-03)

THE ONLY IMPORTANT exploration of the California coast in the seventeenth century took place under the leadership of Sebastián Vizcaíno. A successful merchant in the Manila trade, this explorer was initially drawn to the Californias to exploit the pearl fisheries, whose existence had been known since 1535. Vizcaíno and his partners were granted a license effective March 1, 1594, for four years, to fish and mine from Navidad to California. The license was renewable for a sixteen-year period in a specific ten-league area. Not until 1596 did the expedition leave Acapulco on its northward journey. Exploration of the Baja coast exhausted supplies and brought trouble with the Indians, but little treasure.

By 1599, events had lessened official interest in, and thus financial support of, Vizcaíno's pearl-fishing enterprise. The Dutch corsair, Oliver van Noort, entered the Pacific, and his threat to Spanish shipping brought a new flurry of interest in a safe port for the Manila galleons. Vizcaíno, because of his supposed knowledge of the California coast, was appointed to head the official exploratory party. However, his appointment from Viceroy Gaspar de Zúñiga y Azevedo, Conde de Monterrey, drastically limited Vizcaíno's authority, inasmuch as he was given specific instructions and his decisions were subject to the review of a council of his officers. The viceroy ordered a detailed mapping of the coast. For this important duty, the cosmographer was Geronimo Martin Palacios. The latter's maps, with place names supplied by Vizcaíno, were the most complete and accurate source of information about the California coast for many years. (The originals of Mar-tin's map were lost, but Enrico Martínez, a Mexico City cartographer, used them to make copies).

The three ships of the expedition, the *San Diego* (the flagship), *Santo Tomás* and *Tres Reyes*, left Acapulco on May 5, 1602. It was November 10 before they reached San Diego, where the expedition remained for ten days. Continuing northward, the expedition sighted Santa Catalina on the twenty-fourth, and thus named it in honor of St. Catherine. A brief anchorage at the island and at a bay named San Pedro brought fresh water and food from friendly natives. In the channel, christened Santa Bárbara, friendly Indians in plank canoes were encountered. After the ships passed Punta de Concep-tión (Point Conception), the Santa Lucia Mountains were sighted. On December 16 the fleet entered Monterey Bay (named for the viceroy). Described as "being very secure from all winds," the harbor was extravagantly praised as an ideal place of refuge for the Manila galleons. At Monterey the *Santo Tomás* was returned to New Spain with the sickest of the crew, there to obtain new supplies. Obtaining fresh water from the Carmelo River, the remaining ships sailed northward on January 4, passing two points named Pinos and Año Nuevo, but missing the entrance to San Francisco Bay. Armenho's San Francisco Bay (Drake's Bay) was skirted, as was Punta de los Reyes. Stormy weather between January 5 and 20 separated the two ships and drove the *San Diego* northward to 42° north latitude. At this point the scurvy-ravaged crew turned southward, completing the most important Spanish exploration of the California coast.

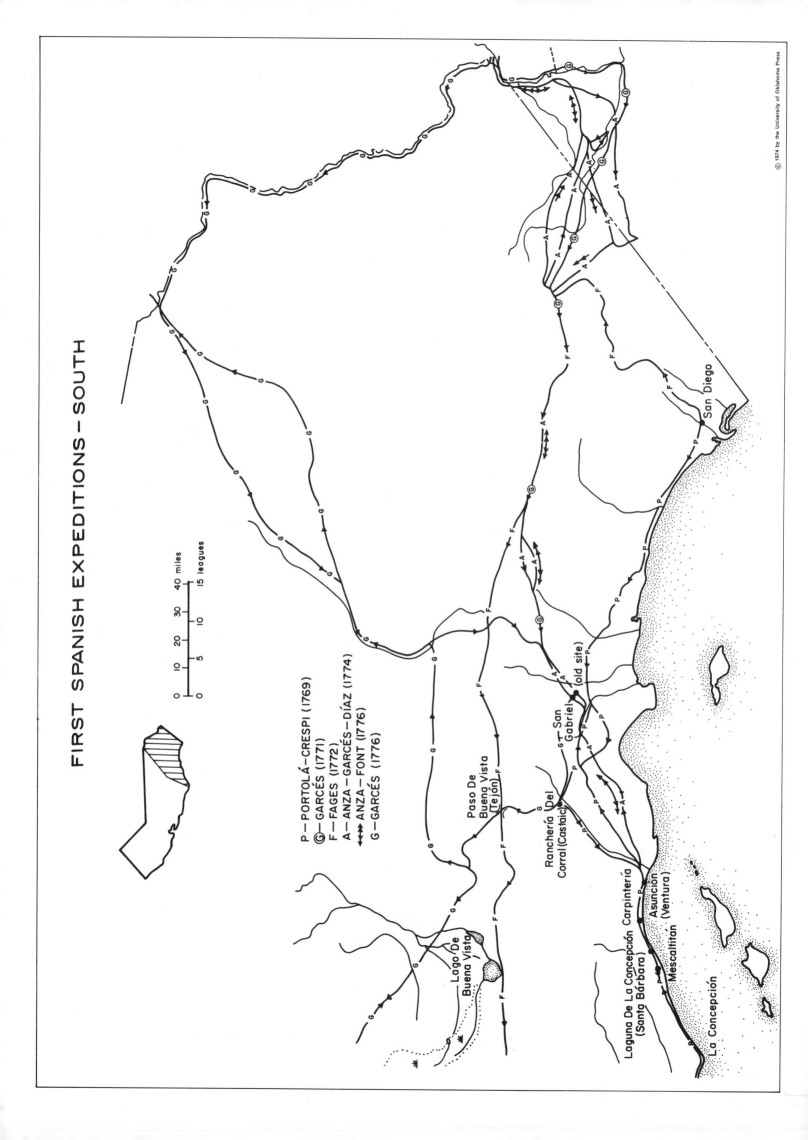

FIRST SPANISH EXPEDITIONS – SOUTH

P — PORTOLÁ – CRESPI (1769)
Ⓖ — GARCÉS (1771)
F — FAGES (1772)
A — ANZA – GARCÉS – DÍAZ (1774)
↔ ANZA – FONT (1776)
G — GARCÉS (1776)

40 miles
30
20
10
15 leagues
10
5
0

San Diego

San Gabriel
(old site)

Ranchería Del
Corral (Castaic)

Paso De
Buena Vista
(Tejón)

Lago De
Buena Vista

Laguna De La Concepción
(Santa Bárbara)
Carpintería
Asunción
(Ventura)
Mescaltitan
La Concepción

© 1974 by the University of Oklahoma Press

15. FIRST SPANISH EXPEDITIONS—SOUTH

FROM THE TIME of the initial settlement at San Diego in 1769, Spanish explorers scattered throughout California and by 1776 had charted most of the trails and had become familiar with most of the southern and coastal areas.

Gaspar de Portolá, accompanied by Friar Juan Crespi, whose diary recorded the route, left San Diego on July 14, 1769, to find and settle Monterey Bay. The party followed a route northward along the coast which was later designated as the King's Highway. On July 28, while the party was on the banks of the Santa Ana River, a strong earthquake was felt, followed by many additional shocks in the following week. August 2 found the group camped on a river near the site of the present city of Los Angeles. From this point the expedition went through the San Fernando Valley to the Santa Clara River, which they followed to the sea at Asunción (Ventura). At Carpintería they found a large pueblo and at Laguna de la Concepción (Santa Barbara) they noted a ranchería. A large village, some ten miles west of Santa Barbara, was named Mescaltitán.

One of the most remarkable Spanish explorers in southern California was Friar Francisco Garcés who made several journeys from the Sonoran missions to the Gila-Colorado area. While searching for mission sites in 1771 he made his way to the Yuma Indians on the Gila River and, crossing the Colorado River at Yuma, he blazed the trail across the Colorado Desert to within sight of the San Jacinto mountains. His trek ultimately became the basic overland route in the Spanish period. This virtually waterless trail was known as El Camino del Diablo (Devil's Road).

Pedro Fages, one of the key figures in the founding of California, charted a new route northward in 1772. Heading eastward from San Diego to the desert, he then turned northward along El Camino del Diablo through Paso de Buena Vista (Tejon Pass) into Antelope Valley and on into the San Joaquin Valley.

The inadequacy of the sea route for settlers and livestock prompted official encouragement for the charting of a land route to the new colony. On January 8, 1774, Juan Bautista de Anza, accompanied by Friar Garcés and Friar Juan Díaz, retraced the route Garcés had followed in 1771 from Sonora. A total of thirty-four persons made up the party, which lost its way in the desert and did not reach Mission San Gabriel until March 22. Anza went on to Monterey using the coastal route, but returned the same way.

Having proven the feasibility of the land route, Anza organized an expedition of colonists totaling 240 persons and more than 1,000 livestock. With Friars Garcés and Pedro Font the group left Tubac in Sonora on October 23, 1775, followed their previous route across the Colorado and the desert, and arrived in Monterey March 10, 1776.

Friar Garcés left the Anza expedition near the junction of the Gila and Colorado rivers and, with only an Indian guide, went up the Colorado. Seeking a better land route to Monterey, Garcés traveled westward along the Mojave River and through Cajon Pass, approximating the route of the latter-day Santa Fe railroad along the thirty-fifth parallel. After resting at San Gabriel, the wandering cleric again tried to reach Monterey via an interior route. Going through Tejon Pass to the vicinity of Bakersfield, he went on nearly to Tulare Lake. At this point he returned to the Colorado, probably via Tehachapi Pass. Difficulty in crossing the Colorado at Yuma possibly prompted Garcés' further search for a new route.

Unfortunately, the land route which Garcés had done so much to blaze was closed by the Yuma uprising in 1781, an event in which the great Franciscan explorer lost his life.

FIRST SPANISH EXPEDITIONS—CENTRAL

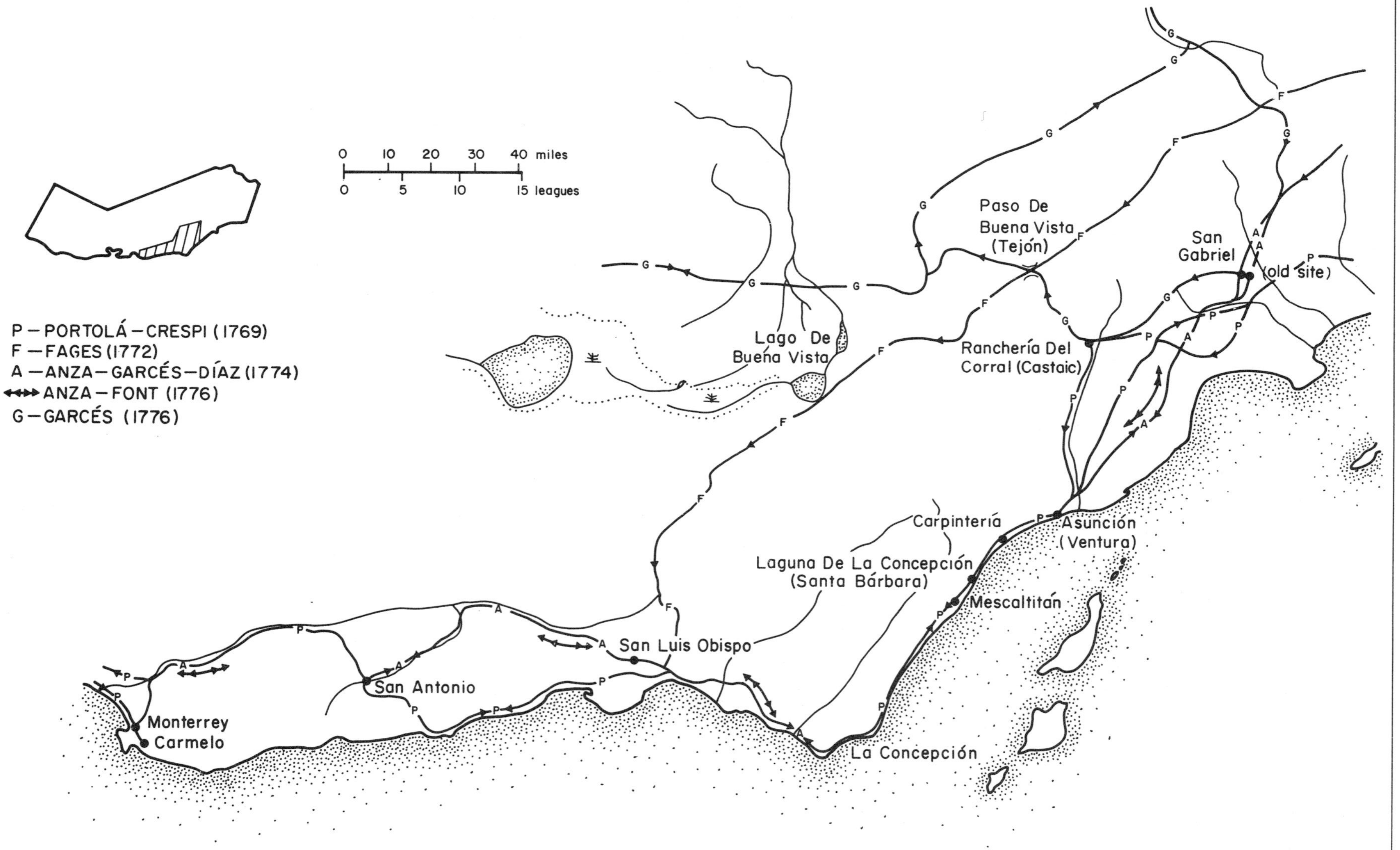

San Gabriel (Old Site)

Paso De Buena Vista (Tejón)

Ranchería Del Corral (Castaic)

Lago De Buena Vista

Asunción (Ventura)

Mescaltitán

Carpintería

Laguna De La Concepción (Santa Bárbara)

La Concepción

San Luis Obispo

San Antonio

Monterrey Carmelo

0   10   20   30   40 miles

0   5   10   15 leagues

P — PORTOLÁ — CRESPI (1769)
F — FAGES (1772)
A — ANZA — GARCÉS — DÍAZ (1774)
ANZA — FONT (1776)
G — GARCÉS (1776)

IN THEIR TRAILBLAZING journey from San Diego in search of Monterey, Gaspar de Portolá and Friar Juan Crespi and their party traced what became the traditional coastal route. From Point La Concepción the explorers stayed close to the ocean past Point Argüello. Near Point Sal, however, they turned inland to avoid the sand dunes and camped near modern San Luis Obispo. Henceforth they would have had easier traveling if they had proceeded inland and followed Anza's route northward up the Salinas Valley, but of course they had no way of knowing this. Instead, the Portolá party struggled through the swamplands along Morro Bay, and over the mountain ranges, which often come down to the ocean. Finding their way blocked by the Sierra of Santa Lucia near Cape San Martin, the travelers were forced to turn eastward and to slowly ascend the mountains. They completed the worst of their journey when they reached the headwaters of the Río de San Antonio, near where the mission of that name was ultimately located. Continuing their trek northeastward, possibly by way of Arroyo Seco, the weary band reached the Salinas River and followed it to the sea.

Pedro Fages, in his effort to find a new route between San Diego and Monterey, entered the San Joaquin Valley through Paso de Buena Vista (Tejon Pass). Proceeding northwestward through Antelope Valley and keeping close to the mountains in order to have water available, the party skirted Lago de Buena Vista. Fages probably crossed the mountains at the La Panza Summit, and then, making his way southwestward, he picked up Portola's trail.

On his first trip northward in 1774, Juan Bautista de Anza, with Garcés and Font, rested for several days at San Gabriel. Then, with only six men, he hastened northward to Monterey, making the round trip between April 10 and May 1, following virtually the same route which Portolà had taken. From San Gabriel his trail was further south, along the inside edge of the Santa Monica Mountains, rejoining Portolá's route a short distance from Ventura. From near San Luis Obispo, Anza took the easier route up the Salinas Valley instead of struggling along the coast. On his second expedition in 1776, bringing settlers and livestock to Monterey, Anza followed the trail he had blazed on his previous trip.

Unable to obtain a military escort and horses after resting at San Gabriel, Friar Garcés left the mission on April 9 with guide Sebastion Tarabal and three other Indians. He entered the upper Santa Clara Valley over the Newhall Pass, stopping at Castaic before crossing the Tehachapis at Tejon Pass. Continuing north, Garcés crossed the Kern River, stopping his trek near Tulare Lake. In leaving the valley he turned eastward across the desert to the Colorado River.

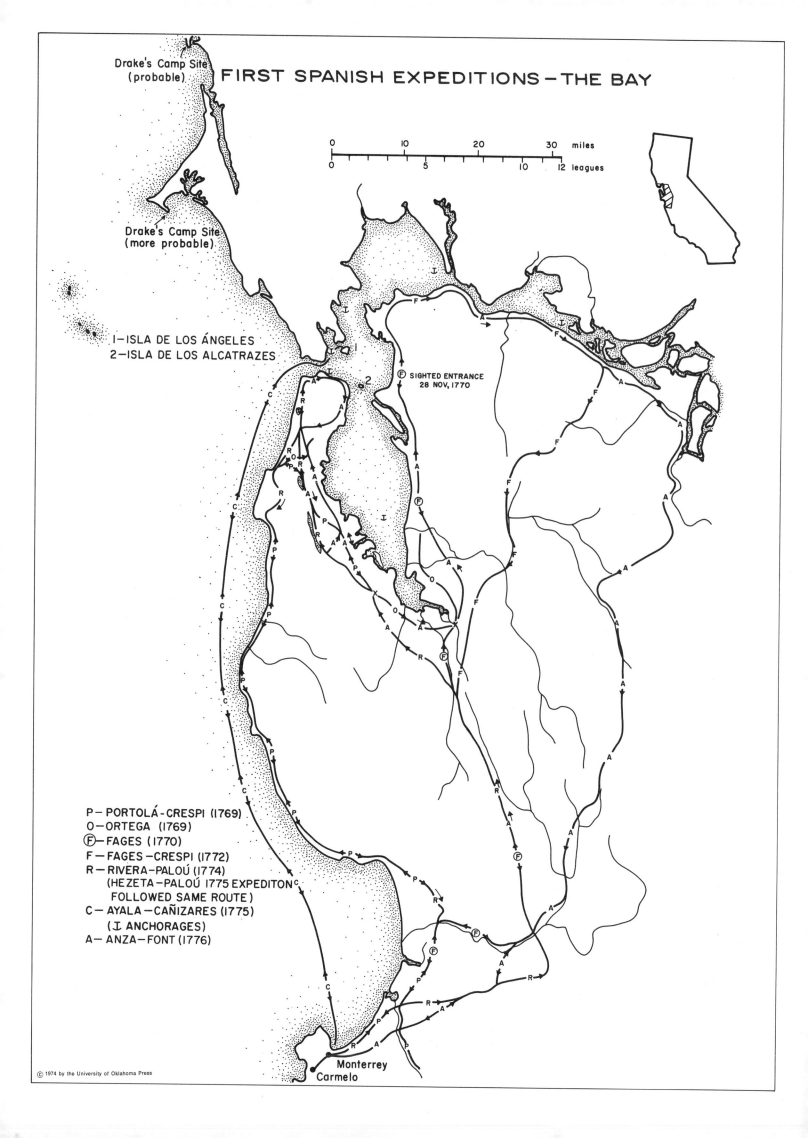

FIRST SPANISH EXPEDITIONS—THE BAY

Drake's Camp Site
(probable)

Drake's Camp Site
(more probable)

1—ISLA DE LOS ÁNGELES
2—ISLA DE LOS ALCATRAZES

Ⓕ SIGHTED ENTRANCE
28 NOV, 1770

0   10   20   30 miles

0   5   10   12 leagues

P — PORTOLÁ-CRESPI (1769)
O — ORTEGA (1769)
Ⓕ — FAGES (1770)
F — FAGES-CRESPI (1772)
R — RIVERA-PALOÚ (1774)
    (HEZETA-PALOÚ 1775 EXPEDITON
    FOLLOWED SAME ROUTE)
C — AYALA-CAÑIZARES (1775)
    (Ⅰ ANCHORAGES)
A — ANZA-FONT (1776)

Monterrey
Carmelo

AFTER FOLLOWING the Salinas River, the Portolá-Crespi party reached the sea on September 30, 1769. However, after exploring the area, they failed to recognize Monterey Bay, possibly because Cabero Bueno had described it as "a fine harbor sheltered from all winds." After a meeting with his officers on Octoger 4, Portolá reluctantly continued the trek northward in quest of the elusive Monterey. Their laborious route was along the coast until October 31, when they sighted the outer San Francisco Bay or the Gulf of the Farallones. Now realizing that they had passed Monterey, the main party camped in San Pedro Valley (Linda Mar of modern Pacifica) while a small group under Sergeant José Francisco Ortega scouted the area. On November 2, deer hunters saw the interior San Francisco Bay from a summit. The Ortega party also sighted the bay between November 1 and 3. Some historians claim that Ortega discovered the Golden Gate, but this assumption is unlikely, although his exact route remains uncertain. On November 4, the reunited group moved southeastward and from Sweeney Ridge viewed the southern arm of San Francisco Bay. On November 7, Ortega was again sent forth to scout and went around the arm of the bay. Returning to the main group, Portolá retraced his route and then returned southward on November 11.

Further explorations were necessary before the Spanish could fully understand the geography of the San Francisco Bay Area. Pedro Fages led a succession of exploratory groups in 1770 in an effort to find a land route to San Francisco Bay. Leaving Monterey on November 17, 1770, he went down the Santa Clara Valley and then along the eastern shore of the bay. From the top of a hill on November 28, 1770, he sighted its entrance (named the Golden Gate in 1846 by John C. Frémont). The following day Fages began the return to Monterey, which he and his small group of seven reached on December 4, 1770.

Seeking a site for a northern mission, Pedro Fages, accompanied by Father Crespi, six soldiers, a muleteer, and an Indian guide, left Monterey on March 20, 1772. The party followed the route Fages had taken before, but continued northward until their march was blocked by Carquines Strait. Turning eastward, they reached a point near Antioch, where they decided to return to Monterey. Seeking a shorter route they crossed the Santa Angela Plain and, via the San Ramon and Amador Valleys and Mission Creek, crossed their outward trails near Mission San José.

Fernando Javier Rivera y Moncada and Father Francisco Palou were next to explore the San Francisco Bay region. From Monterey they followed the route Fages had taken through the Santa Clara Valley, but went up the peninsula side instead of the east shore. They left on November 23 and returned to Monterey on December 13, 1774. A mission site was selected near modern Palo Alto, and although Rivera and Palou reached the Golden Gate they apparently didn't consider it a worthwhile mission or presidio site. Virtually the same route was followed by Bruno de Heceta, a naval captain accompanied by Palou, who, failing to find the Golden Gate from the foggy seas, made an overland journey in 1775.

In August and September, 1775, an extensive nautical survey of the bay was undertaken. Manuel de Ayala, in command of the *San Carlos* with José Cañizares as pilot, took 485 soundings in preparing a chart of the bay.

Anza, who had brought his party of immigrants to Monterey in 1776, left for the Bay Area on March 23, with Father Font, to select the settlement site. Journeying northward, he determined the proper location of the presidio and retraced his steps down the west side of the bay. Going up the east shore, Anza closely followed Fages' route but went farther inland than his predecessor before cutting across country for Monterey.

FIRST SPANISH EXPEDITIONS—NORTH

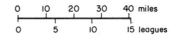

0   10   20   30   40 miles

0   5   10   15 leagues

-Ⓜ- GABRIEL MORAGA, 1810, 1812-1814
- M - GABRIEL MORAGA, 1808
- A - ARGÜELLO - ORDAZ, 1821 (CONJECTURAL)
- S - SÁNCHEZ - ALTIMIRA, 1823

ROSS

BODEGA

SAN RAFAEL

SAN FRANCISCO

MISSION
SAN JOSE

ALTHOUGH SPANISH exploration was concentrated in the San Joaquin Valley, the area north of San Francisco Bay was not totally neglected. Gabriel Moraga, who engaged in forty-two expeditions and campaigns on the California scene, explored extensively in the north country. In addition to the usual reasons for these intrusions into the unknown hinterlands—the quest for new mission sites, to search for runaway neophytes, and to punish hostile Indians—in the north the Spanish were concerned about the challenge of the Russian presence.

In an 1808 visit to the San Joaquin Valley, Gabriel Moraga traveled northward along the Sacramento River. After exploring some distance both up and down the Mokelumne, Cosumnes, and American rivers, the expedition crossed the Feather River. They then went north and northwest along the banks of the Sacramento. They went a short distance beyond Sutter Buttes, possibly to a point opposite modern Glenn or Butte City, before turning southward.

Gabriel Moraga was sent north in September, 1810, to investigate rumors of Russian movement into the area; Indians had reported the presence of the interlopers. But it was Americans, not Russians, which the Spanish explorer met, and Moraga accompanied three deer hunters back to their ship at Bodega Bay. Continuing his explorations into the region, he examined the plain to the northwest and found three streams, the Laguna Santa Rosa, Santa Rosa, and the Russian River. Returning to San Francisco, the party passed the plain of San Francisco Solano, upon which the Sonoma mission was to be built. From 1812 to 1814, Moraga made three overland treks to the Russian settlements at Bodega and Fort Ross. Thus he undoubtedly became familiar with the trails and valleys of Marin and Sonoma counties.

In 1821 an expedition was sent to drive out some Englishmen or Americans rumored to have infiltrated Mexican territory north of San Francisco. Luis Argüello was in command of fifty-five soldiers, accompanied by Father Blas Ordaz and John Gilroy as interpreter. They left San Francisco on October 8 and after crossing the bay followed a northeast by north course to the Sacramento River, reaching that stream a short distance north of Grimes. The group followed the bank of the river northward until they reached Cottonwood Creek. (Their route from this point on can best be classed as conjectural.) After following this stream to its source, they came along the Trinity, Eel, and Russian rivers.

Concern over Russian encroachment and the desire to establish a new mission to serve as an outpost led to an exploration of the country between Suisun and Petaluma in the summer of 1823. Father José Altimira and Alferez José Sánchez led the expedition which left San Francisco on June 25. Passing through San Rafael and Olompali, the travelers explored the Sonoma, Napa, and Suisun plains for possible mission sites. They finally decided on the Sonoma site and returned to San Francisco.

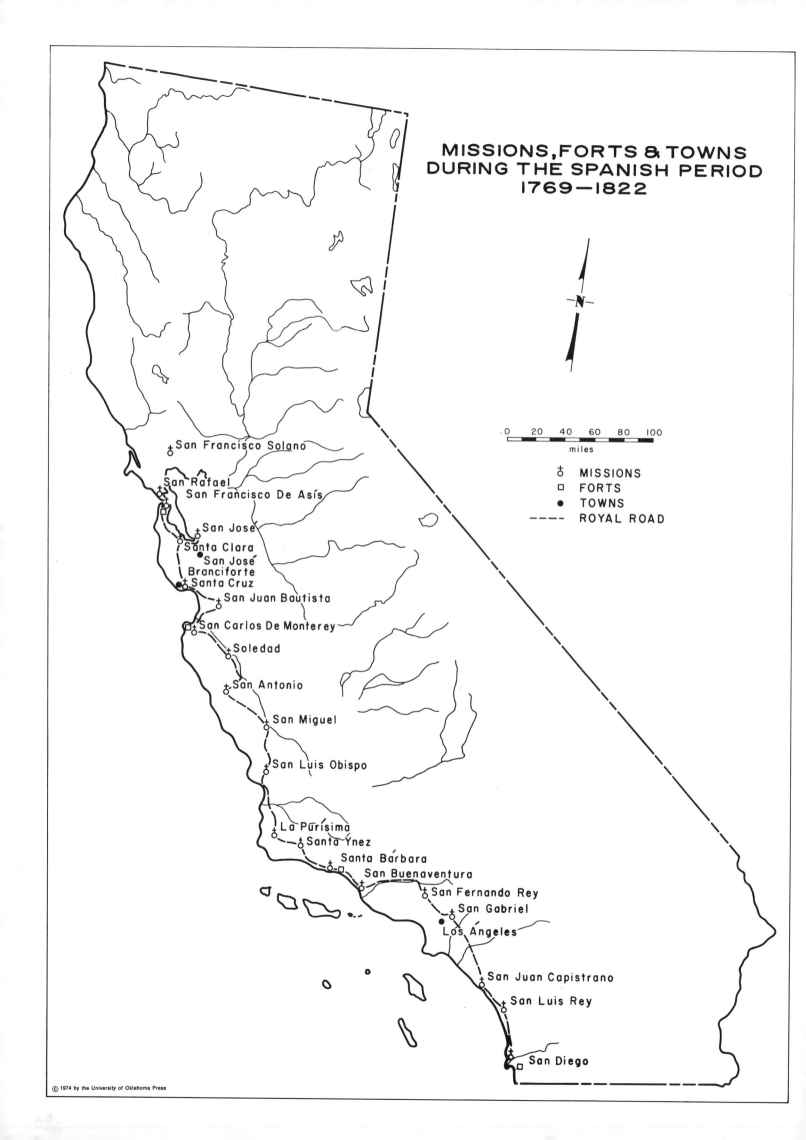

MISSIONS, FORTS & TOWNS
DURING THE SPANISH PERIOD
1769—1822

N

.0   20   40   60   80   100
miles

MISSIONS
FORTS
TOWNS
ROYAL ROAD

San Francisco Solano
San Rafael
San Francisco De Asís
San José
Santa Clara
San José
Branciforte
Santa Cruz
San Juan Bautista
San Carlos De Monterey
Soledad
San Antonio
San Miguel
San Luis Obispo
La Purísima
Santa Ynez
Santa Bárbara
San Buenaventura
San Fernando Rey
San Gabriel
Los Ángeles
San Juan Capistrano
San Luis Rey
San Diego

19. MISSIONS, FORTS, AND TOWNS DURING THE SPANISH PERIOD, 1769–1822

THE MISSION WAS the most important Spanish institution in California. Designed to Christianize the natives, it was also intended to strip them of their aboriginal culture and Hispanize them. Incidentally, the mission also became a significant vehicle by which Spain could advance her frontier, and it was the missionary drive, developed in Mexico, which led to the ultimate settlement of Alta California.

Twenty-one missions were established from San Diego in the south to Sonoma in the north. They were located approximately thirty miles apart, or a single day's journey along the Royal Road. This highway was usually little more than a bridle path and in many places followed the ocean beaches and was all but impassable in rainy weather.

The preferred mission site had timber, good soil, a convenient water supply, and Indians. Partially because of their excellent location, partially because of an ample labor supply, and partially because of the able leadership provided by the Franciscan friars, the missions flourished far more than did secular institutions. Within a few years the missions were producing an abundance of crops and a surplus of livestock. Thus, in actuality, it was the Franciscans who really conquered and settled California.

A Mission Chronology

The missions and the date of their founding were:

July 16, 1769	San Diego de Alcala
June 3, 1770	San Carlos de Monterey (moved to Carmel in 1771)
July 14, 1771	San Antonio de Padua
September 8, 1771	San Gabriel Arcangel
September 1, 1772	San Luis Obispo de Tolosa
November 1, 1776	San Juan Capistrano (First founded November 30, 1775)
October 9, 1776	San Francisco de Asís (or Dolores)
January 12, 1777	Santa Clara de Asís
March 31, 1782	San Buenaventura
December 4, 1786	Santa Bárbara
December 8, 1787	La Purísima Concepción
August 28, 1791	Santa Cruz
October 9, 1791	Señora de la Soledad
June 11, 1797	San José de Guadalupe
June 24, 1797	San Juan Bautista
July 25, 1797	San Miguel Arcangel
September 8, 1797	San Fernando Rey de España
June 13, 1798	San Luis Rey de Francia
September 17, 1804	Santa Ynez
December 14, 1817	San Rafael Arcangel
July 4, 1823	San Francisco Solano

The Spanish fort, or presidio, was intended to protect the missions from savage Indians or from attack by foreign intruders. The four forts were established at San Diego (1769), Monterey (1770), San Francisco (1776) and Santa Bárbara (1782). They were initially well constructed, but with the passage of years were permitted to fall into decay. According to many foreign visitors, their defenses were so weak that any invader could easily capture them. There were but few soldiers in the province (372 in 1812, for example), and these were reported to be of inferior quality. But however weak or small, the presence of a Spanish military force deterred foreign invasion. For an attack on a California fort would constitute an attack on Spain herself.

Spanish towns, or pueblos, were founded at San José (1777); at El Pueblo de Nuestra Señora—which was shortened to Los Angeles (1781), and Villa de Branciforte (1797). The towns were established in the hope that their citizens would raise enough surplus food to feed the military and also to provide a militia to assist in the defense of the province. It was hoped that the towns would be settled by a high caliber of citizenry, who would provide fine examples to the Indians. These hopes were not realized, and often California was something of a penal colony. Together, the towns and the forts provided a secular influence that was resented, sometimes with good cause, by the Franciscan friars.

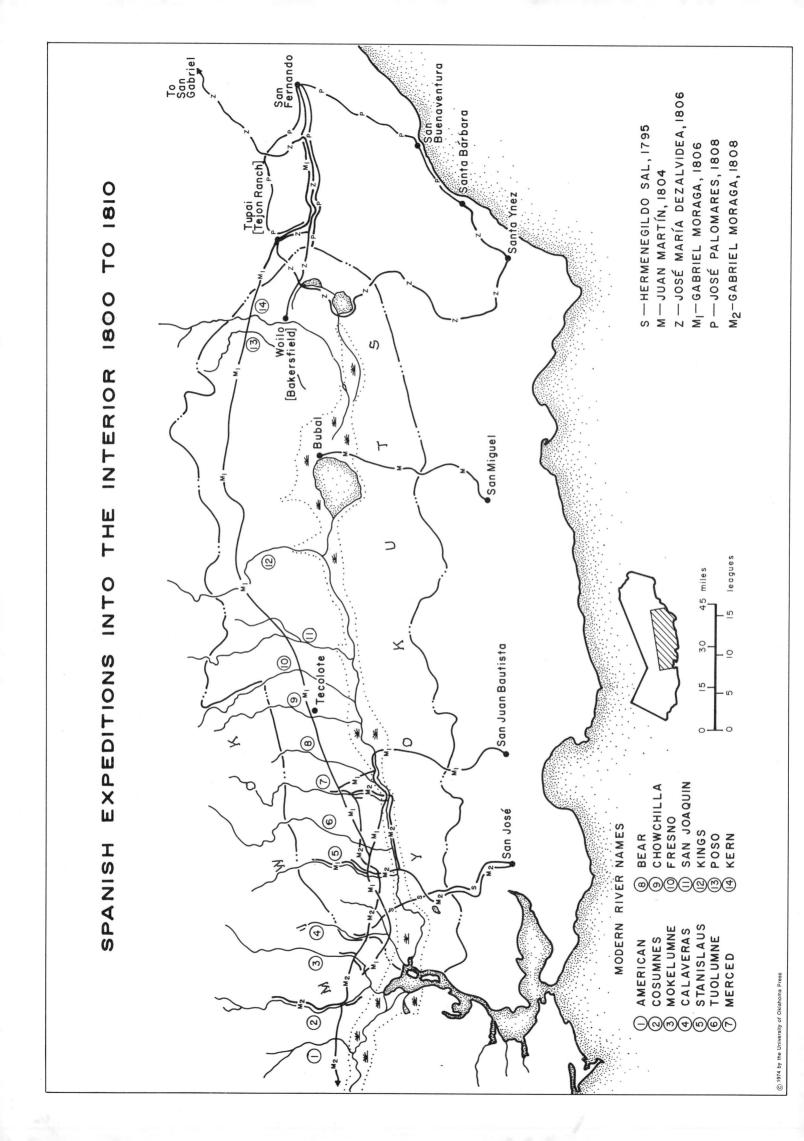

SPANISH EXPEDITIONS INTO THE INTERIOR 1800 TO 1810

S —HERMENEGILDO SAL, 1795
M —JUAN MARTÍN, 1804
Z —JOSÉ MARÍA DEZALVIDEA, 1806
M₁—GABRIEL MORAGA, 1806
P —JOSÉ PALOMARES, 1808
M₂—GABRIEL MORAGA, 1808

MODERN RIVER NAMES

① AMERICAN
② COSUMNES
③ MOKELUMNE
④ CALAVERAS
⑤ STANISLAUS
⑥ TUOLUMNE
⑦ MERCED

⑧ BEAR
⑨ CHOWCHILLA
⑩ FRESNO
⑪ SAN JOAQUIN
⑫ KINGS
⑬ POSO
⑭ KERN

45 miles
leagues
15
30
15
5
10
0

THE SPANISH OCCUPATION of California was mainly coastal with most of the missions being only a few miles from the ocean. Only in the south, as a result of the expeditions of Anza and Garcés, was much known of the interior. However, several exploring parties made their way inland in the first three decades of the nineteenth century to capture runaway neophytes, to punish Indian raiders, and to select new mission sites.

An exploratory party seeking a new mission site left Monterey November 15, 1795, under Hermenegildo Sal, accompanied by Father Antonio Danti. After finding suitable mission sites on the San Benito River and at Gilroy, the explorers went up the east side of San Francisco Bay, probably as far as present-day Oakland. A mission site was marked at San Francisco Solano, and the party returned to Santa Clara on November 25. Sal's report to the governor indicated considerable general knowledge of the rivers and the terrain in general east of the bay.

Interest in the Indians of the interior was evidenced by the unofficial visit of Father Juan Martín to the Tulares in 1804. Hearing that he would be welcomed by the natives, Father Martín traveled east from Mission San Miguel. He reached the rancheria of Bubal on the southeast edge of Lake Tulare. However, Martín's request to take Indian children to the mission was refused, and he was forced to return.

A more successful effort to explore the Central Valley was that of Father José María de Zalvidea who left Santa Barbara on July 19, 1806. From Santa Ynez the party went northward before crossing the mountains into the valley. Although some authorities claim that Father Zalvidea went as far north as Tulare Lake, it is more probable that his party went around the north side of Buena Vista Lake. After going a short distance east and retracing their steps, the explorers went as far as the site of Bakersfield. They went through Tehachapi Pass en route to San Gabriel, which they reached on August 14.

A far more extensive exploration was carried out by a group led by Alferez Gabriel Moraga, accompanied by Father Pedro Muñoz. With a twenty-five-soldier escort the party left San Juan Bautista on September 21, 1806. After crossing the San Joaquin near the present boundary between Merced and Fresno counties, they named a slough Mariposas because of the many butterflies in the area. After dividing into two groups, the explorers named the Merced River and decided it had the most desirable mission site. Moraga went as far north as the Mokelumne River, but then turned southeastward on October 4 and, skirting the edge of the mountains, reached Tejon Pass on November 1 and San Fernando on November 3. In 1808, Moraga made another visit to the San Joaquin Valley to look for suitable mission sites. Leaving San Jose on September 25, the party crossed the San Joaquin and went as far south as the Merced River, which they explored to its source. On this trip they also extensively explored the Stanislaus, Calaveras, Mokelumne, and Cosumnes rivers as they made their way northward.

A minor exploratory party was led by José Palomares from Santa Bárbara in 1808. It made its way into the south San Joaquin via San Buenaventura and San Fernando. This group of explorers followed part of the same route as de Zalvidea.

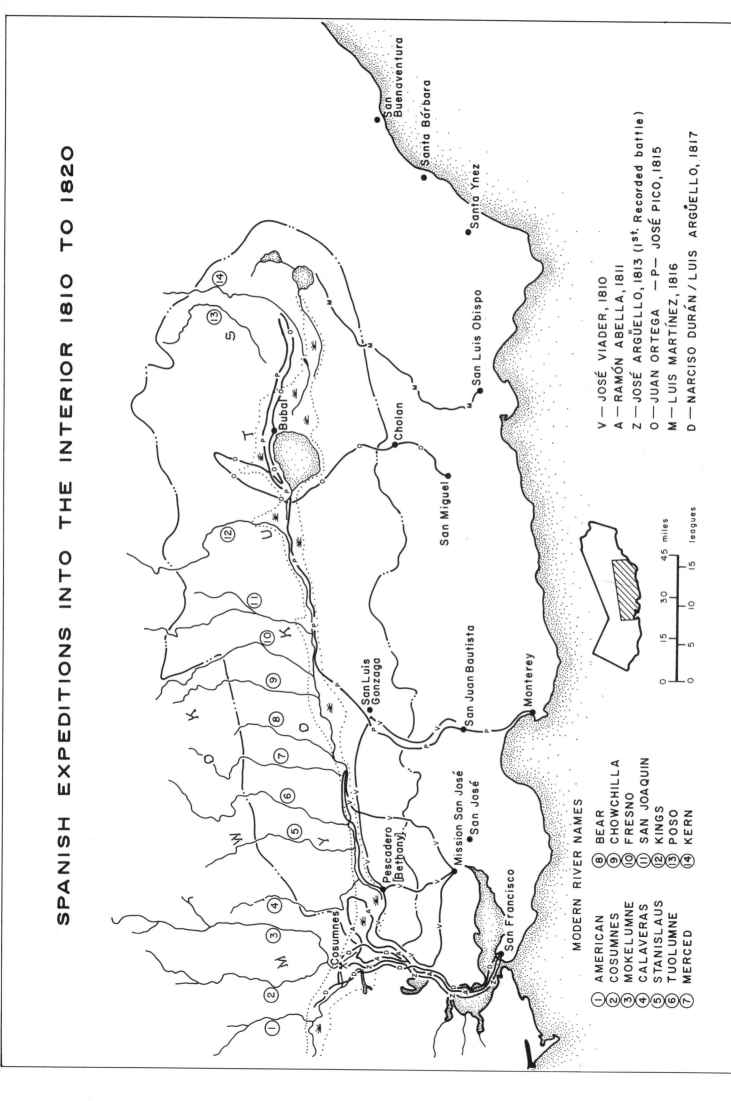

SPANISH EXPEDITIONS INTO THE INTERIOR 1810 TO 1820

San
Buenaventura

Santa Bárbara

Santa Ynez

V — JOSÉ VIADER, 1810
A — RAMÓN ABELLA, 1811
Z — JOSÉ ARGÜELLO, 1813 (1st. Recorded battle)
O — JUAN ORTEGA   —P— JOSÉ PICO, 1815
M — LUIS MARTÍNEZ, 1816
D — NARCISO DURÁN / LUIS ARGÜELLO, 1817

San Luis Obispo

Bubal

Cholan

San Miguel

San Luis
Gonzaga

San Juan Bautista

Monterey

Mission San José

San José

Pescadero
[Bethany]

San Francisco

Cosumnes

MODERN RIVER NAMES

1. AMERICAN
2. COSUMNES
3. MOKELUMNE
4. CALAVERAS
5. STANISLAUS
6. TUOLUMNE
7. MERCED
8. BEAR
9. CHOWCHILLA
10. FRESNO
11. SAN JOAQUIN
12. KINGS
13. POSO
14. KERN

45 miles

leagues

0   15   30   45

0   5   10   15

21. SPANISH EXPEDITIONS INTO THE INTERIOR, 1810 TO 1820

IN THE SECOND decade of the nineteenth century the Spanish continued to send exploratory parties into the interior, mainly into the San Joaquin Valley. They retraced the routes of previous expeditions while still seeking mission sites, runaway neophytes, or the opportunity to intimidate hostile Indians.

Father José Viader, accompanied by Gabriel Moraga, made two reconnaissances in 1810. They first went north from Mission San José into present day Contra Costa County via Valle de San José and Walnut Creek. At Carquines Straits they went eastward to the San Joaquin River. The explorers then followed it upstream, or southward, to San Luis Gonzaga, where they turned west en route to San Juan Bautista, arriving there on August 25. After a brief rest, Viader and Moraga went exploring again. This time they went eastward from Mission San José through Pescadero (Bethany). Going southward from this point the party again examined the Merced River as a possible mission site. Here they turned northward before returning to Mission San José.

In October, 1811, Father Ramón Abella led a water exploration of the lower portions of the Sacramento and San Joaquin rivers, again looking for suitable mission locations. The party went by way of Angel Island, by San Pablo and Point Pinole, following the right side of the straits as they made their way inland. Entering the main channel of the San Joaquin they ascended that stream southward for four days. They then went down the east channel into the Sacramento for the first recorded navigation of that river.

In 1813 José Argüello led the first expedition of punishment against the Indians. Twelve soldiers, later joined by a hundred Indian auxiliaries, left from San Francisco by launch, and went up the straits to capture runaway neophytes. The hostile Indians were reported to be a thousand in number, concentrated on an island protected by dense thickets. Despite the discrepancy in numbers, the Spaniards forced the natives to flee with heavy casualties while they suffered the loss of only one auxiliary. The soldiers had the advantage in such encounters with the Indians because they wore leather jackets of five thicknesses of sheepskins and carried leather shields of two thicknesses of cowhide. Arrows could seldom penetrate these devices.

In 1815 a so-called "grand expedition" was organized to return Indians who had fled the missions. One party, led by Juan Ortega, left Mission San Miguel on November 4. They spent the first night at Cholan and then marched eastward to the San Joaquin. No runaways were apprehended, and "the Spaniards were well received by the Indian villages of Tache and Sumtache by the runaways from La Soledad." On November 15, Ortega joined the group led by José Dolores Pico, and the combined force went to Bubal. Pico, accompanied by Father Jaime Escudo, in charge of the second detachment, marched from Monterey. They entered the valley via San Luis Gonzaga and ascended the San Joaquin (southward) in search of runaways. The expedition returned to their starting point with nine prisoners in all and a large number of horses.

The following year Father Luis Martínez visited the Indian villages of the Tulare in an effort to lure converts to the missions. He left from Mission San Luis Obispo and traveled to the region of Buena Vista Lake, but the unfortunate cleric was only able to obtain one boy "in exchange for beads, blankets, and meat."

In 1817 another maritime exploration of the great rivers took place under Father Narciso Durán and Luis Argüello. Leaving from the beach at the presidio of San Francisco on May 13, the party went across the bay by way of Angel Island and Point San Pedro. They went up the Sacramento for several days and reached a point midway between Clarksburg and Freeport. Here they turned back and went around Brannan Island, planning to ascend the San Joaquin. The going was difficult, and after only a short distance they returned to the presidio.

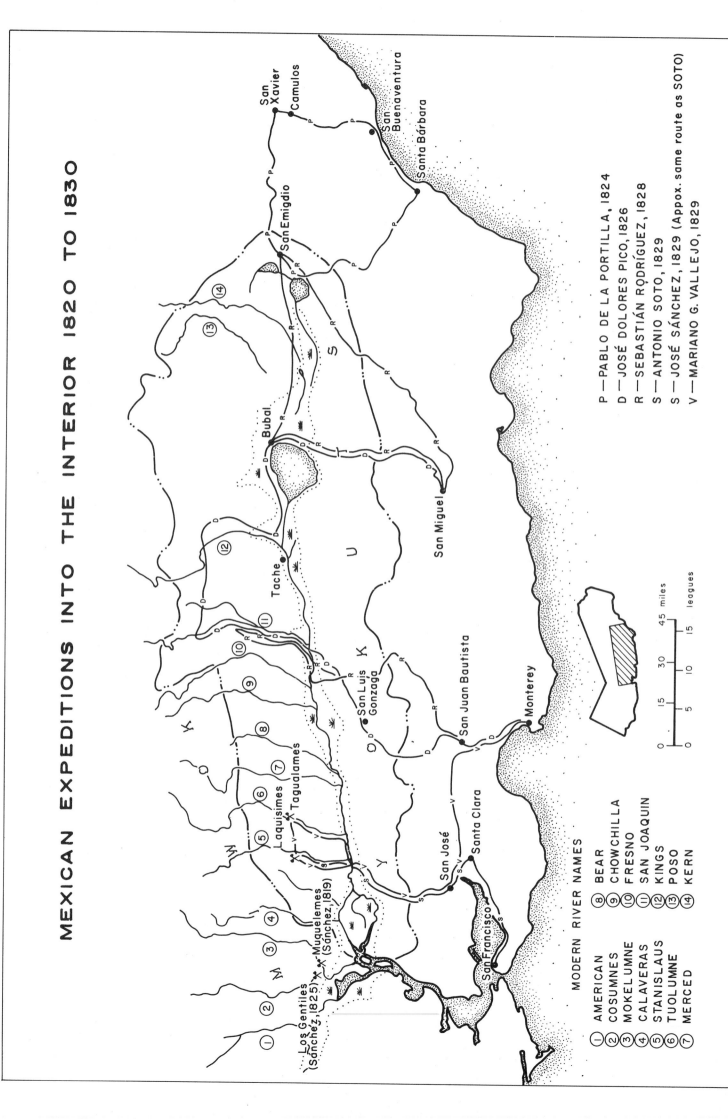

MEXICAN EXPEDITIONS INTO THE INTERIOR 1820 TO 1830

P — PABLO DE LA PORTILLA, 1824
D — JOSÉ DOLORES PICO, 1826
R — SEBASTIÁN RODRÍGUEZ, 1828
S — ANTONIO SOTO, 1829
S — JOSÉ SÁNCHEZ, 1829 (Appox. same route as SOTO)
V — MARIANO G. VALLEJO, 1829

MODERN RIVER NAMES

① AMERICAN   ⑧ BEAR
② COSUMNES   ⑨ CHOWCHILLA
③ MOKELUMNE   ⑩ FRESNO
④ CALAVERAS   ⑪ SAN JOAQUIN
⑤ STANISLAUS   ⑫ KINGS
⑥ TUOLUMNE   ⑬ POSO
⑦ MERCED   ⑭ KERN

San Xavier
Camulos
San Buenaventura
Santa Bárbara
San Emigdio
Bubal
Tache
San Miguel
San Luis Gonzaga
San Juan Bautista
Monterey
Tagualames
Laquisimes
Muquelemes (Sánchez, 1819)
Los Gentiles (Sánchez, 1825)
San José
Santa Clara
San Francisco

0   15   30   45 miles
0   5   10   15 leagues

AFTER CONTROL OF California passed from Spain to Mexico in 1822, expeditions into the interior continued, but with a changed purpose. Interest in an inland area as a possible mission site waned; instead, soldiers were sent into the interior to recover stolen animals and punish hostile Indians, in order to reduce the attacks upon towns, missions, and ranchos.

The march of a force commanded by Pablo de la Portilla in 1824 resulted from Indian revolts in February of that year at Santa Ynez, Purísima Concepción, and Santa Bárbara missions. The military expedition left Santa Bárbara on June 2 to return the runaway neophytes to their missions. Marching via San Buenaventura, the main force went up the Santa Clara Valley through Camulos (a sheep ranch of Mission San Fernando). At San Xavier they turned northeast and followed a route approximating that of the present highway through the Tejon Pass to the valley. At San Emigdio, Portilla met a unit of fifty soldiers under Antonio del Valle that had come from San Miguel to assist. Near Buena Vista Lake the combined forces met the runaway neophytes and through diplomacy were able to convince them to return to Santa Bárbara without bloodshed. The expedition returned, marching westward via modern Maricopa over the mountains to Santa Bárbara.

On December 27, 1825, José Dolores Pico led a force from Monterey via Mission San Juan Bautista and the Hollister valley through San Luis Gonzaga into the San Joaquin Valley. Again the purpose was to return runaway neophytes. The party ascended the rain-swollen San Joaquin River into the mountains, looking for a place to ford. After ferrying the horses across the stream on rafts made for the purpose, Dolores led the expedition southward along the Sierra Nevada to the Kings River, which they followed westward into the Great Central Valley, and then marched southward around the eastern edge of Tulare Lake. From Bubal the well-marked trail to Mission San Miguel was followed. The expedition was "successful" in that a number of hostile Indians were killed, many tribes were intimidated, a number of neophytes were returned, and some horses were reclaimed.

In 1828, Sebastián Rodríguez led two expeditions into the interior mainly searching for stolen horses, which had become an important diet item of the Indians. On April 20 he left San Juan Bautista and entered the valley by way of Little Panoche, reaching the San Joaquin south of modern Dos Palos. Ascending the San Joaquin for some distance, the party recaptured many neophytes, intimidated the natives, and found large numbers of stolen horses before returning to San Juan Bautista on May 6. Rodríguez led a similar military expedition from San Miguel on May 26. Going southeastward over the mountains at La Panza, the group went to Buena Vista Lake, San Emidgio, and then northward to Bubal. Again, a number of horses and Indians were obtained before the return to San Miguel on June 9.

In 1829, three expeditions were sent against Estanislao, a former mission Indian of outstanding talents, who led a strong force of runaway neophytes and wild Indians on the Stanislaus River. Trouble with Indians over horse stealing had led to attacks by José Sánchez on the native villages of Mugelemes in 1819 and Los Gentiles in 1825. Antonio Soto led the first group against Estanislao in 1829, only to turn back when his small force was unequal to the challenge. José Sánchez next led a force of forty men into the impenetrable wilderness along the Stanislaus River with no success. A large force under Mariano G. Vallejo was able to defeat the Indians in a campaign along both the Stanislaus and Tuloumne rivers.

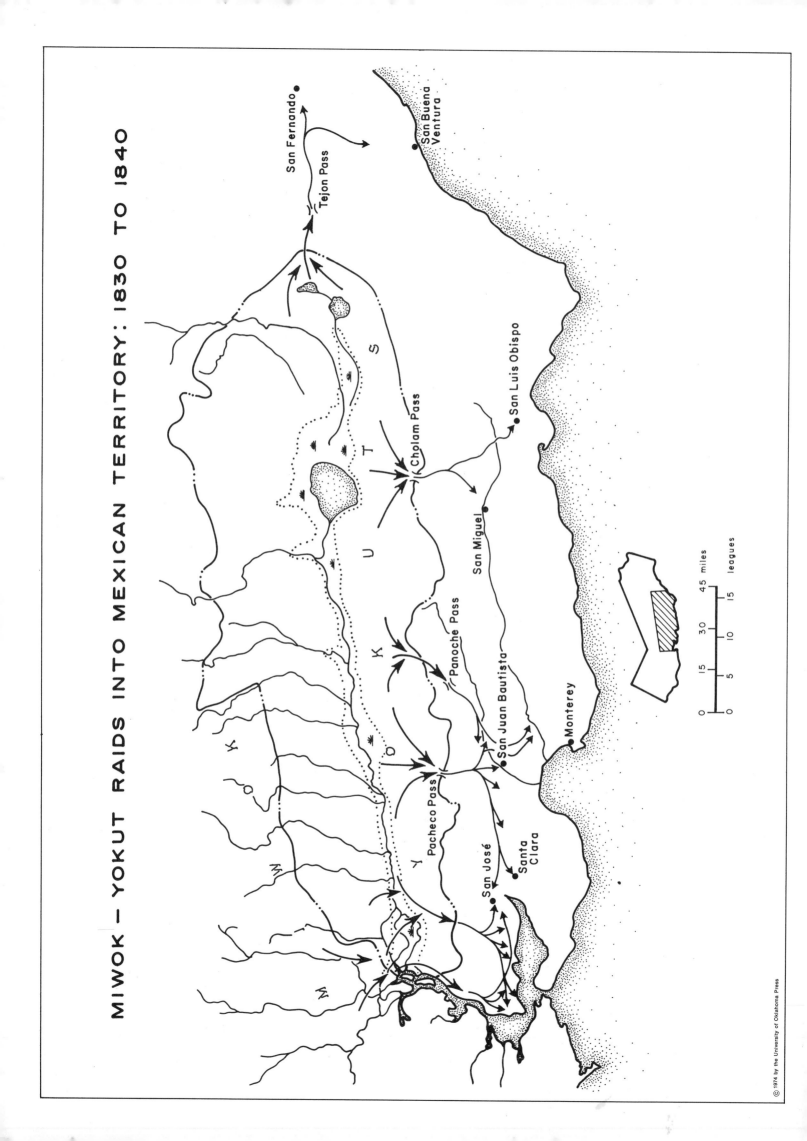

MIWOK – YOKUT RAIDS INTO MEXICAN TERRITORY: 1830 TO 1840

San Fernando

Tejon Pass

San Buena Ventura

San Luis Obispo

Cholam Pass

San Miguel

Panoche Pass

San Juan Bautista

Pacheco Pass

San José

Santa Clara

Monterey

23. MIWOK-YOKUT RAIDS INTO MEXICAN TERRITORY, 1830 TO 1840

THE DECADE OF the 1830's saw the Mexican Californios everywhere on the defensive. From San Fernando to the Bay Area—missions, ranchos, and towns were subjected to a constant series of Indian attacks, with large numbers of horses and cattle being taken and many people killed and injured. Valley Indians, usually Yokuts but also Miwoks, crossed Cholam Pass, Panoche Pass, Pacheco Pass, and Tejon Pass along the riverine area to raid almost at will. After 1833, hardly a year passed without reports of such depredations and petitions to the authorities for help. For example, in 1838 several rancheros were killed near Monterey by Indians; in 1839 the grain storehouse at Santa Clara was attacked; and in 1841 Mission San Juan Bautista was under siege. At San Luis Obispo more than a thousand head of stock were lost in a single raid.

Mexican authorities met the threat by the old policy of expeditions. As these forays frequently punished the innocent Indians as well as the guilty, they made conditions worse. By 1840, the natives were so strong that such inland expeditions were both costly and dangerous. In 1833, Governor José Figueroa ordered that "from every presidio a military expedition shall set out each month and scout those places where the robbers shelter themselves." In 1840, Governor Juan B. Alvarado ordered a military force to patrol the mountain passes and prevent the Indians from using them. And in 1843 it was proposed that a stockade (or fort) be built in Pacheco Pass; in other words, Hispanic officialdom had shifted from the offensive to the defensive as the "first" Californians threatened their very presence.

The basic reason for the Miwok-Yokut raids was the conflict between the California Indian and white civilization. This first arose at the missions when neophytes, unhappy with the confinement, labor, punishment, diet, disease, or just homesick, sought to return to their native state. From the founding of the first mission, Spanish authorities had been kept busy returning such runaways, but as secularization neared in the 1830's and conditions at the missions became increasingly chaotic, the number fleeing increased dramatically. Having been trained by the Spanish, these runaways, such as Estanislao, often provided the wild tribes with superior leadership. In addition, these neophytes desired certain items they were used to at the missions, but which now could only be obtained by raiding.

The heathen or native Indians were at first peaceful and receptive to the Mexican expeditions. However, this early hospitality waned when Indian children were taken for the missions, Indian women were abused by Mexican soldiers, and as a result of hearing horror stories of mission life from fugitive neophytes. The atrocities committed against them by numerous expeditions by Indian auxiliaries as well as by Mexicans, prompted the valley Indians to embark upon a policy of physical resistance. Contact with the Hispanic way of life also triggered a change in the native life style. As Professor Sherburne F. Cook puts it, "A peaceful, sedentary localized group underwent conversion into a semi-warlike, seminomadic group." By 1828 the acorn had been replaced by horsemeat as the staple food item. Perhaps this important dietary change resulted from the influence of neophytes among them. In any event, the only way to obtain this basic food was by raiding Hispanic settlements. The horse made them highly mobile, and in a short time the Indians became expert cavalrymen whose hit and run tactics created havoc among the great herds of the 1830's.

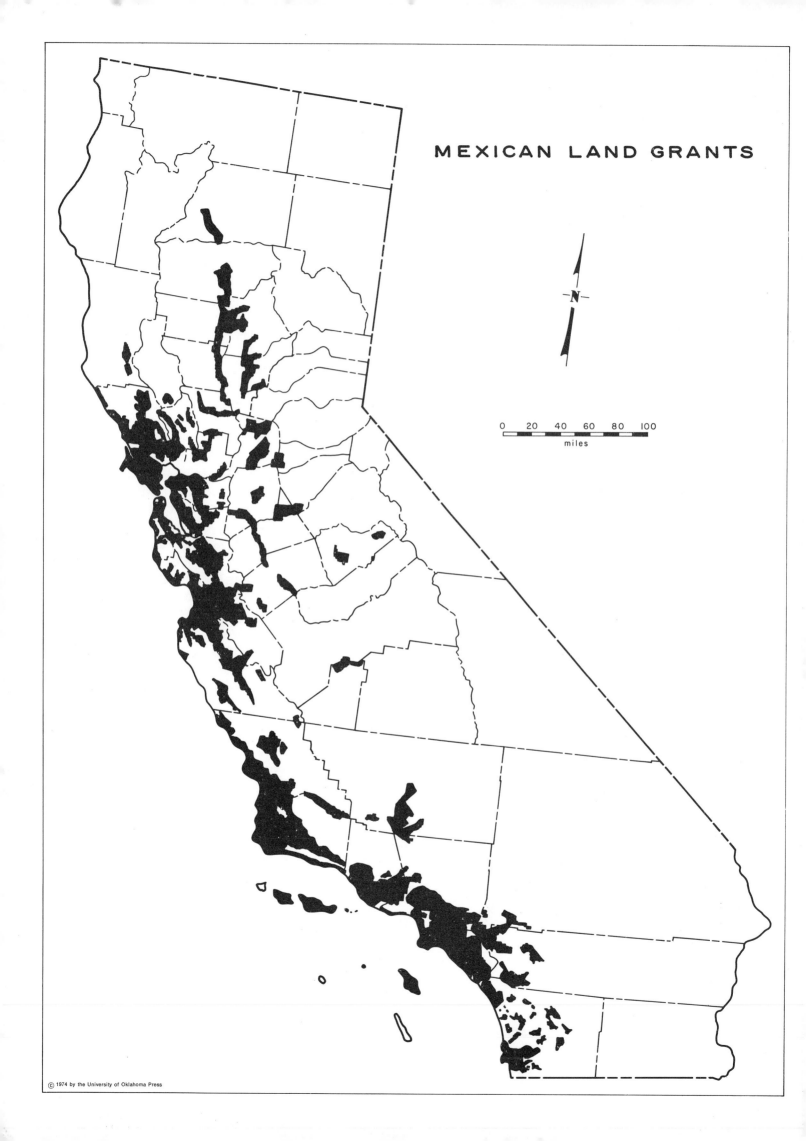

MEXICAN LAND GRANTS

N

0 20 40 60 80 100
miles

© 1974 by the University of Oklahoma Press

24. MEXICAN LAND GRANTS

THE SYSTEM OF Mexican land grants was one of the most important influences upon California history. These ranchos were the prime force in allowing the creation of great feudal baronies in the Anglo era, which, in turn, led to the concentration of California land ownership in a few hands. In fact, many of the large farms and ranch properties today originated in one or more of the Mexican grants. Nineteen of the grants, all of which are in grazing sections, are still intact. At least twelve others are assessed to single ownerships to the extent of two-thirds of their original size, and at least six more single ownerships cover from a third to half of the original area. The grants have left a heritage of confused land ownership that has made necessary a flourishing title insurance business in the state. City streets and country roads often follow the boundaries laid down by a Mexican land grant. For example, Pico Boulevard in Los Angeles runs along the edge of what was once Rancho La Ballona. Hillside Boulevard in San Mateo County runs along the southern boundary of Rancho Cañada de Guadalupe, Visitación y Rodeo Viejo. Such irregular boundaries are in marked contrast to the checkerboard pattern of lands divided on the basis of public land surveys.

Although popularly referred to as "Spanish" ranchos, land grants were only made during the Mexican period. Under Spanish rule some 25 concessions were made which permitted settlement and use of a specified tract of land, but title remained with the crown. Actually, the Spanish concessions were little more than grazing permits, although many were patented under Mexican laws of 1824, 1828, and 1834 which provided the legal base for the grants. Until 1834, only 51 grants were claimed. Of the 813 grants ultimately claimed, 453 were filed between 1841 and 1846, 277 from 1844 to 1846, and 87 in the last few months before United States occupation. Of the total claims presented, 346 (or 42 per cent) were presented by non-Mexicans. The rapid increase in claims for land grants coincided with the rise in importance of the hide and tallow trade and the expectation of land appreciation following American occupation.

In all previous acquisitions of territory, as well as the treaty of 1848 with Mexico, the United States guaranteed existing rights in land. Unfortunately, the Mexican grants were conditional, boundaries were vague and overlapping, legal titles were faulty or did not exist, and the existence of many spurious land claims cast suspicion on valid ones. To settle the complex problem, the Land Act of 1851 established a land commission to adjudicate.

This commission approved 553 claims totaling some 8,850,000 acres. The 197 rejected grantees failed to comply with Mexican law requiring complete documentation, or had their claims rejected for fraud or antedated documents. The other grants were withdrawn, either because of compromise or certain rejection.

Under Mexican law a claim for land was filed by petition to the governor, requesting a specific tract. An individual cited his military service record, proved his citizenship, and presented an argument as to why he should receive the land. Accompanying the petition was a *diseño* or sketch-map of the land desired. Some *diseños* clearly displayed a familiarity with the land being described and were drawn by a person at the area in question. Other *diseños* were fabrications drawn by someone who had never seen the land described. After proper investigation the governor granted a decree known as a *concedo* which was the official order to prepare the land title. Before the title was made final, the grantee was required to erect a permanent building, fence, or otherwise mark boundaries of the land and have the local magistrate define the boundaries by the act of juridical possession, the closest thing to an actual survey. Unfortunately, this measurement was often not carried out, or if it was, documentation to prove it was not filed with the proper authorities. Many rancheros failed to obtain approval of their grants by the territorial legislature or neglected one or more of the steps required by Mexican law to finalize ownership. Thus, the land commission rejected land claims because either the rancheros or the Mexican authorities were negligent. (When land grants overlap counties they are repeated.)

MEXICAN LAND GRANTS

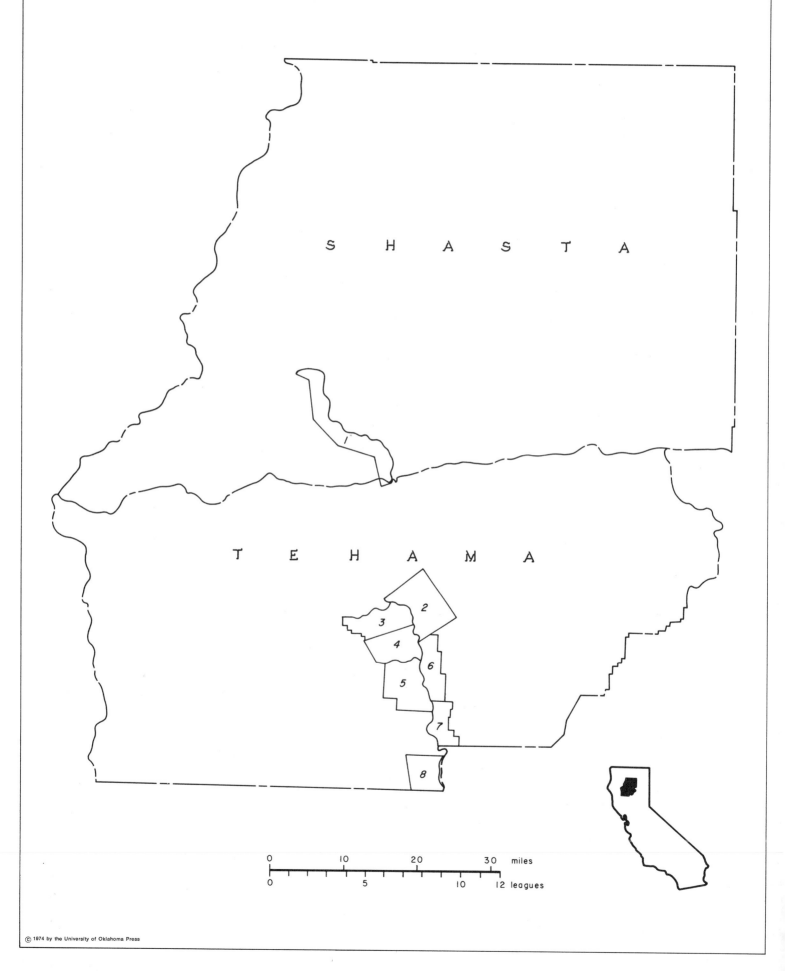

S H A S T A

T E H A M A

2

3

4

6

5

7

8

0	10	20	30	miles
0	5	10	12 leagues	

25. MEXICAN LAND GRANTS—TEHAMA, SHASTA

	TEHAMA COUNTY	
Grant Number	*Name*	*Acres*
7	Bosquejo (Butte)	22,206
8	Capay (Colusa)	44,388
2	Primer Cañon o Río de los Berrendos	26,637

3	La Barranca Colorado	17,707
4	Las Flores	13,315
6	Río de los Molinos	22,172
5	Saucos	22,112
	SHASTA COUNTY	
1	San Buenaventura	26,632

MEXICAN LAND GRANTS

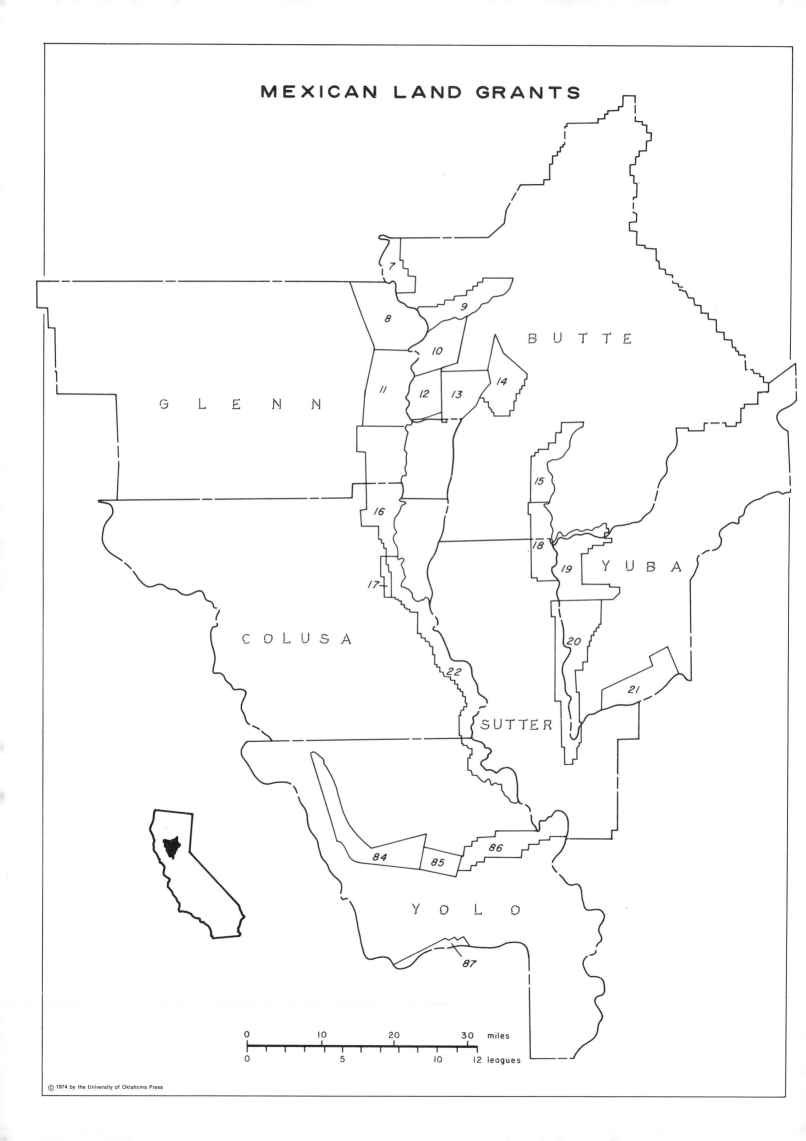

B U T T E

G L E N N

7

9

8

10

14

11

12

13

15

16

18

19

Y U B A

17

20

C O L U S A

22

21

S U T T E R

84

85

86

Y O L O

87

| 0 | 10 | 20 | 30 | miles |
| 0 | 5 | 10 | 12 leagues |

BUTTE COUNTY

Grant Number	Name	Acres
13	Aguas Frias	26,761
9	Arroyo Chico	22,214
18	Boga (Sutter)	22,185
7	Bosquejo (Tehama)	22,206
14	Esquon	22,194
15	Fernandez	17,806
19	Honcut (Yuba)	31,080
12	Llano Seco	17,767
10	Rancho de Farwell	22,194

COLUSA COUNTY

17	Colus	8,876
22	Jimeno	48,854
16	Larkin Children's Rancho	44,364

GLENN COUNTY

Grant Number	Name	Acres
8	Capay (Tehama)	44,388
11	Jacinto	35,488

16	Larkin Children's Rancho (Colusa)	44,364

YOLO COUNTY

84	Cañada de Capay	40,079
22	Jimeno (Colusa)	48,854
85	Quesesosi or Guesisosi	8,894
86	Río Jesus Maria	26,637
87	Río de los Putos (Solano)	17,755

YUBA COUNTY

19	Honcut (Butte)	31,080
21	Johnson's Rancho	22,197
20	New Helvetia (Sutter & Sacramento)	48,839

SUTTER COUNTY

18	Boga (Butte)	22,185
20	New Helvetia (Sacramento & Yuba)	48,839

MEXICAN LAND GRANTS

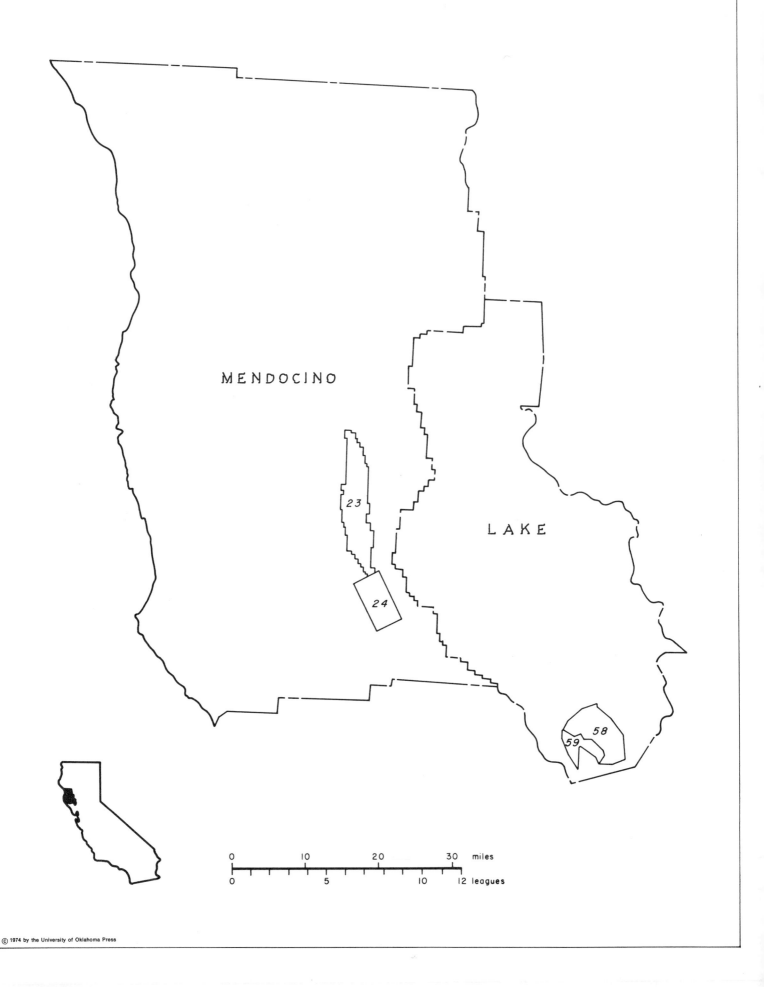

MENDOCINO

LAKE

23

24

58

59

0   10   20   30   miles

0   5   10   12 leagues

27. MEXICAN LAND GRANTS—MENDOCINO, LAKE

	MENDOCINO COUNTY			LAKE COUNTY	
Grant Number	*Name*	*Acres*			
24	Sanel	17,754	58	Guenoc	21,220
23	Yokaya	35,541	59	Collayomi	8,242

MEXICAN LAND GRANTS

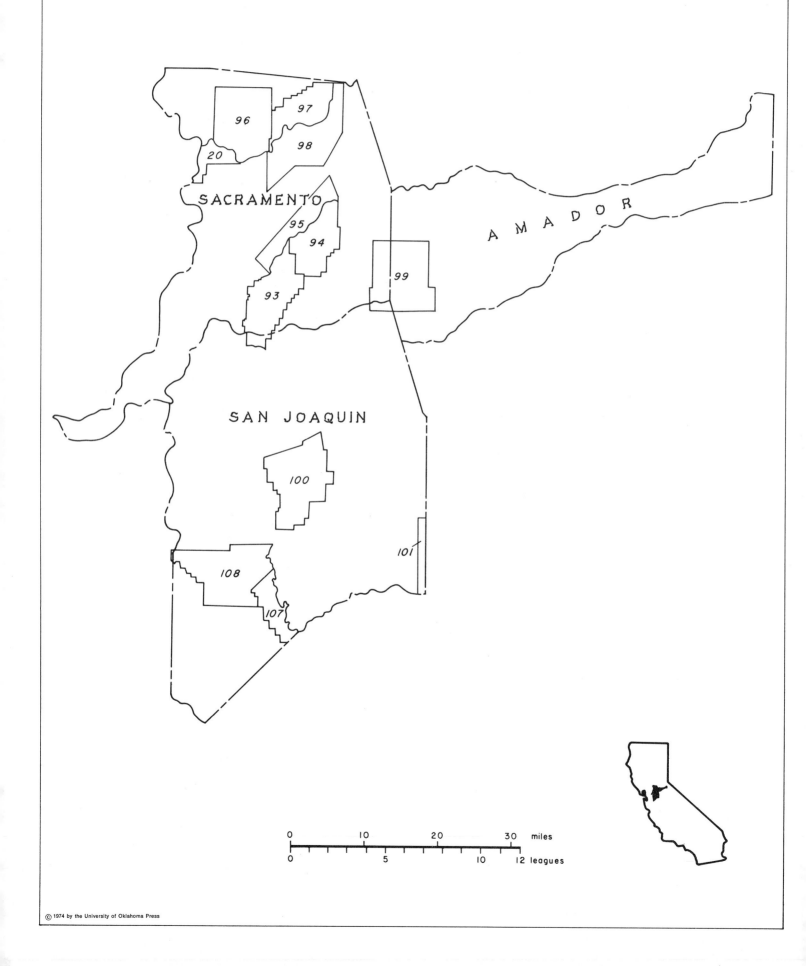

SACRAMENTO

AMADOR

SAN JOAQUIN

96

97

98

20

95

94

93

99

100

101

108

107

0		10		20		30	miles
0			5			10	12 leagues

SACRAMENTO COUNTY

Grant Number	Name	Acres
99	Arroyo Seco (Amador & San Joaquin	48,858
94	Cosumnes	26,605
96	Rancho del Paso	44,371
20	New Helvetia (Yuba & Sutter)	48,839
95	Omochumnes	18,662
98	Río de los Americanos	35,521
93	Sanjon de los Moquelumnes (San Joaquin)	35,508
97	San Juan	19,983

SAN JOAQUIN COUNTY

99	Arroyo Seco (Amador)	48,858
100	Campo de los Franceses	48,747
107	El Pescador (Grimes) (Stanislaus)	35,446
108	El Pescador (Pio & Naglee)	35,546
93	Sanjon de los Moquelumnes (Sacramento)	35,508
101	Thompson's Rancho (Stanislaus)	35,533

AMADOR COUNTY

99	Arroyo Seco (Sacramento)	48,858

MEXICAN LAND GRANTS

SOLANO

NAPA

SONOMA

MARIN

miles

12 leagues

29. MEXICAN LAND GRANTS—MARIN, NAPA, SOLANO, SONOMA

MARIN COUNTY

Grant Number	Name	Acres
29	Blucher (Sonoma)	26,759
35	Las Baulines	8,911
40	Cañada de Herrera	6,658
47	Corte Madero de Novato	8,879
42	Corte Madera del Presidio	7,845
30	Laguna de San Antonio (Sonoma)	24,903
46	Novato	8,871
48	Olompali	8,877
41	Punta de Quentin	8,877
33	Punta de los Reyes	8,879
34	Punta de los Reyes (Sobrante)	48,189
39	San Gerónimo	8,701
45	San José (Pacheco)	6,659
44	San Pedro, Santa Margarita y Las Gallinas	21,679
36	Saucelito	19,572
31	Soulajule	10,898
37	Tomales y Baulines (Phelps)	13,645
38	Tomales y Baulines (Garcia)	9,468
43	Lands belonging to Mission San Rafael	6.48
32	Nicasio	56,620

NAPA COUNTY

Grant Number	Name	Acres
79	Carne Humana	17,962
82	Catacula	8,546
89	Chimiles	17,762
78	Caymus	11,887
74	Entre Napa	5,711
73	Carneros, Rincon de Los (Part of Entre Napa)	2,558
72	Huichicha (Sonoma)	18,704
80	La Jota	4,454
83	Las Putas	35,516
81	Locoallomi	8,873
61	Malacomes or Moristal y Plan de Agua Caliente (Sonoma)	17,743
76	Napa	21,917

Grant Number	Name	Acres
75	Tulucay	8,866
77	Yajome	6,653

SOLANO COUNTY

Grant Number	Name	Acres
88	Los Putos	44,384
92	Los Ulpinos	17,726
87	Río de los Putos (Yolo)	17,755
91	Suisun (Wilson, part of Fine)	17,755 482
90	Tolenas (Napa)	13,316

SONOMA COUNTY

Grant Number	Name	Acres
67	Agua Caliente	3,219
29	Blucher (Marin)	26,759
27	Bodega	35,488
57	Caslamayomi	26,788
65	Cotate	17,239
28	Estero Americano	8,849
25	German	17,580
66	Los Guilicos	18,834
52	Cañada de Jonive	10,787
30	Laguna de San Antonio (Marin)	24,903
60	Malacomes or Moristal (Napa)	2,560
53	Molinos	17,892
72	Huichica (Napa)	18,704
26	Muñiz	17,761
56	Rincon de Musalacon	8,867
49	Petaluma	66,622
51	Cañada de Pogolimi	8,781
62	San Miguel	6,663
63	Cabeza de Santa Rosa	8,885
64	Llano de Santa Rosa	13,316
54	Sotoyome	48,837
55	Tzabaco	15,439
61	Malacomes, or Moristal y Plan de Agua Caliente (Napa)	17,743
50	Roblar de la Miseria	16,887
70	Mission Sonoma	14.20
68	Sonoma Pueblo Lands	6,094
69	Lac	177

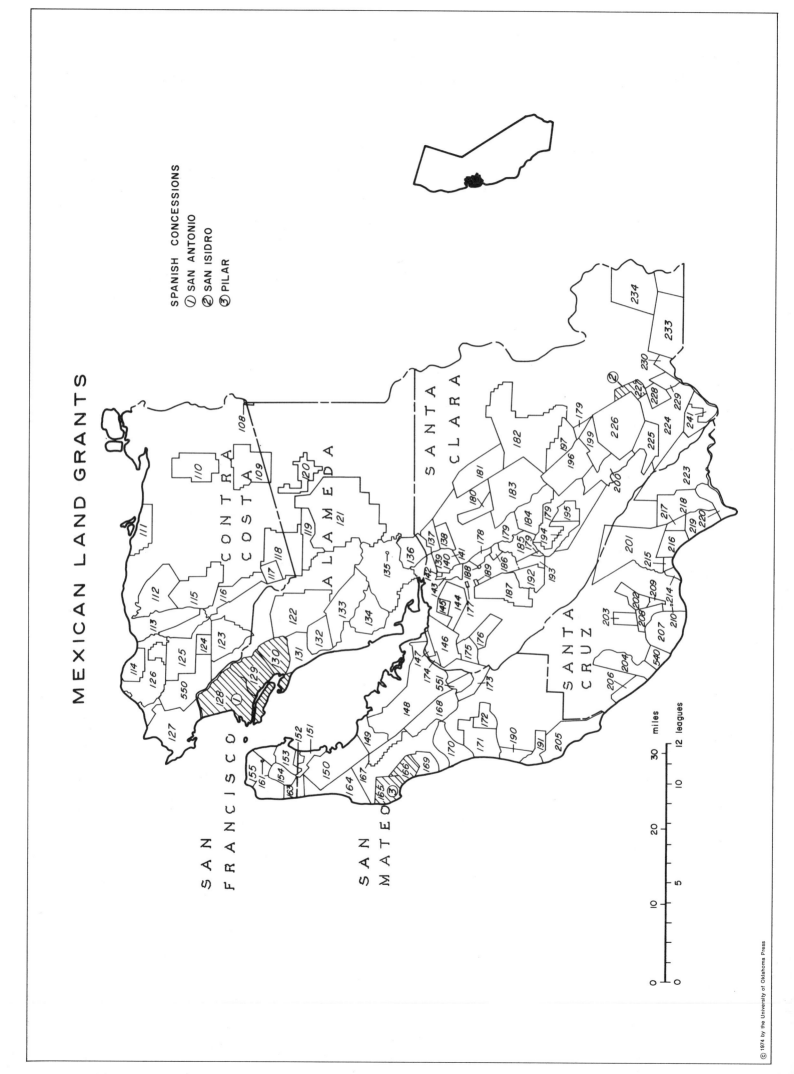

MEXICAN LAND GRANTS

SPANISH CONCESSIONS
① SAN ANTONIO
② SAN ISIDRO
③ PILAR

30. MEXICAN LAND GRANTS—ALAMEDA, CONTRA COSTA, SANTA CLARA, SAN FRANCISCO, SAN MATEO, SANTA CRUZ

ALAMEDA COUNTY

Grant Number	Name	Acres
136	Agua Caliente (Santa Clara)	9,564
133	Arroyo de la Alameda	17,705
109	Cañada de los Vaqueros (Contra Costa)	17,760
120	Las Positas	8,880
135	Mission San Jose	28
134	Potrero de los Cerritos	10,610
128	San Antonio (V. & D. Peralta)	18,849
129	San Antonio (A. M. Peralta)	15,207
130	San Antonio (Y. Peralta)	9,416
122	San Lorenzo (Castro)	26,723
132	San Lorenzo (Soto)	6,686
131	San Leandro	6,830
118	San Ramon (Amador) (Contra Costa)	16,517
119	Santa Rita	8,894
121	Valle de San Jose (Sunol & Bernal)	48,436

CONTRA COSTA COUNTY

Grant Number	Name	Acres
124	Acalanes	3,329
115	Arroyo de las Nueces y Bolbones	17,782
114	Cañada del Hambre Las Bolsas	13,354
109	Cañada de los Vaqueros (Alameda)	17,760
125	La Boca de la Cañada de Pinole	13,316
123	Laguna de los Palos Colorados	13,316
113	Las Juntas	13,293
110	Los Meganos	13,316
112	Monte del Diablo	17,922
127	San Pablo	17,939
118	San Ramon (Amador) (Alameda)	16,517
116	San Ramon (Carpentier)	8,917
117	San Ramon (Norris)	4,451
111	Los Medanos	8,859
126	El Pinole	17,761
550	El Sobrante	20,565

SANTA CLARA COUNTY

Grant Number	Name	Acres
136	Agua Caliente (Alameda)	9,564
233	Ausaymas y San Felipe (San Benito)	35,504
551	Cañada del Corte de Madera (San Mateo)	3,561
194	Los Capitancillos	3,360
181	Cañada de Pala	15,714
197	Cañada de San Felipe y Las Animas	8,788
173	El Corte de Madera (San Mateo)	13,316
241	Juristac (Santa Clara)	4,540
188	Mission Santa Clara	20
199	Ojo de Agua de la Coche	8,927
180	Pala	4,454
144	Pastoria de las Borregas (Murphy)	4,894
	Castro	4,172
145	Posolmi	1,696
178	El Potrero de Santa Clara	1,939
187	Quito	13,310
147	Rinconada del Arroyo de San Francisquito	2,230
192	Rinconada de los Gatos	6,631
141	Rincon de los Esteros (Alviso)	2,200
140	Rincon de los Esteros (Berreyesa)	1,845
139	Rincon de los Esteros (White)	2,308
146	Rincon de San Francisquito	8,418
223	Salsipuedes (Santa Cruz)	31,201
176–A	San Antonio (Dana)	3,542
176–B	San Antonio (Mesa)	4,440
226	San Francisco de las Llagas	22,283
174	San Francisquito (San Mateo)	1,471
179	San José Pueblo Lands	55,892
185	San Juan Bautista	8,880
234	San Luis Gonzaga (Merced)	48,821
177	Santa Clara (Enright)	710
189	Santa Clara (Bennett)	359
184	Santa Teresa	9,647
195	San Vicente (Berreyesa)	4,438
228	San Ysidro (Gilroy)	4,461
229	San Ysidro (Ortega)	4,439

Grant Number	Name	Acres	Grant Number	Name	Acres
201	Shoquel Augmentation (Santa Cruz)	32,702	168	Cañada de Raymundo	12,545
225	Solis	8,875	170	Cañada de Verede y Arroyo de la Purísima	8,906
183	Yerba Buena	24,332	551	Cañada del Corte de Madera (Santa Clara)	3,566
189	Santa Clara (Bennett)	359			
138	Milpitas (Alviso)	4,458	165	Corral de Tierra (Palomares)	7,766
137	Tularcitos (Higuera)	4,394	166	Corral de Tierra (Vasquez)	4,436
230	Llano del Tequisquito (San Benito)	11,016	173	El Corte de Madera (Santa Clara)	13,316
182	Los Huecos	39,951	153	Rincon de las Salinas y Potreo Viejo (San Francisco)	4,446
175	La Purísima Concepción	4,439			
186	Los Coches	2,219	154	San Miguel (Noe) (San Francisco)	4,443
224	Las Animas	26,519			
227	La Polka	4,167	167	Feliz	4,448
143	Ulistac	2,217	163	Laguna de la Merced (San Francisco)	2,219
200	Las Uvas	11,080			
142	Embarcadero de Santa Clara	180	169	Miramontes (San Benito)	4,424
196	La Laguna Seca	19,973	148	Pulgas	35,240
			205	Punta de Año Nuevo	17,753
	SAN FRANCISCO COUNTY		190	San Antonio or Pescadero	3,282
152	Cañada de Guadalupe y Rodeo Viejo (San Mateo)	943	174	San Francisquito (Rodríguez) (Santa Clara)	1,471
151	Cañada de Guadalupe, La Visitacion y Rodeo Viejo (San Mateo Counties)	5,473	172	San Gregorio (Castro)	4,439
			171	San Gregorio (Rodríguez)	13,344
163	Laguna de la Merced (San Mateo Counties)	2,219	149	San Mateo	6,439
543	Las Camaritas	19	164	San Pedro (Sánchez)	8,926
161	Two Tracts at Mission Dolores	9	551	Cañada del Corte de Madera (Santa Clara)	3,566
159	Ojo de Agua de Figueroa	1.77			
153	Rincon de las Salinas y Potrero Viejo	4,446		SANTA CRUZ COUNTY	
			206	Agua Puerca y las Trancas	4,422
154	San Miguel (Noe)	4,443	216	Aptos	6,686
155	San Francisco Pueblo Land	12,643	540	Arroyo de la Laguna	4,418
			214	Arroyo del Rodeo	1,473
	SAN MATEO COUNTY		220	Bolsa del Pajáro	5,496
150	Buri Buri	14,639	208	Cañada del Rincon en el Río de San Lorenzo de Santa Cruz	5,827
191	Butano	4,439			
151	Cañada de Guadalupe la Visitacion y Rodeo Viejo (San Mateo Counties)	5,473	217	Laguna de las Calabazas	2,305
			218	Los Corralitos	15,400
152	Cañada de Guadalupe y Rodeo Viejo (San Francisco)	943	207	Refugio	12,147
			223	Salsipuedes (Santa Clara)	31,201
			219	San Andres	8,912
			202	San Augustín	4,437

Grant Number	Name	Acres	Grant Number	Name	Acres
204	San Vicente (Escamilla)	10,803	203	Zayanta	2,658
215	Shoquel	1,668	210	Mission lands of Santa Cruz	
201	Shoquel Augmentation			(Church)	17
	(Santa Clara)	32,702	209	La Carbonera	2,225

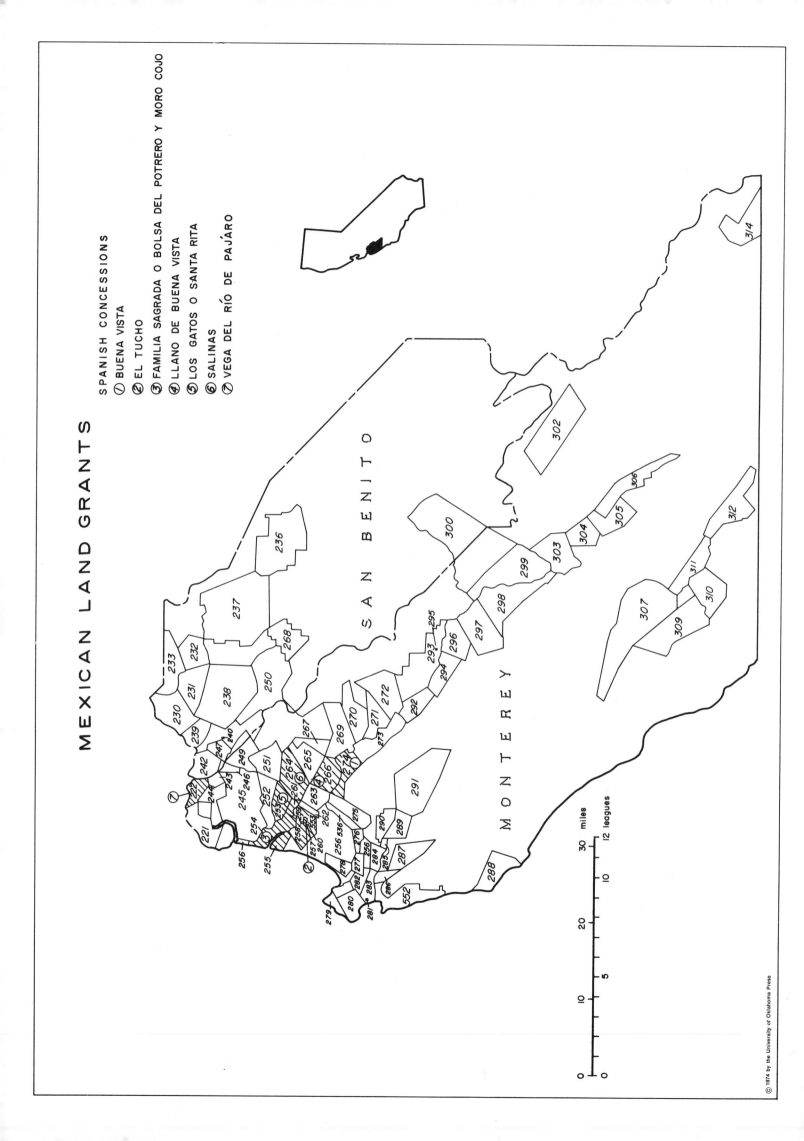

MEXICAN LAND GRANTS

SPANISH CONCESSIONS
① BUENA VISTA
② EL TUCHO
③ FAMILIA SAGRADA O BOLSA DEL POTRERO Y MORO COJO
④ LLANO DE BUENA VISTA
⑤ LOS GATOS O SANTA RITA
⑥ SALINAS
⑦ VEGA DEL RÍO DE PAJÁRO

S A N   B E N I T O

M O N T E R E Y

miles
12 leagues

31. MEXICAN LAND GRANTS—MONTEREY, SAN BENITO

MONTEREY COUNTY

Grant Number	Name	Acres
282	Aguajito	3,323
252	Bolsa de las Escarpines	6,416
297	Arroyo Seco (Torre)	16,523
221	Bolsa de San Cayetano	8,866
254	Bolsa del Potrero y Moro Cojo or La Sagrada Familia	6,916
245	Bolso Nueva y Moro Cojo	30,901
274	Buena Vista	7,726
243	Cañada de la Carpenteria	2,236
283	Cañada de la Segunda	4,367
314	Cholame	26,622
270	Chualar	8,890
290	Corral de Tierra (McCobb)	4,435
265	El Alisal (Bernal)	5,941
267	El Alisal (Hartnell)	2,971
536	El Chamisal	2,737
269	Encinal y Buena Esperanza	13,391
310	El Piojo	13,329
294	Ex-Mission Soledad	8,900
280	El Pescadero (Jacks)	4,426
286	El Potrero de San Carlos	4,307
288	El Sur	8,949
275	El Toro	5,688
259	El Tucho	400
273	Guadalupe y Llanitos de los Correos	8,858
276	Laguna Seca	2,179
251	La Natividad	8,642
257	Las Salinas	4,414
266	Llano de Buena Vista	8,446
244	Los Carneros (Littlejohn)	4,482
246	Los Carneros (McDougal)	1,629
253	Los Gatos o Santa Rita	4,424
296	Los Coches	8,794
311	Los Ojitos	8,900
289	Los Laureles (Beronda)	6,625
285	Los Laureles (Ransom)	718
291	Los Tularcitos (Gomez)	26,581
249	Los Vergeles	8,760
307	Milpitas	43,281
281	Mission Carmelo (Church)	9

Grant Number	Name	Acres
308	Mission San Antonio (Church)	33
295	Mission Soledad	34
256	Monterey, City Lands	30,860
258	Monterey County Tract (Castro)	113
262	Monterey County Tract (Cocks)	1,106
284	Monterey County Tract (Meadows)	4,592
263	Nacional	6,633
278	Noche Buena	4,412
292	Paraje de Sanchez	6,584
312	Pleyto	13,299
298	Posa de los Ositos	16,939
279	Punta de Pinos	2,667
272	Rincon de la Punta del Monte	15,219
255	Rincon de las Salinas	2,220
261	Rincon de Sanjón	2,230
304	San Benito	6,671
303	San Bernabé	13,297
306	San Bernardino (Soberanes)	13,346
287	San Francisquito	8,814
552	San José y Sur Chiquita	8,876
302	San Lorenzo (Randall)	22,264
300	San Lorenzo (Sanchez)	48,286
299	San Lorenzo (Soberanes)	21,884
305	San Lucas	8,875
309	San Miguelito	22,136
293	San Vicente (Munrass)	19,979
277	Saucito	2,212
264	Sauzal	10,242
260	Two Suertes	38
222	Vega del Río de Pajáro	4,310
271	Zanjones	6,714

SAN BENITO COUNTY

Grant Number	Name	Acres
233	Ausaymas y San Felipe (Santa Clara)	35,504
231	Bolsa de San Felipe	6,795
250	Cienega del Gabilan (Monterey)	48,781
268	Cienega de los Paicines	8,918
230	Llano del Tequesquita (Santa Clara)	16,016
242	Las Aromitas y Agua Caliente	8,660

Grant Number	Name	Acres	Grant Number	Name	Acres
246	Los Carneros (McDougal) (Monterey)	1,629	300	San Lorenzo (Sanchez) (Monterey)	48,286
249	Los Vergeles (Monterey)	8,759	237	Santa Ana y Quién Sabé	48,823
239	Lomerias Muertas	6,660	248	Tract Near Mission of San Juan Bautista	401
236	Real de las Aguilas	31,052			
232	San Joaquin	7,425	240	Tracts of Mission San Juan Bautista	55
247	San Juan Bautista (Mission Lands)	4,439	222	Vega del Río de Pajáro (Monterey and Santa Cruz)	4,310
238	San Justo	34,620			

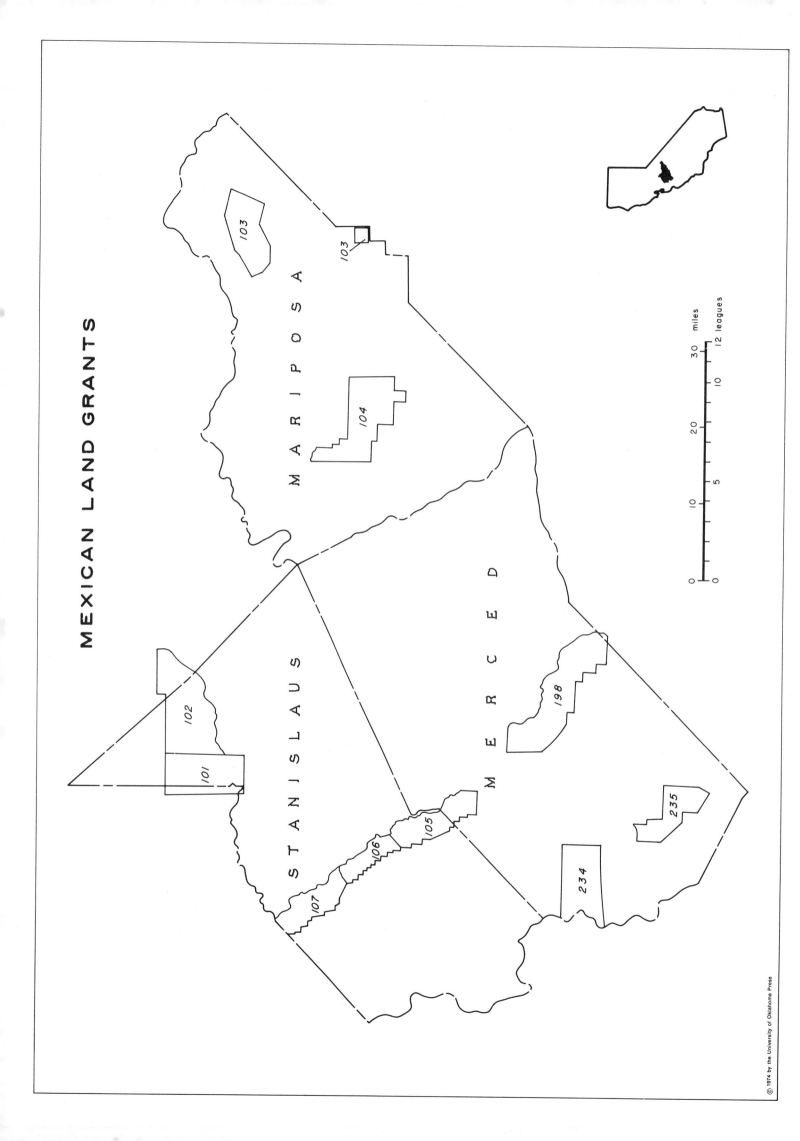

MEXICAN LAND GRANTS

MARIPOSA

103

103

104

STANISLAUS

102

101

MERCED

198

235

105

106

107

234

| | | | | | | | miles |
|0| |10| |20| |30| |

| | | | | | 12 leagues |
|0| |5| |10| | |

32. MEXICAN LAND GRANTS—STANISLAUS, MERCED, MARIPOSA

STANISLAUS COUNTY

Grant Number	Name	Acres
107	El Pescador (Grimes) (San Joaquin)	34,446
105	Orestimba	26,666
106	Rancho del Puerto	13,340
101	Thompson's Rancho (San Joaquin)	35,533
102	Rancheria del Río Estanislao	48,887

MERCED COUNTY

Grant Number	Name	Acres
235	Panocha de San Juan y Los Carrisalitos	22,175
234	San Luis Gonzaga (Santa Clara)	48,821
198	Sanjon de Santa Rita (Fresno)	48,824
105	Orestimba (Stanislaus)	26,666

MARIPOSA COUNTY

Grant Number	Name	Acres
104	Las Mariposas	44,387
103	Yosemite and Big Tree Grants (This was not a private land grant, but a special grant which became the park.)	33,270

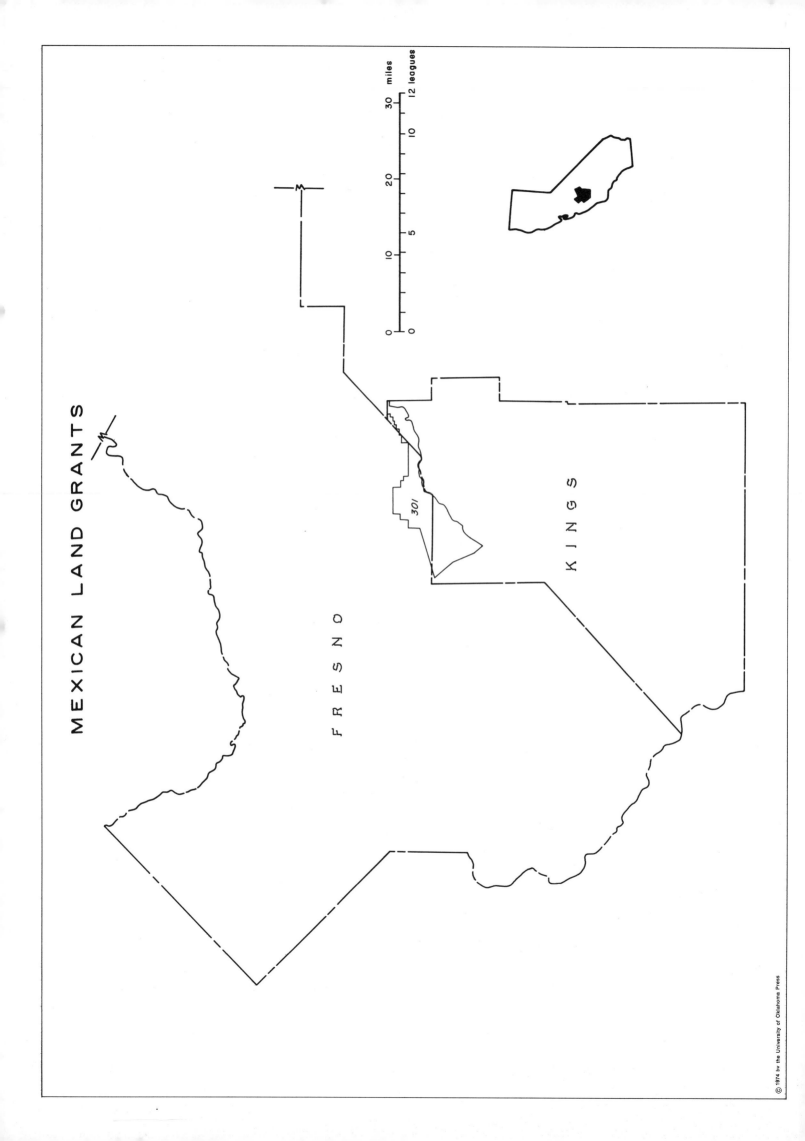

MEXICAN LAND GRANTS

miles

12 leagues

30

20

10

5

10

301

FRESNO

KINGS

33. MEXICAN LAND GRANTS—FRESNO AND KINGS

FRESNO AND KINGS COUNTIES

Grant Number	Name	Acres
301	Laguna de Tache	48,801

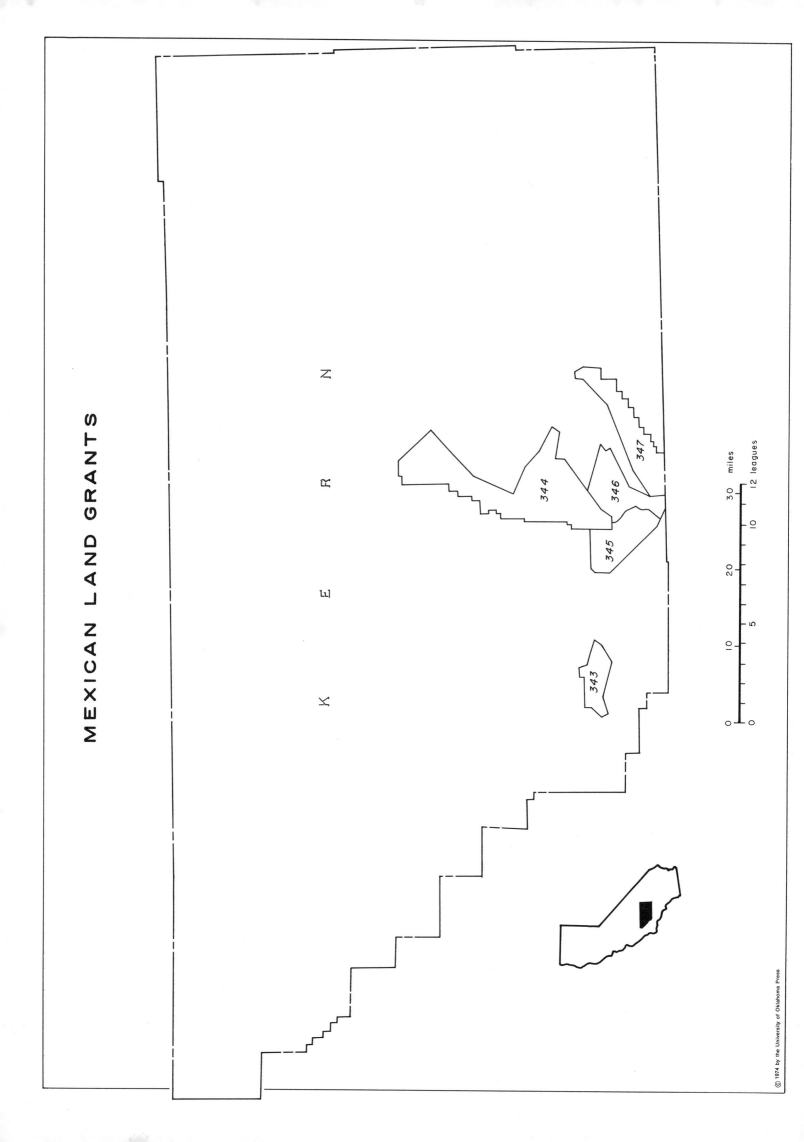

MEXICAN LAND GRANTS

K   E   R   N

344

346

347

345

343

30   miles

0   10   20   30

0   5   10   12 leagues

34. MEXICAN LAND GRANTS—KERN

KERN COUNTY

Grant Number	Name	Acres	Grant Number	Name	Acres
			347	La Liebre (Los Angeles)	48,800
345	Castac	22,178	346	Los Alamos y Agua Caliente	26,626
344	El Tejon	97,617	343	San Emidio	17,710

MEXICAN LAND GRANTS

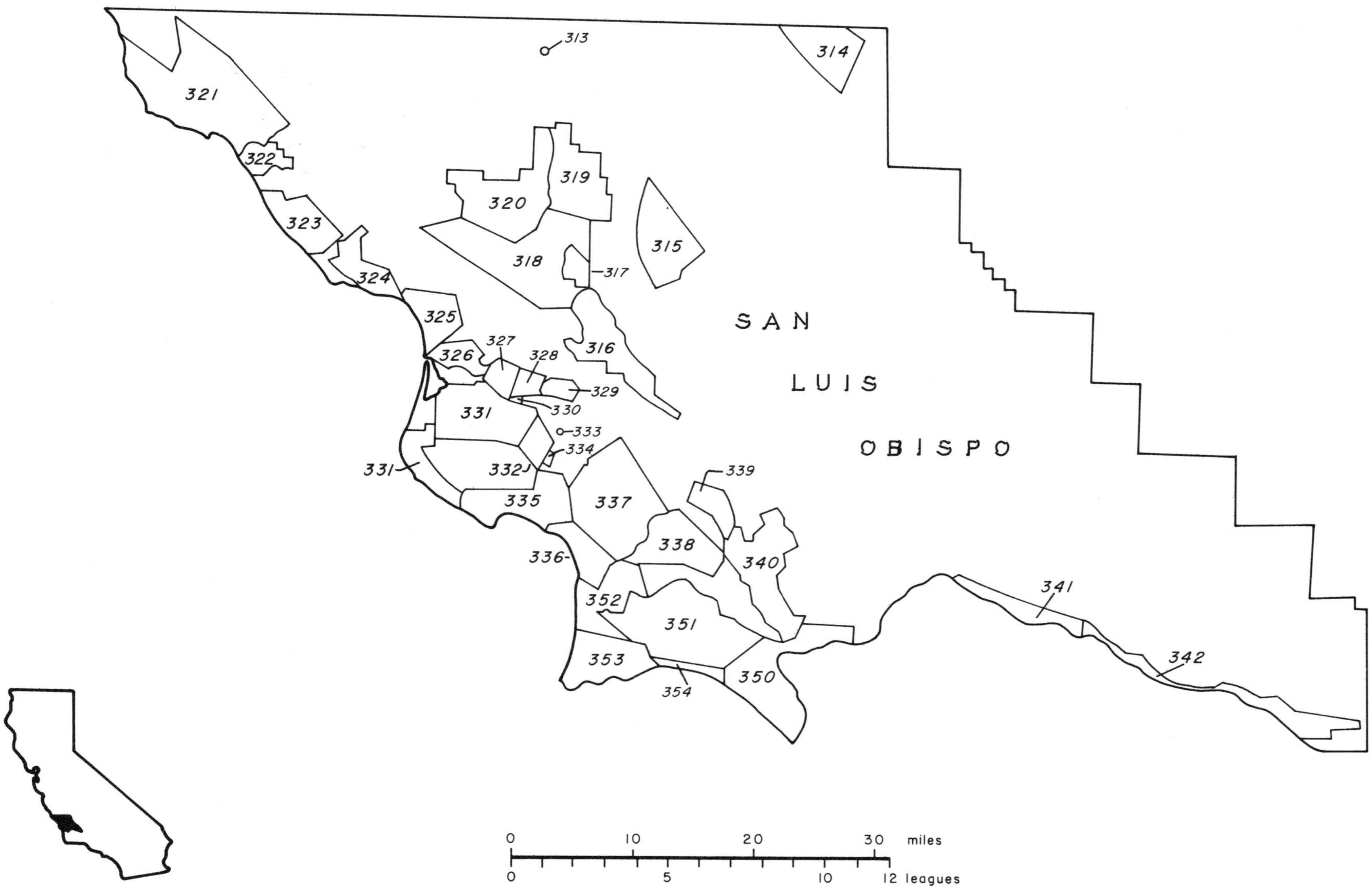

SAN LUIS OBISPO

314

315

313

319

317

316

329

318 320

328 330 333

327 334

326 332 335

331

325 336

324 337

323 338

322 339

340

321 350

351

352 353

354

341

342

miles
0   10   20   30
0   5   10   12 leagues

35. MEXICAN LAND GRANTS—SAN LUIS OBISPO

San Luis Obispo County

Grant Number	Name	Acres
339	Arroyo Grande	4,437
318	Ascunción	39,224
317	Atascadero	4,348
352	Bolsa del Chamisal	14,335
331	Cañada de los Osos y Pecho y Islay	32,431
314	Cholame (Monterey)	26,622
337	Corral de Piedra	30,911
342	Cuyama (Santa Barbara)	48,828
341	Cuyama (Santa Barbara)	22,193
328	El Chorro	3,167
353	Guadalupe	43,682
340	Huasna	22,153
315	Huer-h-uero	15,685
330	Huerta de Romualdo or El Chorro	117
332	Laguna (Church Property)	4,157
333	Mission San Luis Obispo Lot	1 acre
313	Mission San Miguel (Church)	34

Grant Number	Name	Acres
325	Moro y Cayucos	8,845
351	Nipoma (Santa Barbara)	37,888
320	Paso de Robles	25,993
321	Piedra Blanca	48,806
336	Pismo	8,839
334	Ranchito de Santa Fe	166
326	San Bernardo (Cane)	4,379
324	San Gerónimo	8,893
327	San Luisito	4,390
329	Potrero de San Luis Obispo	3,506
354	Punta de la Laguna (Santa Barbara)	26,648
335	San Miguelito	14,198
322	San Simeon	4,469
338	Santa Manuela	16,955
316	Santa Margarita	17,735
323	Santa Rosa (Estrada)	13,184
319	Santa Ysabel	17,774
350	Suey (Santa Barbara)	48,834

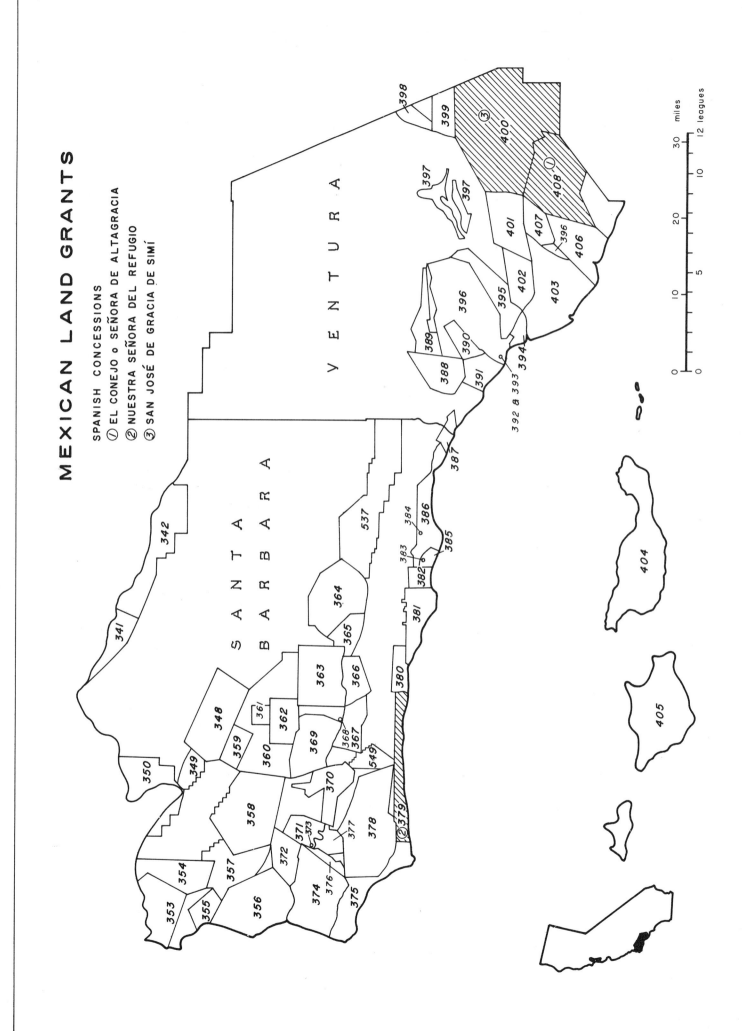

MEXICAN LAND GRANTS

SPANISH CONCESSIONS
① EL CONEJO o SEÑORA DE ALTAGRACIA
② NUESTRA SEÑORA DEL REFUGIO
③ SAN JOSÉ DE GRACIA DE SIMÍ

miles
leagues

VENTURA COUNTY

Grant Number	Name	Acres
407	Calleguas	9,998
391	Cañada de San Miguelito	8,877
390	Cañada Larga o Verde	6,659
408	El Conejo (Los Angeles)	48,672
387	El Rincon (Arellanes) (Santa Barbara)	4,460
406	Gaudalasca	30,594
401	Las Posas	26,623
396	Lands of Ex-Mission San Buenaventura	48,823
392	Lands Belonging to Mission San Buenaventura (Church)	36
393	Mission San Buenaventura	29
389	Ojai	17,717
403	Río de Santa Clara	44,883
399	San Francisco (Los Angeles)	48,612
394	San Miguel (Olivas and Lorenzana)	4,694
388	Santa Ana	21,522
402	Santa Clara del Norte	13,989
395	Santa Paula y Saticoy	17,773
397	Sespe	8,881
400	Simi	113,009
398	Temascal (Los Angeles)	13,339

SANTA BARBARA COUNTY

Grant Number	Name	Acres
380	Cañada del Corral	8,876
363	Cañada de los Pinos or College Rancho	35,499
377	Cañada de Salsipuedes	6,656
355	Casmalia	8,841
362	Corral de Quati	13,322
342	Cuyama (San Luis Obispo)	48,827
341	Cuyama (San Luis Obispo)	22,193
387	El Rincon (Arellanes) (Ventura)	4,460
353	Guadalupe (San Luis Obispo)	43,682

Grant Number	Name	Acres
404	Island of Santa Cruz	52,760
405	Island of Santa Rosa	62,696
356	Jesus María	42,185
382	La Goleta	4,426
360	La Laguna (Gutierrez)	48,704
376	La Mission Vieja de la Purísima	4,414
383	Las Cieneguitas	28
549	Las Cruces	8,888
385	Las Positas y La Calera	3,282
361	La Zaca	4,458
366	Lomas de la Purificacion	13,341
374	Lompoc	42,085
358	Los Alamos	48,803
381	Los Dos Pueblos	15,535
537	Los Prietos y Najalayegua	48,729
373	Lands Belonging to Mission Purísima de la (Church)	14
372	Ex-Mission la Purísima	14,736
384	Lands Belonging to Mission Santa Bárbara	283
368	Lands Belonging to Mission Santa Ynez	17
367	Nojoqui	13,285
379	Nuestra Señora del Refugio	26,529
375	Punta de la Concepción	24,992
354	Punta de la Laguna	26,648
369	San Carlos de Jonata	26,634
378	San Julian	48,222
364	San Marcos	35,573
386	Santa Barbara Pueblo Lands	17,826
371	Santa Rita (Malo)	13,316
370	Santa Rosa	15,526
348	Sisquoc	35,486
350	Suey (San Luis Obispo)	48,834
349	Tepusquet	8,901
365	Tequepis	8,919
359	Tinaquaic	8,875
357	Todos Santos y San Antonio	20,772

MEXICAN LAND GRANTS

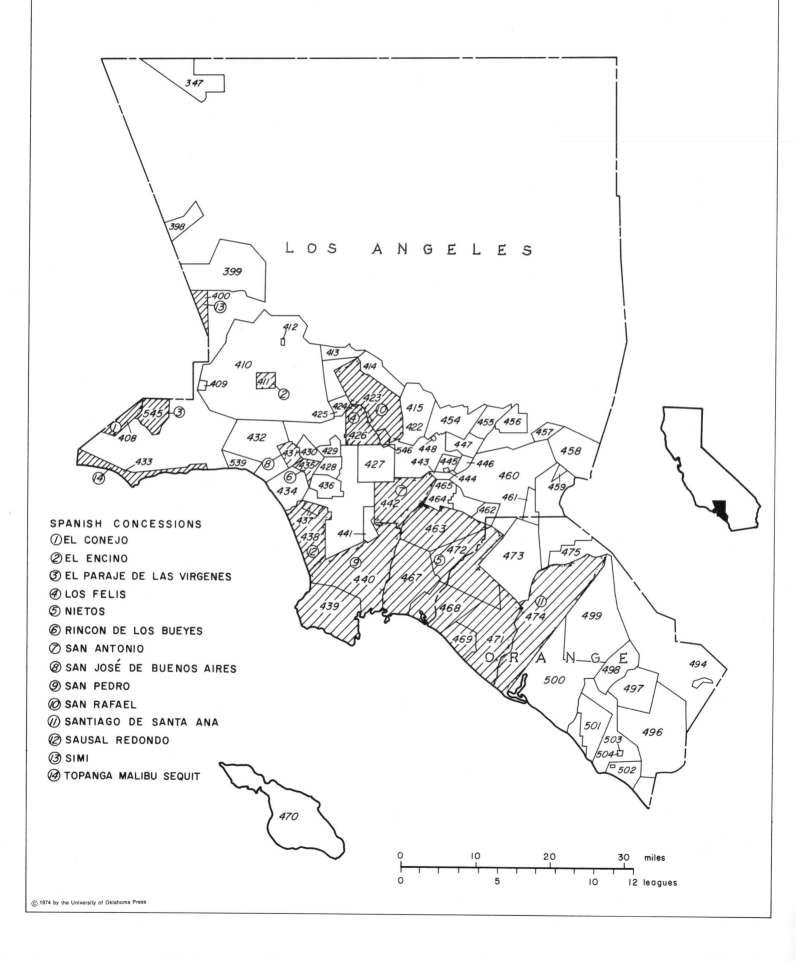

SPANISH CONCESSIONS

① EL CONEJO
② EL ENCINO
③ EL PARAJE DE LAS VIRGENES
④ LOS FELIS
⑤ NIETOS
⑥ RINCON DE LOS BUEYES
⑦ SAN ANTONIO
⑧ SAN JOSÉ DE BUENOS AIRES
⑨ SAN PEDRO
⑩ SAN RAFAEL
⑪ SANTIAGO DE SANTA ANA
⑫ SAUSAL REDONDO
⑬ SIMI
⑭ TOPANGA MALIBU SEQUIT

LOS ANGELES

ORANGE

LOS ANGELES COUNTY

Grant Number	Name	Acres
437	Aguaje de la Centinella	2,219
425	Cahuenga	388
455	Azusa (Duarte)	6,596
456	Azusa (Dalton)	4,431
539	Boca de Santa Monica	6,657
546	Cañada de los Nogales	1,200
436	Cienega O Paso de la Tijera	4,481
408	El Conejo (Ventura)	48,672
411	El Encino	4,461
409	El Escorpion	1,110
470	Island of Santa Catalina	45,820
429	La Brea	4,439
434	Ballona	13,920
414	La Cañada	5,832
462	La Habra	6,699
347	La Liebre (Kern)	48,800
443	La Merced	2,364
460	La Puente	48,791
428	Las Cienegas	4,439
545	Las Virgenes	8,885
468	Los Alamitos	28,027
427	Los Angeles City Lands	17,172
467	Los Cerritos	27,054
472	Los Coyotes	48,806
426	Los Felis	6,647
459	Los Nogales	1,004
439	Los Palos Verdes	13,629
433	Topanga Malibu Sequit	13,316
410	Ex-Mission San Fernando	116,858
412	Mission San Fernando (Church)	77
448	Mission of San Gabriel (Church)	190
465	Paso de Bartolo (Guirado)	876
465	Paso de Bartolo (Sepulveda)	208
464	Paso de Bartolo (Pío Pico)	8,991
446	Potrero de Felipe Lugo	2,042
445	Potrero Grande	4,432
424	Providencia	4,064
461	Rincon de la Brea	4,453
435	Rincon de los Bueyes	3,128
442	San Antonio (Lugo)	29,513
430	San Antonio or Rodeo de las Aguas	4,449

Grant Number	Name	Acres
399	San Francisco (Ventura County)	48,612
447	San Francisquito (Dalton)	8,894
457	San José, Addition to	4,431
458	San José (Dalton & other)	22,340
431	San José de Buenos Aires	4,439
415	San Pascual (Garfias)	13,694
422	San Pascual (Wilson)	709
440	San Pedro (Dominguez)	43,119
423	San Rafael	36,403
454	Santa Anita	13,319
466	Santa Gertrudes (McFarland & Downey)	17,602
463	Santa Gertrudes (Colima)	3,696
432	San Vicente y Santa Monica	30,260
438	Sausal Redondo	22,459
400	Simi (Ventura)	113,009
441	Tajauta	3,560
398	Temascal (Ventura)	13,339
413	Tujunga	6,661

ORANGE COUNTY

Grant Number	Name	Acres
502	Boca de la Playa	6,607
498	Cañada de los Alisos	10,669
475	Cañon de Santa Ana	13,329
469	La Bolsa Chica	8,107
462	La Habra (Los Angeles)	6,699
460	La Puente (Los Angeles)	48,791
471	Las Bolsas	33,460
499	Lomas de Santiago	47,227
468	Los Alamitos (Los Angeles)	28,027
472	Los Coyotes (Los Angeles)	48,806
503	Mission San Juan Capistrano	44
504	Mission San Juan Capistrano Tract	7
496	Mission Viejo or La Paz	46,433
501	Niguel	13,316
497	Trabuco	22,184
474	Santiago de Santa Ana	78,941
473	San Juan Cajon de Santa Ana	35,971
500	San Joaquin	48,803
461	Rincon de la Brea (Los Angeles)	4,453
494	Potreros de San Juan Capistrano	1,168

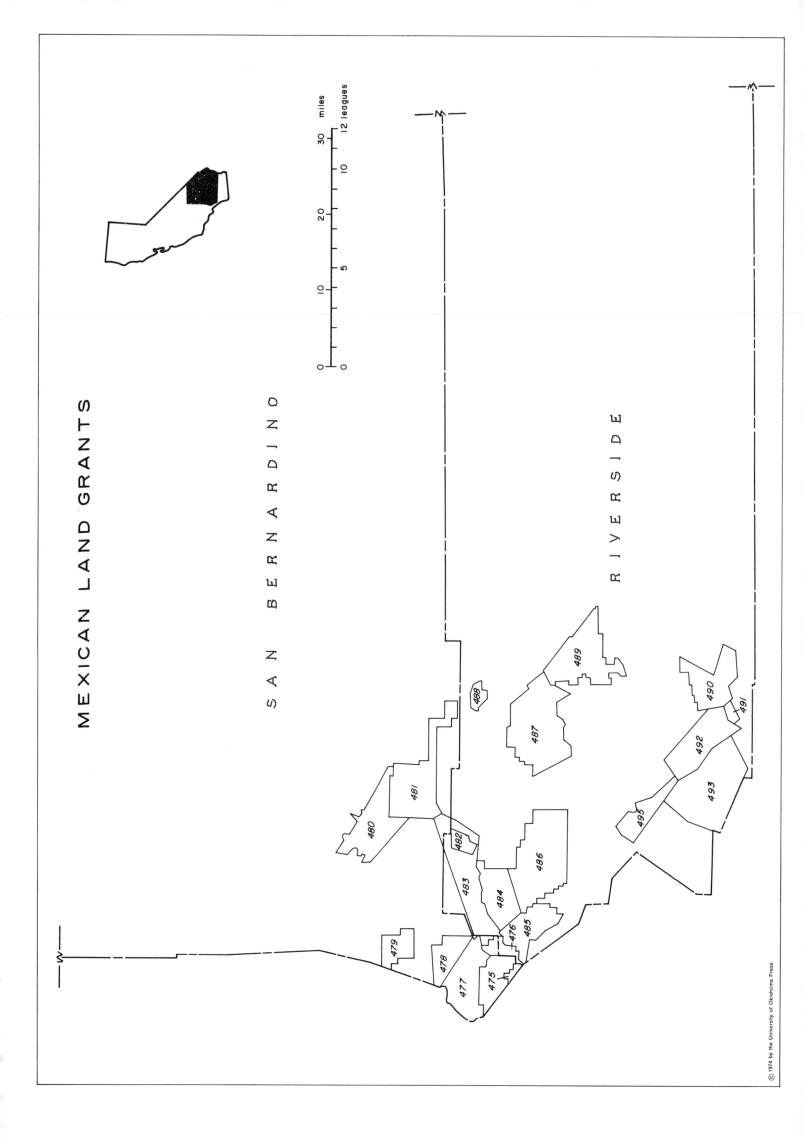

MEXICAN LAND GRANTS

SAN BERNARDINO

RIVERSIDE

30 miles
12 leagues

© 1974 by the University of Oklahoma Press

38. MEXICAN LAND GRANTS—RIVERSIDE, SAN BERNARDINO

RIVERSIDE COUNTY

Grant Number	Name	Acres
476	El Rincon (San Bernardino)	4,431
482	Jurupa (Rubideaux)	6,750
483	Jurupa (Stearns)	33,819
495	La Laguna (Stearns)	13,339
492	Temecula	26,609
491	Land in the Valley of Temecula	2,233
484	La Sierra (Sepulveda)	17,774
485	La Sierra (Yorba)	17,787
490	Pauba	26,598
489	San Jacinto Viejo	35,503
487	San Jacinto Nuevo y Potrero	48,861
488	San Jacinto y San Gorgonio	

Grant Number	Name	Acres
	Tract Between	4,440
493	Santa Rosa (Morino)	47,815
486	Sobrante de San Jacinto	48,847

SAN BERNARDINO COUNTY

475	Cañon de Santa Ana (Orange)	13,329
479	Cucamonga	13,045
476	El Rincon (Riverside)	4,431
483	Jurupa (Stearns) (Riverside)	32,259
480	Muscupiabe	30,145
477	Santa Ana del Chino	22,234
478	Santa Ana del Chino Addition	13,366
481	San Bernardino	35,509

MEXICAN LAND GRANTS

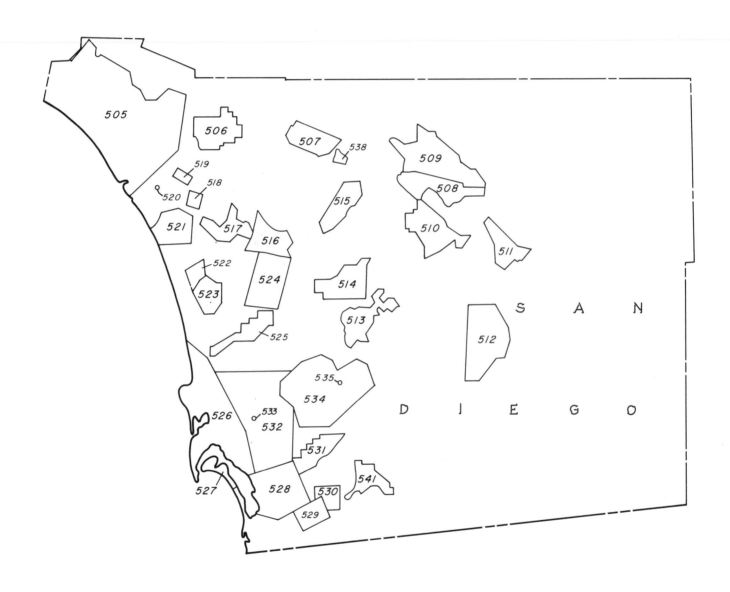

505

506

507 538

509

508

519

518

520

521

517

516

515

510

511

522

524

514

523

513

525

512

S   A   N

535

534

526

533

532

D   I   E   G   O

531

541

527

528

530

529

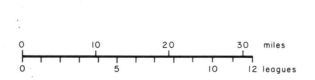

0   10   20   30   miles
0   5   10   12 leagues

39. MEXICAN LAND GRANTS—SAN DIEGO

SAN DIEGO COUNTY

Grant Number	Name	Acres
521	Agua Hedionda	13,311
518	Buena Vista	2,288
535	Cañada de los Coches	28.39
513	Cañada de San Vicente y Mesa del Padre Barrona	13,316
534	El Cajon	48,800
538	Cuca or El Potrero	2,174
512	Cuyamaca	35,501
515	Guejito	13,299
519	Guajomé	2,219
513	Jamacha	8,881
541	Jamul	8,926
522	Los Encenitos	4,431
525	Los Penasquitos	8,486
533	Mission San Diego	22.21
532	Ex-Mission San Diego	58,875

Grant Number	Name	Acres
520	Ex-Mission San Luis Rey	53
506	Monserate	13,323
528	La Nacion	26,632
530	Otay (Dominguez)	4,437
529	Otay (Estudillo)	6,658
507	Pauma	13,310
516	Rincon del Diablo	12,654
524	San Bernardo (Snook)	17,763
527	San Diego, Island of	4,185
523	San Dieguito	8,825
509	San José del Valle	26,689
510	Santa Ysabel	17,719
505	Santa Margarita y Las Flores	133,441
514	Valle de Pamo or Santa María	17,709
511	Valle de San Felipe	9,972
508	Valle de San José (Portilla)	17,634
517	Vallecitos de San Marcos	8,975

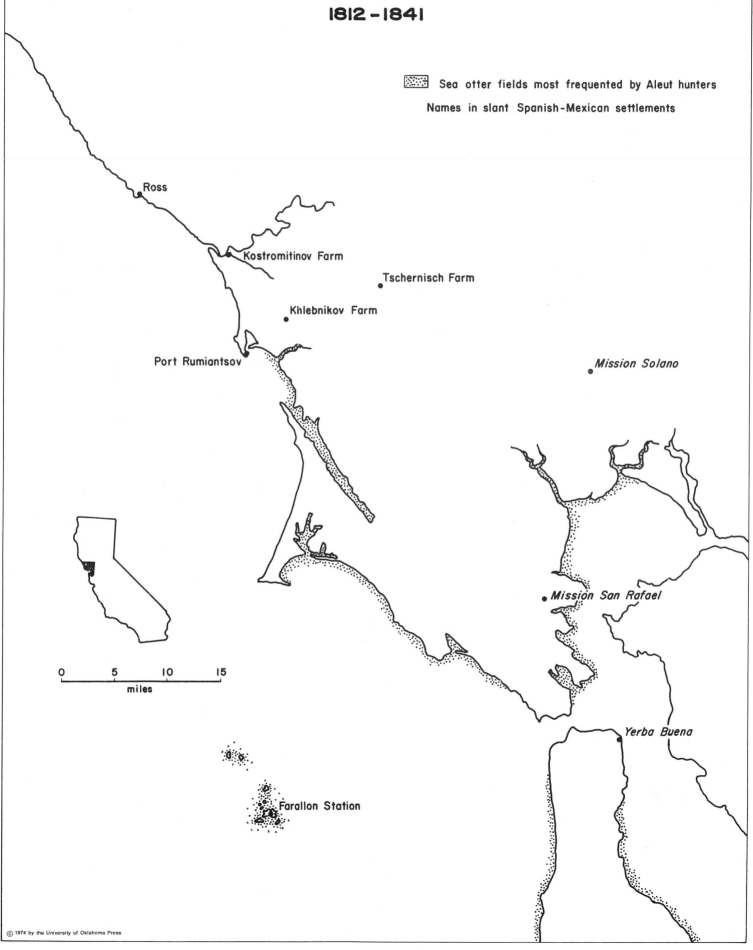

RUSSIAN-AMERICAN COMPANY SETTLEMENT

1812-1841

Sea otter fields most frequented by Aleut hunters

Names in slant Spanish-Mexican settlements

Ross

Kostromitinov Farm

Tschernisch Farm

Khlebnikov Farm

Port Rumiantsov

Mission Solano

Mission San Rafael

0   5   10   15
miles

Yerba Buena

Farallon Station

RUSSIAN SETTLEMENT in California was an outgrowth of that nation's interest in the Pacific fur trade which dated back to 1742. Attention was called to the California coast in 1803, when the Boston trader, Joseph O'Cain, went into a partnership with the Russian-American Company. Using the Aleuts and their canoes to poach for sea otters in Spanish California waters, the undertaking was highly successful.

But the establishment of a southern post was not realized until 1805, when Count Nikolai Petrovich Rezanov, the Czar's chamberlain, inspected the Alaskan fur posts. He found them in desperate need of food, especially the fresh fruits or vegetables needed to ward off scurvy. Often such supplies had to be obtained from a great distance. To Rezanov the solution was to establish a base in California to furnish food for the Alaska installations. But to take care of the immediate shortage the Russian nobleman took a ship laden with trade goods to San Francisco in the spring of 1806. Rezanov knew of the Spanish prohibition upon foreign trade, and while awaiting the arrival of Governor Arrillaga he aroused interest by a careful distribution of gifts from his cargo. In addition, he ardently wooed Maria de la Concepción Argüello y Moraga, the daughter of the port commandant. His whirlwind courtship succeeded in putting food into the stomachs of the starving Russian colonists in Alaska. However, Rezanov's death en route home via Siberia leaves unanswered the question as to his actual marital intentions.

The availability of food in California made imperative the establishment of a base for trade with the Spanish and a colony to also raise crops. In 1809, Ivan Aleksandrovich Kuskov was sent to explore the coast north of San Francisco. He built temporary structures at Port Rumiantsov while the Aleuts gathered two thousand furs from around Bodega Bay. Two years later Kuskov had his Aleuts gather twelve hundred skins from San Francisco Bay, to the dismay of the Californians. More importantly, Kuskov had selected a permanent site for settlement. He bypassed Bodega Bay, fearing it was too susceptible to Spanish attack, because of a lack of timber and fresh water, and paid the Indians three blankets, three pairs of pants, two axes, three hoes, and some beads to rent a settlement site. It was called Rossiya, an ancient term for Russia, but was often mistakenly referred to as Fort Ross by the Spanish Californians and Americans. Formal dedication and construction took place in 1812. Farallon Station was used as a base for the Aleuts hunting sea lion meat. Agriculture, fruit orchards, and stock raising developed around Ross, but the area was not well suited for such activities, and other farms were established at some distance. Lumbering flourished and several ships were built.

The Russians were always considered interlopers by the Californians and were often ordered to leave. However, their presence coincided with the outbreak of the wars for independence, and it was impossible to use force to evict the Russians. Mission Solano and Mission San Rafael were established in an effort to have a buffer against the unwelcome encroachment. However, the Russians were never numerous enough to constitute a real threat; the original settlers at Ross included 80 Aleuts and 95 Russians and was never more than 400 persons. California Indians in the area accepted the new arrivals —causing Spanish officials much concern. Consumer goods from the Russian settlements were exchanged for food, but the colony never prospered. In one year the Russian-American Company spent 72,000 rubles in support while receiving only 8,000 rubles in return (1 ruble = $.96). On December 12, 1841, the moveable properties were purchased by John A. Sutter for 30,000 pesos. However, the Russians were again active in California as traders during the Gold Rush. Their Alaskan warehouses were emptied of shoddy merchandise at inflated prices to satisfy the needs of the miners. But this trade soon collapsed, and the United States bought Russian interests in Alaska for $7,200,000 in 1867.

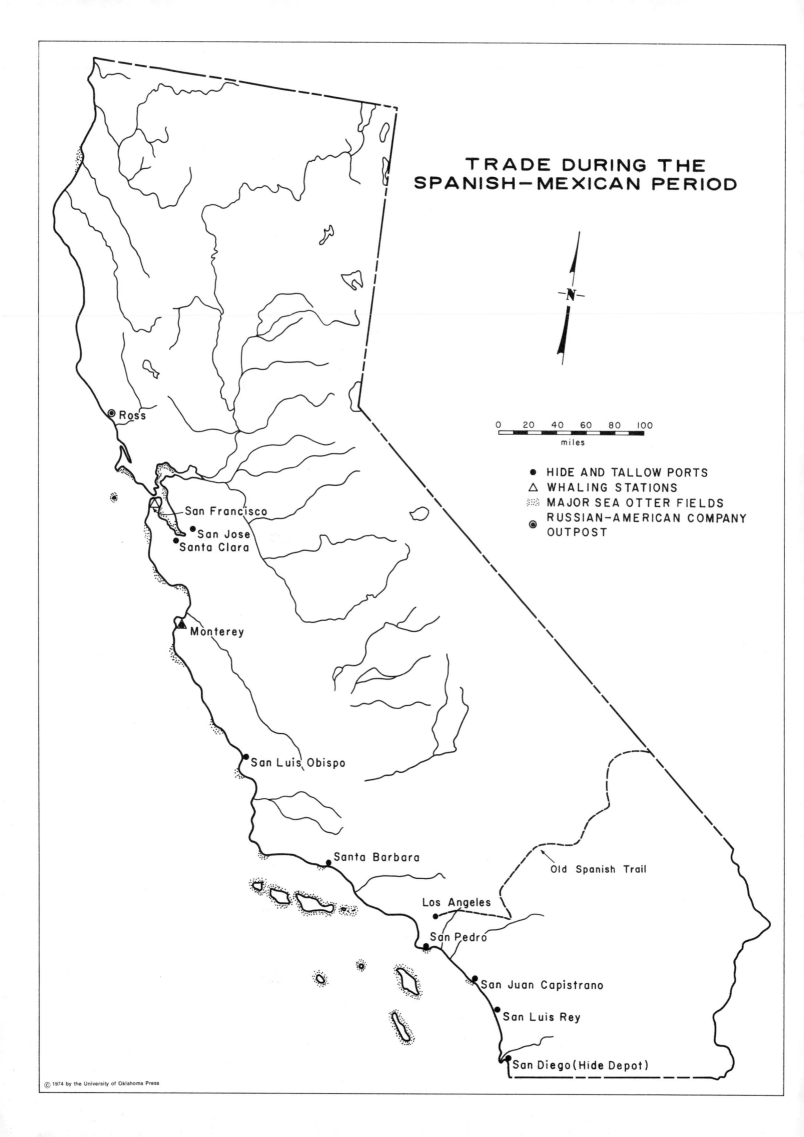

TRADE DURING THE
SPANISH–MEXICAN PERIOD

N

```
0   20   40   60   80   100
         miles
```

● HIDE AND TALLOW PORTS
△ WHALING STATIONS
⬚ MAJOR SEA OTTER FIELDS
◉ RUSSIAN–AMERICAN COMPANY
   OUTPOST

◉ Ross

△ San Francisco
● San Jose
● Santa Clara

▲ Monterey

● San Luis Obispo

● Santa Barbara

Los Angeles ●
Old Spanish Trail

● San Pedro

● San Juan Capistrano

● San Luis Rey

● San Diego (Hide Depot)

As THE SPANISH colony in California grew slowly in size, the ability to furnish it with adequate consumer goods declined. Supply ships from New Spain faced a difficult and hazardous journey to the remote outpost of the empire under the best of circumstances, but when the wars for independence began in 1810 their voyages virtually ceased. Spain's economic policy banned foreign trade, but an illicit commerce developed anyway.

The presence in California waters of valuable fur-bearing animals and of whales in nearby ocean waters provided the initial basis for trade by the province. John Ledyard, an American in the service of Captain James Cook, obtained sea otter pelts on his 1778 visit which sold for $100 in China. The journal of his adventure publicized the possibility of immense profits, and interest grew. Beginning in the 1790's, scores of American, Russian, and British ships invaded North Pacific waters in search of the sea otter. Until 1820, when the trade began to decline, fortunes were made in the exploitation of this exotic animal. Ships of many nations, of which American were most numerous, traded consumer goods for valuable pelts, which brought high prices in the Orient. Such trade was illegal, but Spain lacked the power of enforcement.

Fur from seals was also in great demand, especially as the sea otter declined. Whalers in search of the elusive sperm, right, greyback, and blue whale likewise invaded California shores. Fresh fruit and vegetables were absolute essentials to ship crews of that date, to counter the ravages of scurvy. It was equally necessary to find harbors where ships could be carromed, bottoms scraped and caulked, and sails and running gear repaired.

In an effort to obtain food for their fur trading posts in Alaska, the Russians visited San Francisco in 1806 to initiate trade. In 1812, Fort Ross was established to raise crops and livestock for food, but was always more of a trading center. With a surplus of foodstuff, the Spanish were pleased to trade for Russian cloth, agricultural tools and other hardware items, candles, and even furniture.

The trade in hides and tallow began at the beginning of the nineteenth century, but grew rapidly after Mexican independence. Some fifty to eighty thousand hides were shipped annually. Ships of all nations visited the hide and tallow ports, but again Yankees were most numerous. However, Mexican ships were second in number. Cloth of all types was in greatest demand in California, with shoes, saddles, and hardware items also being important trade items. At first, goods were displayed aboard ship, but traders soon established local offices on shore, which evolved into year-round stores. Foreign merchants, especially American and English, thus became permanent residents of California.

Trade between New Mexico and California was begun in 1829–30 by Antonio Armijo over the Old Spanish Trail and grew slowly but steadily in subsequent years. From Santa Fe came hand-woven serapes and blankets as well as Yankee items such as knives, guns, hardware items, and cloth. The California mules were preferred in exchange, because they were larger and sturdier than their New Mexican cousins. Exact knowledge of this trade is difficult to gather, but apparently some New Mexican traders obtained horses and mules by stealing them or by trading with Indians who had obtained them the same way.

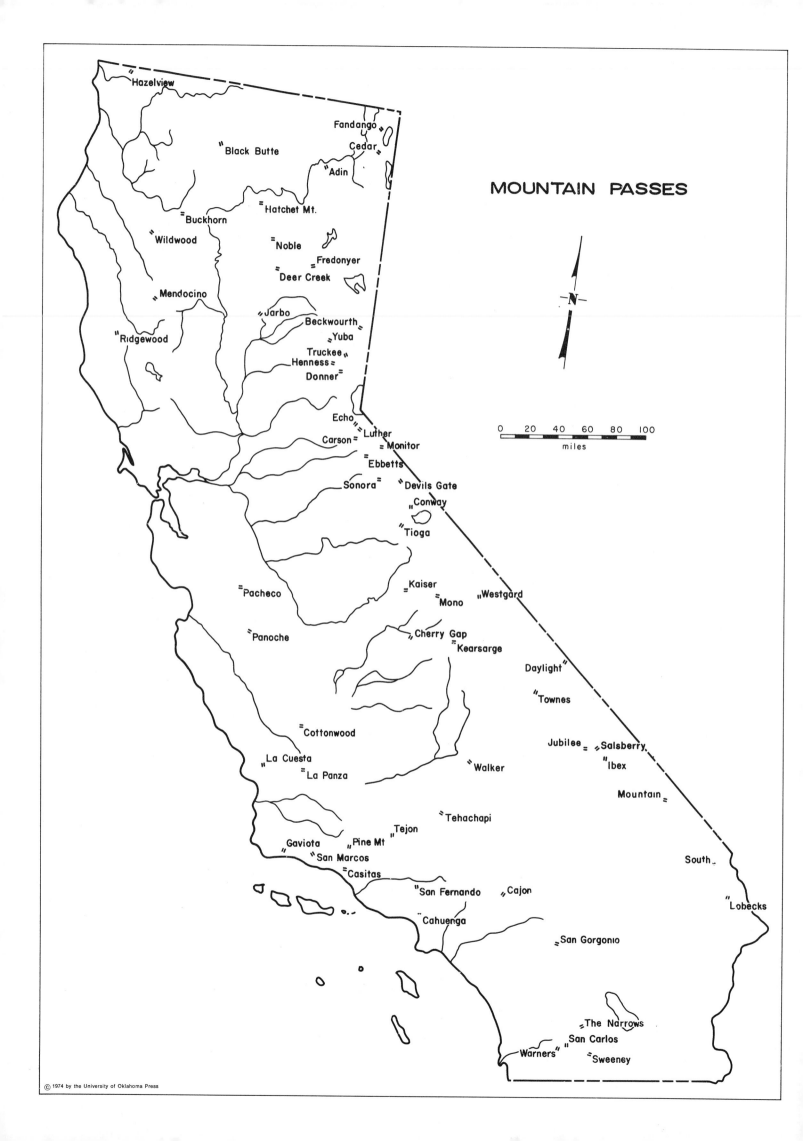

MOUNTAIN PASSES

Hazelview

Fandango
Cedar
"Black Butte
Adin
Hatchet Mt.
Buckhorn
Wildwood
Noble
Fredonyer
Deer Creek
Mendocino
Jarbo
Beckwourth
Ridgewood
Yuba
Truckee
Henness
Donner
Echo
Luther
Carson
Monitor
Ebbetts
Sonora
Devils Gate
Conway
Tioga
Pacheco
Kaiser
Mono
Westgard
Panoche
Cherry Gap
Kearsarge
Daylight
"Townes
Cottonwood
Jubilee
Salsberry
La Cuesta
"Ibex
La Panza
Walker
Mountain
Tehachapi
Tejon
Gaviota
Pine Mt
San Marcos
South
Casitas
San Fernando
Cajon
Lobecks
Cahuenga
San Gorgonio
The Narrows
San Carlos
Warners
Sweeney

N

```
0   20   40   60   80   100
            miles
```

42. MOUNTAIN PASSES

GEOGRAPHY HAS BEEN a prime determinant in the history of California. Most influential have been the rugged mountain ranges which virtually encircle the state. The Sierra Nevada towers like a massive wall on the eastern border, prompting John Bidwell, the leader of the overland emigrant train in 1841, to comment: "If California lies beyond those mountains we shall never be able to reach it." Most early travelers were equally awed by the apparently impassable barrier to the promised land; without the numerous passes which breach the seemingly impregnable Sierras, man could not have made an overland entry. The Coast Ranges and the mountains in the northern and southern parts of the state are not as rugged, but without well-located passes man's adaptation to California would have been far more difficult.

Mountain passes determined the location of Indian trails, the routes of early Spanish explorers, and were the trails by which the Anglo intruders traversed the state seeking beaver. A knowledge of the best route through the mountains often was the difference between life and death for the emigrant trains. In the 1830's, passes such as Pacheco, Panoche, and La Panza were used by the Miwok-Yokut Indians en route to raids on the Mexican missions, ranchos, and settlements. Because certain key passes were vital to the control of the surrounding areas, they were often the site of battles. Bandits used passes as convenient points from which to rob travelers. In the Anglo era, forts were built to guard key passes, and such points were the meeting places for miles around. Today a pass like Cajon has railroads, highways, and aqueducts side by side, as man continues to cross the mountains to his residence in the valleys below.

There is no single important pass through the mountains to the east like the famed Cumberland Gap. There are, instead, many that have figured prominently in the history of the state. Between the Tioga Pass in Central California and Walker Pass there are some fifty passes crossing the Sierra Nevada. (Only the more important are marked on the map). Walker Pass was preferred by emigrants seeking to avoid early snow, but was never as popular or famous as Beckwourth, Truckee, Donner, or Sonora. Farther south, Townes Pass was not only a gateway to California but often to life itself; at least to those seeking to escape from Death Valley this notch through the Panamint Range was indispensable. The Fandango-Cedar passes in the northeast corner of the state formed a significant passage through the rugged Warner Mountains for those coming from Oregon or via the Lassen Cutoff.

The passes through the Coastal Ranges are not as prominent as those through the Sierra Nevada, but many are just as vital to man. Those in the north played a key role in the Gold Rush era. From Pacheco Pass south to La Panza, passes were indispensable to man in moving from the coast to the Great Valley. Gaviota Pass, north of Santa Barbara, has played a significant role from 1861 to the present and was the outlet to the coast for the great sheep ranches of the interior. The highways make extensive use of this pass today. A series of natural passes have enabled the populous Los Angeles Basin to communicate to the east and to the north.

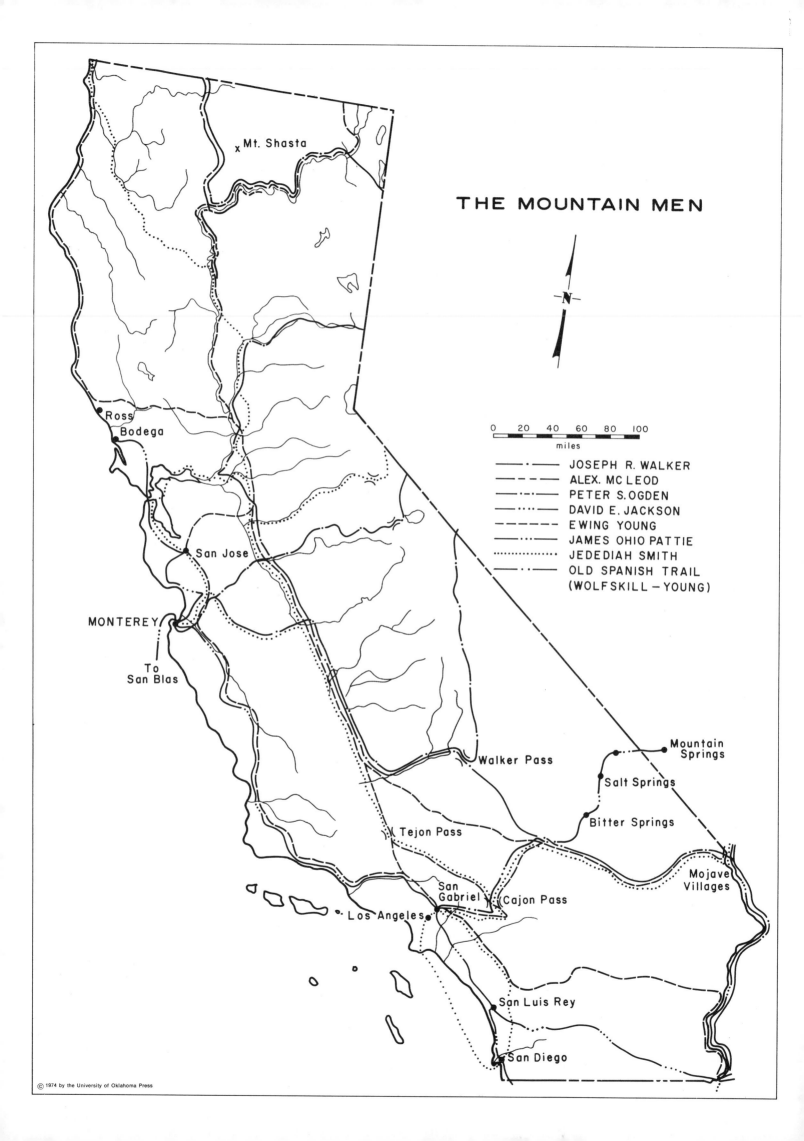

THE MOUNTAIN MEN

x Mt. Shasta

Ross
Bodega

San Jose

MONTEREY

To
San Blas

0   20   40   60   80   100
miles

—·— JOSEPH R. WALKER
— — ALEX. MCLEOD
—··— PETER S. OGDEN
······ DAVID E. JACKSON
— — EWING YOUNG
—···— JAMES OHIO PATTIE
······ JEDEDIAH SMITH
—··— OLD SPANISH TRAIL
(WOLFSKILL — YOUNG)

Walker Pass

Mountain
Springs

Salt Springs

Tejon Pass

Bitter Springs

San
Gabriel

Cajon Pass

Mojave
Villages

Los Angeles

San Luis Rey

San Diego

43. THE MOUNTAIN MEN

THE FIRST OVERLAND intruders into Mexican California were the mountain men. In search of the elusive beaver, these trappers invaded the Spanish Southwest as early as 1817 and, despite official efforts to keep them out, invaded Mexican territory in force in the 1820's. Usually headquartered at Taos or Bents Fort, the mountain men roamed wherever beaver could be found. They might start trapping along the Gila River but, finding game scarce along that stream, decide to try their luck along the Colorado, San Joaquin, Sacramento, or American rivers, or even to venture into the Oregon Territory.

The devout Jedediah Smith, perhaps the greatest of the mountain men, led the parade of Anglo-American intruders into California. Entering at Mojave villages along the Colorado, his party followed the Old Spanish Trail via Cajon Pass to arrive at Mission San Gabriel in November, 1826. Smith was forced to go to San Diego to explain his intrusion to Governor José Maria Echeandia. Released on the promise to leave immediately via the same route he had entered, Smith instead went up the San Joaquin Valley via Tejon Pass. Leaving most of his party camped on the Stanislaus River, Smith and two men returned to Utah, being the first white men to cross the Sierra. After a brief rest, Smith retraced his route to Mission San Gabriel and up the San Joaquin to rejoin his comrades waiting for him on the Stanislaus. Efforts to buy supplies at San Jose brought a brief stay in jail at Monterey, which ended with a stern command to leave California at once. This the party did by following the Sacramento north, exiting into Oregon in the northwest corner of the province.

Soon after Smith was forced to leave California, James Ohio Pattie entered. A trapping party led by his father crossed the Colorado at Yuma and made their way to a mission in Baja California, where they were escorted to San Diego and imprisoned. Released in order to vaccinate the population along the coast, James Ohio Pattie saw much of the province. On his return home, the *Personal Narrative of James Ohio Pattie* helped stir interest in California, bringing many more Americans to the Mexican Southwest.

Ewing Young, one of the ablest and most influential of the mountain men, arrived in Los Angeles in 1832, via the Old Spanish Trail. After otter hunting along the coast, Young and his party trapped for beaver along King's River and the San Joaquin. Going north along the Sacramento he cut overland, reaching the coast above Fort Ross, and continued searching for beaver along the coast into Oregon. Returning southward, Young crossed the Klamath and Rogue rivers to the headwaters of the Sacramento and then returned to Los Angeles.

One of the most spectacular entries into California was made by Joseph R. Walker. On a reconnaissance in Utah and Nevada, Walker's party made their way westward over the Sierra and, at one point, gazed down on the wonders of the Yosemite Valley. Going down the San Joaquin, the party turned eastward through Walker Pass and northward through the Owens Valley.

The explorations of the mountain men opened California to other Americans. The trails they blazed were first followed by traders and, very soon, by permanent settlers. Some mountain men returned as traders themselves or acted as guides to others–or as permanent settlers themselves. Other mountain men escorted wagon trains to California and, in the 1840's, an invading army. The publicity accorded these early explorers made California appealing to the American people and aided the drive of Manifest Destiny, which would add the province to the United States.

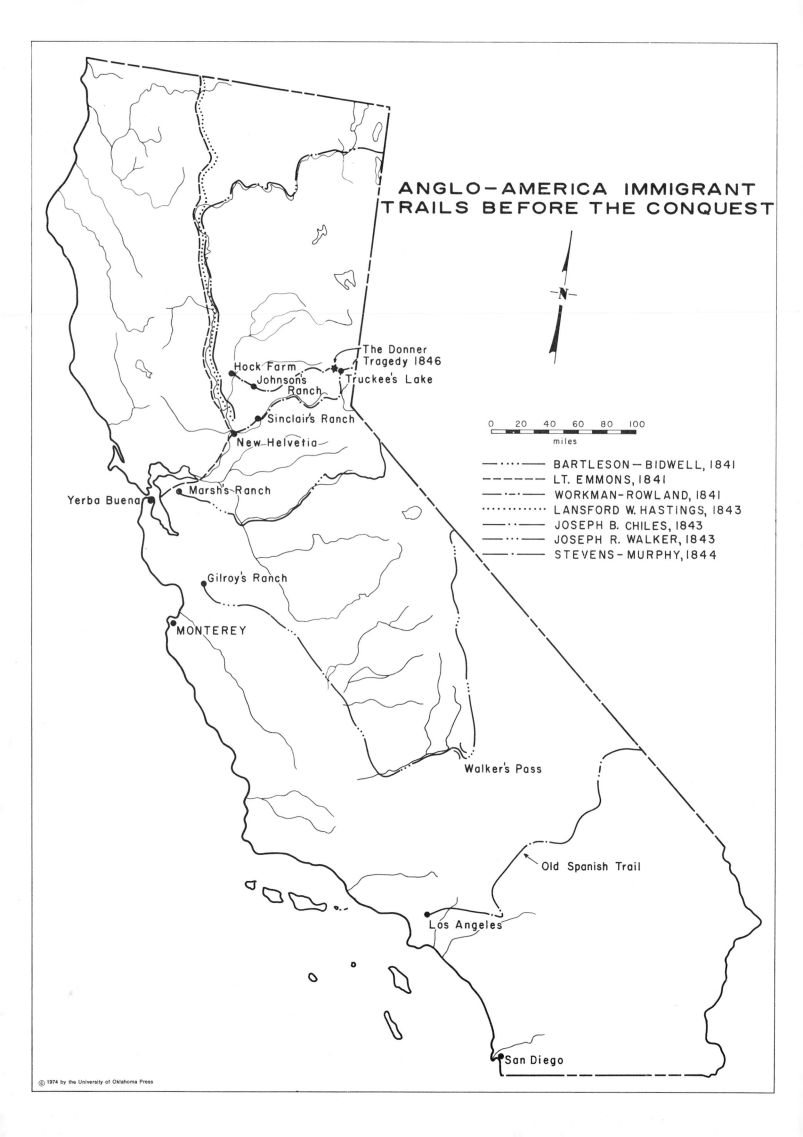

ANGLO—AMERICA IMMIGRANT
TRAILS BEFORE THE CONQUEST

—N—

0   20   40   60   80   100
miles

—————·······————— BARTLESON—BIDWELL, 1841
————— — ————— LT. EMMONS, 1841
—————·—·————— WORKMAN—ROWLAND, 1841
·················· LANSFORD W. HASTINGS, 1843
—————··—————— JOSEPH B. CHILES, 1843
—————···————— JOSEPH R. WALKER, 1843
—————·—·————— STEVENS—MURPHY, 1844

The Donner
Tragedy 1846
Hock Farm
Johnsons
Ranch   Truckee's Lake
Sinclair's Ranch
New Helvetia
Marsh's Ranch
Yerba Buena
Gilroy's Ranch
MONTEREY

Walker's Pass

Old Spanish Trail

Los Angeles

San Diego

© 1974 by the University of Oklahoma Press

THE EXPLOITS OF the mountain men and the growing force of Manifest Destiny led to the entry of American immigrant parties into California during the early 1840's. The first of these overland groups was the Bartleson-Bidwell party. John Bartleson led the group, but John Bidwell, as clerk, kept a superb account of the pilgrimage. This "first emigrant train to California" made its way through the Sierra and down the Stanislaus River to Marsh's Ranch on November 4, 1841. Another party, led by William Workman and John Rowland, took the southern route, fearing that snow would block the Sierra before they could cross, and followed the Old Spanish Trail to Los Angeles, arriving in November, 1841.

In 1843 Lansford W. Hastings led a party of some forty settlers down from Oregon to the Sacramento area. The most important group in 1843 were the Chiles-Walker parties. Joseph B. Chiles, who had come to California with the Bidwell-Bartleson group, led a party of emigrants overland. En route, perhaps near Fort Laramie, he engaged Joseph R. Walker as a guide for his party of some fifty people. At Fort Hall, because of the shortage of provisions, the group divided. Chiles led nine or ten men into California by a new route, via the Malheur and Pit rivers, and then south along the Sacramento. Apparently, the plan was to send supplies back to the rest of the party. Walker, however, knew how to enter California without braving the snow-clad Sierra. He proceeded south along the eastern edge of the mountains to Walker Lake and then westward into the Owens Valley and, via Walker's Pass, into the San Joaquin Valley. It was January before the Walker party reached Gilroy's Ranch in the Santa Clara Valley.

Mexican authorities tried to keep Americans out of California by issuing warnings through the Mexican minister at Washington. However, California officials paid little attention to the directions from Mexico City, and most Americans readily acquired land or went into business with little difficulty.

The Stevens-Murphy party of 1844 was under the leadership of Elisha Stevens but is known by the above name because of the large number of Murphy families included in the group. They were probably the first immigrants to cross the Sierras by the Truckee and Bear rivers, the route which the Central Pacific Railroad followed. They were behind schedule and snow was falling by the time they reached the mountains. In early December they camped near what later was named Donner Lake. From this point one group pushed on to New Helvetia. The others waited for help but, not receiving any, proceeded on to Johnson's Ranch and Hock Farm.

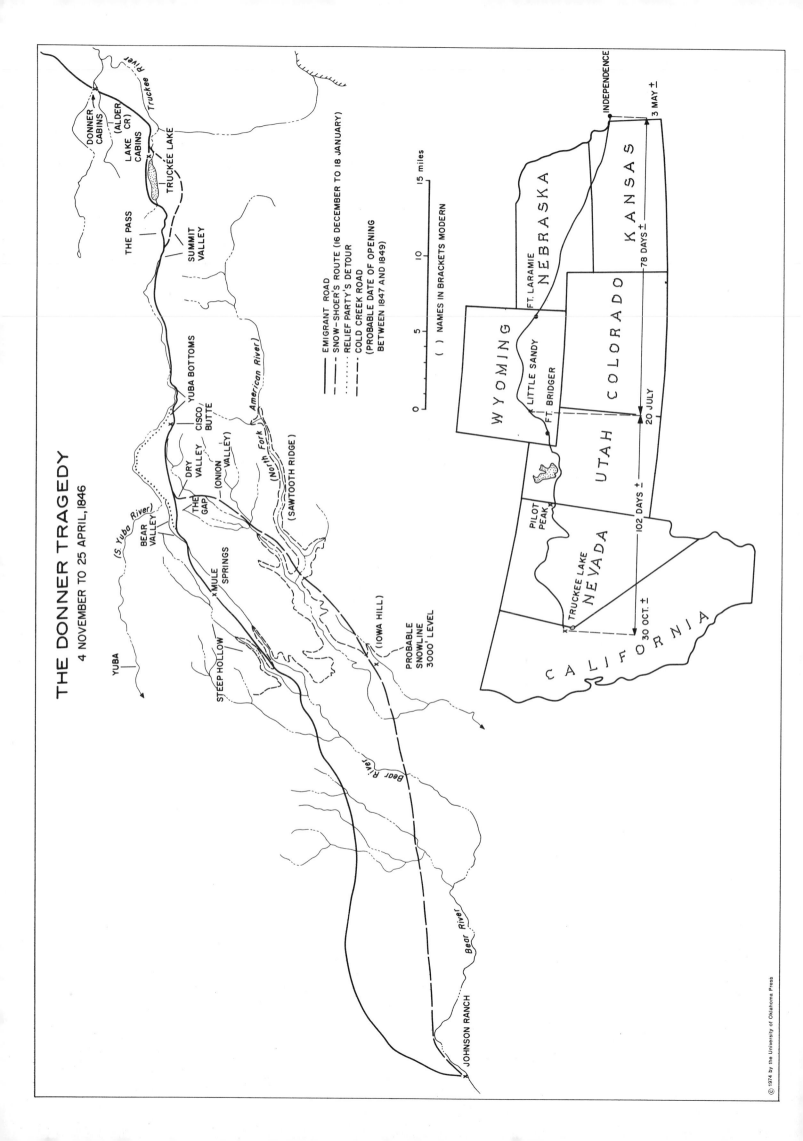

THE DONNER TRAGEDY
4 NOVEMBER TO 25 APRIL, 1846

EMIGRANT ROAD
SNOW-SHOER'S ROUTE (16 DECEMBER TO 18 JANUARY)
RELIEF PARTY'S DETOUR
COLD CREEK ROAD
(PROBABLE DATE OF OPENING
BETWEEN 1847 AND 1849)

( ) NAMES IN BRACKETS MODERN

0   5   10   15 miles

DONNER CABINS
(ALDER CR)
LAKE CABINS
TRUCKEE CABINS
Truckee River
TRUCKEE LAKE
THE PASS
SUMMIT VALLEY
YUBA BOTTOMS
CISCO BUTTE
DRY VALLEY
(ONION VALLEY)
(North Fork American River)
(SAWTOOTH RIDGE)
THE GAP
BEAR VALLEY
(S. Yuba River)
YUBA
MULE SPRINGS
STEEP HOLLOW
(IOWA HILL)
PROBABLE SNOWLINE 3000' LEVEL
Bear River
Bear River
JOHNSON RANCH

INDEPENDENCE
3 MAY ±
NEBRASKA
KANSAS
78 DAYS ±
FT. LARAMIE
WYOMING
COLORADO
UTAH
Little Sandy
FT. BRIDGER
20 JULY
102 DAYS ±
PILOT PEAK
NEVADA
Truckee Lake
30 OCT. ±
CALIFORNIA

45. THE DONNER TRAGEDY

THE DISASTER WHICH befell the Donner Party was the most famous one which happened to any emigrant group en route to California. Their tragedy resulted from bad luck and mistakes in judgment somehow avoided by most of the other emigrants to the Golden State. The original party of thirty-two organized in Springfield, Illinois, under the leadership of George Donner. The latter, along with his brother Jacob, was a wealthy farmer who took along a large supply of merchandise to be sold in California and $10,000 in cash. The Donner brothers were in their sixties, and a fatal weakness of the party was the disproportionate number of elderly people and women and children, which slowed their progress on the trail.

On May 3, 1846, the party left Independence, having grown to about a hundred persons. The first 78 days of the journey passed uneventfully. In fact, Mrs. George Donner recorded, "I could never have believed we could have traveled so far with so little difficulty." At Little Sandy, on July 20, the first decision leading to disaster was made. A messenger from Lansford Hastings, author of *The Emigrants Guide to Oregon and California*, informed them of a cut-off which would save 400 miles. Part of the group remained on the California trail, with the remainder (eighty-seven persons), constituting the ill-fated Donner Party, taking the "short-cut." Before reaching Fort Bridger they met the famed mountain man Joseph Walker, who warned them to return and take the regular trail north of the Great Salt Lake. Despite the fact that they had no experienced guide, the party rejected this sound advice and plunged into the trailless Utah wilderness. It took a month to reach the southern lake shore (it took 21 days to go 36 miles) only to encounter more hardships in the Great Salt Desert. Many wagons were abandoned in the difficult passage as oxen died, wandered off, or were stolen by the Indians. This also meant the decimation of their food supply. Not until September 30 did they reach the Humboldt River and return to the well-marked California Trail. (The group which separated from their party had passed the same point 45 days earlier.)

It was October 30 before the party, its morale shattered by murder, desertion, and death, reached the base of the Sierras. Had they plunged on they probably could have beaten the snow through the pass, but they took five fatal days to rest and were snowed in by November 4. Even then, if firewood had been promptly cut, and the beeves, oxen, horses, mules, and dogs butchered, the party could have survived. Instead, much of the livestock was permitted to wander off to perish in the snow.

The main group camped in the lake cabins on Truckee Lake, while the Donner families were in tents and brushwood huts on Alder Creek. A snowshoe party of fifteen started from lake camp on December 16 to cross the Sierra with rations for six days, but their journey lasted thirty-two days. As members died, they were eaten by the survivors, a practice also in effect at the lake cabins. Once word reached Johnson Ranch (and Sutter's Fort) of the plight of the Donner Party, four relief expeditions came through the snow to the aid of the beleaguered group. However, of the total of eighty-seven only forty-eight reached California.

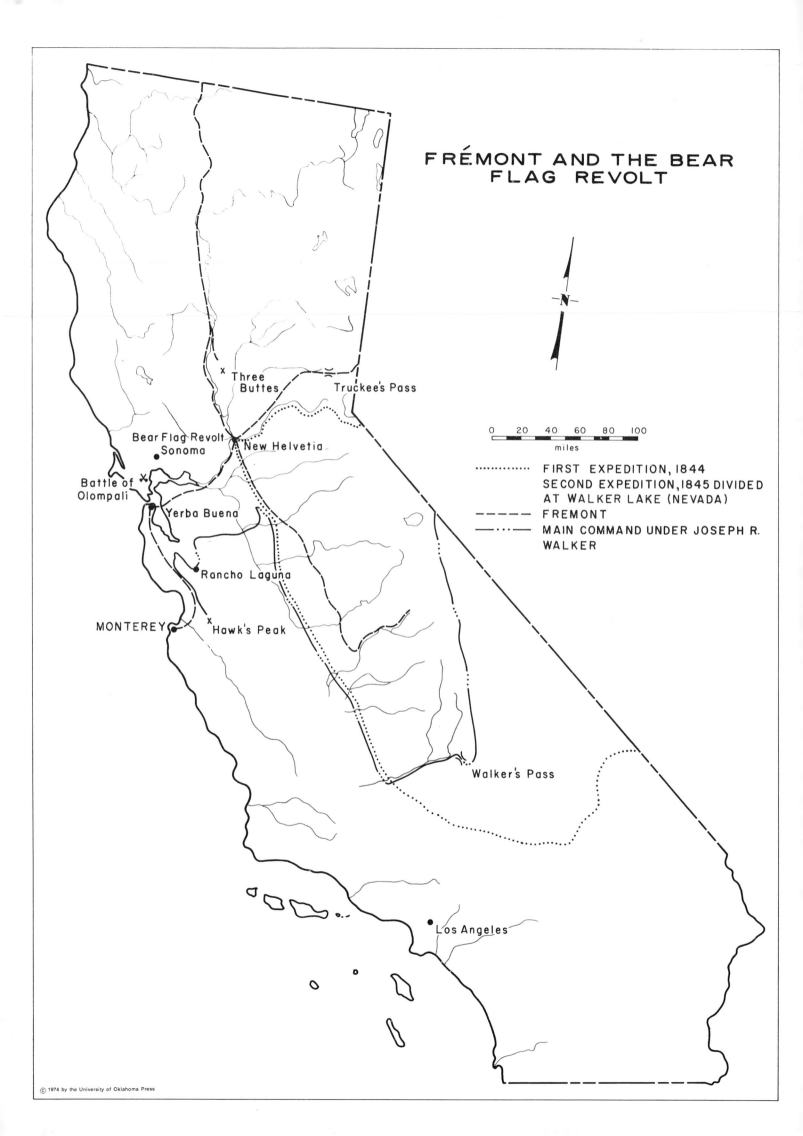

FRÉMONT AND THE BEAR FLAG REVOLT

x Three Buttes

Truckee's Pass

N

Bear Flag Revolt
Sonoma

△ New Helvetia

Battle of
Olompali x

Yerba Buena

Rancho Laguna

MONTEREY

x Hawk's Peak

Walker's Pass

Los Angeles

| 0 | 20 | 40 | 60 | 80 | 100 |
miles

·········· FIRST EXPEDITION, 1844
SECOND EXPEDITION, 1845 DIVIDED
AT WALKER LAKE (NEVADA)
– – – FREMONT
–··–··– MAIN COMMAND UNDER JOSEPH R.
WALKER

46. FRÉMONT AND THE BEAR FLAG REVOLT

THE ROLE OF John Charles Frémont in the Bear Flag Revolt remains a matter of controversy. A son-in-law of the influential Missouri Senator, Thomas Hart Benton, and an officer of the elite Army Corps of Topographical Engineers, Frémont had a national reputation by the time of his California adventures. He was greatly aided by the superb prose of his wife, who converted dull military exploratory reports into high adventure which sold widely to a public fascinated by news of the West.

In January, 1844, while returning from an exploratory trip into the Oregon Territory, Frémont went south along the eastern side of the Cascades and the Sierra. In February the explorers' party crossed the deep snow of the Sierra to the welcome hospitality of New Helvetia. After resting for two weeks, Frémont and his men went southward through the San Joaquin Valley, over the Tehachapi Pass, and then eastward over the Old Spanish Trail.

The winter of 1845 found Frémont back in California. With a small force the "Pathfinder" entered by way of Truckee Pass. Meanwhile, his main command, under Joseph R. Walker, arrived via the Owens Valley. It took some two months for the two groups to find each other at Rancho Laguna. Mexican authorities, justifiably concerned over the presence of a unit of the United States Army in their territory, ordered Frémont to leave. Instead, the party built fortifications and raised the American flag on Hawk's Peak (or Gavilan, but now called Frémont). After three days Frémont abandoned this site and made his way northward towards the Oregon border. En route he was overtaken by a courier, Lieutenant Archibald H. Gillespie. The Marine Corps officer had traveled across Mexico to California posing as a merchant but carrying special messages from Secretary of State Buchanan to Consul Larkin at Monterey. He showed Frémont a copy of the dispatch to Larkin, as well as a packet of letters from Senator Benton, but historians have speculated that he may also have carried special orders from President Polk.

Frémont's version of the messages he received were vague: "The letter of Senator Benton . . . was a trumpet giving no uncertain note. Read by the light of many conversations and discussions with himself and other governing men in Washington, it clearly made me know that I was required by the Government to find out any foreign schemes in relation to California, and to counteract them so far as was in my power. His letters made me know distinctly that at last the time had come when England must not get a foothold; that we *must be first*. I was to *act*, discreetly but positively." In other words, he interpreted his father-in-law's letter as an imperative act in the interests of the United States. In terms of his personal ambitions, Frémont's actions were correct.

While Frémont retraced his steps southward, American settlers started a revolt on their own on June 10, 1846. Hostilities were initiated by seizing a band of horses intended for the Mexican militia. The Bear Flaggers raised the grizzly bear flag and issued a proclamation of independence. A short distance from San Rafael the virtually bloodless "Battle" of Olompali was fought. This action prompted Frémont to place his small detachment (sixty-two) of United States troops on the side of the rebels. The question which remains is whether or not Frémont encouraged the revolt and only waited until success was ensured before overtly joining the conflict. From New Helvetia the small American force made its way to Yerba Buena and on to Monterey, where it joined forces with United States Naval units. The fact that war with Mexico had already begun made Frémont's action acceptable.

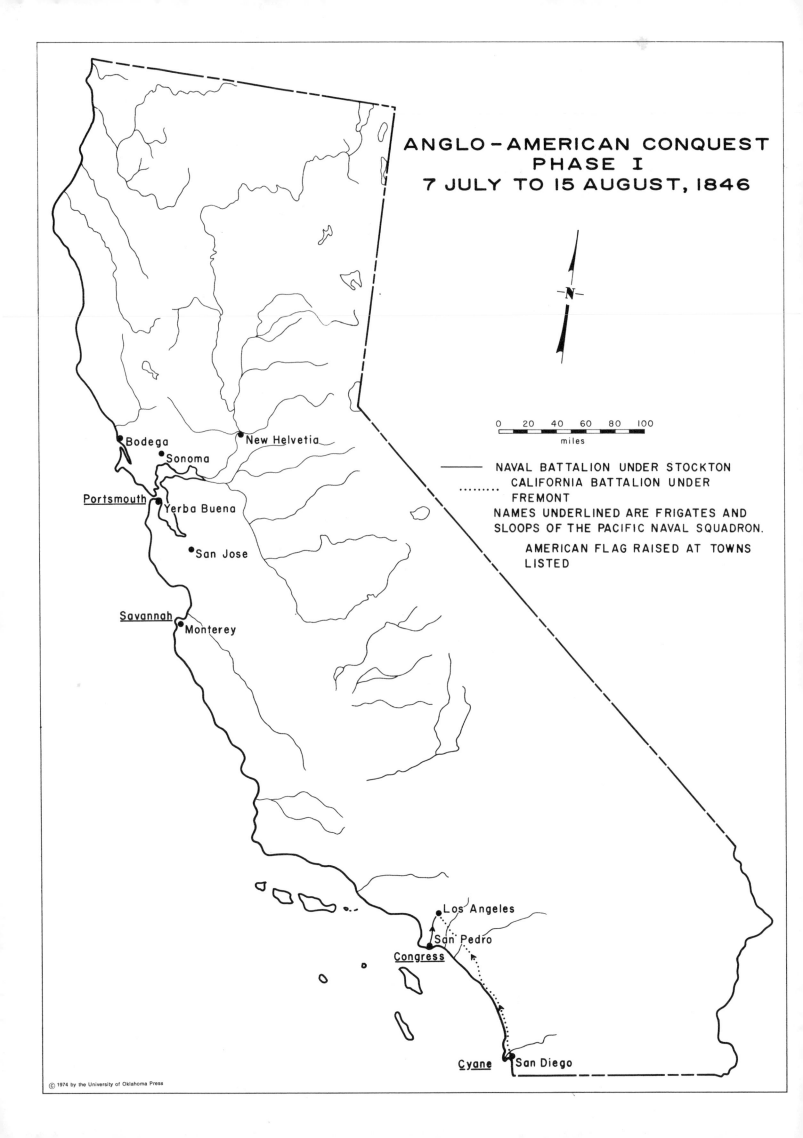

ANGLO-AMERICAN CONQUEST
PHASE I
7 JULY TO 15 AUGUST, 1846

-N-

0   20   40   60   80   100
miles

—————— NAVAL BATTALION UNDER STOCKTON
·········· CALIFORNIA BATTALION UNDER
          FREMONT
NAMES UNDERLINED ARE FRIGATES AND
SLOOPS OF THE PACIFIC NAVAL SQUADRON.

AMERICAN FLAG RAISED AT TOWNS
LISTED

• Bodega
• Sonoma
• New Helvetia

Portsmouth
• Yerba Buena

• San Jose

Savannah
• Monterey

• Los Angeles
• San Pedro
Congress

Cyane • San Diego

47. ANGLO-AMERICAN CONQUEST, PHASE I

July 7 to August 15, 1846

WHILE THE BEAR FLAG "Revolt" was in process, preparations for the actual military conquest of California were being made. Commodore John D. Sloat, in command of the Pacific fleet of the United States, heard rumors of the outbreak of war while at Mazatlan, Mexico. Proceeding northward in his flagship *Savannah*, Sloat reached Monterey on July 1 or 2. He waited for several days before taking possession of the city, possibly to make sure that war was an actuality. On July 7, a force of marines and seamen formally raised the United States flag at the customhouse. A conciliatory proclamation was read and posted in public places.

Captain John B. Montgomery of the *Portsmouth* raised the flag at Yerba Buena on July 9, in accordance with Sloat's instructions. On the same day, an aide of Montgomery raised the flag over Sonoma. On July 11, the stars and stripes were also raised at New Helvetia, with so much cannonading that nearly all the glass at Sutter's Fort was broken. In some communities it was the Bear Flag and not that of Mexico which was lowered before the United States flag could be hoisted with proper ceremony.

With the conquest of central California complete, Commodore Sloat turned his command over to Commodore Robert F. Stockton on July 29. The latter naval officer was more belligerent towards the native Californians than his predecessor and was also more eager to complete the conquest of the southern portion of the province. Stockton sailed from Monterey on August 1, planning to capture Los Angeles. Arriving at San Pedro on August 7, with a poorly trained force of 360, he waited until August 11 before beginning the overland march to Los Angeles. Meanwhile, John C. Frémont, who had previously joined forces with Stockton in Monterey, had sailed southward with a battalion. Taking formal possession of San Diego on July 29, Frémont's force marched north on August 8 and joined Stockton in time for the ceremonial flag raising in Los Angeles on August 13.

One American observed that, "we simply marched all over California from Sonoma to San Diego and raised the American flag without opposition or protest. We tried to find an enemy, but could not." There were many reasons for the inability of the native Californians to offer more resistance during the first phase of the American conquest. First of all, California was a remote outpost of Mexico and had been neglected to the point where there was little in the way of a fighting force available or little funds to purchase essential equipment. Hence, many individuals did not want to participate in a useless struggle. Others also were disenchanted with Mexican domination to the point that they were indifferent to the outcome or even favored American victory. Friction between Governor Pío Pico and General José Castro also made unity against the invaders difficult. Even if a stubborn resistance had been made, Castro's army seldom exceeded a hundred inferior armed men. On August 10, both Pico and Castro fled Los Angeles for Mexico.

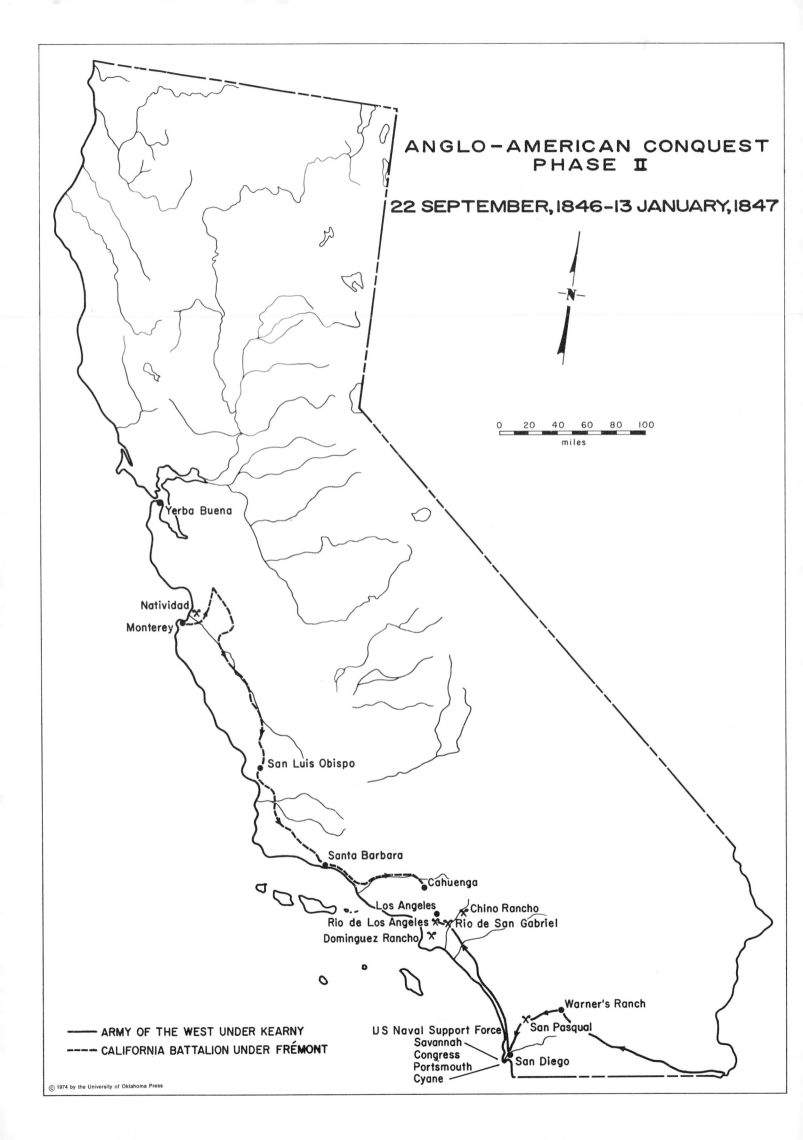

ANGLO—AMERICAN CONQUEST
PHASE II

22 SEPTEMBER, 1846—13 JANUARY, 1847

-N-

0 20 40 60 80 100
miles

Yerba Buena

Natividad
Monterey

San Luis Obispo

Santa Barbara

Cahuenga

Los Angeles
Chino Rancho
Rio de Los Angeles
Rio de San Gabriel
Dominguez Rancho

Warner's Ranch

US Naval Support Force
Savannah
Congress
Portsmouth
Cyane

San Pasqual

San Diego

—— ARMY OF THE WEST UNDER KEARNY
----- CALIFORNIA BATTALION UNDER FRÉMONT

© 1974 by the University of Oklahoma Press

September 22, 1846 to January 13, 1847

THE SECOND PHASE of the Anglo-American conquest of California saw greater bloodshed than the first phase. Hostilities were renewed on the night of September 22, when the Californios laid siege to the small American garrison in Los Angeles. On September 26, some twenty Americans, led by Benjamin D. Wilson, surrendered at Chino Rancho. On September 30, the Los Angeles force, commanded by Lieutenant Archibald Gillespie, was permitted to leave for San Pedro with a promise to sail from California. Instead, the American force joined with a relief party at the port and marched inland in an effort to recapture Los Angeles. On October 9, the Californios defeated the Americans in a battle at Dominguez Rancho, forcing another retreat to San Pedro. This conflict was followed by a temporary cessation of hostilities.

Meanwhile, the army of Stephen Watts Kearny was marching on California. Leaving Fort Leavenworth in June, with a force of more than sixteen hundred men, General Kearny was instructed to capture Santa Fe and California. After a bloodless conquest of New Mexico, Kearny sent most of his troops to aid General Zachary Taylor in Mexico and started for California with only three hundred men. Meeting Kit Carson carrying messages from Stockton to Washington officials relating that the conquest of California had been completed, he sent all but about a hundred of his troops back to Santa Fe. With Carson to guide him, Kearny made the harsh desert crossing, which taxed both men and their mounts.

Near the Indian village of San Pasqual, Kearny's weary force encountered a detachment of Californios under Andrés Pico. Using exceptionally poor judgment, the Americans attacked early on the morning of December 6, despite a cold mist and a fog-shrouded unfamiliar battlefield. Kearny was urged to immediate battle by Carson and Gillespie. Wet gunpowder silenced their guns. Mounted on either worn-out mules or undisciplined horses recently seized from the Mexicans, the Americans were no match for the lance equipped and superbly mounted Californios. Kearny's force lost twenty-one killed and eighteen wounded in the most significant battle on California soil, while Pico's force had but one fatality and eighteen wounded. Kit Carson and Lieutenant Edward F. Beale slipped through hostile country, reached San Diego, and summoned help to the battered American force.

But San Pasqual was to be the last victory for the Californios. Dissension within their ranks made a strong command impossible. They were further weakened by poor quality gunpowder which reduced the effectiveness of their artillery. On December 29 a force of some six hundred Americans under Kearny and Stockton left San Diego overland for Los Angeles. On January 8 there was a brief skirmish on the banks of the Río de San Gabriel. The following day saw the last battle on California soil. The Californios made their final stand on the banks of the Río de Los Angeles but withdrew after light artillery fire.

Frémont, in command of the California Battalion, fought a battle at Natividad in the Salinas Valley, with perhaps the loss of five lives on each side. The battalion marched southward, slowed more by mud and rain than by the enemy. On January 13, 1847, the remnants of the command of Andrés Pico capitulated to Frémont at Cahuenga, formally ending hostilities.

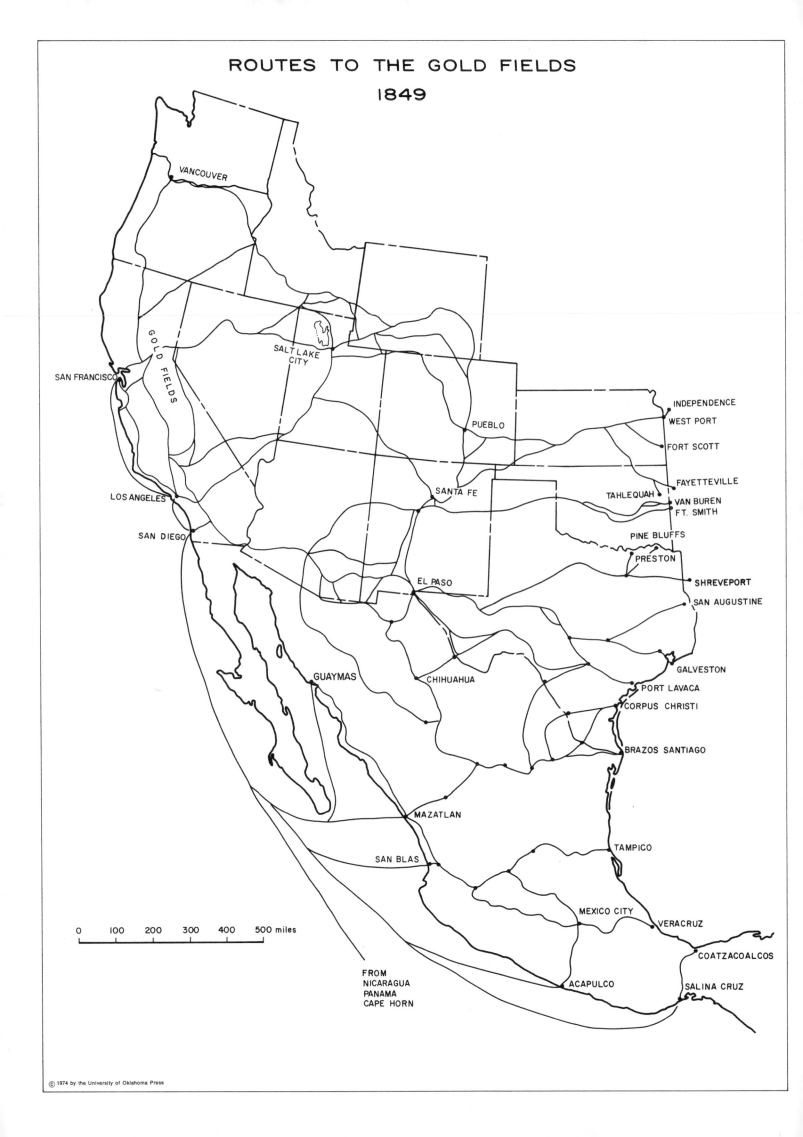

49. ROUTES TO THE GOLD FIELDS

THE ROUTE AROUND Cape Horn to San Francisco from New York initially took from five to eight months. Despite the hazards of such an ocean voyage and the discomforts aboard ship, it was preferred by those who could afford the cash outlay for passage. It was the usual route for the inhabitants for the Atlantic coast.

A more favored sea route was via Panama or Nicaragua. With luck, passage could be effected in six to eight weeks. These routes were the choice of travelers in a hurry to reach the gold fields, despite the hazards of disease in crossing the isthmus. Some Argonauts took the first available ship to one of the Mexican ports. There they made their way westward by a variety of means of land transportation to a Pacific port. Unfortunately, there were frequent delays until a California-bound ship was available. Some were forced to go overland from San Blas to Mazatlan, and even on to Guaymas, and a few, in desperation, went overland to California.

By far the most popular routes to the gold fields were overland. They had the advantage of being available to midwesterners and required little cash outlay to get started. River transportation was available to where the trails began. Most routes west had been publicized during the Mexican War or by the writings of John Frémont and Lansford Hastings.

Overland, the people's choice was the Oregon Trail. The basic starting place was St. Joseph or Independence, but with one spur leaving from Kanesville, Iowa, and joining the Oregon Trail on the Platte. From Salt Lake City, the more common practice was to swing north around the lake and then southwestward to the headwaters of the Humboldt. The most direct route west was over the salt flats known as Hasting's Cut-off, but this was usually avoided. Some went southward from Salt Lake City, especially if the season was late and there was danger of snow in the mountains. This route divided in southeastern Utah, with one spur going through Death Valley and the other into Los Angeles via Cajon Pass. A few Argonauts even went the long way around into Oregon before turning south. Under the most favorable conditions, the overland journey of some two thousand miles took a hundred days.

Perhaps a sixth of all who came to the gold fields used "minor" routes. The Santa Fe Trail was preferred by those who went the southern way. From New Mexico several branches went into Colorado and then northwestward to one of the main trails. A few struck westward at Albuquerque, to Zuñi, and then south to the Gila; while others veered westward at Socorro. The favored route to the Gila went into Mexico via Guadalupe Pass, where it joined a well-traveled trail. The route went down the Gila and crossed the Colorado at Yuma. Many travelers from the southern states left from Fort Smith, Arkansas, and crossed Oklahoma to Santa Fe. Several routes went through Texas to El Paso, to the Mesilla Valley, and then down the Gila. Other routes, possibly publicized by the recent war, led across northern Mexico with one route through Chihuahua and another via Parras.

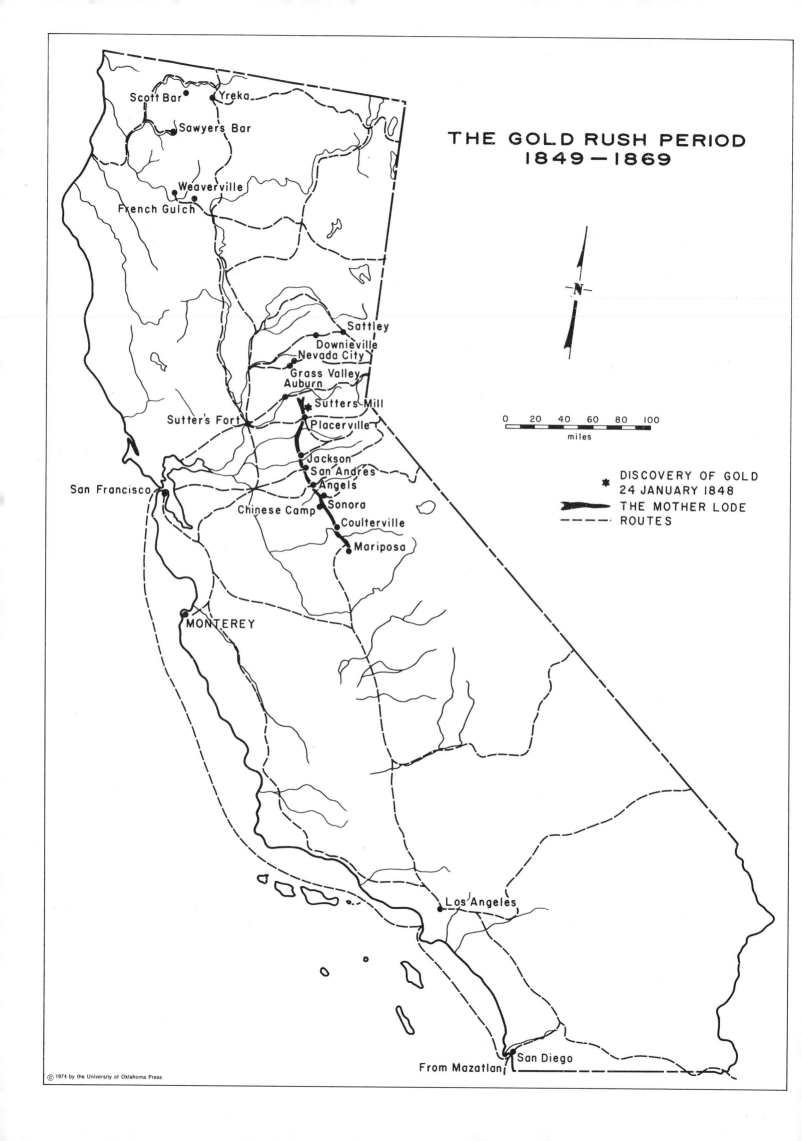

THE GOLD RUSH PERIOD
1849—1869

Scott Bar
Yreka
Sawyers Bar
Weaverville
French Gulch

Sattley
Downieville
Nevada City
Grass Valley
Auburn
Sutter's Mill
Sutter's Fort
Placerville
Jackson
San Andres
Angels
Sonora
Chinese Camp
Coulterville
Mariposa

San Francisco

MONTEREY

Los Angeles

From Mazatlan | San Diego

-N-

0   20   40   60   80   100
miles

★   DISCOVERY OF GOLD
     24 JANUARY 1848
▶   THE MOTHER LODE
- - -   ROUTES

50. THE GOLD RUSH PERIOD, 1849–69

James Marshall discovered gold on January 24, 1848, at Sutter's Mill on the American River. At first there was no mad rush, simply because nothing like this had ever happened before in American history. As late as early May a San Francisco newspaper spoke for many persons, stating that "a few fools have hurried to the [American River], but you may be sure there is nothing in it." But on May 12, Sam Brannan dramatized the discovery by promenading the streets of San Francisco bellowing "Gold, gold, gold from the American River," and within days another San Francisco newspaper moaned: "The whole country from San Francisco to Los Angeles, and from the sea shore to the base of the Sierra Nevadas, resounds with the sordid cry of 'gold, Gold, GOLD!' while the field is left half planted, the house half built, and everything neglected but the manufacture of shovels and pick axes."

By the end of 1848 miners were prospecting from the Feather River to the Tuolumne River along the western slope of the Sierras. By 1850 there was hardly a canyon or small valley in central California that didn't have a small town or a miners' camp. The area known as the "Mother Lode" began north of Sutter's mill and continued as far south as Mariposa. The term possibly originated from the reference of Spanish-speaking miners to the *veta madre*. It rested upon the assumption that there was one great vein from which all of the gold originally came. Because the Mother Lode country was the first to be mined, the name has become synonymous with the gold mining region. However, some of the richest mines were north of the Mother Lode in Nevada, Placer, and Sierra counties. An important but separate gold field was located north and west of the Sacramento Valley. In this area streams such as the Klamath, Trinity, Shasta, and their tributaries were the locales of productive mines.

Fortunately for the novices at mining in California in 1848 and 1849, the gold was easily obtained. The precious metal had been originally created when volcanic action forced hot liquid into the fissures and cracks of the earth's mantle. A subsequent series of geologic cycles after the veins were formed brought erosion, volcanic eruption, and an uplift of the mountain westward which increased the erosive power of the westward-flowing streams. Therefore, gold was found along the banks of streams or in stream beds in tiny particles known as "flour gold" or in nuggets weighing several pounds.

Gold was so easily obtainable in the virgin deposits that it was dug out with a knife, spoon, or shovel and swirled around in a pan to separate the gold from the dross. Being heavier, the gold would sink to the bottom of the pan while the foreign matter was washed over the rim. Naturally, there were many variations of the "panning" process, with devices such as the long-tom, but the principle remained the same. Quartz and hydraulic mining developed once the virgin deposits were worked over, but these innovations demanded much capital, labor, and equipment. Had they been required in the early stages of the gold rush, the entire story would have been different.

The gold rush period of California was characterized by constant change as new fields were discovered. There was a mad stampede to the new area, the hasty building of a tent city, followed by the erection of more durable buildings, and the influx of a large number of people. When the initial high hopes were dashed, there was a mad rush to greener pastures, and the process was repeated. Dame Shirley lamented: "Our countrymen are the most discontented of mortals. They are always longing for 'big strikes!' If a claim is paying them a steady income, by which, if they pleased, they could lay up more in a month, than they could accumulate in a year at home, still, they are dissatisfied, and, in most cases, will wander off in search of better 'diggings.'"

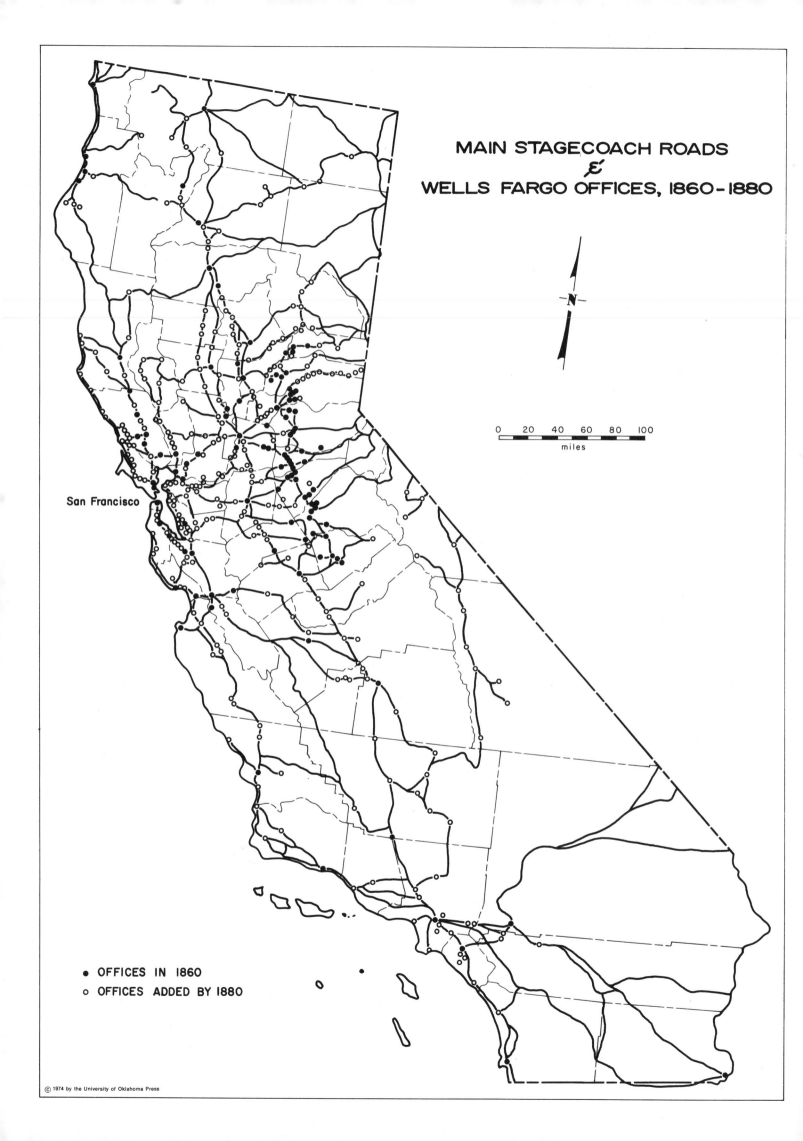

MAIN STAGECOACH ROADS
&
WELLS FARGO OFFICES, 1860-1880

—N—

0   20   40   60   80   100
miles

San Francisco

• OFFICES IN 1860
○ OFFICES ADDED BY 1880

© 1974 by the University of Oklahoma Press

51. MAIN STAGECOACH ROADS AND WELLS FARGO OFFICES, 1860–80

As IN SO MANY other areas, the Gold Rush provided the first great impetus towards the development of roads, the growth of freighting and express companies, and the emergence of a stagecoach system which ultimately covered most of the state. Miners, unwilling to absent themselves from profitable claims, were ready to pay handsomely for someone else to carry their mail, bring them supplies, or transport their gold in safety. Traders hauling freight in the large wagons brought in by the emigrants to the ever-changing mining centers were the first to open many of the roads. Of course, in many instances they followed trails originally laid out by Mexicans or by emigrant parties. For the more rugged terrain of the mines, pack mules were the only possible means of transport.

Before express and stagecoach lines could flourish in California, it was necessary to build bridges and roads. As Professor Winther notes: "There is little to be said in favor of the quality of California's roads between 1848 and 1860." The British traveler Frank Marryat would concur in his observation that, "no one knows what a wagon will undergo until he has mastered California's trails and gulches." Yet, by 1860 the state was knitted together by a system of passable roads with their center at Sacramento. Initially, most of the roads were of private construction. In 1858 there were sixty-four turnpikes, many of the plank or corduroy type. Not until 1859 did the state appropriate much money for roads.

The first stagecoaches began operation in California in 1849. One line operated between San Francisco and San Jose; another ran from Sacramento to towns on the American River. In the early years, many stagecoach efforts began and died in a matter of months as a result of underfinancing, lack of equipment, or accident. But many of the "one man, one horse" operations did flourish and provide the nucleus for larger transportation enterprises. By 1853, Sacramento had twelve stage lines, and few centers of population were without such transportation. Not only was excellent equipment brought in from the east, but also experienced personnel. In 1854 a merger of competing lines created the California Stage Company. This organization soon controlled some five-sixths of the stagecoach business in the state. Since most of the people were in the central and northern parts of the state, this was where the stagelines were located.

The emergence of express companies originally resulted from the inadequacy of the United States Post Office in the rapidly expanding mining frontier. Alexander Todd, discovering that mining was too much for his health, was probably the first to carry mail and supplies from San Francisco for other miners. In a short time Todd had a lucrative business handling the affairs of thousands of miners, scattered through scores of mining camps. Profits of up to $1,000 a day attracted many competitors operating out of Stockton, Sacramento, San Francisco, or Marysville. The usual mergers reduced the number of express firms and finally one, Wells Fargo, dominated the scene. Chartered in New York in 1852, under the leadership of Henry Wells and William G. Fargo, its capital and superior management gave it an advantage over its competitors. Growth was effected through merger, affiliation, purchase, or by driving other firms out of business.

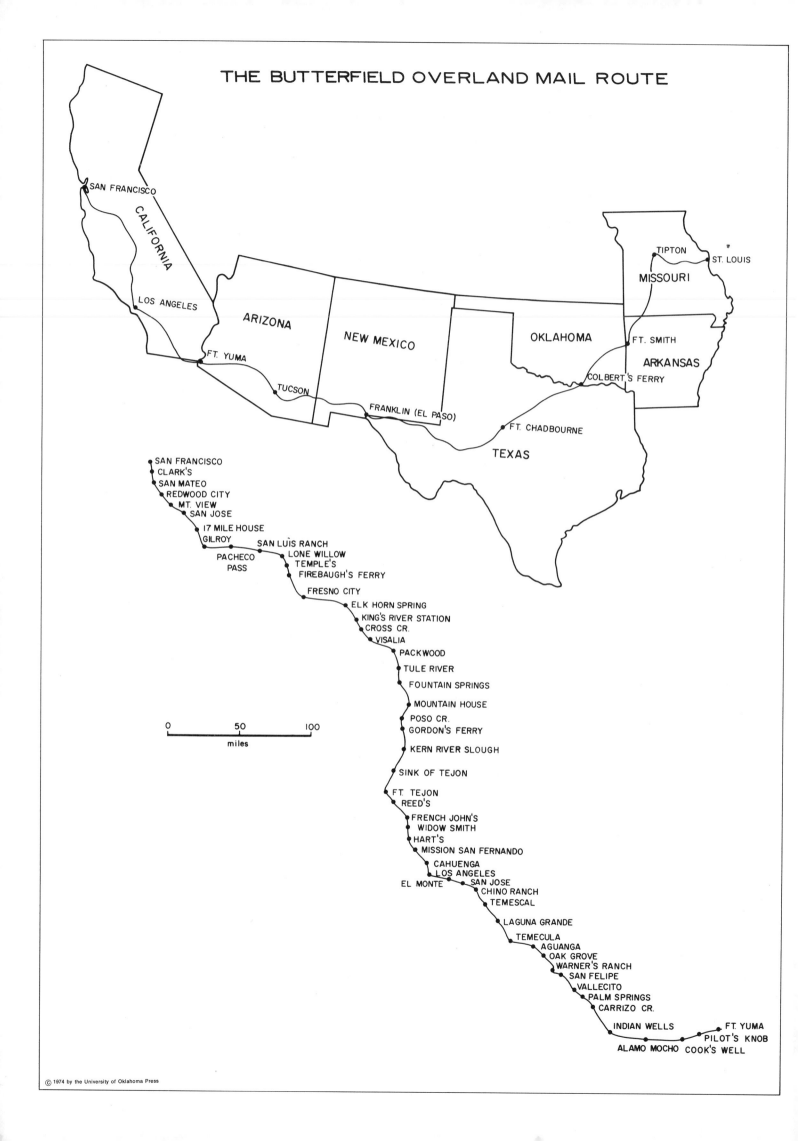

THE BUTTERFIELD OVERLAND MAIL ROUTE

CALIFORNIA

SAN FRANCISCO

LOS ANGELES

ARIZONA

FT. YUMA

TUCSON

NEW MEXICO

FRANKLIN (EL PASO)

OKLAHOMA

FT. SMITH

COLBERT'S FERRY

ARKANSAS

FT. CHADBOURNE

TEXAS

MISSOURI

TIPTON

ST. LOUIS

SAN FRANCISCO
CLARK'S
SAN MATEO
REDWOOD CITY
MT. VIEW
SAN JOSE
17 MILE HOUSE
GILROY
PACHECO PASS
SAN LUIS RANCH
LONE WILLOW
TEMPLE'S
FIREBAUGH'S FERRY
FRESNO CITY
ELK HORN SPRING
KING'S RIVER STATION
CROSS CR.
VISALIA
PACKWOOD
TULE RIVER
FOUNTAIN SPRINGS
MOUNTAIN HOUSE
POSO CR.
GORDON'S FERRY
KERN RIVER SLOUGH
SINK OF TEJON
FT. TEJON
REED'S
FRENCH JOHN'S
WIDOW SMITH
HART'S
MISSION SAN FERNANDO
CAHUENGA
LOS ANGELES
EL MONTE
SAN JOSE
CHINO RANCH
TEMESCAL
LAGUNA GRANDE
TEMECULA
AGUANGA
OAK GROVE
WARNER'S RANCH
SAN FELIPE
VALLECITO
PALM SPRINGS
CARRIZO CR.
INDIAN WELLS
FT. YUMA
PILOT'S KNOB
ALAMO MOCHO   COOK'S WELL

```
0        50        100
miles
```

JOHN BUTTERFIELD, founder of the American Express company and a veteran of staging operations in New York State, was the leader of the company designed to end California's isolation from the rest of the country. Recipient of a government grant of $595,000 annually for carrying the mails semiweekly, the company developed a new route stretching from St. Louis to San Francisco, some 2,750 miles, in an "ox bow."

Service began on September 15, 1858, with the normal operating time between east and west less than twenty-five days for a San Francisco–St. Louis fare of $200. Mail was carried the full distance at three cents for each half-ounce. Coaches carried a maximum of six (hardy) passengers who had to withstand the rigors of the trip, bad food, and perhaps also fight off hostile Indians.

The Butterfield operation was truly a major enterprise in its day. Some eight hundred people were employed to handle the one hundred Concord coaches and fifteen hundred horses and mules or service the relay stations. Usually built approximately 10 miles apart, such stations frequently needed to furnish guards against Indian attack as well as fresh horses and mules.

In addition to effectively closing the travel gap between California and the Mississippi Valley, the Butterfield Route also united the state of California more completely than any other staging project. However, in spite of these accomplishments, the company was deeply resented in the Golden State. No opportunity was overlooked to attack its food,

its coaches, or its service in general. This hostility probably originated as a result of widespread conviction that the line was a result of political favoritism; that southerners dictated the route with an eye to sectional advantage. The Butterfield route also made the southern part of the state closer to the rest of the country. This was resented in the Sacramento-San Francisco region for fear that the economic well-being of their area might be injured. Some northern Californians continued to believe that faster service was possible over a central route. With secession and with war clouds gathering in 1861, the Butterfield Overland Mail, which ran through southern territory, was doomed.

Within California the Butterfield route followed the line of least geographic resistance, so long as water was available. From Fort Yuma the route stretched westward across the difficult sand dunes before dipping southward into Mexico. It re-entered the state near the New River and skirted the inside edge of the mountains into Los Angeles. The most difficult passage in California was the slow and arduous trip northward through the mountains and Tejon Pass into the San Joaquin Valley. It was relatively easy traveling until the route veered northwestward after Fresno, over Pacheco Pass and through Gilroy and San Jose, en route to San Francisco. Everything considered, this stagecoach route was vastly superior to the difficulties that would have had to be met in running stagecoaches through the passes of the Sierra Nevada.

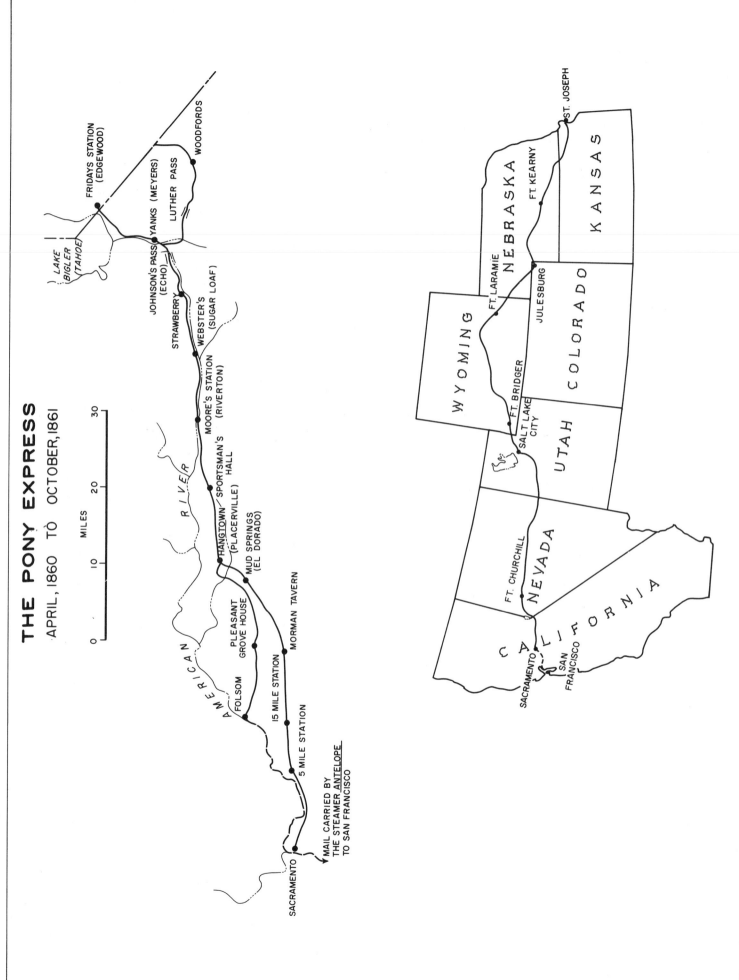

THE PONY EXPRESS

APRIL, 1860 TO OCTOBER, 1861

MILES

0   10   20   30

SACRAMENTO

MAIL CARRIED BY
THE STEAMER ANTELOPE
TO SAN FRANCISCO

5 MILE STATION

15 MILE STATION

MORMAN TAVERN

FOLSOM

PLEASANT
GROVE HOUSE

MUD SPRINGS
(EL DORADO)

HANGTOWN
(PLACERVILLE)

SPORTSMAN'S
HALL

AMERICAN

RIVER

MOORE'S STATION
(RIVERTON)

WEBSTER'S
(SUGAR LOAF)

STRAWBERRY

JOHNSON'S PASS
(ECHO)

YANKS (MEYERS)

LUTHER PASS

WOODFORDS

FRIDAYS STATION
(EDGEWOOD)

LAKE
BIGLER
(TAHOE)

ST. JOSEPH

FT. KEARNY

NEBRASKA

KANSAS

FT. LARAMIE

JULESBURG

WYOMING

COLORADO

FT. BRIDGER

SALT LAKE
CITY

UTAH

FT. CHURCHILL

NEVADA

CALIFORNIA

SACRAMENTO

SAN
FRANCISCO

53. THE PONY EXPRESS

THE PONY EXPRESS remains the most fabled of all forms of western communication. This was true despite the fact that it lasted but a few months and used more horses than ponies. Begun in April, 1860, this unique mail service arose from demands for more rapid communication between California and the East than that available by ship or stagecoach. It was also an outgrowth of the efforts of Russell, Majors, and Waddell's freighting company, the Central Overland California and Pike's Peak Express Company, to compete with the Butterfield Overland Stage. The latter company enjoyed a large government subsidy, and the COC and PP hoped the publicity of the Pony Express would earn federal support for the central route. The drama of this undertaking has become part of American folklore, but the undertaking bankrupted the daring entrepreneurs.

The route ran 1,966 miles from St. Joseph, Missouri to Sacramento. Relay stations to supply fresh horses were stationed about 10 miles apart. Eighty riders (as in the case of jockeys, small men were preferred), half going east and half going west, were employed. Each rider normally rode 50 to 60 miles, but could ride 100 miles if necessary; and in an emergency one rider once rode 280 miles. In its sixteen months of operation these riders traveled 650,000 miles and lost only one shipment, while successfully delivering 35,000 pieces of mail. The mail was wrapped in oiled silk to protect it from the elements. As many as 350 letters were carried initially at ten dollars an ounce, later reduced to two.

The romance associated with the lone rider driving his mount at a gallop over rugged terrain, night and day, in all kinds of weather, pausing only for two minutes to change horses, captured the public imagination. The mail did go through on time (ten days) in spite of all the hazards. But the Pony Express failed to make money for its sponsors.

The Pony Express was soon a victim of technological progress. Shortly after this mail service was inaugurated, Congress authorized a subsidy for a transcontinental telegraph. Express riders repeatedly passed construction crews erecting poles and stringing the wire destined to end their service. The end came shortly after the two telegraph companies building towards each other met on October 24, 1861, in Salt Lake City. But in spite of its short duration of sixteen months, the Pony Express was a significant chapter in efforts to end California's isolation from the rest of the nation.

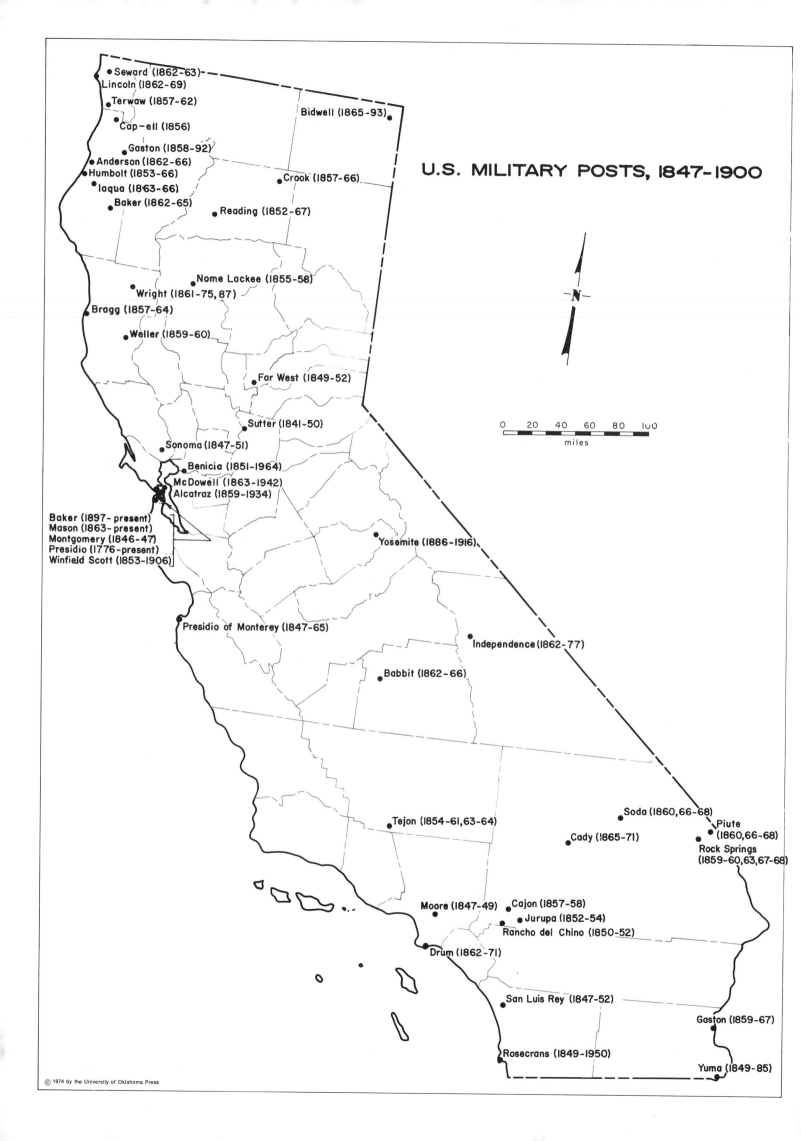

U.S. MILITARY POSTS, 1847-1900

Seward (1862-63)
Lincoln (1862-69)
Terwaw (1857-62)
Cap-ell (1856)
Bidwell (1865-93)
Gaston (1858-92)
Anderson (1862-66)
Humbolt (1853-66)
Iaqua (1863-66)
Crook (1857-66)
Baker (1862-65)
Reading (1852-67)
Nome Lackee (1855-58)
Wright (1861-75, 87)
Bragg (1857-64)
Weller (1859-60)
Far West (1849-52)
Sutter (1841-50)
Sonoma (1847-51)
Benicia (1851-1964)
McDowell (1863-1942)
Alcatraz (1859-1934)
Baker (1897- present)
Mason (1863- present)
Montgomery (1846-47)
Presidio (1776-present)
Winfield Scott (1853-1906)
Yosemite (1886-1916)
Presidio of Monterey (1847-65)
Independence (1862-77)
Babbit (1862-66)
Tejon (1854-61,63-64)
Soda (1860,66-68)
Piute (1860,66-68)
Cady (1865-71)
Rock Springs (1859-60,63,67-68)
Moore (1847-49)
Cajon (1857-58)
Jurupa (1852-54)
Rancho del Chino (1850-52)
Drum (1862-71)
San Luis Rey (1847-52)
Gaston (1859-67)
Rosecrans (1849-1950)
Yuma (1849-85)

0 20 40 60 80 100
miles

-N-

54. U.S. MILITARY POSTS, 1847–1900

ACQUISITION OF California after the Mexican War made the War Department responsible for the protection of the area. The gold rush influx of Americans into every corner of the state caused an intermittent conflict with the Indians. Soldiers, therefore, had to protect the newly-arrived whites from depredations by the "first Californians," but, in many instances, also had to protect the Indians from brutal and senseless attacks by the settlers. To accomplish these objectives the United States Army ultimately dotted California with military installations. The more permanent were usually along the coast, often on the site of a former Mexican facility. Posts were established in the mining country to protect the miners, and garrisons were posted along communication routes, especially at key mountain passes, to protect the large traffic to and from the mines. Many of these establishments existed for only a short time and were built to fill a real or imagined need. When the emergency had passed, they were abandoned and their garrisons moved elsewhere.

Because the terms forts, camps, and barracks, are often used interchangeably to describe the same site, they are omitted on the map. Some installations were of limited significance and these have been omitted at the discretion of the authors. Nor have all of the names by which a facility was known been used. For example, Fort Rosecrans has had various names as well as many sub-forts or associated installations in the San Diego area such as Fort Stockton, Presidio of San Diego, Fort San Diego, Garrison at San Diego, San Diego Barracks, Mission of San Diego and Fort Pío Pico: Fort McDowell was Camp Reynolds (1863–66) and Post of Angel Island (1866–1900), and since 1900, Camp and Fort McDowell.

Among the military installations existing for supply purposes the greatest concentration was, naturally, at San Francisco. Camp Drum (or Drum Barracks, Wilmington Depot, or Camp San Pedro) serviced the Los Angeles area; Fort Rosecrans the San Diego area. Forts Bragg and Humboldt performed similar duties along the north coast, while Fort Gaston acted as a supply point on the Colorado River. Fort Bidwell was located to protect the strategic route into California from the northeast and Fort Yuma performed a similar function in the southeast corner of the state. Camp Cajon and Fort Tejon existed to protect strategic passes. The purpose of Fort Moore, Fort Jurupa, and the detachment at Rancho del Chino was to prevent another Hispano uprising against American rule. The remaining military installations in California, in most cases, were located to deal with conflict with the Indians.

MARIPOSA INDIAN WAR, 1850–1851

DISCOVERY 27 MARCH, 1851

WESTERN MONO

ISBERG PASS

FERNANDEZ PASS

CHIQUITO PASS

YOSEMITE VALLEY

BISHOP CAMP

MIWOK

CRANE VALLEY

COARSE GOLD

FINE GOLD GULCH

FT. MILLER

CAMP BARBOUR

SAN JOAQUIN RIVER

FT. WASHINGTON

CASSADY'S FERRY

RATTLESNAKE CREEK

MAXWELL CREEK

RED BANKS

SOLOMON'S GULCH

RIDLEY'S FERRY

SOUTHERN

BEAR VALLEY

BURN'S DIGGINGS

AGUA FRIA CAMP NO. 1

BRIDGEPORT

CAMP NO. 2 (LEWIS RANCH)

CAMP NO. 3 CAMP FREMONT

MARIPOSA CREEK

FRESNO CROSSING (SAVAGE'S TRADING POST)

CAMP NO. 4 (CAMP McLEAN)

FRESNO RIVER

CHOWCHILLA RIVER

YOKUTS

MERCED RIVER

KUYKENDALL'S FOOT COMPANY TO THE KINGS AND UPPER KAWEAH (ROUTE UNCERTAIN)

x INDIAN ATTACKS

MARIPOSA BATTALION CAMPAIGN ROUTES

1 = 19 MARCH TO 2 APRIL, 1851
2 = 13 APRIL TO 2 MAY, 1851
3 = 4 MAY TO 17 MAY, 1851

0   10   20   30 miles

55. MARIPOSA INDIAN WAR, 1850–51

THE MARIPOSA INDIAN War was the most famed Indian encounter with miners in the southern Sierra region and also led to the discovery of Yosemite Valley. In 1849, as gold seekers invaded the country immediately west of the present Yosemite National Park they found one of the more densely populated Indian areas of the state. This was a region where acorns were abundant and game was plentiful below the winter snow line. Unfortunately, gold was also easily found along the numerous mountain streams. At first the Indians (mainly Miwoks and Yokuts) welcomed the white man and the goods which could be obtained by trade, but resentment grew as virtually every valley was taken over by the newcomers.

To a certain extent, the story of this clash between Indian and white is the saga of James D. Savage, one of the most remarkable of the many characters of the Gold Rush era. A tall blue-eyed blonde who always wore red shirts to better impress the Indians, Savage had been a Bear Flagger, a one-time Sutter employee, and the one who was reported to have excited San Franciscans by hauling a barrel of gold dust through a hotel lobby. Establishing trading posts on the Fresno River and Mariposa Creek, he reportedly traded to the Indians "an ounce of gold [for] . . . five pounds of flour, or a pound of bacon, a shirt required five ounces, and a pair of boots or a hat brought a full pound of the precious metal." Something of a linguist, Savage quickly learned most of the Indian tongues. He further ingratiated himself by taking wives from several different tribes (one authority said thirty-three!) . It is hard to determine if the initial Indian attack was directed against Savage or against whites in general.

Through his wives Savage learned of a planned Indian uprising in September, 1850, but other whites did not take the warning seriously. In De-cember, Savage's Trading Post was destroyed at Fresno Crossing, and three of his men killed. A force under Sheriff James Burney clashed indecisively with the Indians on January 11, 1851. An appeal to the Governor for help led to the organization of the Mariposa Battalion under "Major" James D. Savage, with three companies led by Captain John J. Kuykendall, Captain John Boling, and Captain William Dill. Kuykendall's company went southward to the King and upper Kaweah while the other two companies, in three campaigns, followed the Indians into the mountains.

The Mariposa Battalion was forced to wait before attacking the Indians while a federal Indian commission, composed of Redick McKee, George W. Barbour, and Oliver M. Wozencraft, sought a peaceful solution. On March 19, 1851, the Commissioners signed a treaty at Camp Fremont with six tribes. However, the Yosemites (Miwok) and Chowchillas (Miwok) were absent, so the campaign against them began on March 19. The companies of Boling and Dill moved against the Yosemites, and discovered their valley on March 27. However, the battalion was forced to march in 3- to 5-foot snow drifts and in rain and sleet and found few Indians. The second campaign began on April 13, against the Chowchillas, and destroyed Indian food stores, but again the natives were able to elude their pursuers. However, the death of their chief induced the Chowchillas to surrender and accept reservation status. When the Yosemites refused to come to Camp Barbour and make peace, the third campaign was launched against them, but with no more success than the others. However, as in all Indian wars the result was foreordained; the Yosemites were captured at Lake Tenaija (named for their chief) on May 22, and forced to accept reservation life.

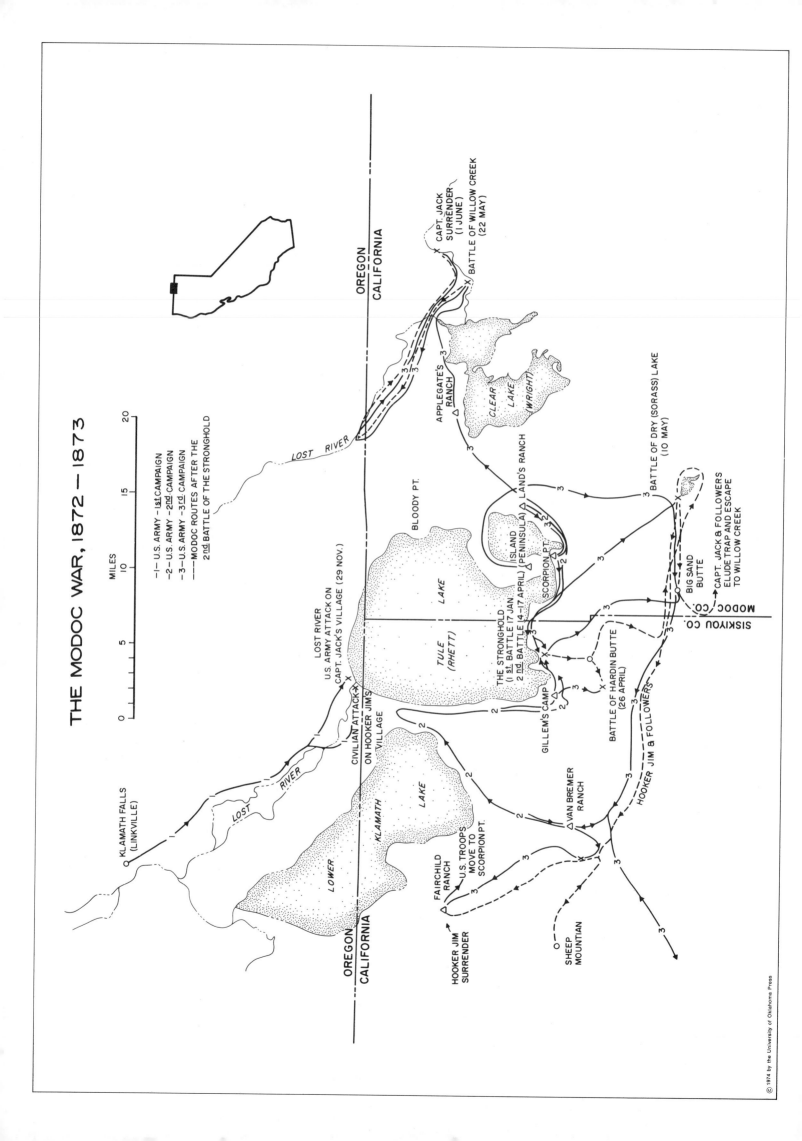

THE MODOC WAR, 1872–1873

MILES

0   5   10   15   20

—1— U.S. ARMY – 1st CAMPAIGN
—2— U.S. ARMY – 2nd CAMPAIGN
—3— U.S. ARMY – 3rd CAMPAIGN
—— MODOC ROUTES AFTER THE
    2nd BATTLE OF THE STRONGHOLD

OREGON
CALIFORNIA

CAPT. JACK SURRENDER
(1 JUNE)

BATTLE OF WILLOW CREEK
(22 MAY)

APPLEGATE'S RANCH

CLEAR LAKE (WRIGHT)

LOST RIVER

LAND'S RANCH

ISLAND (PENINSULA)

SCORPION PT.

BLOODY PT.

BATTLE OF DRY (SORASS) LAKE
(10 MAY)

BIG SAND BUTTE

CAPT. JACK & FOLLOWERS
ELUDE TRAP AND ESCAPE
TO WILLOW CREEK

LOST RIVER
U.S. ARMY ATTACK ON
CAPT. JACK'S VILLAGE (29 NOV.)

CIVILIAN ATTACK ON HOOKER JIM'S VILLAGE

THE STRONGHOLD
(1st BATTLE 17 JAN.
2nd BATTLE (4–17 APRIL)

GILLEM'S CAMP

TULE (RHETT) LAKE

MODOC CO.
SISKIYOU CO.

BATTLE OF HARDIN BUTTE
(26 APRIL)

HOOKER JIM & FOLLOWERS

KLAMATH FALLS
(LINKVILLE)

LOST RIVER

KLAMATH LAKE

LOWER

VAN BREMER RANCH

U.S. TROOPS MOVE TO SCORPION PT.

FAIRCHILD RANCH

HOOKER JIM SURRENDER

SHEEP MOUNTIAN

OREGON
CALIFORNIA

56. THE MODOC WAR, 1872-73

THIS CONFLICT RESULTED from forces common to all Indian wars: the encroachment of whites upon traditional Indian land until the aboriginal way of life was threatened with extinction. However, it was complicated by the appearance of the Ghost Dance religion, which (it was believed) protected the Indians from the white man's bullets and stirred many of the young braves to fanatical deeds, the presence of bitter rivalries among tribal leaders, and the leadership talents of Captain Jack Kientopoos. Roots of the war went back to 1852, when Indians slaughtered sixty-five whites in a wagon train at Bloody Point, and in retaliation forty-one Modocs were murdered by whites at a peace parley. Hostilities continued until 1864, when the Modocs signed a peace treaty and agreed to live on the Klamath reservation in Oregon. Unable to coexist with their enemies, the Klamaths, the Modocs fled the reservation in 1865, returned briefly in 1869, but left finally in April, 1870.

The war began when troops tried to force Captain Jack's band, camped on Lost River, back to the reservation on November 29, 1872. As the Indians fled, they murdered thirteen (or eighteen) settlers. The Modocs retreated to "The Stronghold," a vast lava bed honeycombed with outcroppings, caves, and caverns, making it a virtually impregnable rocky fortress. Efforts to dislodge the Modocs in heavy fog on January 17, 1873, cost the army thirty-five dead and many wounded, with no casualties for the Indians. Weeks of negotiation followed, with the army reluctant to risk more casualties and Captain Jack desirous of stalling until spring so he could more easily maneuver in the mountains. The deadlock ended on Good Friday, April 11, 1873, when General Edward Richard Sprigg Canby was murdered, with other peace negotiators, by Captain Jack, while unarmed and conducting peace negotiations. (Canby thus became the only army general to die in the Indian wars.) The usually astute Captain Jack was goaded to this misdeed by warriors convinced that the army would leave if their leader was gone.

On April 14, 1873, the army laid siege to the Stronghold, and, lacking water, Captain Jack fled southward. After Canby's death, General Jefferson C. Davis, another distinguished Civil War veteran, commanded the troops. At Hardin Butte, on April 26, the bungling army suffered another disaster when a force of some eighty-five men were ambushed and suffered two-thirds casualties. By this time the Modoc leaders had a force that varied from forty-nine but never was reported as more than eighty-nine to ward off more than a thousand army regulars, plus volunteers, and Indian allies. The end was near.

Badly outnumbered, short of supplies, and lacking horses, Captain Jack's followers began to desert him. Hooker Jim led one band to Fairchild Ranch (he knew and trusted the rancher) and surrendered. Braves who had urged a more aggressive policy for the Modoc leader now guided the army in its pursuit. In an attempted ambush of an army unit at Sorass Lake on May 10, the Modocs suffered several casualties, and lost twenty-four pack animals with most of their ammunition. Captain Jack continued to lead the army on a wild chase, but this battle sealed his doom. At Big Sand Butte the resourceful Indian led his band (then only thirty-three) out of an army trap involving more than three hundred soldiers. But one by one the Modocs surrendered, with the guarantee they would be treated as prisoners of war, and on June 1, Captain Jack laid down his rifle.

The Modoc War cost over half a million dollars, the lives of some eighty-three whites, and a total of seventeen Indians. Captain Jack and three others were hanged for the murder of the peace commissioners, while two other Indians had their sentences commuted to life imprisonment. The rest of the Modocs were removed to a reservation in Indian Territory.

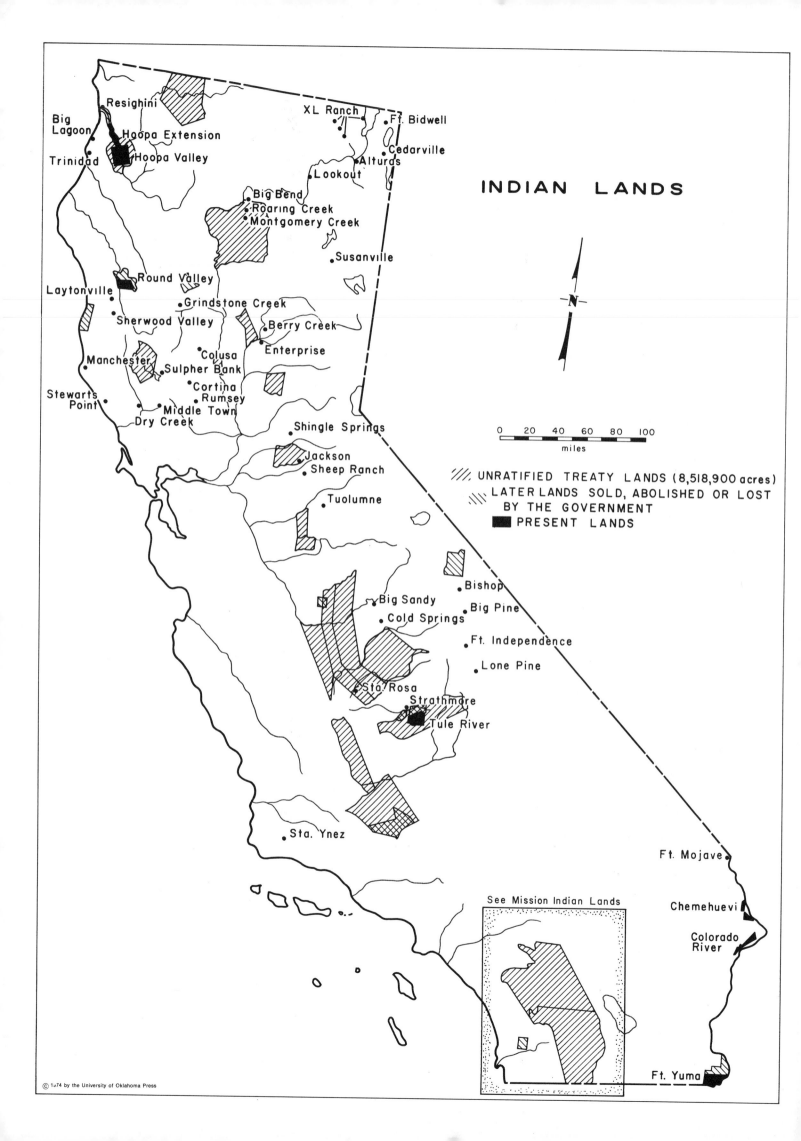

INDIAN LANDS

Resighini
Big Lagoon
Hoopa Extension
Trinidad
Hoopa Valley
XL Ranch
Ft. Bidwell
Cedarville
Alturas
Lookout
Big Bend
Roaring Creek
Montgomery Creek
Susanville
Round Valley
Laytonville
Grindstone Creek
Sherwood Valley
Berry Creek
Manchester
Colusa
Enterprise
Sulpher Bank
Cortina
Rumsey
Stewarts Point
Middle Town
Dry Creek
Shingle Springs
Jackson
Sheep Ranch
Tuolumne
Bishop
Big Sandy
Big Pine
Cold Springs
Ft. Independence
Lone Pine
Sta. Rosa
Strathmore
Tule River
Sta. Ynez
Ft. Mojave
Chemehuevi
Colorado River
See Mission Indian Lands
Ft. Yuma

N

```
0   20   40   60   80   100
        miles
```

/// UNRATIFIED TREATY LANDS (8,518,900 acres)
/// LATER LANDS SOLD, ABOLISHED OR LOST
    BY THE GOVERNMENT
■ PRESENT LANDS

© 1974 by the University of Oklahoma Press

As of June 30, 1971, the Bureau of Indian Affairs had under its jurisdiction in California some 540,000 acres of land. The number of reservations and rancherias, as well as the total acreage, is being constantly reduced as the result of an act of Congress providing for the withdrawal of federal responsibilities and the division of lands among the Indians. The largest is the Hoopa Valley Reservation in Humboldt County, with 84,744 acres, but many have only a few acres. Some of the Indian lands contain substantial resources, mainly timber, but most are unproductive and serve mainly as homesites for some one-sixth of the California Indians. The number living on reservations fluctuates considerably because of the seasonal nature of employment in agriculture or in the lumber industry.

Although Indian residents on tribal lands are full citizens and have the personal freedom to come and go as they please, accept employment wherever they choose, and acquire personal property, the federal government has placed certain restrictions upon the land. Such property is exempt from taxation but cannot be sold or leased without approval. The Bureau of Indian Affairs also constructs and maintains roads, constructs irrigation systems, manages timber and grazing land, sells timber, leases land for agricultural or other uses, collects and distributes rental income, probates Indian estates, supervises membership enrollment, aids in tribal government, and performs other related functions.

Department of the Interior Lands Under Jurisdiction of the Bureau of Indian Affairs as of June 30, 1971	Acres, Tribal	Acres Individually Owned
Alturas Rancheria	20.00	—
Big Bend Rancheria	40.00	—
Big Lagoon Rancheria	5.50	—
Berry Creek Rancheria	33.04	—
Big Pine Rancheria	279.00	—
Big Sandy (Auberry) Rancheria	7.72	—
Bishop Reservation	875.00	—
Cachil Dehe (Colusa) Rancheria	268.68	—
Cedarville Rancheria	17.00	—
Chemehuevi	28,223.87	—
Cold Springs (Sycamore) Rancheria	100.65	—
Colorado River	42,696.00	—
Cortina Rancheria	640.00	—
Dry Creek (Geyserville) Rancheria	75.00	—
Enterprise Rancheria	40.00	—
Fort Bidwell Reservation	3,334.97	—
Fort Independence Reservation	233.85	114.62
Fort Mohave	9,132.79	—
Fort Yuma	8,801.88	—
Grindstone Creek Rancheria	80.00	—
Hoopa Valley Reservation	84,744.16	1,328.88
Hoopa Valley Reservation Extension	3,421.00	3,417.11
Jackson Rancheria	330.66	—
Laytonville Rancheria	200.00	—
Lone Pine Rancheria	237.00	—
Lookout Rancheria	40.00	—
Manchester (Point Area) Rancheria	363.09	—
Middletown Rancheria	108.70	—
Montgomery Creek Rancheria	72.00	—
Public Domain Allotments	408.37	17,389.00
Resighini Reservation (Coast Indian Community)	228.00	—
Roaring Creek Rancheria	80.00	—
Rumsey Rancheria	66.51	—
Round Valley Reservation	13,061.41	5,481.42
Santa Rosa Rancheria	170.00	—
Sheep Ranch	.92	—
Sherwood Valley Rancheria	292.22	—
Shingle Springs Rancheria	160.00	—
Stewarts Point Rancheria	40.00	—
Strathmore (Terminated)	—	—
Sulphur Bank Rancheria	50.00	—
Susanville Reservation	30.00	—
Trinidad Rancheria	54.60	—
Tule River Reservation	54,116.00	—
Tuolumne Rancheria	323.10	—
X.L. Ranch Reservation	9,254.86	—

MISSION INDIAN LANDS

■ San Manuel

⊘ SAN BERNARDINO

Twentynine Palms ■

SAN BERNARDINO CO.

RIVERSIDE CO

⊘ RIVERSIDE

■ Mission Creek

Morongo

BANNING ⊘

Soboba

HEMET ⊘

Agua Caliente

INDIO ⊘

Cabazon ■

■ Augustine

Santa Ynez

Gaviota

Santa Barbara

Ramona

Santa Rosa

Cahuilla

Torres-

Pechanga

RIVERSIDE CO.

SAN DIEGO CO.

Martinez

Pala

Mission Reserve

Pauma

Yuima

Rincon

La Jolla

Los Coyotes

San Pasqual

Mesa Grande

Santa Ysabel

OCEANSIDE ⊘

Inaja

Cosmit

Barona Ranch

Capitan Grande

Laguna

N

Viejas

Cuyapaipe

Sycuan

Manzanita

La Posta

SAN DIEGO CO.

IMPERIAL CO.

SAN DIEGO ⊘

Campo

0   5   10   20

miles

U.S.A.

MEXICO

© 1974 by the University of Oklahoma Press

58. MISSION INDIAN LANDS

THESE LANDS ARE thirty-one small scattered reservations varying in size from 99 acres to 32,353 acres and totaling some 250,000 acres. They were set aside by executive orders between 1875 and 1891 for the remnants of mission Indian bands, and are mainly located in Riverside and San Diego counties. Established during a period of rapid population influx, these reservations were not adequately protected against the encroachment of agricultural, mining, and town expansion. As a result, much land was lost in boundary adjustments. In 1891 the present lands were confirmed by executive order.

Some five thousand Indians lived on the reservations in 1871. Because of the semi-arid environment the land area was never able to sustain an expanding rural economy. Indians began deserting these mission lands immediately, and after 1910, outward mobility increased. Today (1974) only a third of the four thousand Indian band members still reside on reservation lands. Perhaps three-fourths of these earn most of their livelihood from off-reservation work. The advantage of a rent-free and tax-free residence enables the limited earnings of many Indians to stretch farther. Such an arrangement keeps Indian workers from experiencing the economic disadvantages of living in the city. Only marginal utilization of the 250,000 acres is being made.

MISSION INDIAN LANDS	ACRES, TRIBAL	ACRES INDIVIDUALLY OWNED
Agua Caliente (Palm Springs)	2,055.83	23,843.01
Augustine Rancheria	341.80	160.49
Barona Rancheria	5,005.00	—
Cabazon Reservation	1,153.21	548.32
Cahuilla Reservation	18,272.38	—
Campo Reservation	15,010.00	—
Capitan Grande Reservation	15,753.40	—
Cuyapaipe Reservation	4,100.13	—
Inaja Cosmit Rancheria	800.00	—
Laguna Reservation (Originally 320 acres but terminated)		
La Jolla Reservation	7,588.16	639.90
La Posta Reservation	3,672.29	—
Los Coyotes Reservation	25,049.63	—
Manzanite Reservation	3,579.38	—
Mesa Grande Reservation	120.00	—
Mission Reserve	9,470.82	—
Morongo Reservation	30,926.75	1,325.42
Pala Reservation (Old Pala)	6,547.48	1,188.88
Pauma Reservation	250.00	—
Pechanga Reservation	2,860.78	1,236.28
Ramona Reservation	560.00	—
Rincon Reservation	3,612.04	353.75
San Manuel Reservation	653.15	—
San Pasqual Reservation	1,379.58	—
Santa Rosa Reservation	11,092.60	—
Santa Ynez Reservation	99.28	—
Santa Ysabel Reservation	15,526.78	—
Soboba Reservation	5,035.68	—
Sycuan Reservation	370.55	269.45
Torres-Martinez Reservation	18,223.16	7,106.13
Twentynine Palms Reservation	162.13	—
Viejas (Baron Long) Rancheria	1,609.00	—

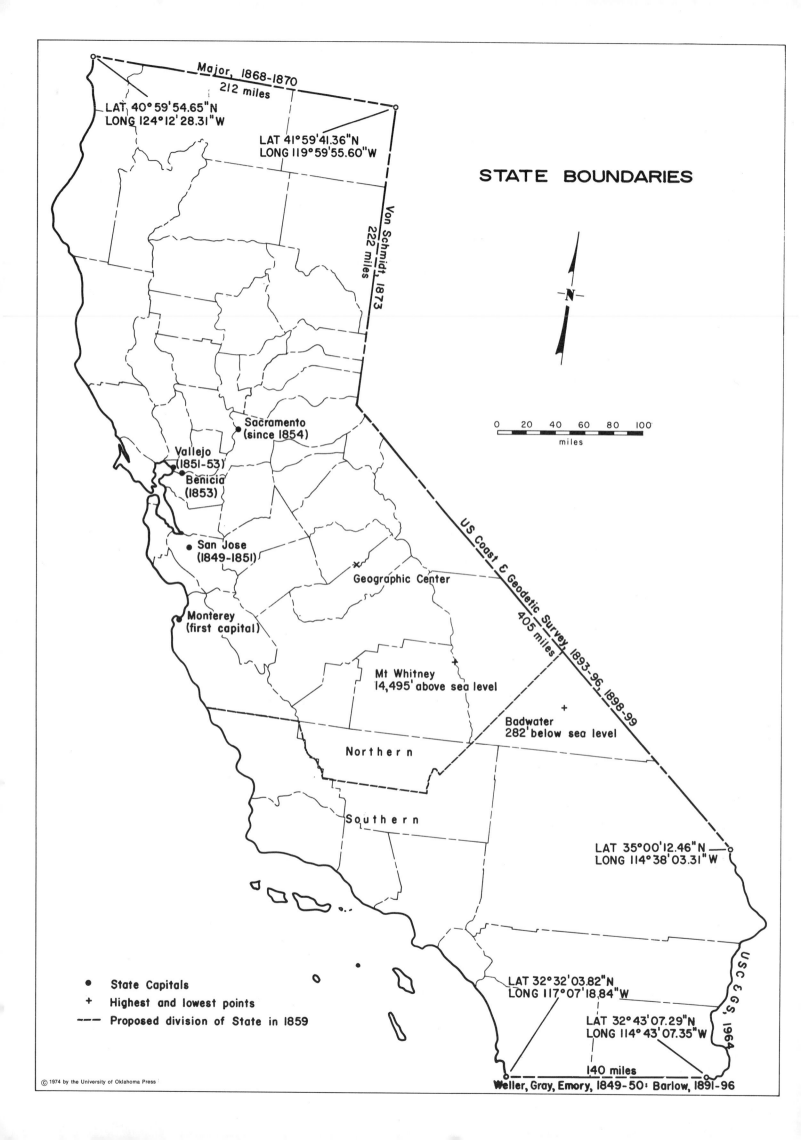

STATE BOUNDARIES

Major, 1868-1870
212 miles

LAT 40° 59' 54.65" N
LONG 124° 12' 28.31" W

LAT 41° 59' 41.36" N
LONG 119° 59' 55.60" W

Von Schmidt, 1873
222 miles

— N —

0 20 40 60 80 100
miles

Sacramento
(since 1854)

Vallejo
(1851-53)

Benicia
(1853)

San Jose
(1849-1851)

Geographic Center

US Coast & Geodetic Survey, 1893-96, 1898-99
405 miles

Monterey
(first capital)

Mt Whitney
14,495' above sea level

Badwater
282' below sea level

Northern

Southern

LAT 35°00' 12.46" N
LONG 114° 38' 03.31" W

USC & GS, 1964

● State Capitals

+ Highest and lowest points

- - - Proposed division of State in 1859

LAT 32° 32' 03.82" N
LONG 117° 07' 18.84" W

LAT 32° 43' 07.29" N
LONG 114° 43' 07.35" W

140 miles

Weller, Gray, Emory, 1849-50; Barlow, 1891-96

59. STATE BOUNDARIES

VIRTUALLY EVERY session of the legislature of the 1850's was concerned with the location of the state capital. As Bancroft puts it, "the seat of government was hawked about for years in a manner disgraceful to the state." This was the basic problem concerning the location of the seat of government: the state could not afford to provide the essential facilities necessary for a state government. Numerous promoters sought to profit from the circumstance by making promises (usually unfulfilled) to entice the capital to their city. San Jose was first able to obtain the capital from Monterey for the first two legislatures (1849–51), and it would probably have remained there if that town had kept its promises to the state. Citing the difficulties of travel to San Jose in rainy weather, a legislative committee recommended Vallejo because of its climate and accessibility by water. But when the new legislature met at Vallejo, disappointment was so keen that after a few days it adjourned back to San Jose, only to reconvene back in Vallejo, but completed its session in Sacramento. In 1853 Benicia received the capital. Continued displeasure with that site brought the oft-moved seat of state government to Sacramento in 1854. Many reasons for the move were given, but political intrigue and the purported bribe of $10,000 were most important. Since 1854, Oakland, San Francisco, San Jose, Berkeley, Los Angeles, and Monterey have made efforts to obtain the state capital.

Every legislature of the 1850's was also concerned with a proposed division of the state on an east-west line. In the Constitutional Convention delegates from Southern California proposed forming a separate territory south of San Luis Obispo. For a decade agitation for separation was renewed on the grounds that the expenses of state government would ruin the landholders of the southland, the thinly populated south would be under the dominance of the more populous north, and the great distance from the north would be a hardship. Petitions to Congress to effect such a division of California triggered futile efforts by southerners who proposed legislation to extend the 36° 30′ line of the Missouri Compromise across California and form the southland into the territory of Colorado. Out of the welter of proposed laws on division, the most serious was passed by the legislature and approved in a general election in 1859. However, the measure died in Congress as a result of the growing tension which culminated in the Civil War. Although serious efforts at state division died in 1860, every decade since has witnessed a renewal of some kind of agitation towards a separation of California. The most recent was in 1965 when northern Californians, angered at surrendering water to the southland, proposed casting the area south of the Tehachapis adrift.

The state boundaries have also been the source of much confusion. The northern border was fixed at 42° north latitude, but the western terminus is south of that point because of a surveying error. Daniel G. Major, who surveyed the Oregon-California line, placed the northeast corner marker more than three miles too far west. This error was corrected in the survey of Allexey W. Von Schmidt, who fixed the location of the border along the 120° W. meridian. Before the "floating" Nevada boundary was established in 1873, there was a border war in which one town acted as the county seat of two different counties (one in Nevada and one in California). The oblique boundary starts in the water of Lake Tahoe and ends in the water of the Colorado River. Because of the continual shifting of that stream, a compact between the states of California and Arizona established a joint commission to fix their border as necessary. The southern border with Baja California in Mexico was fixed by the Treaty of Guadalupe-Hidalgo and surveyed several times.

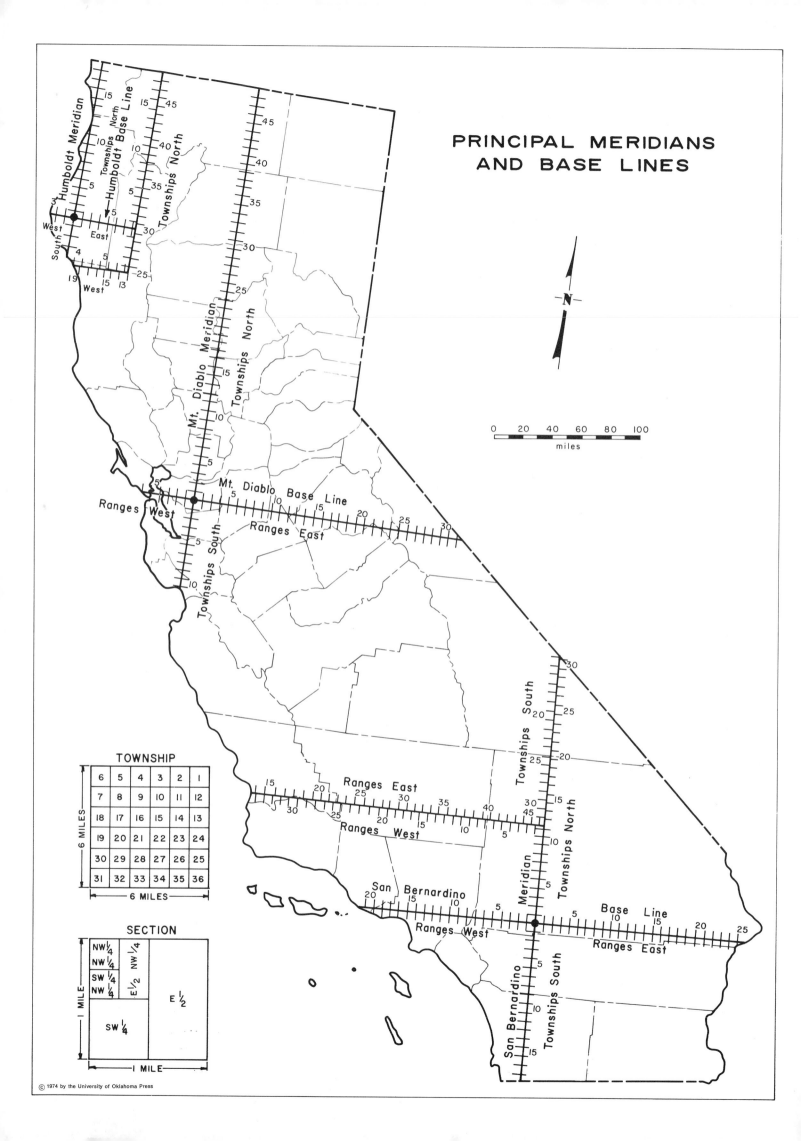

PRINCIPAL MERIDIANS AND BASE LINES

Humboldt Meridian

Humboldt Base Line

Townships North

Townships North

Mt. Diablo Meridian

Townships North

West

East

South

Mt. Diablo Base Line

Ranges West

Ranges East

Townships South

N

0   20   40   60   80   100
miles

TOWNSHIP

6	5	4	3	2	1
7	8	9	10	11	12
18	17	16	15	14	13
19	20	21	22	23	24
30	29	28	27	26	25
31	32	33	34	35	36

6 MILES

6 MILES

SECTION

NW¼ NW¼	E½ NW¼	E½
SW¼ NW¼		
SW¼		

1 MILE

1 MILE

Ranges East

Ranges West

Townships South

Townships North

Meridian

San Bernardino

Base Line

Ranges West

Ranges East

San Bernardino

Townships South

THE PRINCIPAL MERIDIANS and base lines of California are a product of the Northwest Ordinance of 1785. This measure provided for the orderly survey and sale of public lands. During the colonial period, New England had disposed of public lands by surveying them first and then selling them in orderly blocks. A system of "indiscriminate locations and subsequent survey" prevailed in the southern colonies. This permitted a settler to lay out the land he desired where he wished, and then have it surveyed. (This arrangement had certain similarities to practices in Spanish and Mexican California). The southern system bred a welter of conflicting titles as frontiersmen laid out irregular-shaped plots in order to claim the most fertile land and made it impossible for the government to dispose of the less desirable tracts. The survey of public lands was originally evolved in Ohio and well developed by the time California was settled.

The Ordinance of 1785 provided that the public lands of the United States should be divided by lines intersecting true north and at right angles so as to form townships 6 miles square, the townships to be marked with progressive numbers from the beginning. Such townships should be divided into 36 sections, each 1 mile square, containing 640 acres. The sections were to be numbered respectively, beginning with the number one in the northeast sections, and proceeding west and east alternately through the township, with progressive numbers to 36.

In order to carry the foregoing requirements into operation it was necessary to establish independent initial points to serve as a base for surveys. Principal meridians and base lines are then surveyed from these initial points. Guide meridians are initiated at base lines, and standard parallels are initiated at principal meridians so as to form townships. The townships are subdivided into 36 sections by running parallel lines through the township from south to north and from east to west at distances of 1 mile.

Of 35 meridians in the United States, 3 are located in California. They are the Humboldt, the Mount Diablo, and the San Bernardino. The Humboldt initial point is at 124° 07' 10" west longitude and 40° 25' 02" north latitude. The Mount Diablo initial point is at 121° 54' 47" west longitude and 37° 52' 54" north latitude. The San Bernardino initial point is at 116° 55' 17" west longitude and 34° 07' 20" north latitude.

COUNTIES—1852

////// CREATED 1851—1852

I – SIERRA
2 – NEVADA
3 – PLACER

Siskyou

Klamath

Pautan

Tulare

ORIGINAL COUNTIES 1850

BOUNDARY ADJUSTMENTS

61. BOUNDARY ADJUSTMENTS 1850–52

UNDER SPANISH AND Mexican rule little effort was made to politically sub-divide California. Most people lived in a narrow strip along the coast, with the interior left to the non-mission natives. In the Spanish era there were two districts or grand prefectures; the southern district prefect lived in Los Angeles, and that of the north at Monterey. Boundaries were ill-defined, but the southern district probably extended north to Mission La Purísima. Prefectures were later established at Santa Barbara and San Jose. Five districts existed from 1831 to 1840, at San Diego, Los Angeles, Santa Barbara, Monterey and San Francisco. From 1841 to 1845 the division was again formed into a northern and southern district.

The organization of California into counties was assigned to a committee of the first legislature, with General Vallejo as chairman. Their report stressed the difficulty of establishing county boundaries because of the lack of accurate maps. The legislature passed an act creating twenty-seven counties, and it became law on February 15, 1850. The county names were of Indian or Spanish origin except for Suter and Butte counties.

ORIGINAL COUNTIES

5.	Butte	15.	San Joaquin
16.	Calaveras	24.	San Luis Obispo
4.	Colusa	25.	Santa Barbara
14.	Contra Costa	20.	Santa Clara
13.	El Dorado	19.	Santa Cruz
26.	Los Angeles	2.	Shasta
17.	Marin	11.	Solano
23.	Mariposa	6.	Sonoma
3.	Mendocino	9.	Sutter
22.	Monterey	1.	Trinity
7.	Napa	21.	Tuolomne
12.	Sacramento	8.	Yolo
27.	San Diego	10.	Yuba
18.	San Francisco		

The creation of three new counties in 1851 resulted from the rapid increase in population in mining areas. Klamath was created out of the northern part of Trinity County and included all of the Klamath watershed within California. Yuba County surrendered its eastern half to form Nevada County. Placer was carved out of parts of Yuba and Sutter counties. Along with the creation of these new counties, legislation in 1851 adjusted the boundaries of many counties. Most altered was Los Angeles, which absorbed much of San Diego and Mariposa counties. It was expanded to include San Fernando, Tejon, and Tehachapi passes in the north and San Juan Capistrano in the south. It extended westward and then eastward to the state line.

In 1852 three additional counties were created. Siskiyou was organized by taking land from Shasta and Klamath counties. The expansion of mining and, consequently, settlement in the area resulted in this necessary action because the Shasta Mountains made contact with areas to the east very difficult. Yuba County again lost territory, this time to form the mining county of Sierra. Tulare was created by detaching the southern half of the immense Mariposa county. Numerous other counties had their boundaries adjusted by legislative act in 1852: the northern boundary of Napa was accurately defined, the northern side of Sutter was altered, as was also the northern boundary of Nevada.

A most unusual California county, Pautah, existed from 1852 to 1859, for it was beyond the state's boundaries in the territory of Utah. It included territory which was an extension of the state's mining frontier, and it was assumed that Congress would cede the area to California. When this did not occur, the statute creating Pautah County was repealed in 1859.

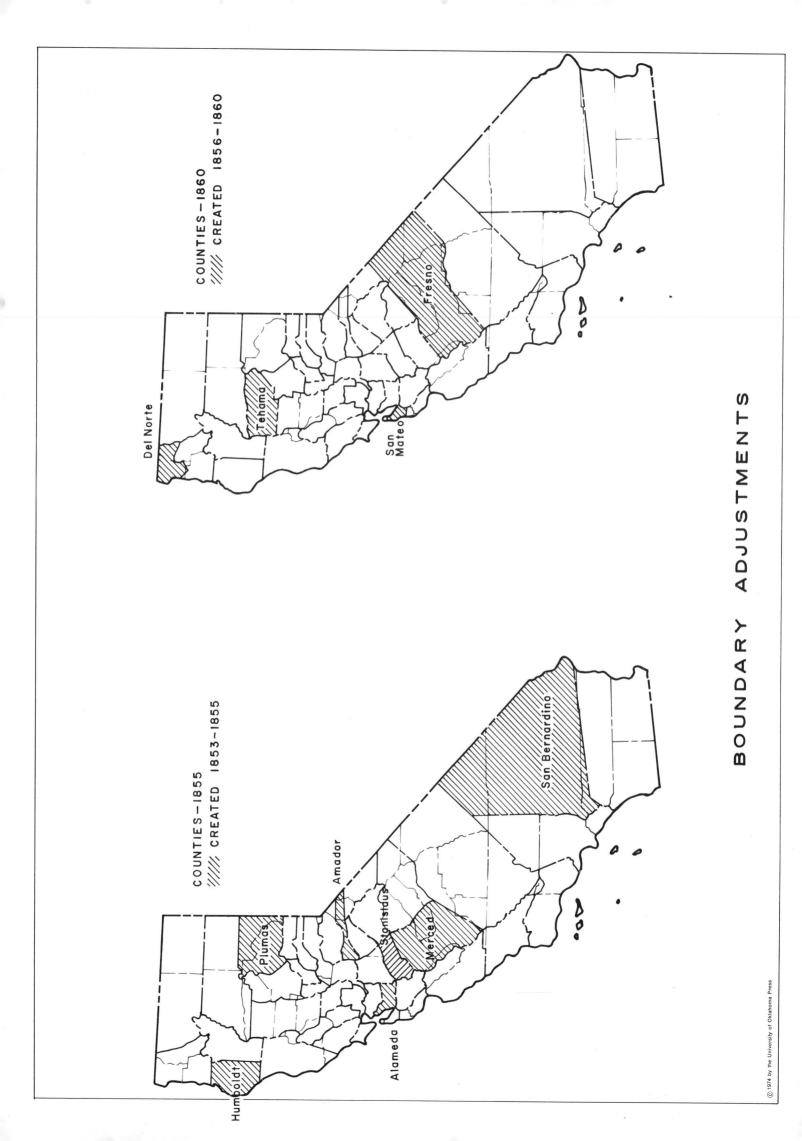

COUNTIES—1860
/// CREATED 1856—1860

Del Norte

Tehama

San Mateo

Fresno

COUNTIES—1855
/// CREATED 1853—1855

Humboldt

Plumas

Amador

Stanislaus

Alameda

Merced

San Bernardino

BOUNDARY ADJUSTMENTS

62. BOUNDARY ADJUSTMENTS 1855-60

THE RAPID INFLUX of population in the decade of the 1850's led to many county changes. Agriculture, instead of mining, led to the creation of three counties. Alameda came into existence in 1853, at the expense of Contra Costa and Santa Clara counties. The name meant "a grove of poplar trees," and the new county reflected the rapid growth of the east side of San Francisco Bay. The immense area of Los Angeles County was reduced to one-third of its former size in 1853 by the formation of San Bernardino County. This action was partially caused by the establishment of a Mormon colony on the San Bernardino rancho in 1851. Humboldt County, named after Alexander von Humboldt, the famed Prussian scientist, was also created in 1853, by dividing Trinity County. The area around Humboldt Bay was rapidly settled after 1850 by farmers and lumbermen who had little in common with the miners east of the mountains on the Trinity River.

Plumas County, made up of area detached from Butte County, was organized in 1854. The name came from the Spanish name for the Feather River, whose headwaters were in the new county, the Río de las Plumas. Expansion of mining in the area and the remoteness from the former county seat justified the legislative action. After much agitation for and against, Amador County was also constituted in 1854. Named for a Spanish pioneer, José María Amador, who came to California in 1771, portions of Calaveras and El Dorado counties were used in its

formation. Stanislaus, the third county created in 1854, was separated from Tuolumne County. The name came from the Indian leader, Estanislao, who with his band fought a bloody engagement with troops under Mariano Vallejo in the area (a river in the area, Estanislao), later corrupted into the English version—Stanislaus. Merced County was formed in 1855 from the western or valley part of Mariposa County. The name was derived from a river, the Nuestra Señora de la Merced, in the area.

In 1856 three more counties emerged by legislative action. San Mateo, meaning St. Matthew, was constructed out of San Francisco County. Fresno County constituted the third and last division of the once immense Mariposa County. Portions were also taken from Merced and Tulare for the new county. Fresno is Spanish for ash tree, which grew along streams in the area. Tehama County was formed in 1856 around Red Bluff, a thriving community at the head of navigation on the Sacramento River. Territory was taken from Colusa, Butte, and Shasta counties for its creation. Tehama was the name of a Wintun Indian village. 1857 saw Del Norte emerge as a new county. Moving the county seat of Klamath County from Crescent City to Orleans Bar precipitated demands for a new county by residents of the former city. It was originally named Buchanan for the then president of the United States, but the name Del Norte evolved from its northern position within the state.

COUNTIES – 1880
///// CREATED 1871–1880

Modoc

San Benito

Ventura

COUNTIES – 1870
///// CREATED 1861–1870

Lassen

Alpine

Mono

Inyo

Kern

Lake

BOUNDARY ADJUSTMENTS

VIRTUALLY EVERY legislative session continued to see the introduction of numerous bills to alter county boundaries. Fortunately, only a small percentage of these measures were enacted into law. Frequent requests for such changes grew out of population mobility as new mining areas continued to open as others closed down, but they also arose from the initial inadequacy of county boundaries and the rivalry between towns desiring the advantages of being the county seat.

Mono County, the first to be created in the mining country east of the Sierra Nevada, resulted from a division of Calaveras County in 1861. The name was derived from a lake in the region and, in all likelihood, comes from *monachi*, a tribal designation of a group of Shoshonean Indians of the Sierra Nevada. Also approved by legislative action in 1861 was the creation of Lake County. It was formed from the northern portion of Napa County. The name came from Clear Lake, the new county's most distinctive natural feature.

In the 1864 legislature additional counties were created east of the Sierra. Alpine emerged at the expense of El Dorado, Amador, Calaveras, Tuolumne, and Mono counties. The name resulted from the mountainous terrain of the region. Far more complex was the creation of Lassen County. A group of settlers near Honey Lake organized an independent entity in 1856 which they named Nataqua. The proposed boundaries included areas whose citizens objected to being included in Nataqua Territory. When Plumas County authorities attempted to administer the area, they were challenged. The result was the "Sage Brush" or "Border Line War" in which some blood was shed. A joint boundary survey by California and Nevada officials placed the Honey Lake region well within the borders of the Golden State, and thus within Plumas County. However, the existing ill-will made it advisable to organize a new county from the area of Plumas east of the Sierra. The eastern half of Shasta was also added to Lassen County, the name given to the new areas. Peter Lassen, who furnished the name, was a pioneer who came to California in 1840, was a Bear-Flagger, and encouraged emigration through the Honey Lake Valley.

Inyo County emerged in 1866 from the portion of Tulare east of the Sierra, a part of Mono County. The name is of Indian origin, probably Shoshonean, and is believed to mean "Dwelling place of a great spirit." Inyo was originally created in 1864 as Coso County, but its organization was not completed. Kern County was also approved in 1866, from portions of Tulare and Los Angeles counties, and named after Edward M. Kern, an artist and topographer who accompanied Frémont's expedition into California in 1845.

In 1872 Ventura County was created from the eastern portion of Santa Barbara County. The name is derived from Mission San Buenaventura. Klamath County was abolished in 1874, a victim of population shifts in mining centers. Its territory was annexed to Humboldt and Siskiyou counties. San Benito (from the Spanish for St. Benedict) County was created from Monterey in 1874, after many years of agitation by citizens of the area. The same year saw the emergence of Modoc County, in the extreme northeast corner of the state, at the expense of Siskiyou County and named after the Modocs. The Klamath people called them Moatokni or "Southerners."

COUNTIES – SINCE 1922
///// CREATED 1907

Imperial

COUNTIES – 1895
///// CREATED 1881–1895

Glenn

Madera

Kings

Riverside

Orange

BOUNDARY ADJUSTMENTS

© 1974 by the University of Oklahoma Press

WITH THE PASSAGE of years, it became increasingly difficult to successfully agitate for the creation of new counties. Each legislative session was marked by the introduction of bills to create new counties, but they failed to be enacted into law. Fifteen years elapsed from the forming of San Benito county in 1874 to the emergence of Orange County in 1889. Legislation finally approved concerning California's counties was limited to the correction of boundaries or to the transfer of territory from one county to another.

The campaign to create Orange County from the southeastern corner of Los Angeles County began as early as 1870. Initially the proposed name for the new county was Santa Ana or Anaheim. The name Orange was taken from the city of that name. It had been originally named by William Glassell, a former Confederate army officer, who had named it for his native county in Virginia, which in turn had been named for the Prince of Orange. In 1891 Glenn County emerged, detached from the northern portion of Colusa County. It was named after Dr. Hugh James Glenn, a California rancher and politician who was defeated for governor in 1879.

Three additional counties were created in 1893. Madera had been that portion of Fresno County lying north and west of the San Joaquin River. The word Madera is Spanish for wood. Kings County was formerly a part of Tulare County. The name is derived from the Spanish, El Río de los Santos Reyes (the river of the Holy Kings). Riverside County was created from sections of San Diego and San Bernardino counties. The county is named after the city of Riverside, which was titled in anticipation of the diversion of the waters of the Santa Ana River.

Legislative reaction over continual pressure to create new counties led to the enactment of two constitutional amendments which limited the passage of special acts forming new counties. The first of these measures, adopted in 1894, provided that: "no new county shall be established which shall reduce any county to a population of less than eight thousand; nor shall a new county be formed containing a population of less than five thousand." The second amendment, enacted in 1910, provided that new counties must have eight thousand population and that the formation of a new county must not reduce the population of an existing county to less than twenty thousand. These amendments virtually ended agitation for changes in county boundaries.

Since the passage of the first amendment limiting the creation of counties, only one new county, Imperial, in 1907, has emerged. Formed from the eastern half of San Diego County, it resulted from the rapid growth of the area following irrigation from the Colorado River. The name was given to the area by the Canadian-born irrigation expert, George Chaffey.

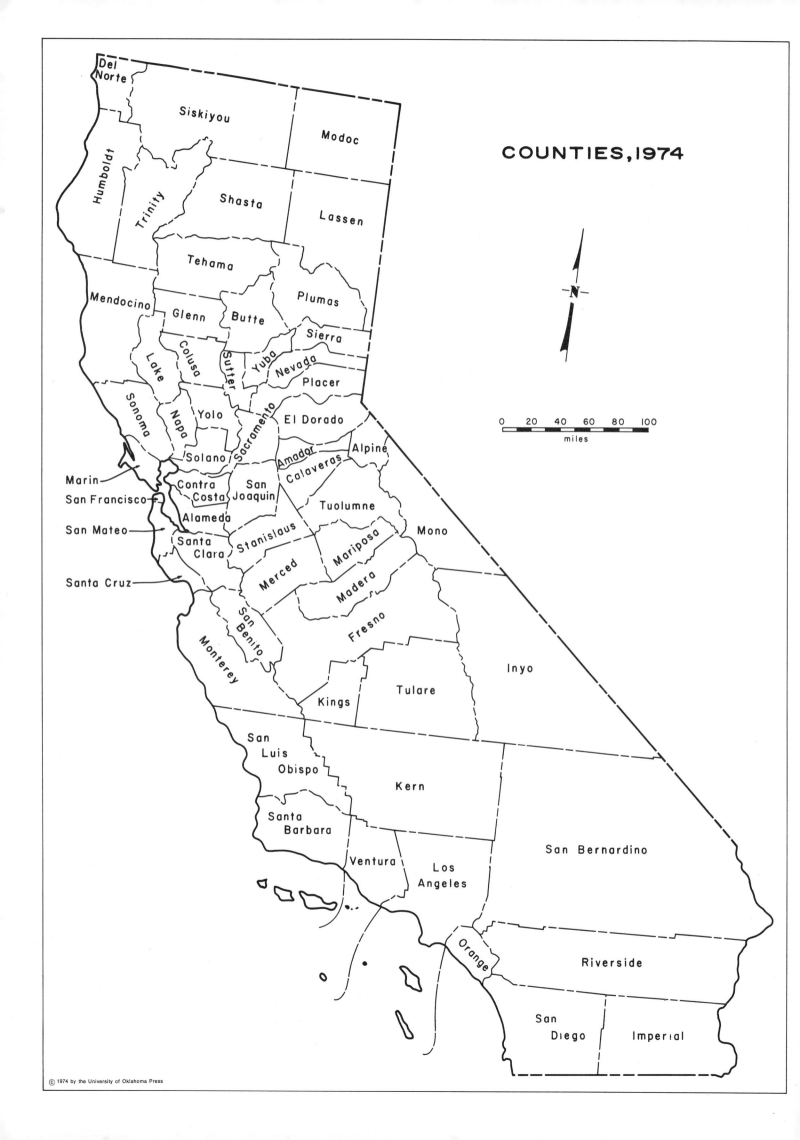

COUNTIES, 1974

Del Norte
Siskiyou
Modoc
Humboldt
Trinity
Shasta
Lassen
Tehama
Mendocino
Plumas
Glenn
Butte
Sierra
Lake
Colusa
Sutter
Yuba
Nevada
Placer
Sonoma
Napa
Yolo
El Dorado
Sacramento
Amador
Alpine
Solano
Calaveras
Marin
Contra Costa
San Joaquin
Tuolumne
San Francisco
Alameda
Mono
San Mateo
Santa Clara
Stanislaus
Santa Cruz
Mariposa
Merced
Madera
San Benito
Fresno
Monterey
Inyo
Kings
Tulare
San Luis Obispo
Kern
Santa Barbara
San Bernardino
Ventura
Los Angeles
Orange
Riverside
San Diego
Imperial

N

0 20 40 60 80 100
miles

No NEW COUNTIES have been created since Imperial in 1907. Perhaps the constitutional amendments have served more to block the necessary elimination of counties than their further creation. Of the state's fifty-eight counties, sixteen have a population less than the twenty thousand minimum suggested by the amendment enacted in 1910, and one of these has a population of less than five hundred. Maintaining such sparsely populated political units in the era of the stagecoach, when it was both time-consuming and costly to journey to a distant county seat, was understandable. In this day of high-speed highways and air transportation, California needs to eliminate many of its present counties through consolidation.

COUNTY POPULATION

	TOTAL POPULATION 1970	TOTAL POPULATION 1960	PERCENT CHANGE 1960 TO 1970
Alameda	1,073,184	908,209	18.2
Alpine	484	397	21.9
Amador	11,821	9,990	18.3
Butte	101,969	82,030	24.3
Calaveras	13,585	10,289	32.0
Colusa	12,430	12,075	2.9
Contra Costa	558,389	409,030	36.5
Del Norte	14,580	17,771	−18.0
El Dorado	43,833	29,390	49.1
Fresno	413,053	365,945	12.9
Glenn	17,521	17,245	1.6
Humboldt	99,692	104,892	−5.0
Imperial	74,492	72,105	3.3
Inyo	15,571	11,684	33.3
Kern	329,162	291,984	12.7
Kings	64,610	49,954	29.3
Lake	19,548	13,786	41.8
Lassen	14,960	13,597	10.0
Los Angeles	7,032,075	6,038,771	16.4
Madera	41,519	40,468	2.6
Marin	206,038	146,820	40.3

	TOTAL POPULATION 1970	TOTAL POPULATION 1960	PERCENT CHANGE 1960 TO 1970
Mariposa	6,015	5,064	18.8
Mendocino	51,101	51,059	0.1
Merced	104,629	90,446	15.7
Modoc	7,469	8,308	−10.1
Mono	4,016	2,213	81.5
Monterey	250,071	198,351	26.1
Napa	79,140	65,890	20.1
Nevada	26,346	20,911	26.0
Orange	1,420,386	703,925	101.8
Placer	77,306	56,998	35.6
Plumas	11,707	11,620	0.7
Riverside	459,074	306,191	49.9
Sacramento	631,498	502,778	25.6
San Benito	18,226	15,396	18.4
San Bernardino	684,072	503,591	35.8
San Diego	1,357,854	1,033,011	31.4
San Francisco	715,674	740,316	−3.3
San Joaquin	290,208	249,989	16.1
San Luis Obispo	105,690	81,044	30.4
San Mateo	556,234	444,387	25.2
Santa Barbara	264,324	168,962	56.4
Santa Clara	1,064,714	642,315	65.8
Santa Cruz	123,790	84,219	47.0
Shasta	77,640	59,468	30.6
Sierra	2,365	2,247	5.3
Siskiyou	33,225	32,885	1.0
Solano	169,941	134,597	26.3
Sonoma	204,885	147,375	39.0
Stanislaus	194,506	157,294	23.7
Sutter	41,935	33,380	25.6
Tehama	29,517	25,305	16.6
Trinity	7,615	9,706	−21.5
Tulare	188,322	168,403	11.8
Tuolumne	22,169	14,404	53.9
Ventura	376,430	199,138	89.0
Yolo	91,788	65,727	39.7
Yuba	44,736	33,859	32.1
Total	19,953,134	15,717,204	27.0

COUNTY SEATS

Crescent City
Yreka
Alturas
Eureka
Weaverville
Redding
Red Bluff
Susanville
Quincy
Willows
Oroville
Downieville
Ukiah
Lakeport
Colusa
Nevada City
Yuba City
Marysville
Woodland
Auburn
Santa Rosa
Placerville
Markleeville
Napa
Sacramento
Fairfield
Jackson
San Andreas
Bridgeport
San Rafael
Martinez
Stockton
San Francisco
Oakland
Sonora
Redwood City
Modesto
San Jose
Mariposa
Santa Cruz
Merced
Hollister
Madera
Salinas
Fresno
Independence
Hanford
Visalia
San Luis Obispo
Bakersfield
Santa Barbara
Ventura
Los Angeles
San Bernardino
Riverside
Santa Ana
San Diego
El Centro

N

0   20   40   60   80   100
miles

66. COUNTY SEATS

COUNTY SEATS IN California are every bit as diverse as the counties themselves. They vary in size from the tiny hamlet of Markleeville in Alpine County, which counts its citizens in the hundreds, to Los Angeles, with a population in the millions. Some seats are small trading communities serving the surrounding farmers or ranchers, while others are great manufacturing or financial centers.

The historical role of county seats is little understood in a day when counties are great metropolitan centers with the limits of cities all but extinguished and open spaces virtually non-existent. (The fact that 91 per cent of Californians resided in urban areas in 1970 illustrates this point). The ease with which the modern citizen can transact his business at the county seats today, via modern highways or freeways, has also prompted him to overlook the importance of this area of government. Before the advent of the motor car and hard surface roads, the location of the county seat was a vital matter, especially in counties of great geographic expanse or in those divided by mountain ranges. Isolation from the county seat could mean the inconvenience of a long trip on horseback and the expense of a night or two away from home while essential official business was transacted. In the Gold Rush Era there was often fiery competition between rival towns as to which would be designated the county seat. Political pressure, sometimes augmented by outright bribery, was used in Sacramento to influence such decisions. Prestige played a role in this vigorous quest to have your community become the seat of county government. Usually, county seats also became the *de facto* business centers of the county. It was common to sell gold dust (or farm produce) as well as visit the county courthouse on the same trip to town.

The county seat has continued to function as an important unit of government. Although counties were originally formed by the state as a subdivision for administrative purposes, they have increasingly become significant units of local self-government. People have turned to the county to help solve problems of water supply, airport development, air pollution—to cite only a few examples of the developing role of counties. In addition, counties continue to exercise their historic role in performing such state functions as the administration of elections; the carrying out of public health services; law enforcement and the administration of justice; upkeep of roads; relief administration; and the maintenance of vital statistics and property records.

Forty-seven of California's counties are general law counties organized under general laws enacted by the state legislature. These acts have established the statewide pattern by which the voters in each county elect a board of supervisors (the chief legislative and administrative county body), sheriff, district attorney, coroner, tax assessor, tax collector, treasurer, auditor, county clerk, recorder, public administrator, superintendent of public instruction, and judges of the superior, municipal, and justice courts.

Eleven of the state's counties operate under charters authorized by a state constitutional amendment in 1911. These counties must have their charters approved by the legislature and, in general, must follow the state laws governing the structure and operation of all counties. However, charter counties have shortened their ballots by making many elective offices appointive and have insisted on some kind of trained managers for their administrative agencies. It is claimed that such an arrangement makes for greater efficiency, and it has been the larger counties which have preferred the charter government: Los Angeles, San Bernardino, Butte, Tehama, Alameda, Fresno, Sacramento, San Diego, San Mateo, and Santa Clara (San Francisco is a chartered city-county).

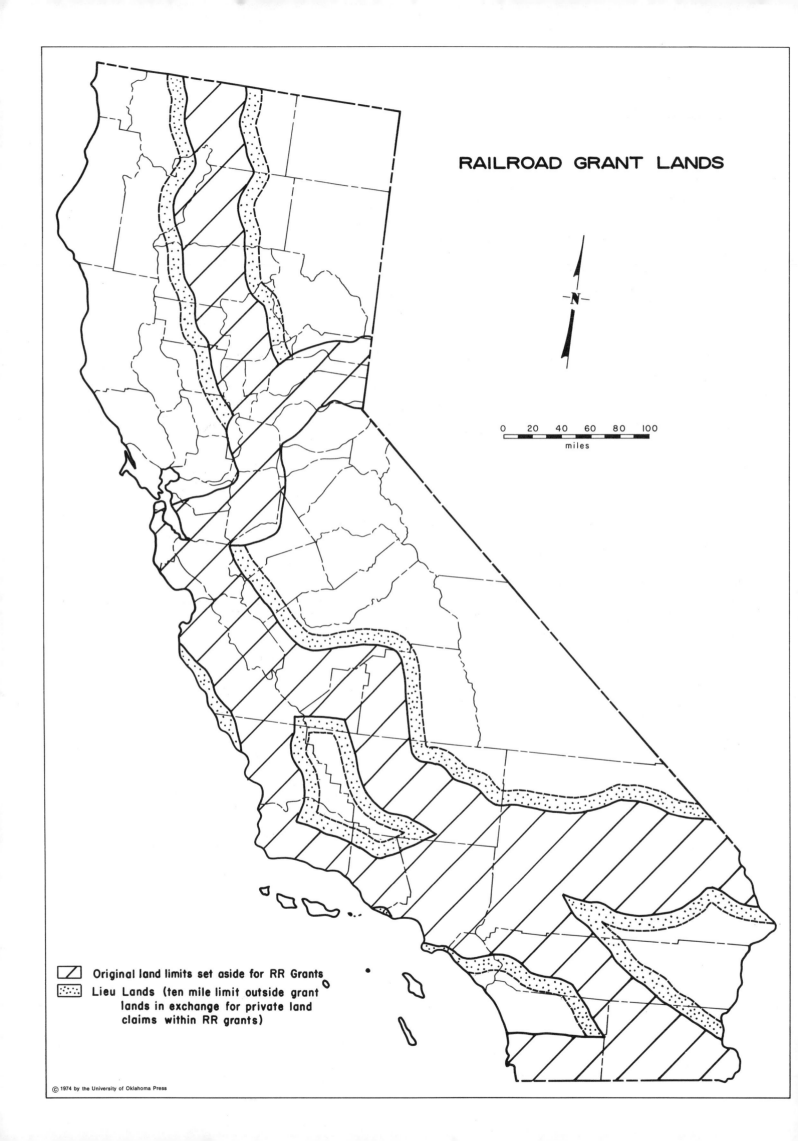

RAILROAD GRANT LANDS

0 20 40 60 80 100
miles

▨ Original land limits set aside for RR Grants
⣿ Lieu Lands (ten mile limit outside grant
   lands in exchange for private land
   claims within RR grants)

67. RAILROAD GRANT LANDS

THE BUILDERS OF California's main railroads received, by act of Congress, 12,800 acres (or twenty sections) of land from the public domain for every mile of track laid. The land granted was to be checkerboarded (to keep the railroad from obtaining exclusive control) in strips extending 20 miles on either side of the tracks. The government's purpose in making the initial land grants was to have the companies sell it to settlers to help pay for the cost of railroad construction. It was also assumed that the sale of these lands at low prices on attractive terms would rapidly bring in settlers whose agricultural produce would help make the railroads a paying proposition. It didn't always work this way, because settlers were often slow to buy, and the railroads were driven to mortgaging grant lands to remain solvent. Also hampering the ability of the railroads to easily sell their grant lands was the slowness of government surveys. Not an acre could legally be sold until the land had been surveyed and patented.

Lieu lands were in place of those areas granted to the railroad which were already occupied. (In California much of the land was covered by Mexican land grants). Lieu lands could usually be selected in an area ten or twenty miles beyond the initial area of the land grant, the outer line being the "indemnity limit."

All of the railroad grant lands in California ultimately came under the control of the Central Pacific–Southern Pacific system. A grant made to the Atlantic and Pacific (later taken over by Atchison, Topeka and Santa Fe) was voided by Congress. The Central Pacific received grants from Sacramento to the Nevada line (within California). The California and Oregon received grants from Roseville north to the Oregon line. The Oregon and California railroad grant also became a part of Southern Pacific holdings, but reverted back to the federal government in 1916. The Southern Pacific was granted lands for the "Main" line from San Jose to Mojave and Needles and a second grant for the "Branch" line from Mojave to near Yuma. The total land acreage ultimately patented was substantially less than the original grants and probably totaled 11,588,000 acres in California, or a little more than 20 per cent of the public domain in the state.

The lands granted to the Central Pacific and Southern Pacific varied widely in quality and value. Some of the land was excellent for agricultural purposes, some of the land had rich timber resources, and much of the land was good only for grazing. Although most land grants to the railroads excluded existing mineral rights, minerals found after the patent had been issued belonged to the railroad. Railroad lands in the Southern San Joaquin Valley later became valuable for oil production.

The railroad usually sold its lands to settlers at fair prices. However, the Mussel Slough incident in 1880 gave the Southern Pacific an evil reputation in its handling of land that still lingers. On this occasion, farmers were promised land at the usual rate of $2.50 an acre by railroad officials and settled it, making improvements while legal disputes delayed the issuance of patents. When the railroad sought to collect $11.00 to $40.00 an acre when the land was patented, an armed encounter cost eight lives and led to the eviction of many settlers.

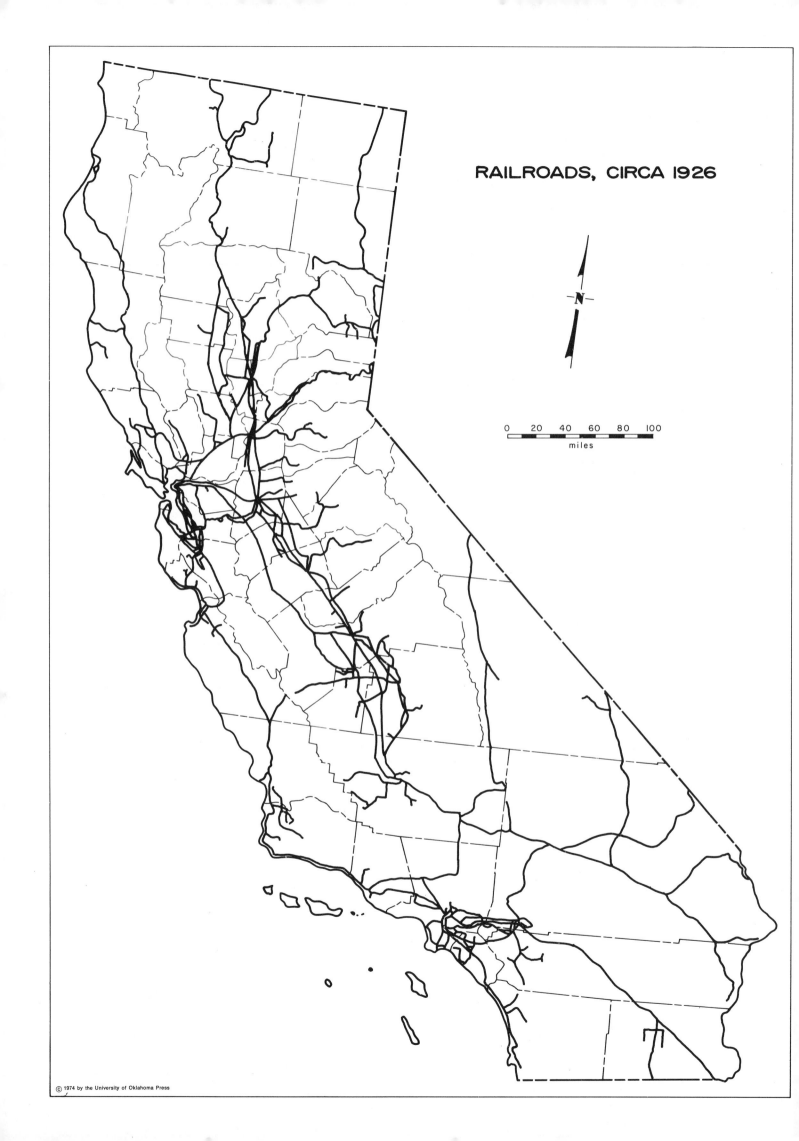

RAILROADS, CIRCA 1926

N

0 20 40 60 80 100
miles

THE IMMENSE SIZE of California and the lack of navigable rivers, together with its remoteness from the other population centers of the nation, combined to make railroads vital to the state's development. In the years since statehood, some 200 railroads have been constructed and operated, and more than 4,000 have been chartered. Many communities flourished or vanished in direct proportion to their ability to provide a transportation link via rails with the outside world. While historians have stressed the more glamorous role of the transcontinental railroads, the local "one engine—one man" lines were indispensable to the economy of many towns.

Since Sacramento had emerged as the stagecoach and express center of the state, it was natural that it should be the first railroad center. The state's first railroad was the modest Sacramento Valley line from the capitol to Folsom. Only 22 miles long, it substantially reduced the cost of freighting to the mines. The San Francisco and San Jose, a paper promotion since 1852 (as were many California railroads), began service in 1864. In Southern California a line connected Wilmington's port facility to Los Angeles in the Civil War period.

But most Californians were far more concerned with the construction of a transcontinental railroad than with local lines. The gold rush triggered a rapid migration into the state, necessitating a more effective link with the rest of the nation than the long, costly, and hazardous sea or overland journeys. However, bitter sectional rivalry between North and South over the location of the route in the 1850's delayed action by Congress until 1862. Theodore Judah, who had been chief engineer of the Sacramento Valley Railroad, charted the railroad route through the seemingly impassable Sierra Nevada. The actual building and control of the railroad became the responsibility of four Sacramento merchants: Leland Stanford, Charles Crocker, Collis Huntington, and Mark Hopkins. The transcontinental line was completed in 1869 (but it was 1876 before Los Angeles was linked by rail). Because the rugged terrain caused high construc-

tion costs, many sizable towns were slow to receive rail service.

Mergers reduced the number of operating roads from the very beginning of the railroad era. However, since 1926 passenger traffic in the state has rapidly declined, along with the railroad mileage operated in California.

RAILROAD MILEAGE OPERATED IN CALIFORNIA DECEMBER 31, 1971

	WITHIN STATE
Class I Line-Haul Railroads:	
Atchison, Topeka & Santa Fe System	1,507
Burlington Northern	100
Northwestern Pacific RR	324
Southern Pacific Co.	4,174
Union Pacific RR	351
Western Pacific RR	580
Total Class I	7,036
Class II Line-Haul Railroads:	
Almanor RR	13
Amador Central RR	12
Arcata & Mad River RR	8
California Western RR	40
Camino, Placerville & Lake Tahoe RR	8
Central California Traction Co.	53
Holton Inter-Urban Ry.	10
McCloud River RR	94
Petaluma & Santa Rosa RR	30
Quincy RR	5
Sacramento Northern Ry.	343
San Diego & Arizona Eastern Ry.	136
Santa Maria Valley RR	18
Sierra RR	56
Stockton Terminal & Eastern RR	14
Sunset Ry.	46
Tidewater Southern Ry.	57
Trona Ry.	31
Ventura County Ry.	11
Visalia Electric RR	34
Yreka Western RR	9
Total Class II	1,028
Total Class I and II	8,064

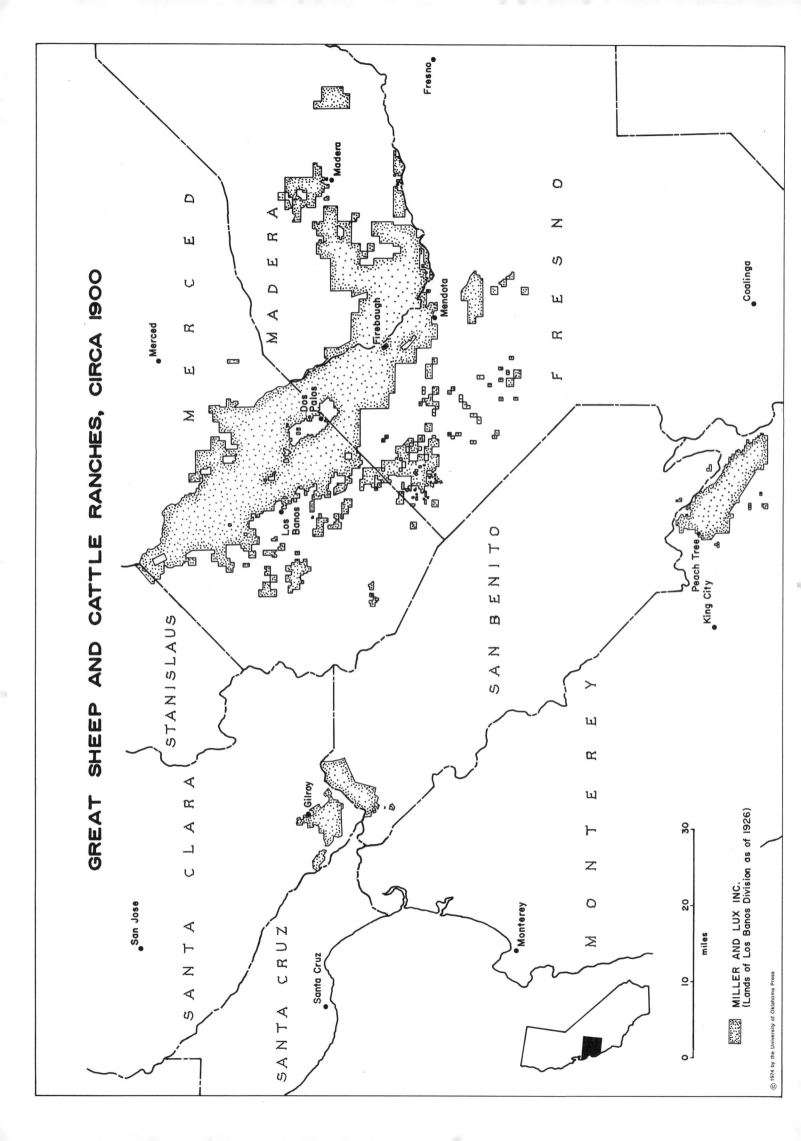

GREAT SHEEP AND CATTLE RANCHES, CIRCA 1900

MADERA

MERCED

STANISLAUS

SANTA CLARA

SANTA CRUZ

MONTEREY

SAN BENITO

FRESNO

Fresno

Madera

Mendota

Firebaugh

Dos Palos

Merced

Los Banos

Peach Tree

King City

Coalinga

San Jose

Santa Cruz

Monterey

Gilroy

MILLER AND LUX INC.
(Lands of Los Banos Division as of 1926)

miles

0   10   20   30

© 1974 by the University of Oklahoma Press

THERE HAS BEEN much emphasis placed upon the great ranchos of the Spanish-Mexican era. Yet the usual maximum size of these landholdings was eleven leagues, or approximately 48,000 acres, and only a few were larger. Far more important to the development of California were the great Anglo ranches, some of which were several hundred thousand acres in extent. The authors have arbitrarily selected what they considered the most important ranches. While every effort has been made to accurately show the exact extent of the selections, some of the landholdings were so extensive and so complex that it is probable many of the owners weren't sure of what they owned.

The greatest of the Anglo landlords were Miller and Lux. Their total acreage in California, Nevada, and Oregon may have been over 3 million acres. In California it was approximately 1 million acres, with some 700,000 of this being in the San Joaquin Valley. Their largest holdings were in Merced and Madera counties accounting for 350,000 acres. More than 20,000 acres were in the Gilroy area, with many smaller tracts widely scattered. Henry Miller reckoned their holdings by the square mile and not by the acre. In court testimony he once stated, "in Santa Clara County we have thirty-six miles north and south, and then about thirty-two miles east and west." It was commonly stated that Henry Miller could travel from Idaho to Mexico by horse and sleep on his own land every night.

Henry Miller (born Heinrich Kreiser) came to America from Germany as a penniless butcher. He plied his trade during the California Gold Rush and became interested in land acquisition as a part of his meat business. Miller did not want land for speculative purposes or just to own land, but he needed it to graze his cattle or to raise alfalfa or grain feeds. He was a partner of Charles Lux, an Alsation immigrant, until Lux died in 1887. However, Miller acquired and managed the ranch end of the business.

The great landholdings were amassed in a variety of ways. One, was to buy out one or more of the heirs to a Mexican land grant. This gave Miller the right to range his cattle on the land, and it was an excellent means of controlling vast areas with a minimum cash investment. In some instances Miller would buy bankruptcies or loan money to settlers who would be ultimately foreclosed. Many farmers who homesteaded lacked the capital investment necessary to succeed in California agriculture. Land script issued to Civil War veterans was purchased, as were school lands. Miller received patents to thousands of acres of alleged swamplands upon testimony before the land officers that he had been over the area in a boat. However, it was claimed that the boat in which he was riding was mounted on a wagon! Regardless of how the land was obtained, Miller pioneered in the draining of actual swamp areas, and was among the first to understand the richness of the San Joaquin Valley when irrigated.

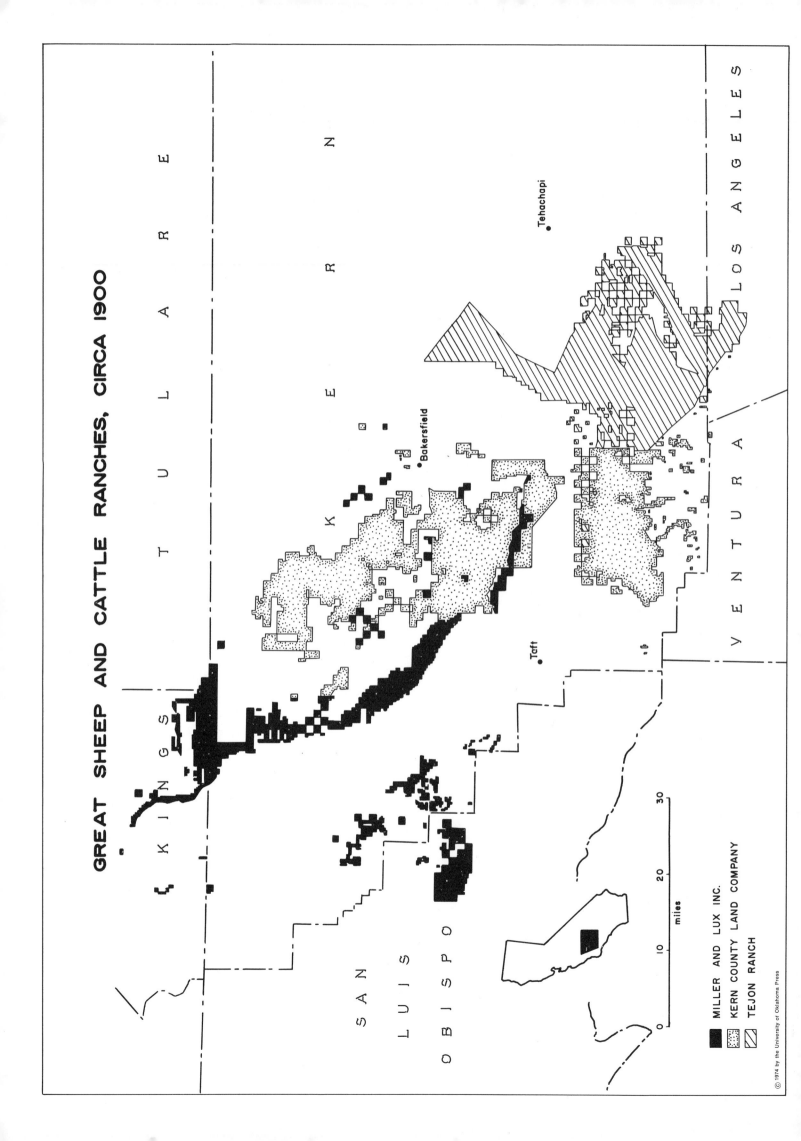

GREAT SHEEP AND CATTLE RANCHES, CIRCA 1900

T U L A R E

K E R N

K I N G S

S A N   L U I S   O B I S P O

V E N T U R A

L O S   A N G E L E S

•Tehachapi

Bakersfield•

Taft•

MILLER AND LUX INC.

KERN COUNTY LAND COMPANY

TEJON RANCH

0   10   20   30
miles

© 1974 by the University of Oklahoma Press

THE EXPANSION OF Miller and Lux into Kings, San Luis Obispo, and Kern counties was a natural extension of their holdings in the San Joaquin Valley. In Kern County their holdings constituted 140,000 to 150,000 acres, mainly along the Kern River or near Lake Buena Vista, at Conner's Station, Millry, and Buttonwillow. Cattle were the mainstay of the ranch, but irrigation was also indispensable for the growing of alfalfa and feeder grains. In 1872, in conjunction with other land owners, Miller and Lux had built the largest and longest canal, which extended for 75 miles across Fresno, Merced, and Stanislaus counties. The Kern Valley Water Company, soon acquired by Miller and Lux, built a canal north from Buena Vista. The canal was 125 feet wide and 7 feet deep and was designed to carry all of the waters of the Kern River that would cover 100,000 or more acres. Meanwhile, James Ben Ali Haggin and his partner, Lloyd Tevis—precursors of the Kern County Land Company—had built canals to carry water to lands not adjoining the river. The drought of 1877 did not leave enough water for both factions and triggered a historic battle over riparian water rights. In "Lux vs. Haggin" the initial court decision favored Haggin, but the State Supreme Court declared for Miller and riparian rights. Miller and Haggin settled their differences by dividing the available water among themselves and thirty-one other land corporations and fifty-eight individual farmers. This bitter contest helped end the supremacy of English Common Law riparian rights in California.

The Kern County Land Company grew out of the land acquisitions of James Ben Ali Haggin, who amassed an immense land empire west and south of Bakersfield in the 1870's and 1880's. Haggin had several partners at different stages of his enterprise; the most important were W. B. Carr and Lloyd Tevis, a San Francisco banker. The stated purpose of Haggin's real estate empire was to drain or irrigate and improve the land and then sell it to small farmers. Subdivision began in earnest after the water rights fight with Miller was settled in 1888, and the company was incorporated in 1890. Sales agencies in the east and in England brought settlers enticed by attractive brochures. Rosedale was the most successful of the small farm developments, but lands were also sold at Greenfield and elsewhere. In 1967, Kern County Land Company was sold to Tenneco and is now known as Heggblade-Marguleas-Tenneco Inc. The company remains basically an agrarian enterprise, but also has tremendous earnings from oil, gas, urban development, and manufacturing companies.

Tejon Ranch Company was originally put together by General Edward Fitzgerald Beale, who figured prominently in the history of California. From service in the Mexican War Beale brought the first gold east, was Superintendent of Indian Affairs, made several important surveys, managed the Camel Corps, and served as Surveyor-General. In 1865 he began amassing a land empire by buying the La Liebre grant of 48,299 acres for three cents an acre. The 26,626-acre Los Alamos y Agua Caliente grant was acquired for about $2,986 in 1865. The 97,612-acre El Tejon grant was obtained in the same year for $21,000. Rancho Castac, 22,178 acres, cost some $65,000 but that included the sheep and cattle. In 1891 Beale's holdings totaled 265,215 acres, since he had added contiguous lands. The area of the ranch has played a vital role in the state's history because three important mountain passes, Tehachapi, Tejon, and Grapevine are located on it. Initially a sheep enterprise, Tejon Ranch stressed cattle after the 1880's. In 1912 Beale's son and heir, Truxton, sold the ranch of 271,300 acres to a group headed by Harry Chandler, and in 1936 the enterprise became a public corporation. Its 1971 annual report has livestock accounting for 47 per cent and farming rents 25.9 per cent of its income, thereby suggesting the retention of agrarian pursuits. The coming of water from the California Water project will greatly alter the future of the Tejon Ranch, as it will also change the pattern of development of the Kern County Land Company.

GREAT SHEEP AND CATTLE RANCHES, CIRCA 1900

FLINT, BIXBY AND COMPANY
IRVINE RANCH
STEARNS HOLDINGS, 1842-1868

L O S   A N G E L E S

S A N

B E R N A R D I N O

R I V E R S I D E

O R A N G E

• Los Angeles

0   10   20   30

miles

71. GREAT SHEEP AND CATTLE RANCHES, *CIRCA* 1900

THE GREATEST OF the Anglo ranchers in Southern California was Abel Stearns. Before drouth brought ruin in the 1860's, his far-flung land empire embraced more than 200,000 acres of the choicest land in the Los Angeles area. In 1842 Stearns, originally a merchant, acquired the 26,000-acre Rancho Los Alamitos for less than two cents an acre, and this property remained the nucleus of his holdings. Taking advantage of his close connections with native Californios resulting from his marriage and long residence in the area, Stearns acquired numerous ranches by loaning money and foreclosing, and by buying the mortgages or claims before the land commission. He purchased the 11,000-acre Rancho La Laguna for only $3,125. An interest in the seven-square-league Rancho Las Bolsas resulted from Stearn's assistance in obtaining a patent for the rancho before the United States Land Commission; he ultimately obtained full title to the entire property. A small loan brought possession of the 6,800-acre Rancho La Bolsa Chica. An interest in Rancho Temescal cost only $1,500. Foreclosure of Pío Pico's $15,000 note added Los Coyotes to Stearn's holdings. Partial interest in the vast Ranchos, Santiago de Santa Ana and San Juan Cajon de Santa Ana, resulted from loans. Rancho La Laguna de Temecula, Rancho Sierra, and Rancho Jurupa in Riverside completed the Stearns empire. The great drouth of the 1860's started the break-up of the great cattle kingdom.

After the Civil War, sheep raisers in central California sought to take advantage of the distress of the cattlemen in the southland and expand into the area. In 1855 Llwellyn Bixby, of Maine, and his cousins, Dr. Thomas and Benjamin Flint, formed the Flint-Bixby Company and purchased the 54,000-acre San Justo Rancho near San Juan Bautista. In 1866 the company acquired Juan Temple's 26,000-acre Rancho Los Cerritos for $20,000. Later the same group acquired a large part of Rancho Los Palos Verde, and Rancho Cajon de Santa Ana and were, for a time, partners with fellow sheepman James Irvine. Jotham Bixby came from San Justo

Rancho as manager of the ranch in Southern California and ultimately became the main owner. In 1878 John William Bixby, a cousin, leased Rancho Los Alamitos, with the backing of I. W. Hellman, Jotham Bixby, and the Flint-Bixby Company; however, the new acquisition was operated as a separate entity. It was purchased in 1881. In 1888 Rancho Los Alamitos was divided three ways: Jotham Bixby annexed his third to Rancho Los Cerritos, the middle third remained in the hands of John Bixby's heirs, and the southeast third of I. W. Hellman's was sold. In 1910 the remainder of Rancho Los Alamitos was divided between Fred Bixby and Susanna Bixby Bryant. Although much of the land was sold to form Long Beach and adjacent communities, the Bixbys continued to be important California landholders.

James Irvine, the founder of the Irvine Ranch, was a Scotch-Irish emigrant who succeeded in the grocery and produce business during the Gold Rush and in San Francisco real estate speculation. With Irvine holding 50 per cent, the Flint-Bixby Company bought the 48,803-acre Rancho San Joaquin from José Sepulveda in 1864 for $18,000; the 47,226-acre Rancho Lomas de Santiago was obtained from William Wolfskill in 1866 for $7,000; a narrow strip of land from Rancho Santiago de Santa Ana totaling 12,157 acres came to the group as a result of complex court proceedings, thus completing the holdings of Irvine Ranch.

In 1876 James Irvine bought out his partners to become sole owner of the ranch to which he gave his name. Originally a sheep spread, the operation was diversified through the years. Cattle, field crops, vegetables, citrus fruit and walnut groves have been added to the sheep, and the ranch is still essentially an agrarian enterprise. However, the sale of land in the 1880's to form the communities of Tustin and Santa Ana pointed the way for future development. Today, the Irvine Ranch has a campus of the University of California, an extensive residential and industrial development, office buildings, and shopping centers.

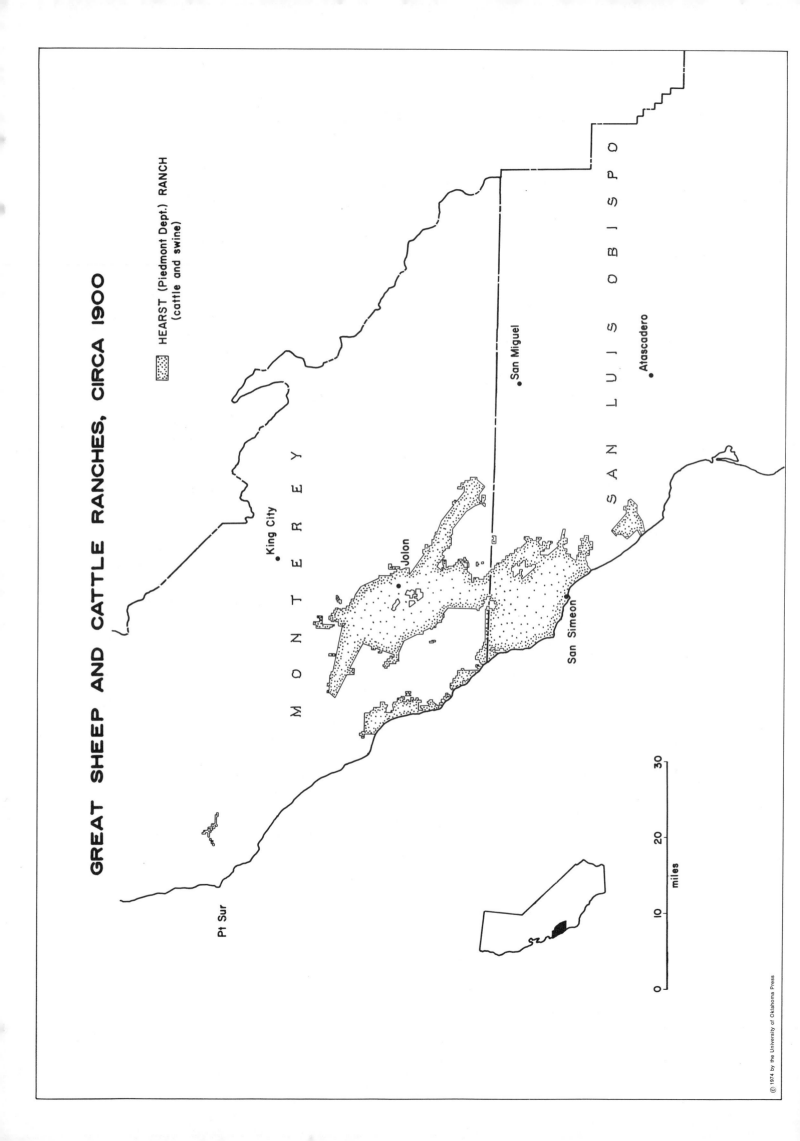

GREAT SHEEP AND CATTLE RANCHES, CIRCA 1900

HEARST (Piedmont Dept.) RANCH
(cattle and swine)

Pt Sur

King City

Jolon

San Miguel

Atascadero

San Simeon

M O N T E R E Y

S A N   L U I S   O B I S P O

0   10   20   30
miles

THE VAST HEARST ranch in San Luis Obispo and Monterey Counties grew out of Senator George Hearst's real estate activities in the nineteenth century. The senior Hearst fortune came mainly from highly successful mining ventures in Nevada, South Dakota, and elsewhere, but he was also fortunate in his real estate dealings. He was a partner of James Ben Ali Haggin and W. B. Carr, who amassed several hundred thousand acres of valley land. In addition, he was associated with Lloyd Tevis, the San Franciscan banker, who financed many of Hearst's real estate speculations. Profits from mining made it possible for the senior Hearst not only to acquire land throughout California but also in Arizona, New Mexico, and Mexico.

The nucleus of what came to be called the San Simeon Ranch was the 48,806-acre Piedra Blanca Rancho purchased in 1865. The San Simeon Rancho of 4,469 acres was soon added, along with the 13,184-acre Santa Rosa Rancho. All three ranchos had been a part of San Miguel Mission lands. Through the years more acres were added, until the total came to some 240,000 acres in the Piedmont section.

The Piedra Blanca Rancho was Senator Hearst's favorite possession, and he visited it as often as possible, bringing along groups of friends. A preferred experience was camping out among the oak trees on *La Cuesta Encantada* (The Enchanted Hill), the site of the fabled castle built by William Randolph Hearst. A new wharf was built at San Simeon in 1878, to make the trip from San Francisco easier and to ship wool and tallow. The same site had once been used by Aleuts while they poached in Spanish waters for sea otters and also as a way station for whalers.

The ranch, however, was more than a delightful recreation center where friends could hunt deer or fish for trout under pleasant circumstances. Senator Hearst made Piedra Blanca into one of the finest stock farms in the state, with prize blooded cattle being sold for premium prices. Some sheep were raised, but the ranch was more famed for its hogs. Early in swine ranching the herd contracted tuberculosis and was almost lost. The ranch finally developed a blue strain hog which was immune to the disease but which was "meaner and tougher than hell." Hogs were turned out to graze acorns in late fall and left to fend for themselves in the steep, oak-shrouded Santa Lucias. In late spring, much to the dismay of the veteran cowhands, who hated such chores, the hogs were rounded up. It was no easy task to get the pigs out of the mountains, much less try to herd them to fattening pens, where they were fed barley for a couple of weeks to harden the meat, and then shipped to market. Senator Hearst also used the ranch to breed race horses and Arabians, and even built a track to train horses.

With the death of the Senior Hearst in 1891, the ranch began to lose its productive character, although William Randolph Hearst liked to consider himself a rancher. On one occasion he answered queries about his political plans stressing this role: "I am a rancher enjoying life on the high hills overlooking the broad Pacific. If you want to talk about Herefords I will talk with you, but not about politics." But to the younger Hearst the ranch was a pleasant wilderness to which he could retire from the cares of the world and entertain numerous and famed guests. After the death of his mother in 1919, Hearst began lavishing the earnings of his publishing empire on building his fabled castle and filling it with the art treasures of the world.

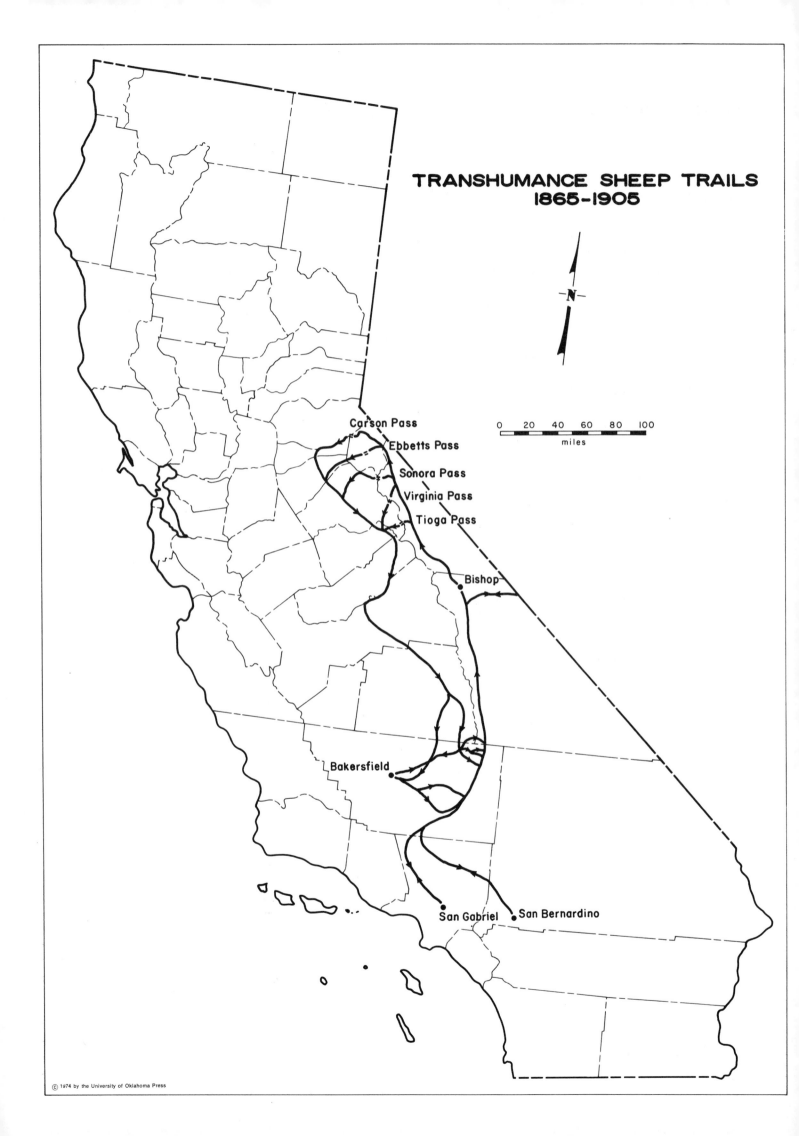

TRANSHUMANCE SHEEP TRAILS
1865-1905

—N—

0   20   40   60   80   100
miles

Carson Pass
Ebbetts Pass
Sonora Pass
Virginia Pass
Tioga Pass

Bishop

Bakersfield

San Gabriel   San Bernardino

SHEEP TRAILS IN California were (and still are) used for the seasonal migrations of flocks, a practice also common in Spain. During the hot dry summers in the San Joaquin Valley and other parts of Southern California, pasture is limited, so the flocks are driven to the green grasslands of the many high valleys of the Sierra Nevada. In addition to improved grazing, the mountains increase the wool clip one and a half pounds per head and result in more twinning among the pregnant ewes.

As soon as lambing, shearing, and dipping are completed in the spring, the annual drive to the highlands begins. Traveling in bands of 1,200 to 4,000 they average 8 to 10 miles a day (the sheep must move at least 5 miles daily so that no one band cleans out sections of the trail), and take 30 to 40 days to reach the mountain meadows.

The southern trails began in San Gabriel and San Bernadino, with a stopover in the Antelope Valley, where men and animals could recuperate. Bakersfield was the focal point of the trails in the San Joaquin Valley. The Tehachapi and Walker passes were used to cross the mountains. The trail into the Owens Valley followed a route approximating that of the Los Angeles Aqueduct and highway 395. Near Owens Lake the trail narrowed so the tax collector could levy a fee of two to five cents a head. (Today

the fee is ten cents for using the trail.) Near Bishop the trails started to fan out. In wetter years some shepherds worked their way eastward into Nevada. However, most preferred to drive their sheep northward on the eastward slope of the Sierras, often to some valley known only to the shepherd, where, it was believed, the grass was greener. In late summer the divide was crossed, usually via Tioga Pass, but passes as far north as Carson were also used. The sheep then grazed their way homeland on the western side of the Sierras through the San Joaquin foothills, the King's River country, or the Kern Valley.

The basic sheep trail from Bakersfield via Walker Pass and Mojave northward into the Owens Valley to the Mono Lake area is still in use. With the decline in numbers of sheep in the state and with changing technology, the pattern of transhumance has been altered, but it remains important. The century-old California Sheep Trail was marked and set aside by the Bureau of Land Management. Some 75,000 sheep graze their way to the mountains annually, guided by Basque shepherds. To truck 3,000 sheep 400 miles to the highland meadows would cost $10,000 more than it does to drive them overland. However, in the fall, trucks are now used to transport the sheep to their home pasture.

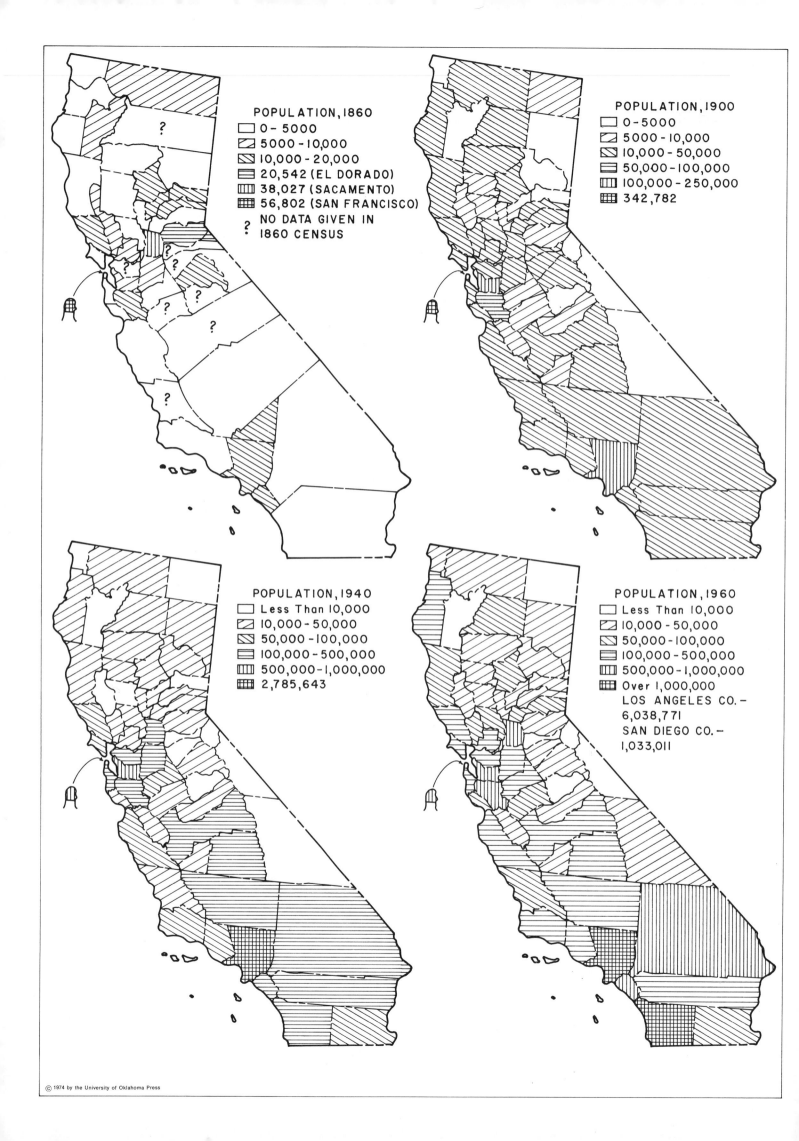

POPULATION, 1860
☐ 0 - 5000
▨ 5000 - 10,000
▧ 10,000 - 20,000
▤ 20,542 (EL DORADO)
▥ 38,027 (SACAMENTO)
▦ 56,802 (SAN FRANCISCO)
? NO DATA GIVEN IN
  1860 CENSUS

POPULATION, 1900
☐ 0 - 5000
▨ 5000 - 10,000
▧ 10,000 - 50,000
▤ 50,000 - 100,000
▥ 100,000 - 250,000
▦ 342,782

POPULATION, 1940
☐ Less Than 10,000
▨ 10,000 - 50,000
▧ 50,000 - 100,000
▤ 100,000 - 500,000
▥ 500,000 - 1,000,000
▦ 2,785,643

POPULATION, 1960
☐ Less Than 10,000
▨ 10,000 - 50,000
▧ 50,000 - 100,000
▤ 100,000 - 500,000
▥ 500,000 - 1,000,000
▦ Over 1,000,000
LOS ANGELES CO. -
6,038,771
SAN DIEGO CO. -
1,033,011

74. POPULATION DISTRIBUTION

FROM A HISPANIC population of some 14,000 in 1848, California has grown to the most populous state in the nation, with some 20 million inhabitants. This growth rate has fluctuated, but population has approximately doubled every two decades, with the greatest rate of growth (66 per cent) coming in the 1920's. The lowest rates of increase came in the 1890's and 1930's, with rates of 22 per cent. As the number of inhabitants has grown, the percentage rate of increase can be anticipated to decline. In the 1950's the rate was 49 per cent, but fell to 27 per cent in the 1960's.

In the Hispanic era population was concentrated in the missions, forts, towns, and ranchos along the coast. This disparity in the distribution of the state's people, a result of climate, topography, and natural resources, has continued down to 1972. In 1860, the year of the first census, over half of the state's residents were concentrated in the Sacramento Valley or in nearby gold-bearing areas of the Sierra Nevada. Another 22 per cent were located in the San Francisco Bay Area. Population shifted dramatically during the Gold Rush era, with some communities becoming metropolises of more than ten thousand people only to collapse into ghost towns with the vicissitudes of the gold fever. Very few people lived in southern California, with Los Angeles, the largest city, having only 4,385 citizens. In some counties the population was so small or in such a state of flux, that it was not even counted.

As late as the 1880's two-thirds of all Californians lived north of the Tehachapis. Those who left the mining areas usually settled in the Bay Area. The boom of the eighties in Southern California helped redress the population imbalance with the central part of the state. The 1880's saw Los Angeles County triple in population (despite the loss of 30,000 when Orange County was created in 1889). The city of Los Angeles jumped from 12,000 in 1884 to an estimated 100,000 in 1887, while cities like Santa Barbara, Pasadena, and San Diego increased tenfold. The boom was triggered by a railroad rate war, and was aided by an extensive propaganda campaign which lured large numbers of health-seekers. Continued increase in population in the southland resulted from the ability to solve the water needs of the arid region, the growth of the citrus industry, and the rapid rise in importance of petroleum. By the 1920's, southern California became the most populous area of the state, and since then the imbalance has grown. By 1940, 55.7 per cent lived south of the Tehachapis.

Concentration in urban centers is another feature of California's population. A large proportion of the state's inhabitants have lived in cities from very early days, and this pattern has continued down to the present. Furthermore, the concentration has centered in the metropolitan centers of San Francisco and Los Angeles, which accounted for 62.4 per cent of the state's population in 1950. The gravitation towards these areas has accelerated.

After slowing in the 1930's, the rate of in-migration skyrocketed during the years of World War II. The rush of newcomers hit a peak of 582,000 in 1944. There was a slight curtailment in the mass movement of people to California immediately after the war, but the 1940 population of 6,950,000 soared to 10,586,000 in 1950, for a 53 per cent gain. In 1960 it reached 15,717,000, for a 48 per cent increase.

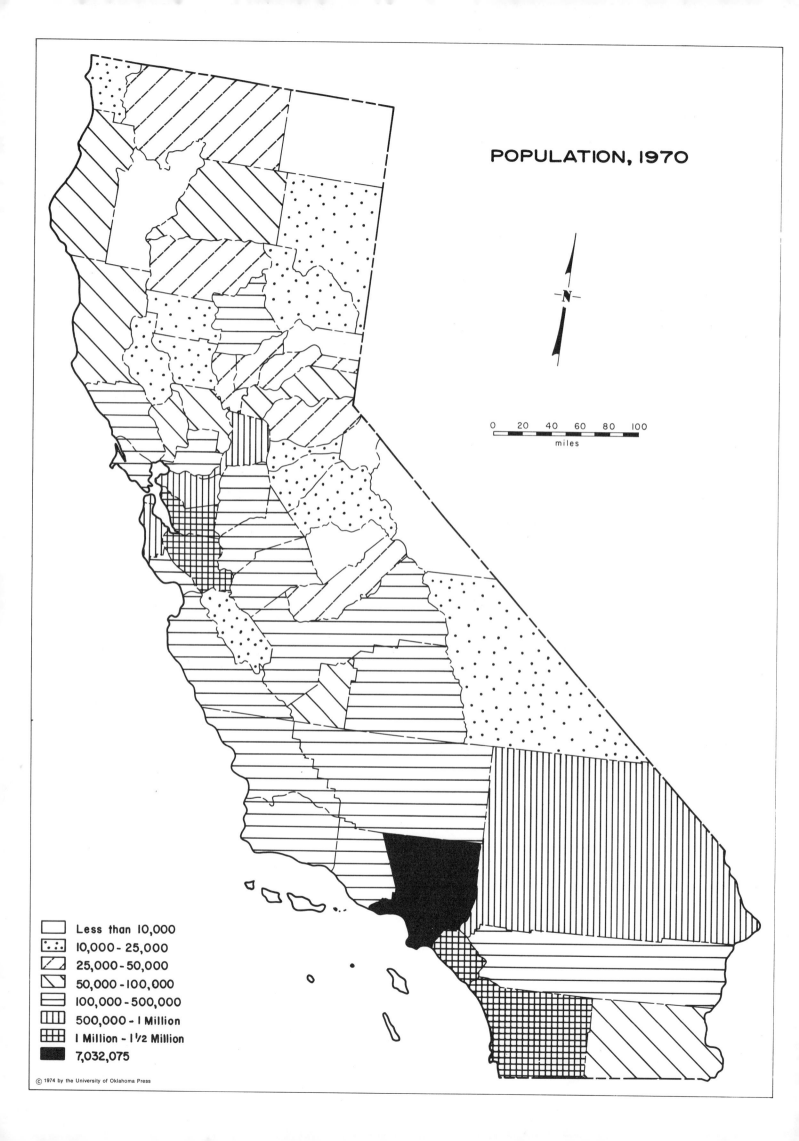

POPULATION, 1970

0   20   40   60   80   100
miles

Less than 10,000
10,000 - 25,000
25,000 - 50,000
50,000 - 100,000
100,000 - 500,000
500,000 - 1 Million
1 Million - 1½ Million
7,032,075

© 1974 by the University of Oklahoma Press

75. POPULATION, 1970

THE POPULATION FIGURES for 1970 suggest many changes for the future of California. The rate of growth dramatically declined in the decade of the 1960's: the 1960 figure of 15,717,000 went up only 27 per cent, to 19,953,000. The decade began as though the growth rate of the preceding twenty years would continue. In 1963 the net migration gain was 356,000, but this was the peak year; in 1969 the net population gain was only 27,000. In 1964 the Budget Division of the State Department of Finance had projected the 1970 population as 21,690,000 and that of 1975 as 24,816,000.

The obvious question was: what had caused these predictions to fall short? A national magazine suggested in an article that "The Golden State Loses Its Glow." Among the many explanations for this change in population growth was the strong emphasis upon zero population growth which has caused a sharp decline in the birthrate. Air pollution and crowded conditions in California made the state no longer an ideal place in which to live, and probably discouraged many potential migrants. More importantly, people stopped coming to the state in the 1960's for the same reason that they had in the 1890's and 1930's; economic conditions simply were not attractive. Jobs for which newcomers had been enticed in the past were not available. Employment in the important aerospace industry dropped from its peak of 617,000 in 1967 to around 400,000 in 1970. The population boom had been self-generating, as each new arrival needed housing and a host of other services. Once the boom spent itself, the number of jobs contracted. Teachers were re-cruited throughout the country for years, but suddenly California found itself with a large surplus. An educational system which had experienced nothing but growth since statehood has had to adjust to declining student population and reduced revenue. Unless the economic picture should change abruptly—and the possibility of this happening does not appear promising—California cannot attract migrants. There is even the possibility that there will be enough out-migration in the 1970's so that this decade may be the first one during which the state's population declined.

The 1970 population figures also show that people continue to be concentrated in a very small part of the state. Urban areas had 91 per cent of the people. Los Angeles County had some 30 per cent of the state's population, with 6,938,453, while Alpine County counted only 484 citizens. Orange County, second in size, showed the sharpest rate of increase among the larger counties, with a growth of 101.8 per cent to 1,420,386. San Diego was the third largest county, with 1,357,854 and a percentage increase of 31.4. Los Angeles, the state's largest county, had a growth rate for the decade of only 16.4 per cent. On the other hand, San Francisco County had a 3.3 per cent decline in population. However, the Bay Area metropolitan region experienced the same kind of growth as Southern California. Alameda County grew to 1,073,184 for an 18.2 per cent increase; Contra Costa to 558,389 and 36.5 per cent; Marin to 206,038 and 40.3 per cent; and Santa Clara to 1,064,714 for a 65.8 per cent increase.

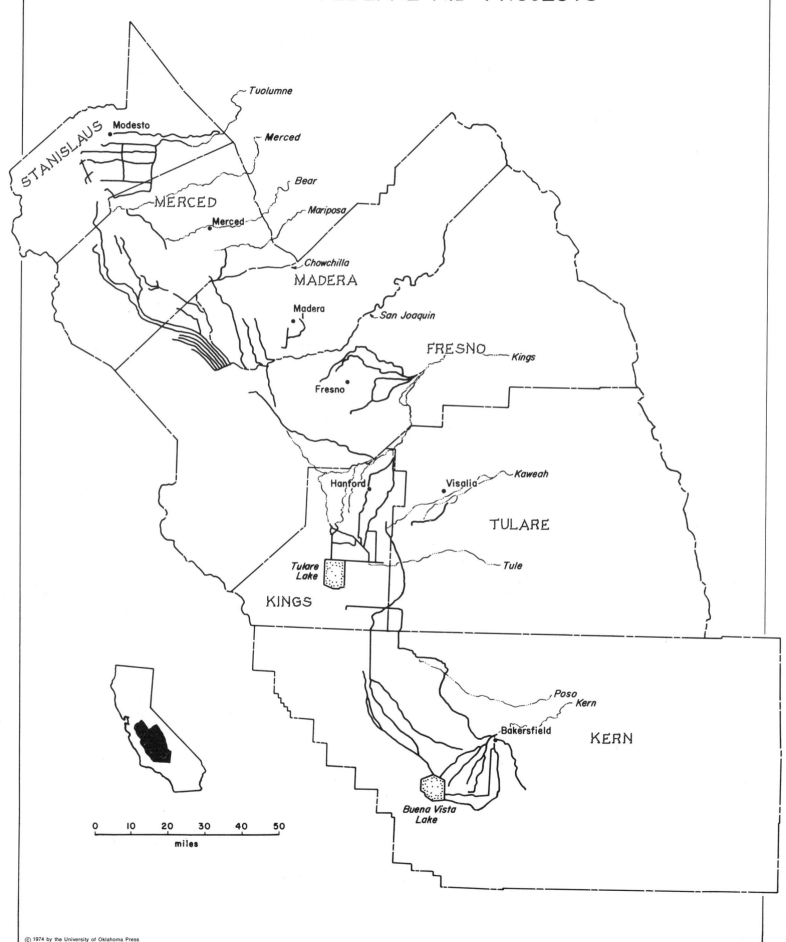

MAJOR IRRIGATION SYSTEMS IN THE SAN JOAQUIN VALLEY
PRIOR TO FEDERAL AID PROJECTS

THE EXTENSIVE SYSTEM of irrigation in San Joaquin Valley under private auspices during the latter half of the nineteenth century resulted from grandiose plans to build a single great canal, from the efforts of individuals to obtain water for their lands, and from the activities of land speculators.

Large landholders who often had acquired their property for a few cents an acre desired irrigation because it could appreciate their land value to as much as $100 an acre.

In Kern County irrigation is dominated by the river of the same name. The Kern River divided near Bakersfield, with part of the flow going south through different channels into Buena Vista Lake and part going north in times of high water to empty into Goose or Tulare Lake. The first irrigation ditches were built in 1858, with the Kern Island canal being finished in 1861.

Henry Miller saw the potential of this land if it could be drained and the surplus water moved by canals to irrigate other areas. Utilizing the provisions of the Swamp Land Act of 1850, Miller and his partner controlled a tract of land extending for 50 miles along the Kern River and containing well over 100,000 acres. Meanwhile, James Ben Ali Haggin's Kern County Land Company had acquired comparable vast landholdings, most of which were not riparian to the Kern River, and built a system of canals to irrigate these lands. Conflict over water between Miller and Lux and Kern County Land Company was inevitable.

Riparian water rights originated in English common law and granted to owners of land along streams prior right to the use of the water; the state legislature adopted this concept in 1850. The clash between Miller and Haggin grew out of the drouth of 1877 and finally reached the Superior Court of Kern County in 1881 as "Lux vs Haggin." After a lengthy trial, Haggin's right to the water was upheld. The case was appealed by Miller, and in 1886 the State Supreme Court reversed the lower court and declared in favor of Miller and riparian rights. Before a retrial could be held, however, Miller proposed a compromise which Haggin accepted. This Miller-Haggin Agreement divided Kern River water between 31 corporations and 58 individuals and remains in force to the present day. Confusion over water rights remained for years, but one side effect of the Lux vs. Haggin conflict was the passage of the Wright Act in 1887. This measure enabled local citizens to organize irrigation districts.

Irrigation from the Kings River began in 1866, with several canals being built in the 1870's and 1880's. The Fresno Canal, as well as the Peoples, Last Chance, and Lemoore, irrigated some 85,000 acres in 1882 in Kings, Fresno, and Tulare Counties. Ultimately, the Kings River provided irrigation water for some 1 million acres.

Irrigation of Fresno, Madera, Merced, and Stanislaus counties came from the Merced and Tuolumne Rivers and facilitated the construction of the San Joaquin and Kings River Canal. Extending for some 100 miles from Mendota, it constituted the largest single irrigation system in the state in the 1880's, although it never materialized as a part of the state transportation system.

Miller, who controlled the canal company stock, ordered the construction of the Outside Canal in 1896, from Mendota Pool (China Slough) northwesterly. By 1903 the canal company had obtained title to Mendota Dam, Mendota Pool, and Outlet Canals 1, 2, and 3 (which carried water from the Outside Canal to the Main Canal). The building of the Parallel Canal in 1905, sometimes called the Inside Canal, doubled the cubic feet of water the Main Canal could carry. Miller and Lux organized mutual canal companies to control the water of the area. The one irrigating the Helm, Firebaugh, Silaxo, Poso, East Santa Rita, Lucerne, and Riverside areas was the Poso Canal Company. The main artery of the Poso system was the Helm Canal, running northwesterly from the Mendota Pool.

The great private water companies have continued in existence, but the involvement of the federal government in the Central Valley Project in the 1930's led to a curtailment of their size.

MAJOR MAN-MADE
WATER SYSTEMS

N

0 20 40 60 80 100
miles

Upper Feather
Lakes

Oroville Dam

Pardee Res.
Mokelumne Aqueduct
Bethany Res.
Hetch Hetchy Res.

Hetch
Hetchy
Aqueduct

San Luis Res.

Cent. Vall. Proj

Tinemaha Res.

Delta
Mendota
Canal

CALIFORNIA

AQUEDUCT

State Water Proj

Friant
Kern
Canal

Los Angeles
Aqueduct

Castaic Lake

Van Norman Res.

Parker
Dam

Lake Perris
Lake Mathews

Colorado River
Aqueduct

Coachella
Canal

San Vincente Res.

All American
Canal

© 1974 by the University of Oklahoma Press

CONTROL OF A water supply has been the single most important factor in the rapid development of California. With precipitation limited and usually occurring during a few winter months, man had to develop his own water systems if population was to grow and cultivated acreage was to increase. Efforts to irrigate California are as old as the Spanish settlement, and irrigation was probably practiced on a limited scale by the native Californians. The American era brought rapid expansion of irrigation programs, especially in the 1850's. William Wolfskill successfully irrigated vineyards and orange groves in Los Angeles County, as did the German settlers at Anaheim, and the Mormons at San Bernardino. Irrigation was also utilized in the Sacramento area. John Wesley North and George Chaffey were leading irrigation pioneers in southern California. The passage of the Wright Law in 1887 brought stability to districts, allowing the development of irrigation. Since that date the number of acres under irrigation in California has continued to grow, helping make agriculture the leading industry. More than 90 per cent of the current cropland is watered artificially.

The first of the major man-made water systems was projected in 1901 to meet the needs of San Francisco, then the state's first city. Plans called for dams and reservoirs on the Tuolumne River in the Hetch Hetchy Valley of Yosemite National Park. Vigorous but futile opposition to the project from conservationists who opposed the desecration of the beauties of Yosemite delayed its start until 1913. It was 1931 when the 186-mile aqueduct carried the first water from Hetch Hetchy to San Francisco. The Pardee Reservoir on the Mokelumne River and the Mokelumne Aqueduct are also integral parts of the Bay Cities water supply system.

Parker Dam formed Lake Havasu on the Colorado River and its aqueduct brought water 242 miles to Lake Mathews by 1941. A branch aqueduct carries water to the San Vincente Reservoir for the San Diego metropolitan area. Colorado River water was also utilized to irrigate farmland in the Imperial Valley in 1901. Settlers swarmed into the area, but from 1903 to 1907 the river went on a rampage. It was controlled only by great effort and the expenditure of several millions of dollars. The All American Canal was constructed to bring irrigation waters from the river without having to go through Mexico. The Coachella Canal is a branch extending 48.9 miles north to the valley of the same name.

The Central Valley Project grew out of the 1920 proposals of Robert Bradford Marshall, chief hydrographer of the United States Geological Survey. The project proposed redistributing water from the wet north to the dry south with a series of canals. This water plan was approved in 1931, but bonds could not be marketed on the depression market. However, the New Deal turned the Central Valley Project into a federal undertaking. Construction of dams and reservoirs began in the late 1930's. An integral part of the project is the Delta-Mendota Canal, which carries water from the Sacramento River south for 117 miles. The Friant-Kern Canal takes impounded San Joaquin River water southward along the base of the Sierras for 156 miles to the arid region around Bakersfield.

The California State Water Project originated as the Feather River Project. The 3,600-square-mile watershed was subject to frequent flooding, and in 1955 the Feather River caused a major disaster. This calamity increased support for the project, since one of the first steps was the erection of the giant Oroville Dam, which was completed in 1967; in addition, smaller dams and reservoirs were built on the Upper Feather Lakes. The California Aqueduct main line runs along the west side of the San Joaquin Valley, bringing water to the southland. The North Bay Aqueduct, the South Bay Aqueduct, Coastal Branch, and West Branch supplement the main line. Storage facilities at Castaic Lake and Perris Lake are important units in the distribution of water in southern California. When completed, the California Water Project will be the most elaborate system of water control in the world. Included will be 21 dams and reservoirs, 6 main aqueducts, 6 power plants, and 22 pumping stations.

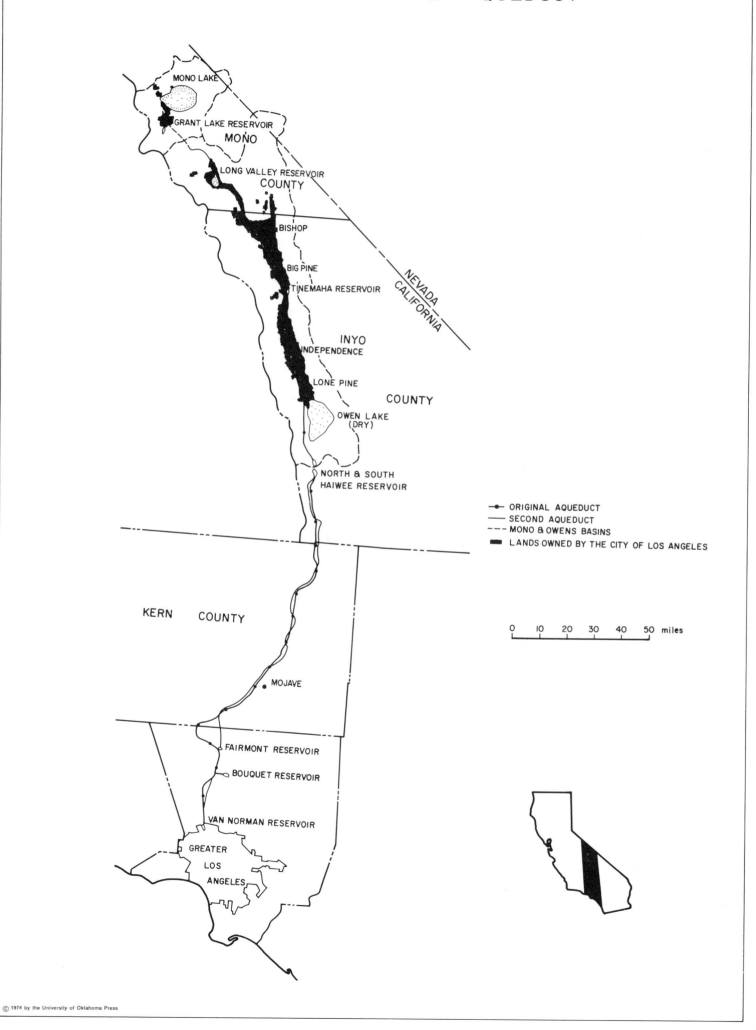

LOS ANGELES-OWENS RIVER AQUEDUCT

MONO LAKE

GRANT LAKE RESERVOIR

MONO

LONG VALLEY RESERVOIR

COUNTY

BISHOP

BIG PINE

TINEMAHA RESERVOIR

NEVADA
CALIFORNIA

INYO
INDEPENDENCE

LONE PINE

COUNTY

OWEN LAKE
(DRY)

NORTH & SOUTH
HAIWEE RESERVOIR

● ORIGINAL AQUEDUCT
—— SECOND AQUEDUCT
- - - MONO & OWENS BASINS
▮ LANDS OWNED BY THE CITY OF LOS ANGELES

KERN   COUNTY

0 10 20 30 40 50 miles

MOJAVE

FAIRMONT RESERVOIR

BOUQUET RESERVOIR

VAN NORMAN RESERVOIR

GREATER
LOS
ANGELES

78. LOS ANGELES–OWENS RIVER AQUEDUCT

SINCE ITS FOUNDING Los Angeles has been frequently plagued by a water shortage. Periods of adequate rainfall were matched by comparable periods of drought; a report for 1840–41 even claimed that no rain fell for eighteen months. However, water from the Los Angeles River was usually adequate for the needs of the small community. A rapid increase in population from 10,000 to 200,000 in the last two decades of the nineteenth century greatly expanded water needs, and several years of below average precipitation prompted a search for a more reliable source than the river.

Construction of the Owens River aqueduct was started in 1907 and completed in 1913. The initial aqueduct, 233 miles in length, passes over foothills, through mountains, and across the Mojave Desert. It includes 142 tunnels totaling 52 miles in length. Its successful completion was one of man's most remarkable engineering feats and brought 320,000 acre-feet of water per year to Los Angeles. Later, the aqueduct was extended to tap the waters of the Mono Basin, with reservoirs being built at Long Valley and Grant Lake. By the time the Mono Basin project was completed, in 1940, the Los Angeles Aqueduct system totaled 338 miles. A second aqueduct to supplement the original was begun in 1964 and completed in 1970 and brings an additional 152,000 acre-feet of water per year. Portions of the route parallel the earlier aqueduct, but in several locations a shorter, more direct route is followed. Both Fairmont and Bouquet Reservoirs hold water for periods of peak demand.

The Owens River Valley was a prosperous irrigated farming and ranching community when Los Angeles began acquiring water rights in the area. Ultimately, the Department of Water and Power purchased 302,000 acres in Inyo and Mono counties. Of this total some 222,000 acres are leased, but only 19,000 acres are irrigated; the remainder being used for dry land grazing. The manner in which Los Angeles authorities acquired land from Owens Valley residents triggered open hostility by enraged citizens who were unwilling to sell their homes at any price. During the 1920's the aqueduct was dynamited several times and armed guards exchanged frequent shots with local opponents of the Department of Water and Power. Whether there was "A Rape of Owens Valley," as many writers contend, remains a matter of bitter controversy. All that is certain is that the City of Los Angeles harvested ill-will which still exists.

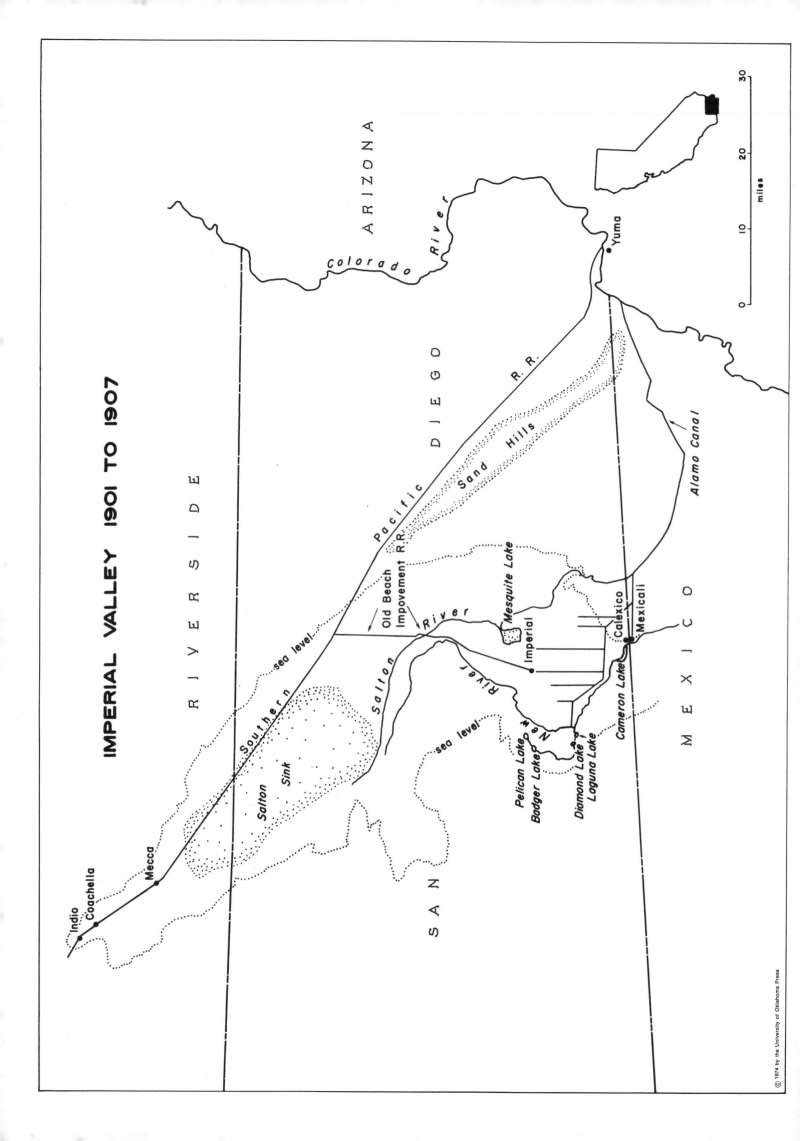

IMPERIAL VALLEY 1901 TO 1907

R I V E R S I D E

A R I Z O N A

Colorado River

Indio
Coachella
Mecca

Salton Sink

Southern

sea level

Pacific R.R.

S A N   D I E G O

Sand Hills

Old Beach
Impovement

River

Salton

sea level

Pelican Lake
Badger Lake
Diamond Lake
Laguna Lake

New River

Mesquite Lake

Imperial

Cameron Lake

Calexico
Mexicali

M E X I C O

Alamo Canal

Yuma

miles
0   10   20   30

79. IMPERIAL VALLEY, 1901–1907

THE IMPERIAL VALLEY, the state's richest agricultural region, is a product of the Colorado River and modern technology. The river created the valley by erecting a barrier across an arm of the Gulf of California which once included all of the Salton Sink and reached north of the present city of Indio. Through the centuries the Colorado River carried in its stream many tons of silt. As the stream lost momentum as it neared the sea-level, it gradually built a dike closing off the northern end of the gulf. The deposits of sand, gravel, clay and silt accumulated in many layers up to two miles thick. The water evaporated from the vast area we know today as the Imperial and Coachella Valleys, and it became a dry basin, up to 297 feet below sea level in the Salton Sink. Since the Colorado River was from 100 to 300 feet higher, it often flooded the area, cutting new channels as it swung northward to fill the depression. The Alamo Canal and Salton River, as well as the New River, were channels that the Colorado had periodically used as it flowed northward. After refilling the valley the stream would again become so choked with silt that it would be obliged to swing towards the sea, leaving the inland lake to evaporate once more.

As early as 1851 the San Diego *Herald* reported on the strange course of the New River and discussed streams which flowed north and west until they were lost in the desert. Public land surveys along the Mexican border during the decade of 1850's confirmed the existence of drainage channels and water courses which could connect the depression with the Colorado River. Few, however, understood the relationship between the two. Dr. Oliver Meredith Wozencraft was the first to grasp the fact that the rich alluvial soil of the Imperial Valley would be-

come a veritable Garden of Eden if irrigated by the nearby waters of the Colorado. The Ohio born physician also understood that to irrigate this potentially fertile desert the water from the higher-elevated river would naturally flow to the valley of its own accord. Wozencraft was not to realize his dream, and it was 1901 before the water of the Colorado caused the Imperial Valley to bloom.

The first settlers poured into the former desert area along with the water, and the agricultural returns were fabulous—despite the hardships. In 1904 dairy yields were $100,000; barley $150,000; hay $125,000; and other crops totaled $700,000. The prosperity brought settlers faster than the water could come from the Colorado, and the canal rapidly silted up. In order to get more water an additional intake was cut to the river without the construction of proper flood control gates. The result, combined with flood conditions early in 1905, brought disaster to the Imperial Valley as the whole Colorado River poured into the depression. As far back as 1853, such a result had been predicted by William P. Blake, who stated: "It is indeed a serious question, whether a canal would not cause the overflow once more of a vast surface, and refill . . . the dry valley of the ancient lake." The river soon created a lake eight to ten miles wide, forcing the Southern Pacific to move its tracks to higher ground five times. Four hundred and eighty-eight square miles of farmland were flooded, and the irrigation company went bankrupt. It took two years and six attempts by the railroad before the Colorado River was returned to its former channel to the sea. The building of several dams has lessened the possibility of the river going on another rampage.

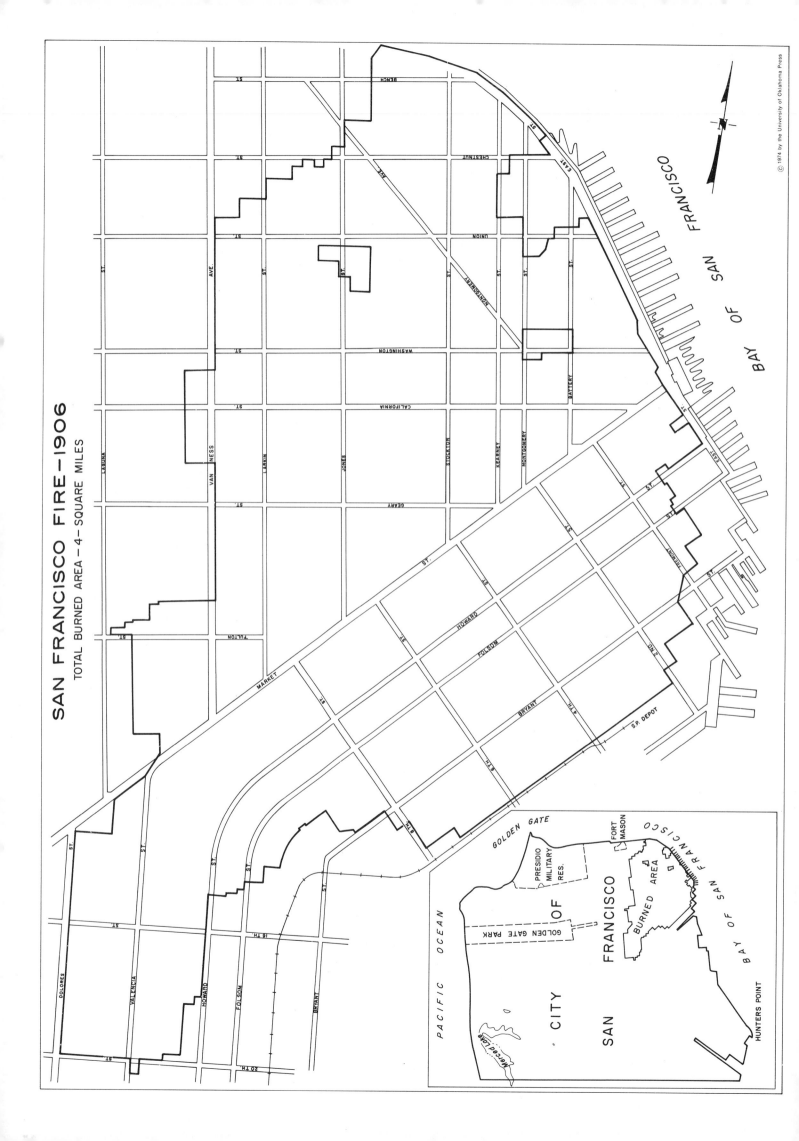

SAN FRANCISCO FIRE—1906
TOTAL BURNED AREA – 4 – SQUARE MILES

80. SAN FRANCISCO EARTHQUAKE AND FIRE, 1906

THE SAN FRANCISCO earthquake and fire remains the most spectacular disaster in the history of the state, and perhaps of the nation. The earthquake struck at 5:12 A.M., April 18, 1906. The first shock lasted for some 40 seconds, ceased for 10 seconds, and returned for another 25 seconds; after-shocks continued for much of the day. It has been estimated that the earthquake measured 8.3 on the Richter scale. The quake felled some 5,000 buildings and twisted roads, railways, sidewalks, gas, water, and electric lines into useless shapes. No estimate of the number of lives lost in the quake is possible, because of the fire which followed. The worst damage was caused to buildings erected on fill; where structures were anchored in solid rock, damage was less severe.

Sporadic fires broke out shortly after the quake, but it was two or three hours before authorities realized a major conflagration was at hand. The earthquake had shattered the pipes leading from the basic water supply at Crystal Springs Lake and San Andreas Lake. The undermanned fire department of only 565 men and some 50 pieces of equipment relied on the little water available from cisterns, reservoirs, and what could be pumped from the bay. Desperate initial efforts to contain the fire by dynamiting buildings were usually ineffective because of the lack of experienced personnel. Some 74 hours after it started, the fire ended. Dynamite, heroic firemen, a change in the wind, and hasty repairs to the water system combined to produce victory. In the smoldering city a tally of the disaster was made.

The fire cost some 450 lives, destroyed 28,000 buildings (about a third of San Francisco) and 490 blocks, totaling more than 4 square miles. Property damage was estimated from $350 to $500 million. Gone were the city's financial district, its retail district, Chinatown, the City Hall with its records, libraries and art collections, and many of the city's schools and churches. Many businesses were totally destroyed and many prominent families financially ruined. Some $229 million in insurance helped ease the burden, but some companies refused to pay, claiming fires caused by earthquake were not covered.

Actually, the great earthquake of 1906 was a California phenomenon and was not restricted to San Francisco. A swath of destruction along the San Andreas fault extended from Salinas on the south to Point Arena on the north. (At some points along the fault, horizontal land movement measured 23 feet.) Fort Bragg and Eureka, far to the north of the San Andreas fault, were ravished by the earthquake and then swept by fire; far to the south, Brawley, in the Imperial Valley, was leveled by the earthquake. Of the scores of towns smashed by the earthquake, hardest hit were Santa Rosa, with 75 dead, and San Jose, where 119 died—most of the latter deaths occurred at the Agnew Asylum. All peninsula towns were badly damaged, with the entire business section of Palo Alto wiped out. Stanford University was almost totally destroyed. Fortunately, destruction to the East Bay was limited, and thousands of persons found refuge in Oakland.

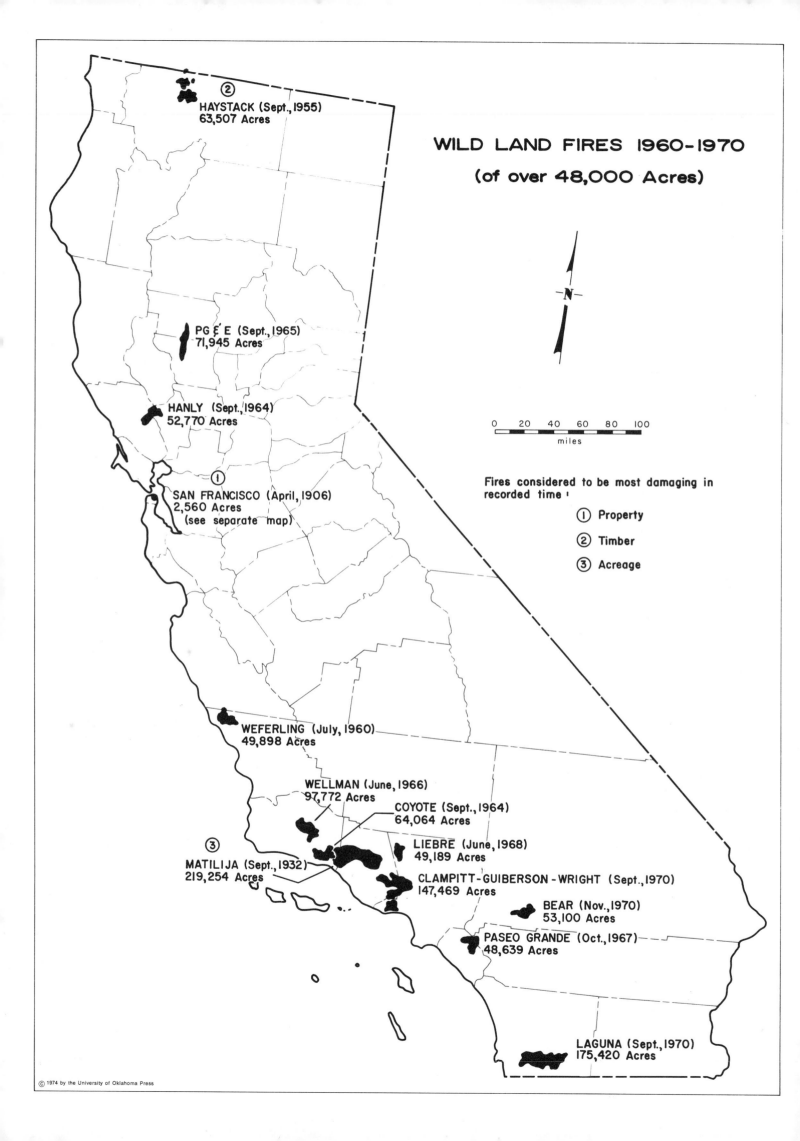

WILD LAND FIRES 1960-1970

(of over 48,000 Acres)

HAYSTACK (Sept.,1955)
63,507 Acres

PG & E (Sept.,1965)
71,945 Acres

HANLY (Sept.,1964)
52,770 Acres

SAN FRANCISCO (April,1906)
2,560 Acres
(see separate map)

WEFERLING (July,1960)
49,898 Acres

WELLMAN (June,1966)
97,772 Acres

COYOTE (Sept.,1964)
64,064 Acres

LIEBRE (June,1968)
49,189 Acres

MATILIJA (Sept.,1932)
219,254 Acres

CLAMPITT-GUIBERSON-WRIGHT (Sept.,1970)
147,469 Acres

BEAR (Nov.,1970)
53,100 Acres

PASEO GRANDE (Oct.,1967)
48,639 Acres

LAGUNA (Sept.,1970)
175,420 Acres

-N-

0 20 40 60 80 100
miles

Fires considered to be most damaging in
recorded time :

① Property

② Timber

③ Acreage

81. WILD LAND FIRES, 1960–70

NOWHERE ELSE IN the world is the potentiality of fire damage as great as it is in California. The combination of months without precipitation, high temperatures, and low relative humidity caused by "Santa Ana" winds create conditions wherein the tiniest spark can mean a destructive conflagration. Fire was a concern in primeval days, but in an age of sophisticated fire protection they are bigger and more destructive than ever. This is because the accumulation of dead and fallen undergrowth is kept from burning off and because of the carelessness of man. Destructive blazes are a worry in late spring and summer, but it is in the fall when most of California is on a fire alert. In addition to the loss of valuable timber and grazing lands, recent fires have taken a growing toll in lives and property.

In 1933 a small fire in Los Angeles' Griffith Park took the lives of twenty-nine firefighters for the largest human toll (except for the earthquake-caused San Francisco disaster). With the expansion of suburbs and resorts into brush-covered hills and forested highlands, the danger has increased. Perhaps the most spectacular of this new kind of fire (which the state Division of Forestry is reluctant to designate a forest fire) was the blaze which began in mountainous Los Angeles County on November 6, 1961. Actually two separate fires which soon joined, it roared westward through the Santa Monica Mountains into Bel Air. Destroyed were 456 homes, with an insurance valuation of some $25 million. Included were the mansions and possessions of movie stars, wealthy industrialists, and many of the leading citizens of Southern California.

The most destructive fire in the state's history (in terms of acres) was the blaze which began in the Matilija Canyon in September, 1932. It destroyed a vast area in Ventura and Santa Barbara counties before being contained. The Haystack Fire of September, 1955, in Siskiyou County consumed the greatest amount of timber. The Weferling Fire (July, 1960) was started by careless campers along the Nacimiento River in Monterey County and de-stroyed most of the watershed for the Nacimiento Reservoir. Hot, dry Santa Ana conditions in September, 1964, brought two disastrous conflagrations in widely separated areas. The Hanly Fire began near Mount Saint Helena in Napa County, country famed as the residence of Robert Louis Stevenson. It spread westward into Sonoma County, joining other minor fires to devastate a vast area. The second major blaze began at the national forest boundary on Coyote Road near Santa Barbara. This city, often threatened by fire, was in real danger as fire raged through the Santa Ynez Mountains. The P. G. & E. fire (also known as Sites) of September, 1965, was unique because of the rapidity with which it spread. Fanned by winds of 60–70 miles an hour, it quickly spread from its point of origin 9 miles northeast of Willows in Glenn County southward into Colusa County. (One motorist claimed that the flames kept up with his car on the highway!). The Wellman fire of June, 1966, was caused by the crash of a light plane in a relatively inaccessible area of Los Padres National Forest in Santa Barbara County.

In October, 1967, conditions existed which the state Division of Forestry described as "A Week of Wildfire." Santa Ana winds helped trigger more than a score of blazes from Ventura County southward to the Mexican border. Prompt action restricted all of them to minimum damage except the Paseo Grande Fire. Originating south of Corona in Riverside County, it quickly spread to Orange County. Of the acreage burned, 1,486 acres were within corporate limits of cities, resulting in the loss of $3 million in homes. In June, 1968, the Liebre Fire in Angeles National Forest near Gorman in Los Angeles County disrupted traffic on the vital Ridge Route (Interstate 5). An exceptionally hot dry summer and severe Santa Ana winds in the fall of 1970 resulted in a record in the number of fires and total acreage burned. The Laguna fire devastated the second largest area in the state's history, while the Clampett-Guiberson-Wright blaze was in third place.

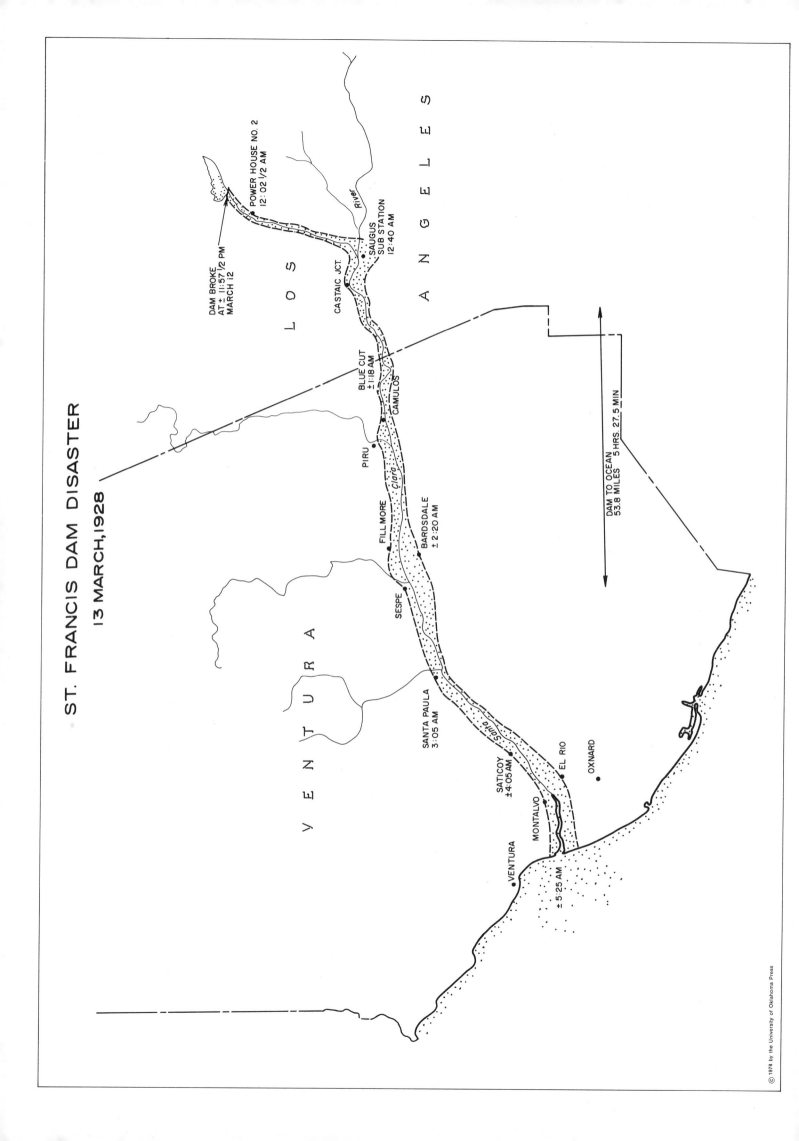

ST. FRANCIS DAM DISASTER

13 MARCH, 1928

POWER HOUSE NO. 2
12:02 1/2 AM

DAM BROKE
AT ± 11:57 1/2 PM
MARCH 12

SAUGUS
SUB STATION
12:40 AM

CASTAIC JCT.

L O S   A N G E L E S

BLUE CUT
±1:18 AM

CAMULOS

PIRU

Santa Clara

FILLMORE

BARDSDALE
± 2:20 AM

SESPE

V E N T U R A

SANTA PAULA
3:05 AM

Santa Paula

SATICOY
±4:05 AM

EL RIO

MONTALVO

OXNARD

VENTURA

± 5:25 AM

DAM TO OCEAN   5 HRS. 27.5 MIN
53.8 MILES

River

82. ST. FRANCIS DAM DISASTER

THE COLLAPSE OF the St. Francis (San Francisquito) Dam just before midnight on March 12, 1928, was the second worst disaster to strike modern California. (Only the San Francisco earthquake and fire was worse). The huge dam, built to impound water from the Owens Valley brought in by the Los Angeles aqueduct, was 600 feet long, 180 feet high, and held 38,000 acre-feet of water. It was located on the San Francisquito canyon near Saugus. When the entire structure gave way, all of the water was released to cascade through the Santa Clara Valley to the sea. Near the dam the crest of water was 60 feet high, but fell in height as it moved onward. However; it was still 25 feet high when it reached Santa Paula. The massive flood carried everything before it. Included in the debris were trees, telegraph poles, bridges, railway tracks, fences, buildings of all kinds, and the bodies of victims, most of whom were swept away without warning as they slept. In all, 385 lives were known to have been lost. (Some authorities put the figure as high as 450, since more bodies have been unearthed through the years.) Some 1,240 homes were destroyed or seriously damaged, 7,902 acres of land were flooded, and the loss of livestock and damage to farms and orchards was likewise great. Some farmland was completely washed away, while other land was badly eroded or piled 10 feet high with silt and debris; some orchards were totally destroyed, while in others some trees were uprooted or only partially damaged.

The St. Francis Dam disaster was not a natural calamity, but was the result of human error. Investigators soon determined that the structure had been erected astride a fault which even the most cursory geological survey would have revealed. Even worse was the fact that residents in the area reported hearing strange noises which suggested that the dam was breaking up. Muddy water was also sighted seeping through the abutments, and cracks appeared on the downstream face of the dam. But these indications of possible disaster were ignored by everyone in authority, although they worried residents of the area. In fact, William Mulholland, chief engineer for the Los Angeles Department of Water and Power, and an associate inspected the dam the day of the disaster and found nothing wrong. Mulholland, a self-trained engineer whose building of the Los Angeles Aqueduct won him fame as the "Goethals of the West," refused to believe that the dam he had completed only two years before was in danger. At the subsequent investigation it was claimed, but never proven, that high officials of the Department of Water and Power knew that the dam was unsafe but did nothing about it.

At the coroner's inquest Engineer Mulholland accepted full responsibility for the disaster, and the city of Los Angeles paid a series of claims possibly totaling as high as $5,500,000. No claims reached court, sometimes being discouraged by questionable practices, but were instead settled by a claims commission. There remain many aspects of the St. Francis Dam disaster that have not been decided and probably never will be. Charles Outland, who has written the most complete study of the event, concluded: "A past generation did an effective job of sweeping the dirt under the rug . . . . The evidence in the St. Francis Dam story is not unlike the Bible; one can prove or disprove any point of view he dislikes."

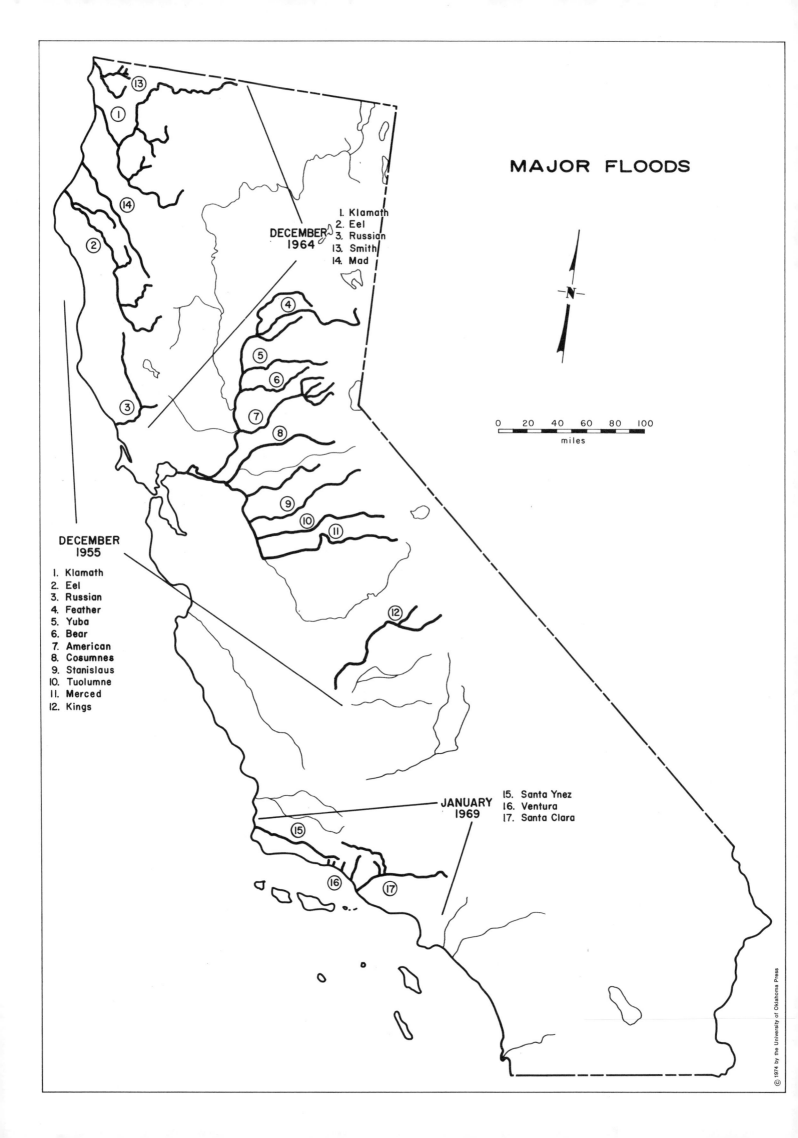

MAJOR FLOODS

N

| 0 | 20 | 40 | 60 | 80 | 100 |
miles

DECEMBER
1964

1. Klamath
2. Eel
3. Russian
13. Smith
14. Mad

DECEMBER
1955

1. Klamath
2. Eel
3. Russian
4. Feather
5. Yuba
6. Bear
7. American
8. Cosumnes
9. Stanislaus
10. Tuolumne
11. Merced
12. Kings

JANUARY
1969

15. Santa Ynez
16. Ventura
17. Santa Clara

83. MAJOR FLOODS

CALIFORNIA HAS always been ravaged by floods. Father Juan Crespi recorded in his diary in 1770 that the Los Angeles River left its banks and flooded the surrounding countryside. During the nineteenth century there were at least sixteen major floods in the state. The most devastating one occurred in 1861–62 throughout the state; it was reported that the San Joaquin Valley was an inland sea the size of Lake Michigan, and boats could sail over the tops of telegraph poles in the Sacramento Valley. Floods continued to take a heavy toll of lives and property in the twentieth century, with a most severe one in the San Diego area in 1916. All of southern California suffered in the great storm of 1938. As the state has increased in population, and subdivisions have proliferated on hillsides subject to mudslides and in valleys subject to periodic flooding, the loss of life and property has increased. Among the most disastrous floods in the state's history were those of 1955, 1964, and 1969.

Atmospheric conditions bringing flood-causing precipitation in recent years and probably causing those of an earlier day have been virtually the same. First there is a cold air mass out of Alaska moving in a cyclonic bend over the southern Gulf of Alaska and the states of Washington and Oregon; second, there is the westerly movement of a warm, moist air mass over the Pacific from near Hawaii toward the California coastline; third, there is a low pressure trough off the coast. When the two air masses collide, there is a strong flow of moist air towards the coast which is increased by the presence of the low pressure trough. The result is record precipitation; San Diego recorded 16 inches in a 24-hour period in 1916, and in 1955 many stations had more than 12 inches of rainfall in a single day.

According to some experts, the flood of December, 1955, recorded flood-water highs which equaled or exceeded those of the legendary 1861–62 disaster. Coastal and valley areas from Santa Barbara north to the Oregon line were badly damaged. More than 1 million acres of land were inundated, and thousands of head of livestock were lost. Property dam-

ages exceeded $200 million and 64 lives were lost. Some communities in the north coastal area were totally destroyed. Hardest hit were Yuba City, Stockton, Fresno, Visalia, Santa Cruz, Watsonville, Eureka, Klamath, Santa Rosa, Guerneville, and the towns in the Sacramento–San Joaquin Delta. Most of the flood damage occurred along streams essentially unregulated by reservoir storage. One result of the disaster was increased flood protection through enactment of what came to be known as the California Water Plan.

The floods of December 1964–January 1965 were similar to those of 1955. Runoff from the streams of the northern coastal range (Smith, Klamath, and Eel), and from the Feather, Yuba, and American rivers surpassed all previous records. Thirty-four counties incurred damage, but six counties suffered complete havoc: Del Norte, Humboldt, Mendocino, Siskiyou, Trinity, and Sonoma. In these counties the damage was several times that of the record flood of 1955. Ten communities were totally destroyed. Of the 24 lives lost, 19 perished in Humboldt County. Destruction in the Central Valley area was extensive, but far below that of the 1955 disaster. The construction of dams, reservoirs, channels, bypasses, and levees since that flood has aided man in his endless struggle with high water.

During January, 1969, precipitation ranged from 195 per cent of normal in the northern part of the state to 550 per cent in the south coastal area. The result was the most severe flood in southern California since 1938. Forty counties were declared disaster areas, but most severely damaged were Santa Barbara, Ventura, Orange, Los Angeles, San Bernardino, and Riverside counties. Many of the 47 deaths recorded were a result of mudslides—which also accounted for much of the property losses. The greatest devastation was in or near heavily populated communities, in contrast to the 1955 and 1964–65 floods. Since most people live on the floodplains of southern California, it is reasonable to anticipate more such disastrous floods.

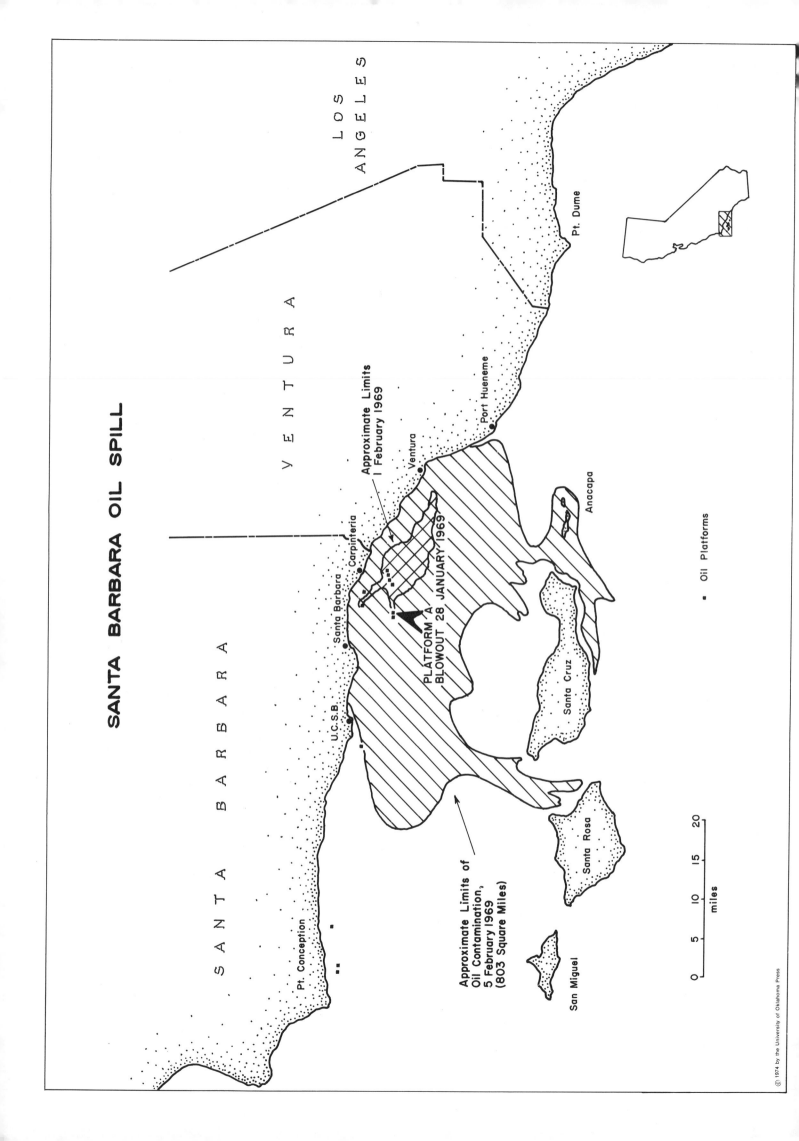

SANTA BARBARA OIL SPILL

S A N T A   B A R B A R A

V E N T U R A

L O S
A N G E L E S

Pt. Conception

Santa Barbara

U.C.S.B.

Carpinteria

Ventura

Port Hueneme

Pt. Dume

PLATFORM A
BLOWOUT 28 JANUARY 1969

Approximate Limits
1 February 1969

Approximate Limits of
Oil Contamination,
5 February 1969
(803 Square Miles)

San Miguel

Santa Rosa

Santa Cruz

Anacapa

■ Oil Platforms

0   5   10   15   20

miles

84. SANTA BARBARA OIL SPILL

IN THE MORNING of January 28, 1969, a blowout occurred at the fifth well drilled from Platform A in the Santa Barbara Channel. The huge platform was as high as a twenty-story building and was located some 5 miles offshore in about 180 feet of water. It marked the beginning of work on the seventy-one leases sold by the federal government to several oil companies in 1968 for the record sum of $603 million. The oil industry believed the channel was one of the richest petroleum fields in the nation and that they would soon recoup their investment. Thus, the blowout was a disaster to the oil men. However, it was an absolute catastrophe to Santa Barbara and the surrounding communities.

The great pressure in the well ruptured the bottom of the channel, and within twenty-four hours of the blowout, oil and gas were seeping from several fissures in the ocean floor and spreading in an east-west zone some 250 feet west of the platform and about 1,050 feet east of the platform. The oil-contaminated zone grew to the area marked on the map by February 1, and by February 5 covered an approximate area of 803 square miles. The massive slicks stretched more than 20 miles down the coast and, in some places, as much as 40 miles to sea. By the end of March, two months after the blowout, most of the mainland shores of the Santa Barbara Channel and much of the Channel Islands had been contaminated. Eventually, all of the mainland channel beaches were affected by the oil.

The oil industry was slow in halting the flow of oil and was incapable of doing anything about the oil once it had been released into the channel. The best solution was to throw straw on the oily waters to absorb the petroleum. More than a thousand men then piled the oil-soaked straw on the beaches until it could be hauled away. And only a small percentage of the oil could be removed; most of it settled to the deep basin of the channel. Meanwhile, more than 3,600 birds died as a result of the pollution and the long run effect on the ecology of the channel may ruin it for marine life for years to come. The stench from the gooey mass drove many residents from coastal homes (Santa Barbara is one of the preferred residential areas in the world). Tourism declined because of the fouling of the beach, and fishing, both commercial and sport, virtually came to a halt. The oil companies spent some $5 million to clean up the mess.

The long-range impact of the Santa Barbara oil spill is impossible to determine at this writing. One study (carried out by a University of Southern California foundation) found that damage to beaches, flora, and fauna was "much less than predicted" and that "The area is recovering well." It was claimed that tests "failed to reveal any effects of oil pollution" on the channel's zooplankton and phytoplankton. Conservationists vigorously challenge the accuracy of this study and accuse the researchers of "selling out to the oil companies." At least one significant result of the oil spill has been to dramatize man's effort to clean up his environment. One observer contends that the oil industry has fired "the ecological shot heard around the world." Since the blowout more progress has been made by ecologists than in any previous period in the nation's history. The oil in Santa Barbara Channel helped shock Congress into passing the National Environmental Policy Act, a cornerstone of federal legislation on this issue. Efforts of enraged Santa Barbara citizenry to halt all oil drilling in the channel through the organization, Get Oil Out (GOO), has not been successful at this writing. Perhaps the only thing sure about the future of oil drilling in the Santa Barbara Channel is that the highly faulted and earthquake-prone ocean floor likely will be the scene of many more such spills.

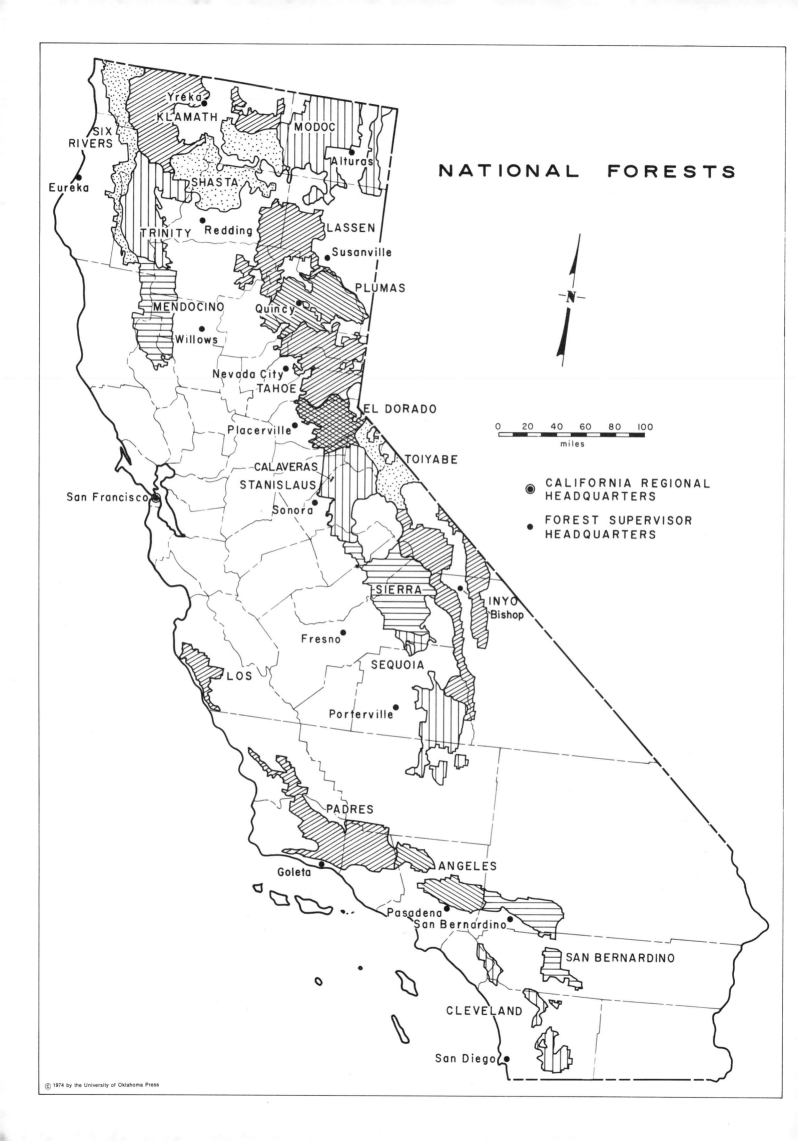

NATIONAL FORESTS

SIX RIVERS

KLAMATH

Yreka

MODOC

Alturas

SHASTA

Eureka

TRINITY

Redding

LASSEN

Susanville

PLUMAS

MENDOCINO

Quincy

Willows

Nevada City

TAHOE

EL DORADO

Placerville

TOIYABE

CALAVERAS

STANISLAUS

Sonora

San Francisco

SIERRA

INYO

Bishop

Fresno

SEQUOIA

LOS

Porterville

PADRES

Goleta

ANGELES

Pasadena

San Bernardino

SAN BERNARDINO

CLEVELAND

San Diego

0 20 40 60 80 100
miles

◉ CALIFORNIA REGIONAL
   HEADQUARTERS

● FOREST SUPERVISOR
   HEADQUARTERS

85. NATIONAL FORESTS

Angeles National Forest (648,866 acres). Headquarters: Pasadena, California.

Calaveras Bigtree (379 acres). Headquarters: Sonora, California.

Cleveland National Forest (393,085 acres). Headquarters: San Diego, California.

Eldorado National Forest (652,527 acres). Headquarters: Placerville, California.

Inyo National Forest (1,835,960 acres, partly in Nevada). Headquarters: Bishop, California.

Klamath National Forest (1,696,965 acres, partly in Oregon). Headquarters: Yreka, California.

Lassen National Forest (1,045,624 acres). Headquarters: Susanville, California.

Los Padres National Forest (1,724,108 acres). Headquarters: Goleta, California.

Mendocino National Forest (872,237 acres). Headquarters: Willows, California.

Modoc National Forest (1,689,508 acres). Headquarters: Alturas, California.

Plumas National Forest (1,146,732 acres). Headquarters: Quincy, California.

San Bernardino National Forest (616,315 acres). Headquarters: San Bernardino, California.

Sequoia National Forest (1,115,858 acres). Headquarters: Porterville, California.

Shasta National Forest (1,003,265 acres). Headquarters: Redding, California.

Sierra National Forest (1,293,180 acres). Headquarters: Fresno, California.

Six Rivers National Forest (939,399 acres). Headquarters: Eureka, California.

Stanislaus National Forest (896,312 acres). Headquarters: Sonora, California.

Tahoe National Forest (696,777 acres). Headquarters: Nevada City, California.

Toiyabe National Forest (694,661 acres) (Administered from Ogden).

Trinity National Forest (1,062,989 acres). Headquarters: Redding, California.

National forests comprise the largest single forest area in California, including approximately half of the timber acreage. More than 24 million acres are included in the total. Some of this area comprises the finest timber-growing land in the state, but much of it is relatively inaccessible high mountain land with little or no timber.

The national forests are managed for multiple use. Commercial cutting of timber under prescribed regulations is permitted. The national forests yield more than 1.3 billion board feet of timber each year, most of it as processed lumber, and more than 100,000 cattle and 85,000 sheep annually graze on national forest rangeland. Grazing land and mineral rights are leased. Watershed is another important function. One of the greatest attractions of the national forests is for recreation purposes, for winter as well as summer sports.

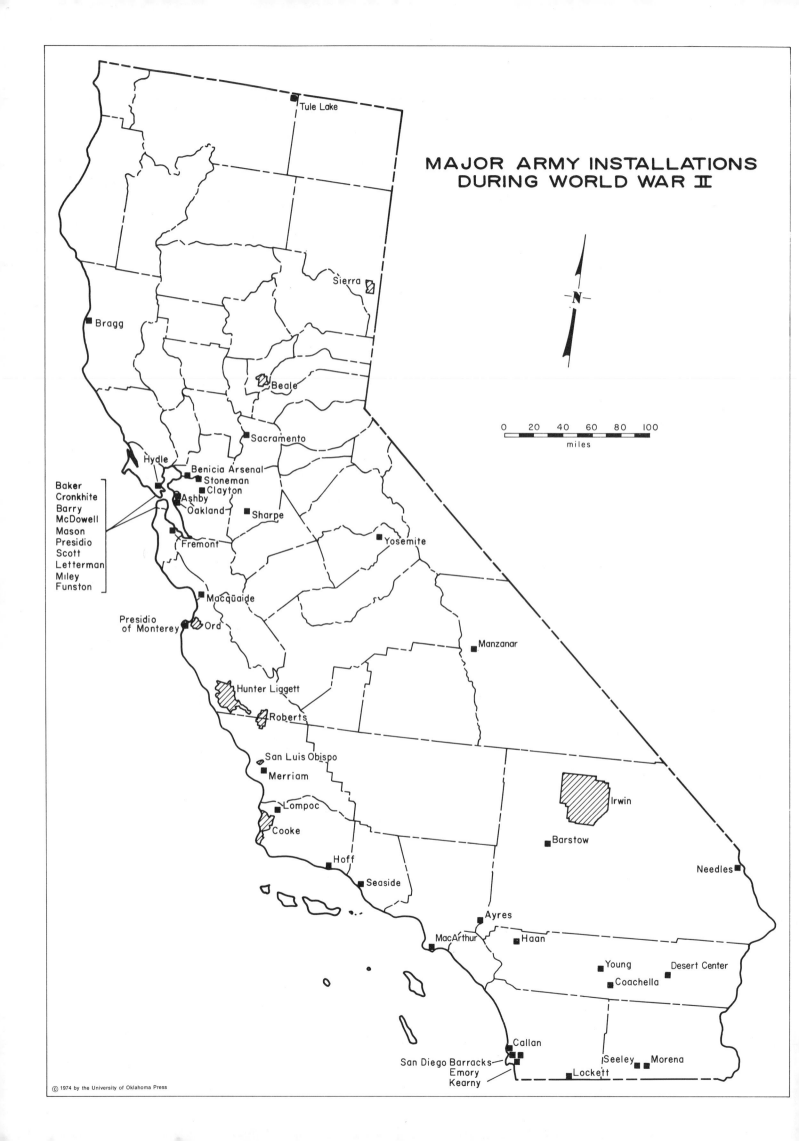

MAJOR ARMY INSTALLATIONS
DURING WORLD WAR II

-N-

0   20   40   60   80   100
miles

Tule Lake

Sierra

Bragg

Beale

Sacramento

Hydle
Benicia Arsenal
Stoneman
Clayton
Baker
Cronkhite   Ashby
Barry   Oakland
McDowell   Sharpe
Mason
Presidio
Scott   Fremont
Letterman
Miley
Funston

Yosemite

Macquaide

Presidio   Ord
of Monterey

Manzanar

Hunter Liggett

Roberts

San Luis Obispo

Merriam   Irwin

Lompoc

Cooke   Barstow

Hoff   Needles

Seaside

Ayres

MacArthur   Haan

Young   Desert Center
Coachella

Callan

San Diego Barracks   Seeley   Morena
Emory   Lockett
Kearny

THE UNITED STATES Army used California extensively to train men for both the Atlantic and Pacific theaters. To supply the Asian war there were numerous arsenals, ammunition and supply depots, and ordnance centers such as: the Benicia Arsenal, Oakland Army Terminal, Sacramento Army Depot. Sharpe Army Depot, The Sierra Army Depot, and Yermo Depot (near Barstow).

Old established installations were greatly expanded to meet wartime demands. Included were these in the San Diego area: San Diego Barracks. Fort Emory, Camp Kearny, and Fort Rosecrans. some of which dated back to the Mexican War era. Camp Callan, near La Jolla, is a World War II facility. Fort MacArthur was commissioned in 1917 to guard Los Angeles harbor, but was on or near the site of earlier military facilities. Named after General Arthur MacArthur, it was originally a coast artillery post. The large number of military centers around San Francisco, some of which date from Spanish days, attest to the importance of that area. They include Forts Baker, Cronkhite, Barry, McDowell (on Angel Island), Mason, the Presidio, Scott, Letterman General Hospital, Miley, and Funston. World War II training centers include the following camps: Hydle, Stoneman, Clayton, Ashby, and Fremont.

One of the largest training centers was located at Fort Ord. Sub-posts of Ord include the temporary facilities at Camp MacQuaide, the venerable Presidio of Monterey, the Hunter Liggett Military Reservation (until 1940 a part of the William Randolph Hearst ranch), and Camp Roberts. Farther south, Camp San Luis Obispo, which had been activated as a national guard camp in 1928, was greatly expanded as an infantry division training center. Camps Merriam, Lompoc, and Cooke were nearby training posts. Hoff General Hospital, in Santa Barbara, was one of the leading army hospitals in the state. Camp Beale, with 86,488 acres, was one of the larger training camps.

A basic reason why California had such a large concentration of army installations during World War II was the large amount of sparsely occupied land which could be purchased or leased for minimum fees. Geographic conditions also made it possible to prepare troops for desert combat, mountain climbing, or test survival techniques in snow and cold. Fort Irwin (originally Camp Irwin) includes some of the most rugged and difficult terrain of the Mojave Desert among its 1,000 square miles. Originally used as an anti-aircraft range, it housed such distinguished units as the "Desert Commandos." It was (and still is), the best training ground for armored units in the United States. Camp Young (near Indio), occupied land similar to that of Fort Irwin, and was the nucleus of the far-flung Desert Training Center. Most important in this complex were camps at Coachella and Needles. General George S. Patton, Jr. used the 162,000 square miles of this center to prepare his armored units for their fabled exploits in North Africa. Camps Seeley, Morena, and Lockett were also desert training facilities. Camp Haan, near March Field, was an infantry training center which also utilized rugged terrain.

Other army facilities included the Manzanar and Tule Lake Evacuee Reception Centers used to house the Japanese internees. Camp Ayres (near Chino), and Fort Bragg were used as prisoner of war encampments.

MAJOR ARMY AIR FORCE
INSTALLATIONS DURING
WORLD WAR II

—N—

0   20   40   60   80   100
miles

Redding

Chico

Oroville

Marysville

McClellan
Mather
Santa Rosa
Suisun
Hamilton
Concord
Oakland   Stockton
Crissy
Alameda
Hayward

San Jose

Castle (Merced)

Bishop

Salinas

Hammer

Lemoore   Visalia

Porterville

Estrella   Delano

Minter
Gardner   Bakersfield

Santa Maria

Muroc

Palmdale

Victorville   Needles

Oxnard

Ontario   San Bernardino
Mines
Rice
March
Santa Ana   Palm Springs
Long Beach   Desert Center
Thermal   Blythe

CALIFORNIA WAS a preferred area for Army Air Force installations for two reasons: first, bases had to be located for purposes of continental defense, and there was fear of a Japanese attack on the West Coast during the first two years of war; second, the state was a desirable area for training because weather conditions seldom curtailed flying. Most air fields in California were multi-purpose; they had to be suitable for employment by bombardment, fighter, and air support aviation. After the emergency created by Pearl Harbor, the Air Force utilized municipal air fields extensively. In addition, the Army Air Force maintained commands at several naval installations at various periods during the war. In some instances, the services even exchanged or loaned their facilities. For example, Moffett Field (Sunnyvale) was originally built as a naval dirigible base in 1930 but was transferred to the Army in 1935. However, it was returned to navy control in 1941, but the Army Air Force continued a command at the base. After 1943, several Army Air Fields were used by the Navy. The Army Air Force trained pilots at private flying schools (under military supervision), mechanics at civil or factory training schools, and meteorological instruction was given at colleges and universities. Thus, Army Air Force installations in California were so numerous that only the most important have been designated.

Some airfields, like March, dated back to World War I, but most were built just before or during the first two years of World War II. Hamilton Field was constructed early in the 1930's to protect the San Francisco area and became headquarters for the 4th Air Support Command. The Sacramento Air Depot (McClellan Field) was activated in 1939. San Bernardino was the site of a second air depot. The dry lake bed at Muroc was first used as a bombing and gunnery range in 1933, but was used to train B–29 pilots in 1945 (later Edwards AFB). Stockton airport was taken over by the military in 1940. Gardner, Hammer, Mather, and Minter Fields were authorized in the fall of 1940 and were active by the following spring. Lemoore, Chico, Merced (Castle), and Victorville (George) were planned but not finished before the outbreak of war. Salinas became the base for the observation squadrons when Moffett Field was regained by the Navy. Fairfield-Suisun (later Travis) was an important part of the Air Transport Command. The facility at Santa Maria was the first authorized in California after Pearl Harbor. In early 1942 Air Force tactical units moved to airports at San Bernardino, Long Beach, Bakersfield, Oakland, Sacramento and Mines Field (Inglewood). The Santa Ana Army Airbase opened in February, 1942, as the aviation cadet classification center for the West Coast.

All of the Army Air Force installations had subbases and auxiliary fields to handle the increased personnel assigned to them. Some, such as Rice, were small, with quarters for only 20 officers and 100 enlisted men and a single airstrip. Others utilized tents, field kitchens, and similar temporary facilities. This was especially true of the bases used to support desert training. Small fields were also necessary adjuncts to army ground forces training installations.

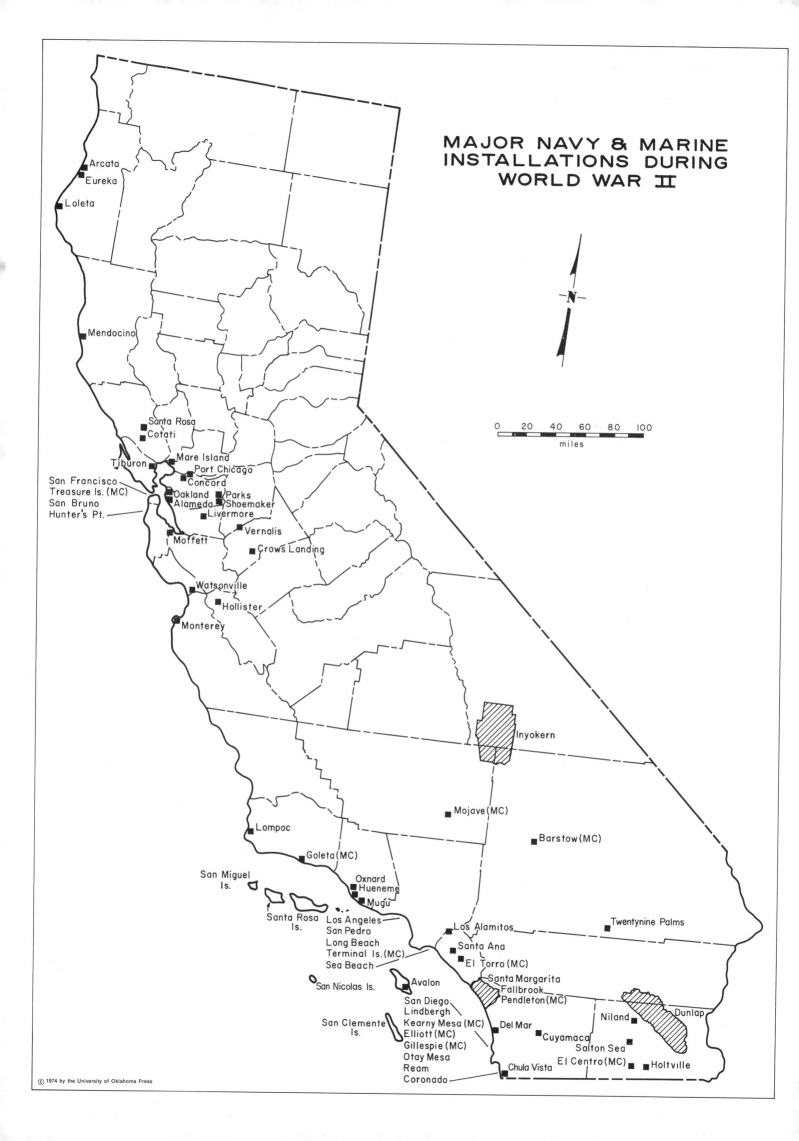

MAJOR NAVY & MARINE
INSTALLATIONS DURING
WORLD WAR II

N

0 20 40 60 80 100
miles

Arcata
Eureka
Loleta

Mendocino

Santa Rosa
Cotati

Tiburon
Mare Island
Port Chicago
Concord
San Francisco
Treasure Is. (MC)
Oakland   Parks
San Bruno   Shoemaker
Alameda
Hunter's Pt.   Livermore
Moffett
Vernalis
Crows Landing

Watsonville
Hollister
Monterey

Inyokern

Mojave (MC)

Lompoc

Barstow (MC)

Goleta (MC)

San Miguel
Is.

Oxnard
Hueneme
Mugu

Santa Rosa
Is.

Los Angeles
San Pedro
Long Beach
Terminal Is. (MC)
Sea Beach

Los Alamitos

Twentynine Palms

Santa Ana
El Torro (MC)

San Nicolas Is.

Avalon

Santa Margarita
Fallbrook
Pendleton (MC)

San Clemente
Is.

San Diego
Lindbergh
Kearny Mesa (MC)
Elliott (MC)
Gillespie (MC)
Otay Mesa
Ream
Coronado

Del Mar

Niland

Dunlap

Cuyamaca
Salton Sea
El Centro (MC)   Holtville

Chula Vista

THE UNITED STATES Navy, reflecting the fact that much of the war was fought in the Pacific theater, had hundreds of installations in California during World War II. They included numerous shipyard facilities (public and private) , a bewildering array of coastguard shore stations, ordnance and supply depots, naval and marine training centers, naval and marine aviation shore facilities, as well as many hospitals and receiving centers. They are so numerous that it is impractical to list them all. In the San Diego area alone there were more than a hundred navy facilities, including the headquarters of Eleventh Naval District. The San Pedro–Long Beach area likewise was dotted with naval bases of all types. R.O.T.C. and V–12 units were found on many college campuses. San Francisco, headquarters of the Twelfth Naval District, had an even greater concentration. Many installations which ostensibly were independent units were actually sub-divisions of parent bases. Then, too, a Marine detachment was assigned to each naval unit for guard duty.

Naval Auxiliary Air Stations (NAAS) had as their function "operational training for fleet units." They were located at: Brown Field, Chula Vista, Camp Kearny, Salton Sea, Holtville, Los Alamitos, Ream Field, San Ysidro, San Clemente Island, San Nicolas Island, Twenty-nine Palms, Oxnard, Arcata, Hollister, and Oakland. Naval Air Stations (NAS) also did fleet air training, served as headquarters for naval district commanders, were major shipping centers for aircraft and aircraft supplies, and acted as assembly and overhaul centers. NAS locations in California were at San Diego, Alameda, and Terminal Island. Auxiliary Air Facilities (NAAF) under the Alameda headquarters command were located at: Livermore, Vernalis, Crow's Landing, Mills Field, San Francisco, Monterey, and Santa Rosa. A Naval Air Facility (NAF) at the Naval Ordnance Test Station at Inyokern was mainly experimental, but was also used for training purposes. Naval bases were also located as adjuncts to other activities, such as the bases on the Port Hueneme complex and Terminal Island. Similar facilities were also at Lindbergh Field (San Diego) and Mendocino. Marine Corps Air Stations (MCAS) were located at: El Centro, El Toro, Goleta, and Mojave. A Marine Corps Air Depot (MCAD) was at Miramar (San Diego) and a Marine Corps Aviation Base at Kearny Mesa (San Diego).

The Naval Air Station at Santa Ana had as its function shore patrol against submarines utilizing lighter than air (LTA) equipment. Auxiliary (to Santa Ana) LTA bases were at Del Mar and Lompoc. Moffett Field at Sunnyvale was the LTA center in northern California, with auxiliary fields at Eureka and Watsonville.

Headquarters for Marine Corps training was at Camp Elliott, but actually embraced the entire San Diego area. Rancho Santa Margarita (near Oceanside) , which became Camp Joseph H. Pendleton, was the largest installation, with some 38,000 officers and men. Camp Dunlap was another important training center, but amphibious practice was also conducted along the coast and on the islands of southern California. Barstow was (and is) the main Marine supply depot. An area near Lake Cuyamaca was utilized to train Marines for jungle warfare. Camp Gillespie was originally used for parachute training, but was designated as a Marine Corps Air Facility in February, 1944.

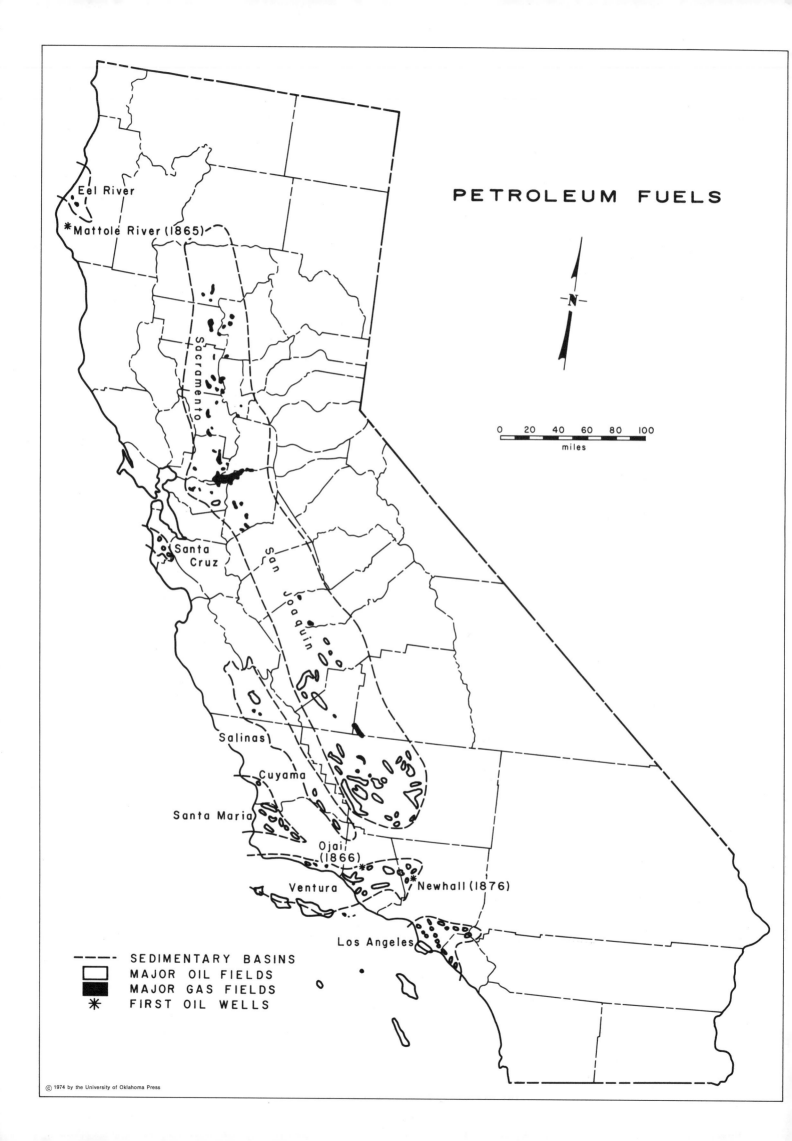

PETROLEUM FUELS

Eel River

* Mattole River (1865)

Sacramento

Santa Cruz

San Joaquin

Salinas

Cuyama

Santa Maria

Ojai (1866)

Ventura

* Newhall (1876)

Los Angeles

- - - SEDIMENTARY BASINS
□ MAJOR OIL FIELDS
■ MAJOR GAS FIELDS
* FIRST OIL WELLS

N

0 20 40 60 80 100
miles

89. PETROLEUM FUELS

PETROLEUM HAS JUSTLY been labeled "Black Gold," for its value in California has several times exceeded that of the more romantic gold. Indians found many uses for it before the arrival of the white man. Lighter oils were used for the treatment of burns and cuts. Heavier oil waterproofed baskets and roofs. In 1855 Andrés Pico collected tar seepings in a canyon near Newhall and sold it for medicine, as a lubricant, and for lamp fuel.

The expanded use of oil in the East in the late 1850's caused a growing interest in California petroleum. When the Civil War curtailed the supply of kerosene from the East, efforts to exploit local oil were increased. The first drilled well was near Petrolia, on the Mattole River, in 1865. The second was near Ojai the following year. There were also early wells in the Newhall area, but by 1867 the first oil boom was over. For the next two decades promising wells were found in most of the sedimentary basins, and a pattern was developed in the California oil fields which was repeated many times: an infusion of money from the East accompanied by oil experts would occur, but the high hopes were seldom realized. Much of California's oil was in small pockets which were soon exhausted, and the drilling techniques were not yet sufficiently advanced to deal with the faulted, fractured, and folded source rocks. Neither were refining techniques sufficiently advanced to handle the petroleum of the Golden State. California oil contained more carbon and less paraffin than eastern crude oils, and thus was less desirable for either lighting or lubrication.

Numerous efforts to solve these drilling and refining problems met with some success, and a production of 40,000 barrels in 1880 increased annually to 377,000 barrels by 1886. The 1890's saw a continued expansion in production, with rich new fields in Los Angeles and the San Joaquin Valley. New uses for oil, besides kerosene, were provided when oil-burning equipment was installed in the power plants of Los Angeles and was developed for steam locomotives and ships. Asphalt was also used for street surfacing. After 1900, the advent of the automobile provided a rapidly expanding market for petroleum products. In 1903 California led the nation in oil production, a position it held until 1936. Oil production and refining became one of the state's leading industries. In the second half of the twentieth century, the southern part of the San Joaquin Valley and Los Angeles County fields were most important. However, offshore oil production accounts for an increasing share of the state's oil production, rising from 8.9 per cent in 1959 to 17.9 per cent in 1967. Despite the importance of such offshore drilling and the key role of petroleum in the state's economy, the disastrous leakage from wells in the ocean near Santa Barbara in 1969 prompted many Californians to question this method of obtaining oil.

Natural gas production is mainly in the Sacramento Valley, with minor fields in the San Joaquin Valley. Production has risen steadily, but demands have far exceeded California's supply. Hence, much of the natural gas consumed in the state is piped from New Mexico.

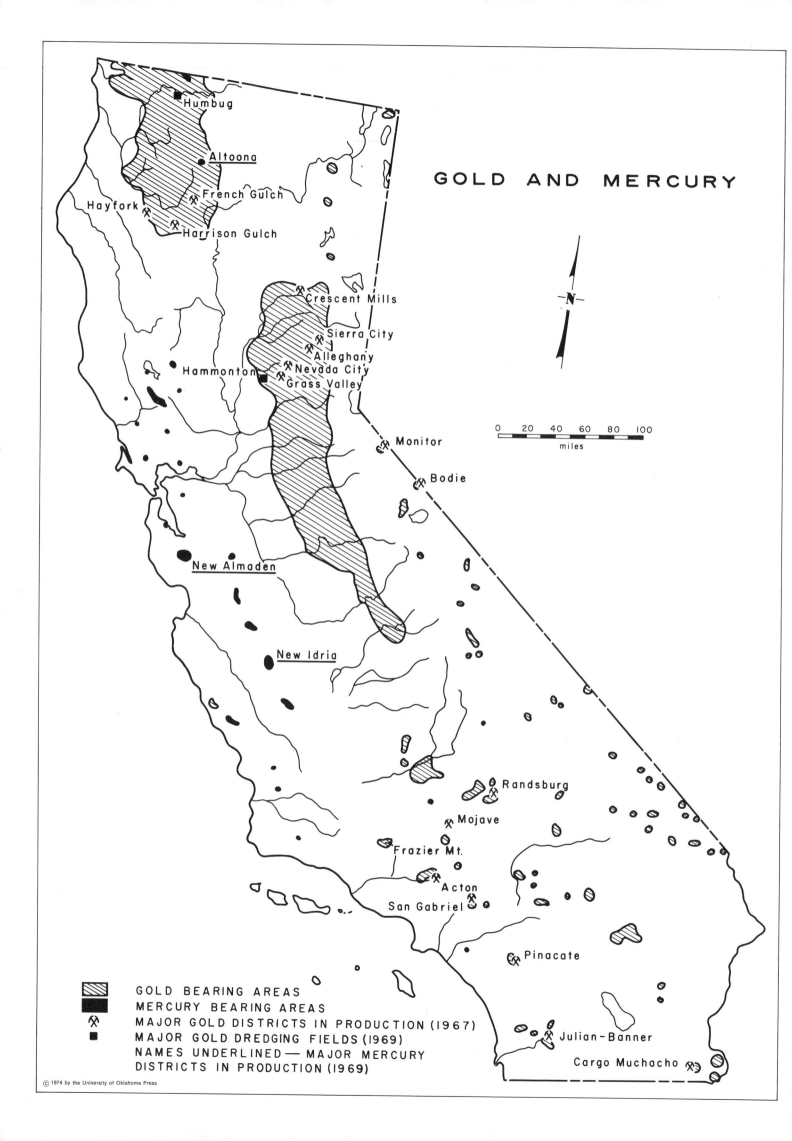

GOLD AND MERCURY

Humbug

Altoona

French Gulch

Hayfork

Harrison Gulch

Crescent Mills

Sierra City

Alleghany

Hammonton

Nevada City

Grass Valley

Monitor

Bodie

New Almaden

New Idria

Randsburg

Mojave

Frazier Mt.

Acton

San Gabriel

Pinacate

Julian-Banner

Cargo Muchacho

0 20 40 60 80 100
miles

-N-

GOLD BEARING AREAS
MERCURY BEARING AREAS
MAJOR GOLD DISTRICTS IN PRODUCTION (1967)
MAJOR GOLD DREDGING FIELDS (1969)
NAMES UNDERLINED — MAJOR MERCURY
DISTRICTS IN PRODUCTION (1969)

90. GOLD AND MERCURY

As Professor John Walton Caughey has put it, "gold is the cornerstone of California." It was gold that triggered the mass influx of people between 1848 and 1860, which saw the population jump from 14,000 to 300,000. Nowhere else in the world has so much gold been laid out by nature for the taking, and take it the Argonauts did! A boy of fourteen cleared some $3,400 in a few weeks' mining. Some placers produced $30,000 to $50,000 a day. In 1860 there were 83,537 men who listed their occupation as mining.

By 1852, gold production was worth more than 80 million dollars. The average annual value of the output in the period from 1850 to 1865 was 50 million. After 1865 to the end of the century, gold production was relatively stable, averaging from 10 to 20 million dollars a year. By 1970, California had produced almost 2.5 billion dollars worth of gold or some 35 per cent of the nation's total.

Most of the metal obtained in the early days of the gold rush came from placer deposits. Because of its high specific gravity and resistance to weathering, gold was concentrated in placers. All of the streams flowing through the gold bearing region have been productive. The gold particles vary in size from microscopic (flour gold) to nuggets weighing seven or eight pounds. Gold was initially easy to obtain from such deposits, and only a pick and shovel, a pan, and water were necessary for the amateur miners. However, after placer gold, which had been accumulating for centuries, had been taken, more sophisticated technology had to be evolved for hydraulic and quartz mining. Such changes made necessary tremendous capital investment, thus eliminating the individual prospector.

The Sierra Nevada, the dominant mountain range in California, has been the source of most of the state's gold output. Second are the Klamath Mountains, with the Klamath, Trinity, and Salmon rivers having the richest deposits. But gold is also found in scattered areas of the state, and hardly a decade passed between 1870 and 1910 without a gold rush somewhere in California. However, no really rich deposits were discovered, and modern technology has not yet found it profitable to mine low-grade ores, especially with inadequate supplies of water. Gold production, which declined rapidly during World War I, experienced a sharp upturn in the 1930's but collapsed during World War II and has not recovered. The last large mine on the Mother Lode was closed in 1953, and the large mines at Grass Valley ceased operation in 1956. Mines at Alleghany, the last quartz mining region, have curtailed operations and are now virtually shut down. The last major dredging field at Hammonton is also barely operative. The some $2 million in gold California still produces annually is either a byproduct of other mining, produced by skin divers or a few prospectors, or by small-scale dredging or placer mining operations. Truly, gold mining in California belongs to the past.

Mercury, the silver-colored liquid metal commonly known as quicksilver, has many industrial uses today. However, it was first sought because it was indispensable in the amalgam processing of gold and silver ore. California produces about 85 percent of the United States production. The New Alamaden mine is the state's leading producer. Indians are believed to have worked the mine, but it was first discovered by white men in 1824 and began production in 1846. The New Idria mine, which began operation in 1853, is second in importance. As gold and silver production expanded in the nineteenth century there was increased demand for mercury. Mines in Lake, Napa, Sonoma, Trinity, Inyo, Santa Barbara and Orange counties came into production. Some of these mines produced mercury during periods of high prices and, though inoperative today, could again be tapped to expand mercury production.

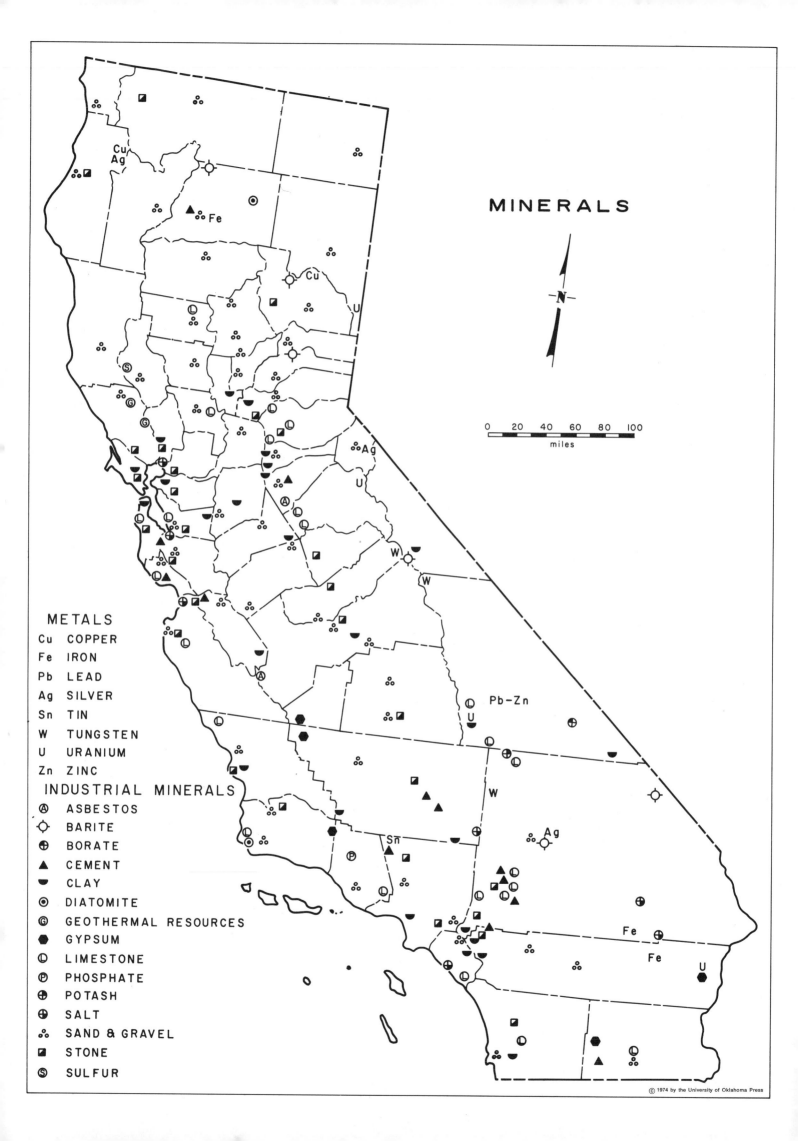

MINERALS

—N—

0   20   40   60   80   100
miles

METALS

Cu COPPER
Fe IRON
Pb LEAD
Ag SILVER
Sn TIN
W   TUNGSTEN
U   URANIUM
Zn ZINC

INDUSTRIAL MINERALS

Ⓐ ASBESTOS
◇ BARITE
⊕ BORATE
▲ CEMENT
◗ CLAY
◉ DIATOMITE
Ⓖ GEOTHERMAL RESOURCES
⬢ GYPSUM
Ⓛ LIMESTONE
Ⓟ PHOSPHATE
⊕ POTASH
⊕ SALT
∴ SAND & GRAVEL
◪ STONE
Ⓢ SULFUR

91. MINERALS

As the map indicates, California is rich in the variety of mineral resources found in virtually every part of the state. More than 700 different species have been identified in California, and there are even 45 minerals that do not occur elsewhere in the world. In recent years California was ahead of all other states in the production of asbestos, boron, cement, diatomite, mercury, pumice, rare earths, sand and gravel, talc, and tungsten. In addition, the state has been among the top three states in the production of the following:

Bromide	Peat
Calcium chloride	Petroleum
Chromite	Platinum
Feldspar	Potash
Gold	Pyrite
Gypsum	Sodium carbonate
Iodine	Sodium sulfate
Iron ore	Strontium
Lithium salts	Sulfur ore
Refractory and	Tin
caustic magnesia	Wollastonite
Natural gas liquids	

Among the metals mined in California, copper is of little importance. Most of the production was between 1891–1930, with a peak production of 25,000 tons in 1909. Active mines which have been important in the past are in Plumas and Humboldt Counties. There are ample copper reserves in the state, but with the high cost of mining and smelting and the recent emphasis on anti-pollution there is litle likelihood of expanded production. Only small quantities of iron ore were produced in California before World War II. The building of the Kaiser Steel plant at Fontana provided an outlet for iron ore that has continued. Ninety-nine per cent of the ore comes from the Mojave Desert in San Bernardino and Riverside counties. Iron ore is exported to Japan at present, and future production will undoubtedly increase.

Silver is second only to gold as the most glamorous of the precious metals. It was mined along with gold from the 1850's on, and was found in approximately the same area (i.e., the Mother Lode country of the Sierra Nevada and the Klamath Mountains). However, there were rich silver mines opened at Calico in 1881, at Mojave in 1894, and at Randsburg in 1919. Like gold, it has declined in importance in recent years, and today 90 per cent of production is a by-product of other mining operations, with the major installations in the Mojave Desert in San Bernardino County, and in Humboldt County.

Tin was reportedly mined in California in the 1850's and 1860's, but the first production of record was in 1891. Wartime shortages led to some mining in the Gorman district at the edge of Kern County from 1943 to 1945. Activity was renewed in 1963, but with only a few tons produced annually. Tungsten is an important ferroalloy essential in the manufacture of high-grade steel. Production figures in recent years have been classified, but it is assumed that California leads the nation. Tungsten mining in the state began in 1905 at Atolia, San Bernardino County, a district still important. Productive mines are also found in Inyo and Madera counties, with extensive reserves available. Uranium was first mined in California in 1954, from deposits in Kern and San Bernardino counties, and ore has been shipped from seventeen different districts in the state. However, limited production is recorded in Inyo, Tuolumne, and Lassen counties.

Total value of mineral production in California has risen in the twentieth century despite the decline in importance of the exotic metals. Cement, sand and gravel, stone, and boron minerals account for 90 per cent of the value of industrial minerals. The tremendous influx of population triggered by World War II and the post-war boom, along with a rapid expansion of industry, has led to a constantly spiraling demand for industrial minerals. Fortunately, the state is rich in such minerals and has the potential to meet most foreseeable demands. Even in new fields such as geothermal energy, California is well endowed.

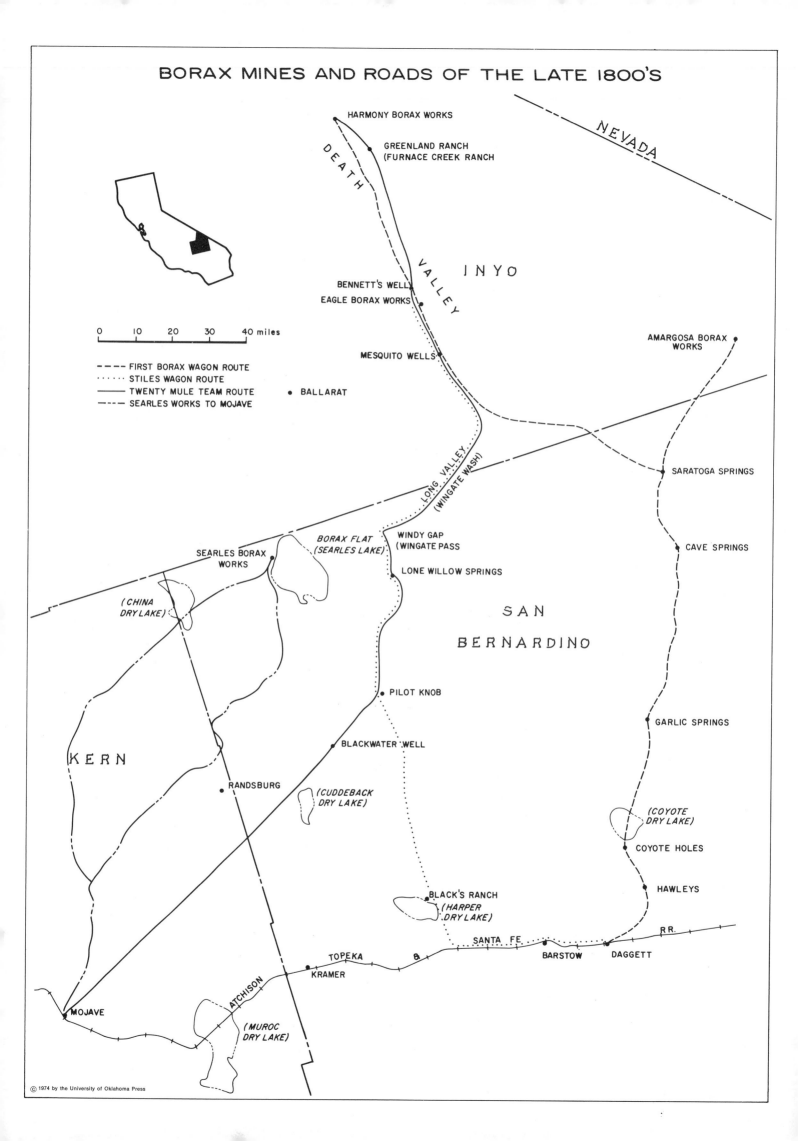

BORAX MINES AND ROADS OF THE LATE 1800'S

HARMONY BORAX WORKS

GREENLAND RANCH
(FURNACE CREEK RANCH

DEATH

VALLEY

INYO

NEVADA

BENNETT'S WELL
EAGLE BORAX WORKS

AMARGOSA BORAX
WORKS

0   10   20   30   40 miles

– – – FIRST BORAX WAGON ROUTE
· · · · STILES WAGON ROUTE
——— TWENTY MULE TEAM ROUTE
– · – SEARLES WORKS TO MOJAVE

MESQUITO WELLS

• BALLARAT

LONG VALLEY
(WINGATE WASH)

SARATOGA SPRINGS

BORAX FLAT
(SEARLES LAKE)

WINDY GAP
(WINGATE PASS

CAVE SPRINGS

SEARLES BORAX
WORKS

LONE WILLOW SPRINGS

(CHINA
DRY LAKE)

S A N

B E R N A R D I N O

• PILOT KNOB

GARLIC SPRINGS

K E R N

• BLACKWATER WELL

(CUDDEBACK
DRY LAKE)

(COYOTE
DRY LAKE)

• RANDSBURG

COYOTE HOLES

HAWLEYS

BLACK'S RANCH
(HARPER
DRY LAKE)

SANTA FE   R.R.

TOPEKA   BARSTOW   DAGGETT

ATCHISON   KRAMER

MOJAVE

(MUROC
DRY LAKE)

© 1974 by the University of Oklahoma Press

CALIFORNIA CONTAINS some of the richest deposits of borax in the world, but its location taxed the ingenuity of man in marketing the product. Borax was first produced north of San Francisco during the Civil War, but the great treasures were to be found in or near Death Valley. In the 1870's Isidore Daunet headed a group producing at Eagle Borax Works, but this operation only lasted two years.

In 1881 gold prospector Aaron Winter discovered a major deposit in Death Valley. William T. Coleman, the leading sales agent for borax, bought him out and built the Harmony Borax Works at the site. The borate mineral was refined by dissolving it in boiling water, and when the solution cooled the borax would precipitate out. However, it was so hot in Death Valley that the solution would not cool sufficiently, so operations ceased in the hottest weather. Fortunately, another strike was made at Amargosa, where the temperature was a "cool" 110° F. Therefore, production took place at Amargosa in summer and moved back to the richer deposits of Harmony when the weather was cooler.

The greatest problem was how to get the borax to the railroad and then to market from one of the dryest and hottest areas of the United States. Advanced technology and resourceful individuals resolved the challenge. Edward Israel Stiles was the first man to drive a 12-mule team outfit from Eagle Borax Works to Daggett and, also, probably pioneered the 20-mule team route from the Harmony Borax Works to Mojave, 165 miles away. It was 26 miles from Harmony to the first water at Bennet's Wells, 5 miles more to Mesquite Wells, 53 miles to Lone Willow Springs, 26 miles to Pilot Knox, 6 miles to Blackwater Well, and finally, a 50-mile waterless stretch to Mojave. Because the loaded mule train could travel only 17 miles a day, it was necessary to cache hay, grain, and water along the route. The round trip took 20 days.

The wagons drawn by the famed 20-mule teams were massive vehicles 16 feet long, 4 feet wide and 6 feet deep. Each wagon weighed 7,800 pounds empty, and loaded with borax, 31,800 pounds. Two such loaded wagons, plus the water tank, made a total load of 73,200 pounds, or 36 1/2 tons, for the 20-mule team to pull (actually, 18 mules and 2 horses). The rear wheels were 7 feet in diameter and the front wheels 5 feet. Many parts of the wagon were made of steel, since wood dried out rapidly in the desert air. Built in Mojave, a wagon cost $900—a very large sum in 1882. They were so well constructed that they withstood the rigors of the primitive roads over mountainous terrain with heavy loads, and 90 years later some wagons are still operative.

The first 20-mule team rigs were not used on the Death Valley route, where they attained their fame, but to haul borax from Searles Borax Works to Mojave in the 1870's. However, the Searles Lake–Mojave run was only half as long as the Harmony–Mojave run and the terrain was much easier to travel. Then too, the route was only briefly in use. The coming of the railroad ended the picturesque era of the 20-mule team, but it has been preserved as the symbol of borax and as a part of American folklore. The Death Valley borax deposits ceased production in 1927, when lower production costs were achieved at Kramer and later at Boron. Deposits at Searles Lake (near Trona) are still worked, and it is possible that another generation may activate the Death Valley deposits again.

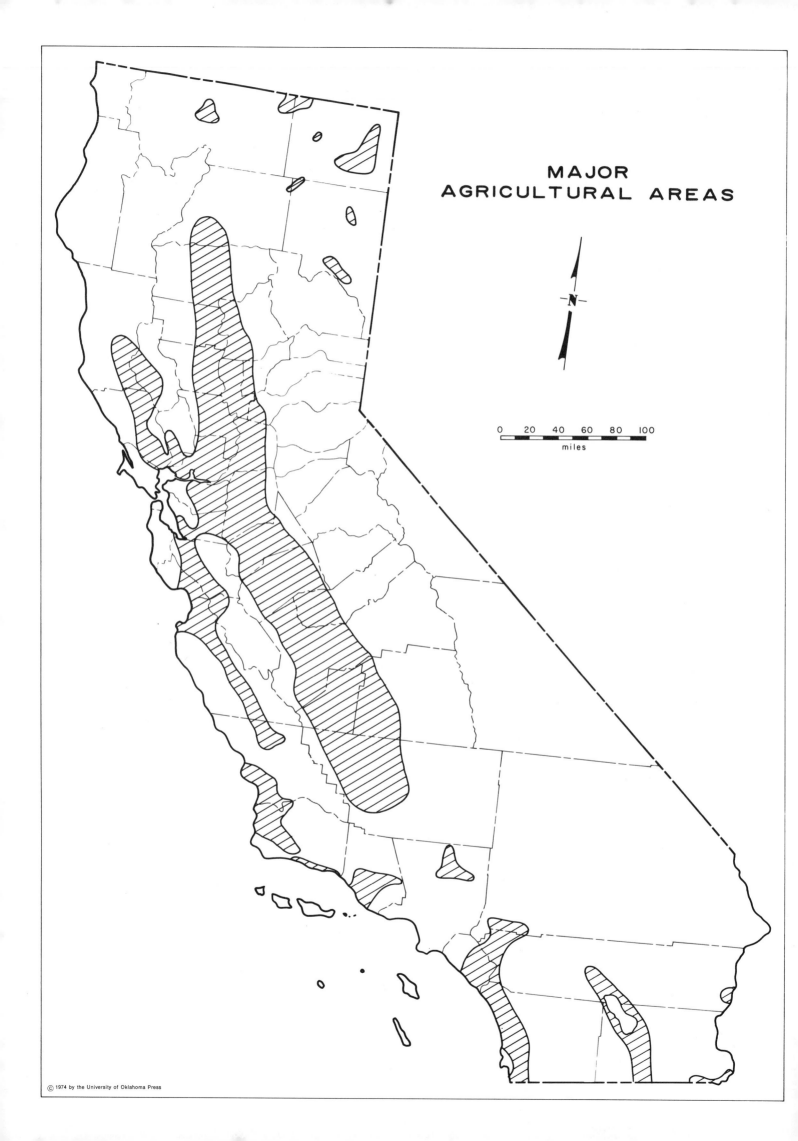

MAJOR
AGRICULTURAL AREAS

N

0   20   40   60   80   100
miles

© 1974 by the University of Oklahoma Press

93. MAJOR AGRICULTURAL AREAS

CALIFORNIA IS THE first state in the nation in terms of the value of agricultural products. This position is the more remarkable when one considers the large areas of the state unsuited to any kind of agricultural activity. Of California's total land area of more than 100 million acres, the land use is approximately as follows: 10 per cent is in cultivated crops; 31 per cent is in pasture and non-forest range lands; 45 per cent is in forest rangeland and timber; and 14 per cent is cities, highways, and wasteland.

The natural environment is of primary importance in establishing the state's agrarian wealth, for the growing season is long enough for several crops, and the soils are very productive. But the favorable natural habitat has not been enough. Man's ability to improve upon nature has been indispensable in California. The ability to irrigate otherwise arid land, the development of improved crops and livestock, the development of new and sometimes unique agricultural implements, and the evolution of an efficient system for processing, distributing, and marketing, are the human elements in the state's agricultural story. All of the major agricultural areas reflect man's alteration of the environment.

The heartland of California's agriculture is in the San Joaquin Valley which accounts for 43 per cent of the state's total. Fresno County leads the state as well as the nation in agricultural income. The other major agricultural regions are: scattered areas in the northeastern corner, the north coast, central coast, south coast, and irrigated areas in the southeast.

Agriculture in California was started at the missions, where basic European flora and fauna were introduced. But after secularization of the missions, cultivation of vineyards, orchards, and fields was neglected. In the Mexican era, during the heyday of the ranchero, the economy stressed the production of hide and tallow. Anglo migrants first viewed California as a sterile, mountainous, sandy region, which was parched with drought for half of the year and flooded during the other half. The San Joaquin Valley was even labeled a desert. But distance from other agricultural regions and high prices for what produce was available led to efforts to till the soil. By 1860 California farmers were able to satisfy the wants of the expanding population and even export a surplus.

The pioneer farmer in California faced many problems. First of all, he had to forget most of his agricultural experience, for farming in this strange land was different from anything he previously had known. He had to learn to adjust to the two seasons, the wet and dry, instead of the four of the East and Midwest. He had to develop irrigation practices unfamiliar to him. He frequently even had to cultivate crops and orchards which he had never seen before. Many observers contend that the success of the first citrus growers came from their willingness to innovate because they had no previous farming experience to unlearn. The pioneer farmer also had to do much experimenting to learn which crops could be grown on certain soils and in specific areas. He had to solve very difficult marketing and transportation problems. Finally, he had to finance his activities, sometimes for five or six years, before obtaining a return on his investment. The success story is obvious today, but there were many failures too.

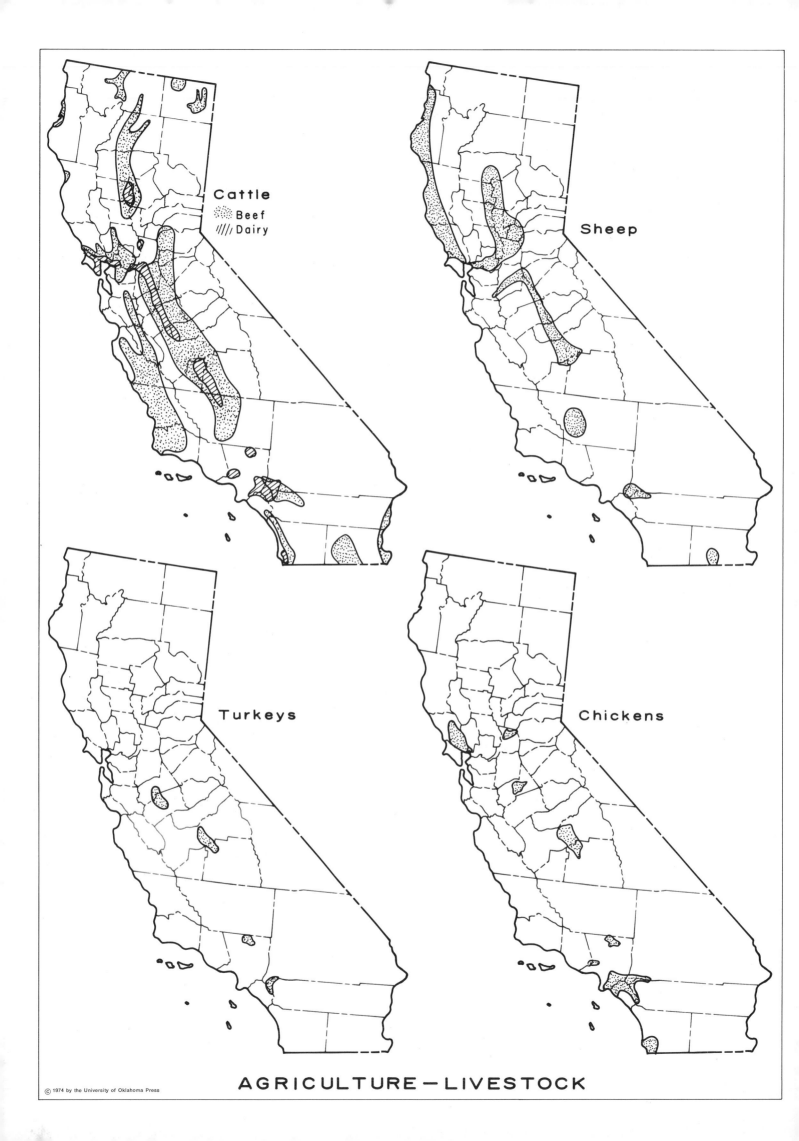

Cattle
Beef
Dairy

Sheep

Turkeys

Chickens

AGRICULTURE—LIVESTOCK

94. AGRICULTURE—LIVESTOCK

RECEIPTS FROM CATTLE and calves in 1970 were first in value (18.6 per cent) among agricultural commodities, and those from dairy products ranked second (11.9 per cent). Thus, livestock raising remained the leading agrarian activity in California. In the Mexican era great herds roaming the open range provided the hide and tallow for a profitable trade and much of the basis of the folklore of the romantic past. Today, open range grazing is decidedly limited, and the raising of cattle is big business. Most of the cattle are ranged outside the state and shipped in as yearlings to one of the many feedlots. There they spend 120 to 150 days being fattened for market on a diet of alfalfa, barley, cottonseed products, and sorghum supplemented with vitamins to speed up the fattening process. Imperial Valley is the greatest cattle area in the world, but there are similar cattle feeding lots in the San Joaquin Valley and in other regions throughout the state.

Dairying came in with the Anglos and early developed a different aspect from that found elsewhere. Lacking the green pasture areas (except in a few regions north of San Francisco) found in other parts of the country, milk cows were fed in feedlots. These "milk factories" were once adjacent to the large cities, but growing urbanization and refrigerated transportation has made it possible to locate them in more remote areas.

Raising sheep for mutton and wool has historic roots and was common in the Spanish and Mexican eras. The Spanish tradition of sheep raising flourished in a California, where cool summers and mild winters provided ample grazing land. In addition, the dry climate discouraged foot rot and other diseases common in more humid areas. Sheep raising prospered under the Anglos, and by 1876 there were some 7,700,000 head in the state. Since that year, the number of sheep raised have steadily declined; in the past decade the number has fallen so rapidly that in 1970 sheep and lambs ranked only thirty-third among the state's agricultural commodities and wool only sixty-second. Along the coastline north of San Francisco there is excellent year-round grazing. However, transhumance is practiced in the Great Valley. In May sheep are moved to mountain meadows to stay until November. One interesting aspect of the California sheep industry is the driving of flocks more than 300 miles to summer pasture over trails marked and set aside by the Bureau of Land Management.

In 1970 turkeys were eighteenth in value among agricultural commodities, but California is the leading state in their production. Because of their susceptibility to respiratory illnesses, turkeys flourish in the drier portions of the state. California also leads the nation in egg production. In fact, poultry ranches are virtually "egg factories," where the products goes from chicken to frying pan virtually untouched by human hands. Chickens are raised in several areas, but Sonoma County is easily the leader, with Petaluma claiming to be the "World's Egg Basket."

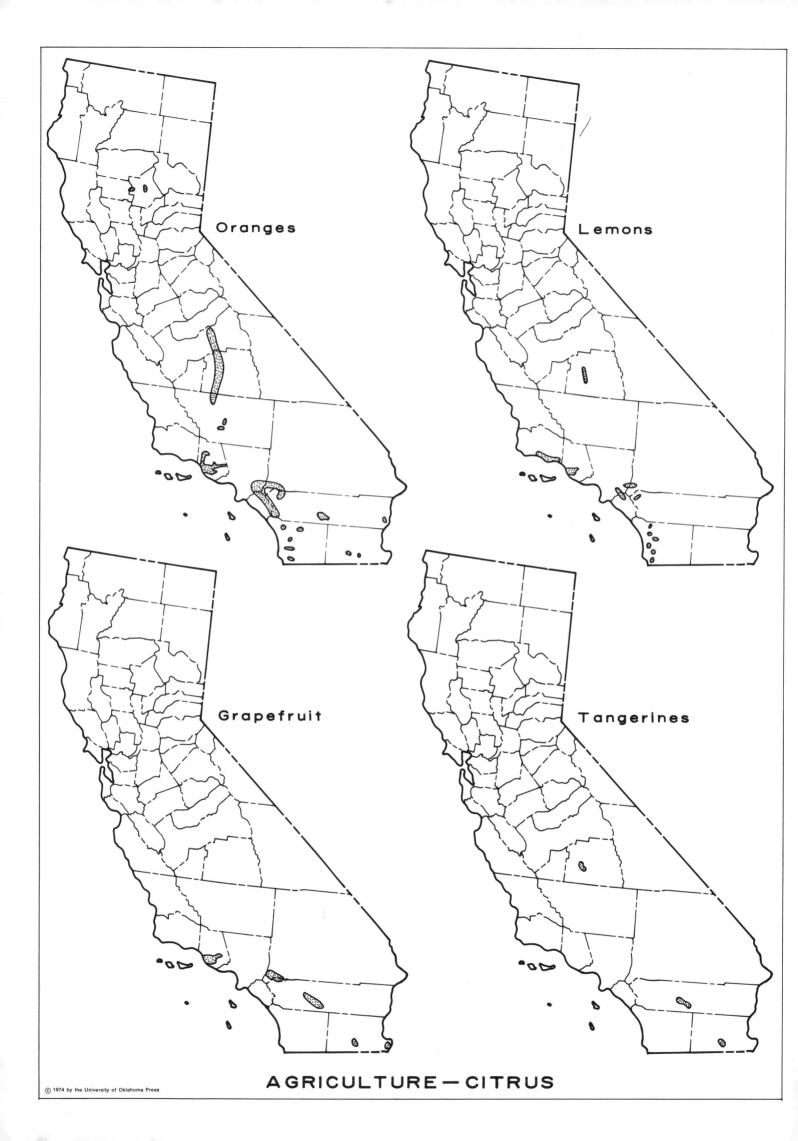

Oranges

Lemons

Grapefruit

Tangerines

AGRICULTURE—CITRUS

95. AGRICULTURE—CITRUS

THE ORANGE IS the most typical of California's agricultural products. Originally introduced by the mission fathers, the first commercial orchard was planted by William Wolfskill in Los Angeles in 1841. By 1862 there were an estimated 2,500 trees in the state, and by 1877 oranges were shipped eastward. In the 1870's two varieties of orange were introduced which triggered California's citrus boom. The Valencia came from Spain and is used mainly for juice. Harvested from April to November, it can be grown under a wide range of climatic conditions. The Navel was brought from Brazil and, being seedless with a high sugar content, is the preferred eating orange. Marketed under the Sunkist brand by the California Fruit Growers Exchange, the state's oranges have long dominated the nation's markets despite growing competition from Florida and Texas producers.

The Los Angeles Basin was once the most favored location for orange trees, with production concentrated in the foothills of Orange County but extending into Los Angeles, Riverside, and San Bernardino counties. The Santa Clara Valley in Ventura County is another important growing area. However, continued urban expansion has witnessed the uprooting of orange trees in these preferred locations. At the same time, orange tree acreage has steadily increased in the San Joaquin Valley, mainly in Tulare and Fresno counties. Oranges are grown in pockets throughout the state from as far south as the Imperial Valley and as far north as Oroville in Butte County—the latter site famed for its exceptionally sweet and early maturing Navels. In 1970 California produced some 18 per cent of the nation's oranges on 160,000 acres, and oranges ranked eleventh in value among the commodities marketed.

Lemons are a more sensitive fruit than oranges, so they were slower to develop as a major California crop. Highly susceptible to frost and wind, they also cannot tolerate conditions that are too hot and too dry. Thus, the areas in which they can be grown are limited. Small pockets of lemon groves are found in the same areas as oranges but are usually located on hillsides in order to promote air circulation and reduce frost danger. The most important lemon producing areas are on the Oxnard Plain in Ventura County and along the coast in Santa Barbara County, where the moderating influence of ocean breezes lessens frost danger. Lemons are raised in the San Joaquin Valley on high ground east of Terra Bella in Tulare County. However, as urbanization crowds out the lemon tree, its flight to less settled areas will be difficult unless hardier varieties can be developed. From a virtual monopoly of American's lemon industry, California's share has been reduced to 82 per cent of the national total by 1970, and further decline can be anticipated.

Grapefruit trees must have soil free from alkali and require special protection against wind, frost, and sunburn. This means high production costs, and in 1970 California had less than 13,000 acres in cultivation and accounted for less than 8 per cent of the nation's production. Grapefruit is principally grown in the southwestern corner of San Bernardino County, in Riverside County, and in Ventura County. Although acreage is limited, it is also the most important fruit crop in the Imperial Valley.

The tangerine (Chinese Orange or Mandarin) is another citrus fruit produced on a limited basis in California. In 1970 some 8,000 acres accounted for 16 per cent of the national total. Tulare and Riverside counties, along with the Imperial Valley, are the major producing areas.

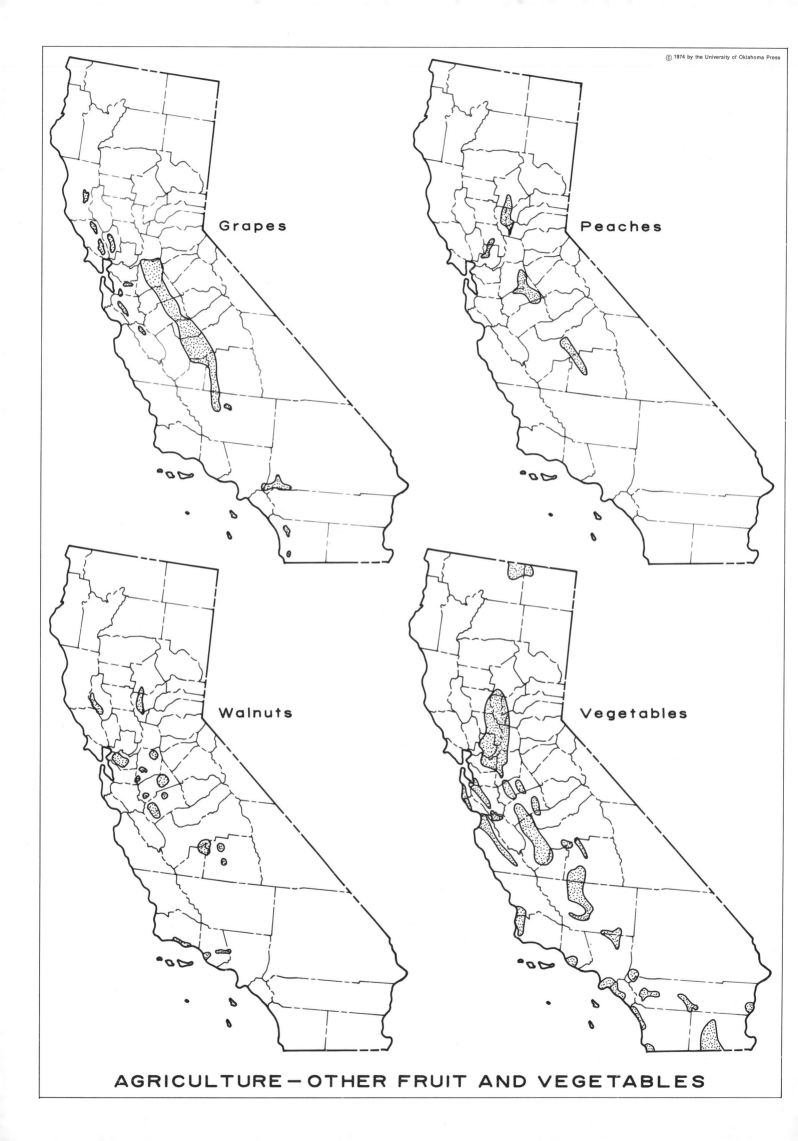

Grapes

Peaches

Walnuts

Vegetables

AGRICULTURE—OTHER FRUIT AND VEGETABLES

CALIFORNIA IS THE nation's leader in grape production with some 89 per cent of the total. This commodity was third in value among crops marketed in the state in 1970, earning an annual income of $236,747,000, but was first in value of field crops. California's present vineyard area covers some 450,000 acres scattered through many counties but with a concentration in the San Joaquin Valley. Grapes are marketed fresh as a table fruit, as raisins, or as juice, either fresh or as wine. The profit per acre is greatest from the table grape. Surplus which cannot be marketed as table grapes or dried as raisins can be crushed for wine. Dry table wines of high quality are made from grapes grown in Napa, Sonoma, Mendocino and other counties.

The Franciscan missionaries first introduced viticulture, and each of the missions had its vineyard and winery. Several diseases had to be conquered, and the correct combination of climate and soil had to be found. Marketing problems for raisins were solved by the Sun Maid Cooperative, and research, largely at the state university, solved the problems of disease and introduced improvements in planting, cultivation, pruning, and processing.

Peaches thrive in the low humidity, ample sunshine, and rather high temperatures of the San Joaquin Valley. Canning varieties dominate production in Sacramento and Sutter counties. Fresh, or table, peaches are grown on the east side of the valley in Tulare and Fresno counties, while peaches for drying are more common in San Joaquin, Stanislaus, and Merced counties. California is the national leader with 61 per cent of the total; peaches rank fifteenth in value among commodities marketed.

Walnuts are another of the many crops of which California leads the nation, growing some 96 per cent of the total. Grown in many different areas of the state, they were once a leading crop in Ventura, Los Angeles, Orange, and San Diego counties. But urbanization and warm winters have crowded them out, and expansion of acreage in the San Joaquin Valley has followed. The leading nut crop, walnuts, was probably introduced as early as 1786, and walnuts were plentiful at most missions by the end of the Mexican period. Most of the crop is marketed under the trade mark "Diamond Brand" by the cooperative California Walnut Grower's Association. In 1970 146,000 acres produced 103,000 tons of walnuts valued at $51,912,000.

Vegetable production is found in California wherever there is farming. Another product of the mission era, it was once concentrated in the vicinity of cities, in order to be easily marketed. Rapid transportation, improved packaging (often utilizing preservatives), and sophisticated marketing techniques make possible the shipment of fresh garden produce for great distances. California provides a vast market itself, but still ships large quantities to eastern points. Distant marketing requires produce of high quality and low cost, or it must reach these distant markets at an off season.

Tomatoes, lettuce, and potatoes are the most valuable of California's vegetables. Tomatoes ranked sixth among the state's commodities, with a value of $186,102,000 in 1970. Lettuce ranked eighth with a value of $148,104,000. Irish Potatoes ranked thirteenth with a value of $88,980,000.

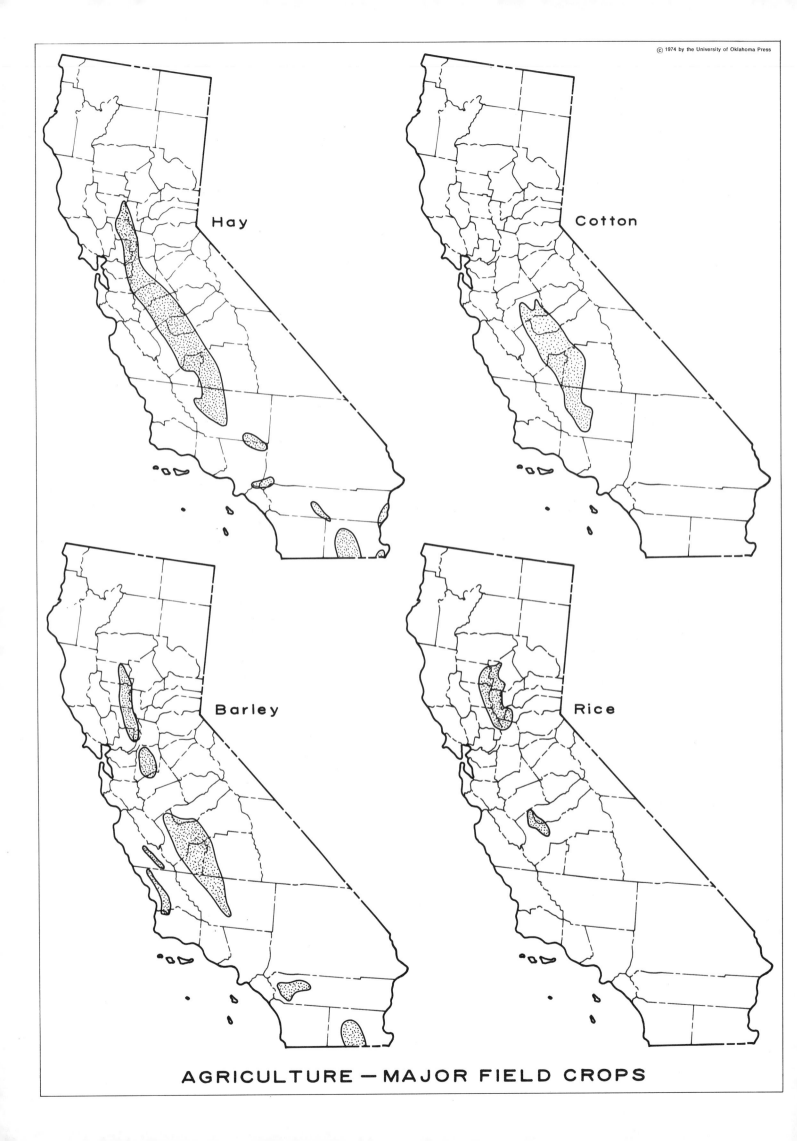

Hay

Cotton

Barley

Rice

AGRICULTURE — MAJOR FIELD CROPS

97. AGRICULTURE—MAJOR FIELD CROPS

HAY WAS THE fourth ranked agricultural commodity in California in 1970 and among field crops was second only to grapes. Alfalfa is the leading hay crop, because it makes excellent livestock feed and because of its role as a soil builder. A member of the legume family, it restores nitrogen naturally to the soil. Thus, it is a part of all systems of crop rotation. It is common practice to plant field crops for a maximum of four successive years and to sow alfalfa in the fifth year. Irrigated, alfalfa will produce five to eight cuttings a year, and one field can last as long as six years. In 1970 hay was valued at $229,333,000.

Cotton raising dates back to mission days, but in spite of an excellent natural environment for it, production was slow to develop. With the shortages growing out of the Civil War, there was great interest in raising cotton, and some was grown. Yet, by 1870 there were only about 2,000 acres planted to the crop, most of it in Los Angeles County. There were many reasons for the reluctance of Californians to become cotton planters, but most important was the lack of cheap labor, especially at harvesttime. Indians were used to pick cotton, but did not prove satisfactory. Efforts were made to bring Negroes from the American South for such labor. Some did come, but after a single season or so they moved into the cities. Not until the 1920's did the crop become important. Cotton prospered with the advent of the mechanical picker. The San Joaquin Valley is an ideal region for cotton culture because of the long, hot growing season and the lack of rain during the harvest period. Cotton ranked seventh in importance in 1970, with a value of $179,293,000.

Barley is the state's most important grain. It is a dry farm crop but is also grown under irrigation, especially in the San Joaquin and Imperial Valleys. Ninety per cent is grown as livestock feed and the rest is used as malting barley. In 1970 barley ranked seventeenth among the state's commodities, with 1,188,000 acres yielding a crop valued at $69,807,000.

The main area of rice growing stretches along both sides of the Sacramento northward; to Artois on the west side of the river and Butte City on the east side. A sizeable producing area is also found in Fresno County. California has the proper environmental conditions for rice production, with plenty of level land, impervious subsoil, abundance of manageable water, and high summer temperature. But the importance of rice growing in the state can be attributed to man's ability to apply technology to the environment. Rice production is perhaps the most progressive example of agricultural engineering in the world. A special seed was developed for the California scene, fields are flooded to kill the weeds, and seeding and fertilizing are performed by low-flying, specially equipped biplanes. Self-propelled combines harvest the crop after the field has been drained, and complex machinery dries it, making the requirements of human labor minimal. In 1970 rice ranked twelfth among California's commodities, with 331,000 acres producing a crop worth $89,205,000.

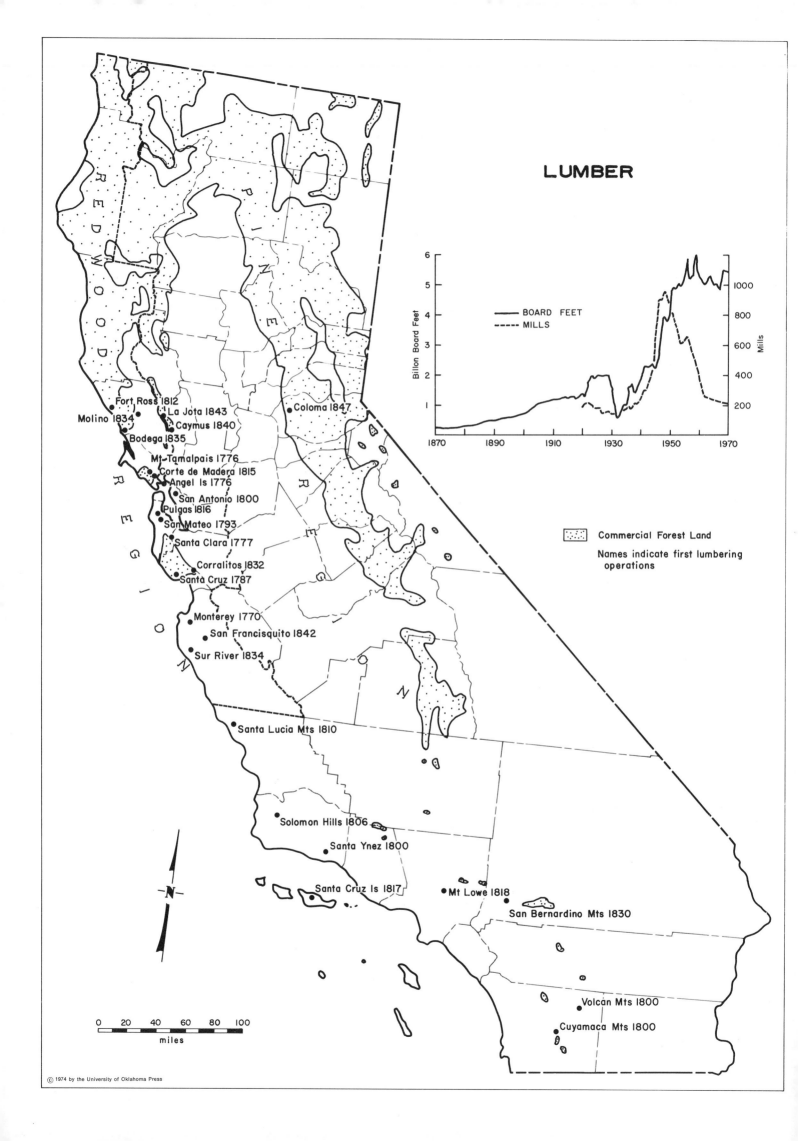

LUMBER

Fort Ross 1812
La Jota 1843
Molino 1834
Caymus 1840
Bodega 1835
Mt Tamalpais 1776
Corte de Madera 1815
Angel Is 1776
San Antonio 1800
Pulgas 1816
San Mateo 1793
Santa Clara 1777
Corralitos 1832
Santa Cruz 1787

Coloma 1847

Monterey 1770
San Francisquito 1842
Sur River 1834

Santa Lucia Mts 1810

Solomon Hills 1806
Santa Ynez 1800

Santa Cruz Is 1817

Mt Lowe 1818
San Bernardino Mts 1830

Volcan Mts 1800
Cuyamaca Mts 1800

REDWOOD REGION

PINE REGION

Commercial Forest Land

Names indicate first lumbering operations

BOARD FEET
MILLS

Billion Board Feet
6
5
4
3
2
1

Mills
1000
800
600
400
200

1870 1890 1910 1930 1950 1970

0 20 40 60 80 100
miles

−N−

THE FOREST LAND of California coincides roughly with the main mountain ranges and the north coastal region. The redwoods, remarkable for their great size and age, are found along the coast (sequoia sempervirens) and in the Sierra (sequoia gigantea). The coastal redwoods are in a narrow strip 10 to 30 miles wide, from the northern corner through Del Norte, Humboldt, and Mendocino counties and a part of Sonoma and small areas of Marin counties. The redwood belt is less dense in San Mateo and Santa Cruz counties, and the once great stands in Monterey County and the East Bay area have all but disappeared. The Sierra redwood occurs along the west slope of the Sierra Nevada between elevations of 4,500 and 8,000 feet, and extends from Placer County in the north to the southern part of Tulare County. In this 250-mile strip the trees occur in small groves, with most of them being in Tulare and Fresno counties. Several different varieties of pine are found east of the coastal redwood belt; south of San Francisco there is a sparse and intermittent continuation of the timber stand until it curves eastward, near Los Angeles, to join the Sierra timber region. The remaining important pine region follows the Cascade and Sierra Nevada ranges extending over approximately half the length of the state.

Lumbering operations in the early Spanish period corresponded to the need for timber to build missions, presidios, small boats, and bridges. Pine and cypress were cut from nearby forests, with the first authenticated use of redwood being in 1776 to build Mission Dolores and the presidio at San Francisco. Adobe bricks were, of course, used for the walls, but wood was necessary for rafters, joists, and window and door lintels. Pine beams were shipped from Monterey to San Diego and Santa Barbara in the 1780's. Logging operations were expanded in the 1790's as Spain rebuilt the presidios against possible foreign aggression. By 1813 ships were hauling lumber to Lima, Peru. In 1816 Spanish logging attracted English and American loggers whose greater technical skill increased production. The Russians, possibly because they had better craftsmen and superior tools, logged more extensively than did the Spanish. They built four relatively large ships, stockades, and comfortable homes from an estimated cut of 1,547,000 board feet of timber.

Lumbering in California became a significant enterprise in the Mexican era. Thomas O. Larkin, Monterey merchant and American consul, dominated trade in lumber products by providing stores on credit to independent lumbermen and buying their production. Boards, doors, and door and window frames were shipped to Los Angeles and Santa Barbara, and even to Hawaii. When John Sutter acquired the resources of the Russian settlement, the lumber facility was probably the most valuable. It was near Coloma that James Marshall discovered gold while building a sawmill for Sutter. Cutting of the central redwoods flourished in the Mexican period, but pine in the San Gabriel and San Bernardino mountains was also converted to lumber. Imported technology also expanded lumber production as whip-sawyers gave way to sawmills. The first water-powered sawmill was at Mission San Gabriel in 1824; another was built at Molino in 1834; and by 1845 there were half a dozen in operation. The first steam-powered sawmill was perhaps built at Bodega in 1844.

Lumber to meet the demand for homes, mining needs, and railroad construction made the industry immediately important in the American period. From 1850 to 1880 the average cut was perhaps a hundred million board feet a year, with a steady increase in each decade thereafter. In 1951 a record cut of 4.8 billion board feet was recorded. Today, Humboldt County is the leading area, accounting for some 25 per cent of the state's total. Since 1951 there has been a decline in the market for lumber and an increase in the use of wood products such as plywood and pulp. These changes have caused a decline in the number of mills. Redwood production has also steadily declined in recent years as production of pine and Douglas fir has increased.

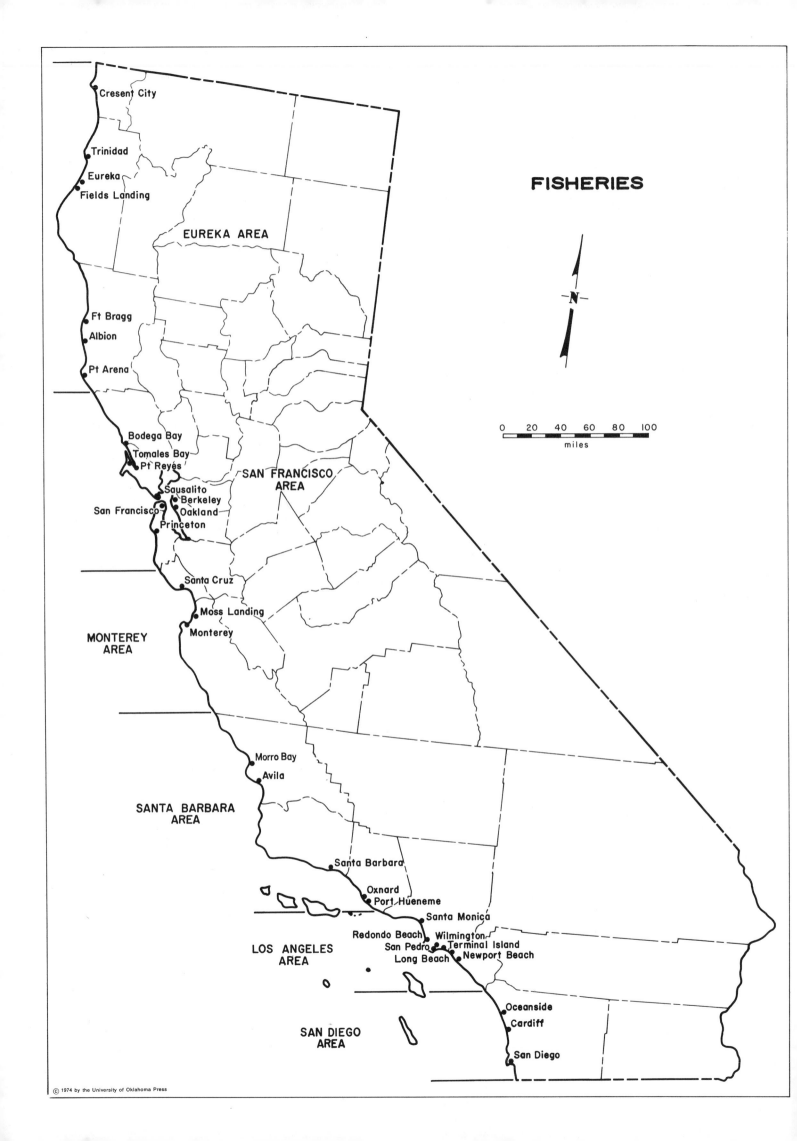

FISHERIES

Cresent City

Trinidad

Eureka

Fields Landing

EUREKA AREA

N

0   20   40   60   80   100
miles

Ft Bragg

Albion

Pt Arena

Bodega Bay

Tomales Bay

Pt Reyes

SAN FRANCISCO
AREA

Sausalito

Berkeley

San Francisco

Oakland

Princeton

Santa Cruz

Moss Landing

Monterey

MONTEREY
AREA

Morro Bay

Avila

SANTA BARBARA
AREA

Santa Barbara

Oxnard

Port Hueneme

Santa Monica

Redondo Beach

Wilmington

San Pedro

Terminal Island

Long Beach

Newport Beach

LOS ANGELES
AREA

Oceanside

Cardiff

San Diego

SAN DIEGO
AREA

99. FISHERIES

AN EXTENDED COASTLINE has ensured an important fisheries industry for California. Commercial enterprises began in coastal waters with the killing of sea otters for pelts. Once these lovely creatures were virtually exterminated, seals and whales suffered the same fate. The small-scale fishing in the late nineteenth century has given way to large-scale operations in the twentieth century. Meatless days during World War I educated the American public to the eating of fish, and improved canning techniques and refrigeration helped make it possible. Fishing operations increased in efficiency with larger vessels, floating lights used as lures, powered net pullers, refrigeration aboard ship, radio telephones, fathometers, direction finders, improved nets, and, recently, the use of helicopters to better locate schools of fish. A catch of 1,764,899,890 pounds in 1936 represented peak production. A slight decline began after that year, and became sharp after 1951.

The Los Angeles area was the first to develop commercial fishing, with the establishment of a sardine processing plant at San Pedro in 1893, and it continues as the leader in California and, in most years, of the nation. Some 2,000 commercial boats based in Los Angeles harbor fish the coastal waters as far south as Peru. "Fish harbor," on Terminal Island, is the site of several canneries and processing plants, with San Pedro handling most of the fresh fish trade. Sardines have fluctuated in importance and have frequently become scarce; after a decline in the early twentieth century they provided the largest tonnage from 1934 to 1947 and then all but disappeared. Several varieties of tuna, plus mackerel, seabass, and anchovies are the leading commercial varieties. A once flourishing port like Newport Beach has all but ceased operations; and it is feared that continual controversy with Latin American nations over the off-shore limits plus the building of American owned canneries in Puerto Rico, Peru, and Samoa may portend the same fate for all of the Los Angeles area fishing centers.

San Diego is the state's second ranking fishing port (it is fourth in the nation). Four-fifths of the catch is some variety of tuna, with mackerel having some importance. More than a hundred million pounds of fish have been landed annually, to make seafood canning a significant economic activity. However, the catch in San Diego has declined because of the growing scarcity of tuna, foreign competition, and for the same reasons plaguing the Los Angeles area.

The Santa Barbara area has an annual catch less than one-third that of San Diego, but with most of it coming from coastal waters. Port Hueneme accounts for more than half of this total, with anchovies, jack mackerel, and squid the leading species. Morro Bay has one-fourth of the catch of the area, with albacore, rockfish, and abalone most important. Santa Barbara is third in the area, rockfish and abalone accounting for over half of the total. Avila has a catch of more than half a million pounds of albacore, with the total from the other ports being insignificant.

The picturesque Chinese fishermen who made Carmel and Monterey leading centers with catches of salmon, sardines, and squid are gone. The fabled "Cannery Row" of Monterey is also a relic of the past, but fishing, though declining, still has some importance. Squid accounts for two-thirds of the small catch of Monterey. Anchovies constitute half of the total catch at Moss Landing; salmon and albacore account for the other half. The once flourishing San Francisco area fisheries have dwindled into insignificance, with a catch of less than ten million pounds annually. Most of the area ports have salmon as the valuable fish except Tomales Bay, which specializes in oysters.

Fishing in the Eureka area is in third place in the state, behind Los Angeles and San Diego. Crescent City leads the area with about half the catch in market crab; Eureka has about the same percentage also in market crab. In Fort Bragg salmon leads in value and weight, but market crab, albacore, Dover sole, and rockfish are also important. At Fields Landing most of the catch is in Dover sole. At Trinidad the small catch is in market crab and salmon; salmon are most important at Albion and Point Arena.

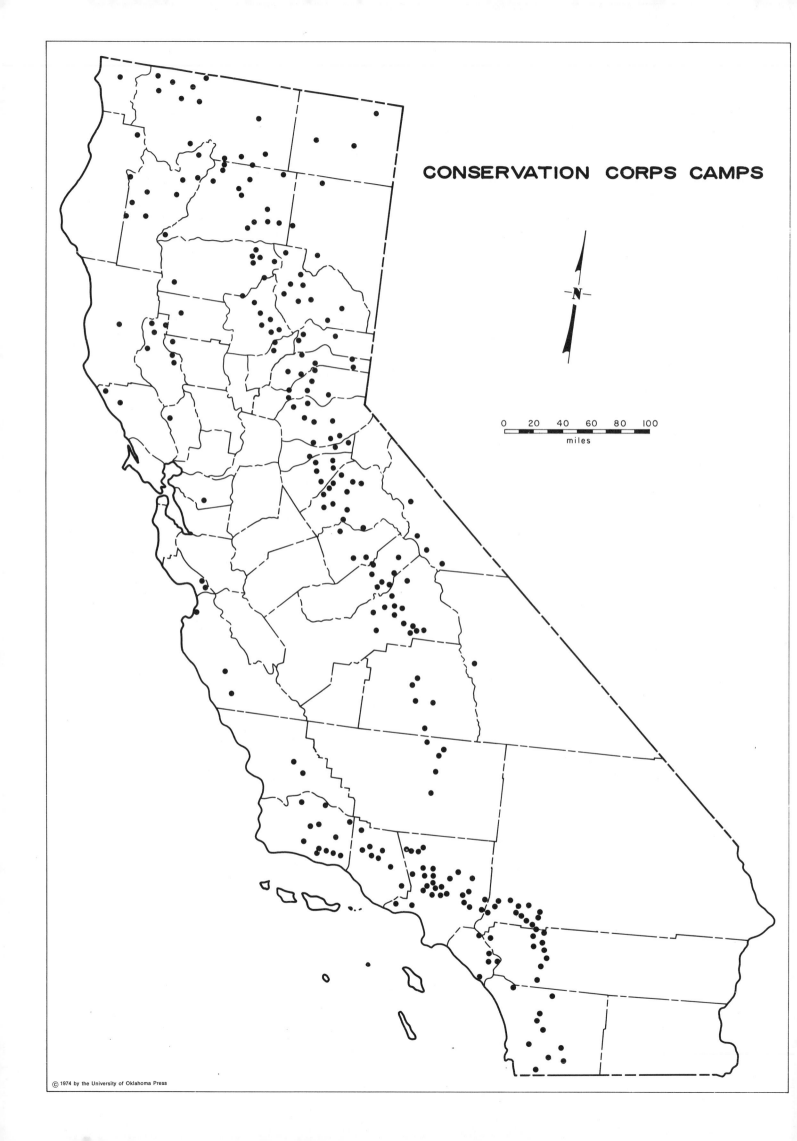

CONSERVATION CORPS CAMPS

0 20 40 60 80 100
miles

-N-

100. CONSERVATION CORPS CAMPS

THE ACT ESTABLISHING the Civilian Conservation Corps Camps in March, 1933, provided "for employing citizens of the United States who are unemployed, in the construction, maintenance, and carrying out of works of a public nature in connection with the forestation of lands . . . , the prevention of forest fires, floods, and soil erosion, plant pest and disease control, the construction, maintenance or repair of paths, trails, and fire lands." These objectives were realized in the nation as a whole, but especially in California, and the CCC became the most popular of all New Deal measures.

California usually had the largest number of camps of any state, the normal high being 150 camps. As the map indicates, the camps were primarily located in wilderness areas along the coast range or in the Sierra. Members of the California Civilian Conservation Corps were kept busy planting trees. In fact, a popular nickname of the CCC was "Roosevelt's Tree Army." They were so successful in this area that fully half of all trees planted in the history of the nation, public and private, was done by the Corps. Their work also included forest protection and forest improvement. Fire fighting was a significant part of the protection programs, and the many CCC enrollees were indispensable in combating various wild fires (49 lost their lives). For example, in 1934, 1,400 men were dispatched to a fire near Los Angeles with such speed that a potential holocaust was quickly controlled. Fire prevention was improved by the Corps' construction of roads, trails, fire lanes, fire breaks, telephone lines, and lookout towers. One fire break in California, was 600 miles long and separated the brush-covered foothills, where fires usually started, from the timbered mountain slopes.

The control of forests against disease and insects was less spectacular than reforestation or fire fighting, but was of equal of importance. In addition, wilderness areas were made more accessible by the building of roads and trails and with the construction of public campsites. Dams of all kinds were built to improve fishing, for flood control, and to assist irrigation within the National Forests. Some were small earthen structures, while others were huge concrete edifices built under the direction of the Army's Corps of Engineers. The CCC also reseeded thousands of acres of grassland and developed and put into operation several rodent control schemes. Soil conservation was another area in which much successful work was done. Still another activity of the Corps was its role in the conservation of wildlife, performed under the direction of the Bureau of Biological Survey in the Department of Agriculture.

The National Park Service benefited directly from the work of the Corps and similar work was performed in state parks. When CCC camps were first springing up in the early summer of 1933, the Park Service supervised 70 emergency camps in national monuments, and 105 camps on state park lands. One park official commented that the CCC boys "permitted the accomplishment of work that had been needed greatly for years, but which was impossible . . . of accomplishment under the ordinary appropriations available." Bridges, roads, and trails were built to open up camp areas: fireplaces, picnic tables, swimming pools, and other facilities made them more useable. Restoration of historical sites was a high priority activity. The restoration of La Puríuma Mission was an example of that work. The carving of Mount Theater at Mount Tamalpais State Park, from the solid rock of the mountainside, was a lasting tribute to the constructive ability, engineering talents, and creativity of the Corps' labor. Truly, the cause of ecology in California was well served by the members of the Civilian Conservation Corps.

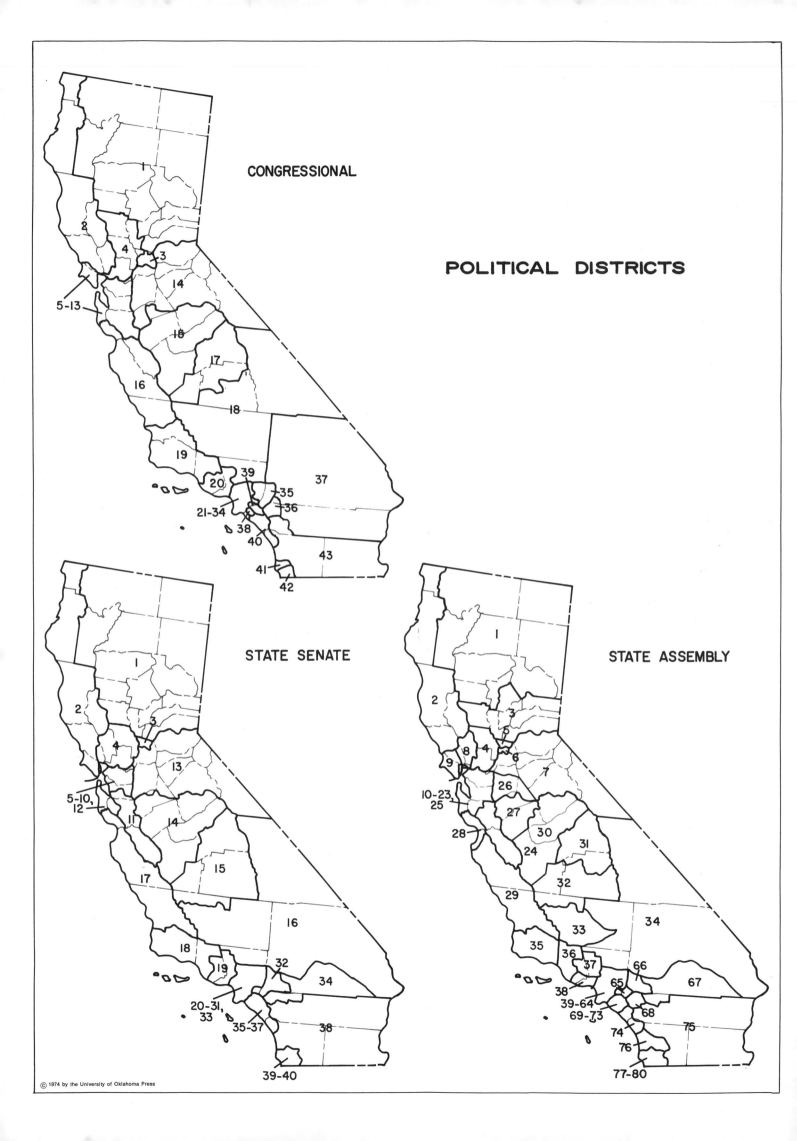

CONGRESSIONAL

POLITICAL DISTRICTS

STATE SENATE

STATE ASSEMBLY

© 1974 by the University of Oklahoma Press

101. POLITICAL DISTRICTS

HISTORICALLY, CALIFORNIA has often feuded over the proper way in which to apportion representation in the state's legislative bodies. The constitutions of 1850 and 1879 had both stipulated that population should be the basis of representation in both legislative houses. The system was accepted until the 1910 census revealed that Alameda, Los Angeles, and San Francisco counties had 48 per cent of the state's population. Numerous efforts on the part of what the city dwellers contemptuously referred to as "cow counties" to prevent their political demise finally resulted in the enactment of the federal plan of 1926. (It was so-named because of its similarity to the national constitution, where the upper house represents areas and the lower house represents people.) Under this plan the eighty members of the legislature each represented one-eightieth of the state's population, while the forty members of the Senate were elected from counties, no county having more than one Senator and no Senatorial District containing more than three counties. When the federal plan first went into effect in 1930, Los Angeles lost seven out of its eight seats in the Senate, San Francisco six of seven, and Alameda three of its four. With mass migration of people to the state during and after World War II, inequitable representation in the Senate grew with the expansion of urban centers and the decline in population of rural areas. In the 1961 apportionment one mountain Senatorial District had 14,196 citizens, while Los Angeles County had more than six million.

The historic "one man–one vote" decision of the United States Supreme Court in 1964 forced California to base representation in the Senate on population. A special session of the legislature meeting in October, 1965, reapportioned both houses on the basis of population. The populous counties gained dramatically as a result. Los Angeles County, to cite an example, received fourteen Senate seats instead of its previous one.

The relative ease with which reapportionment was accomplished in 1965 could not be duplicated in 1971, when the new census returns dictated that the task be repeated, for the governor and the legislative majority were now of opposite political parties. After long and difficult deliberations, the legislature enacted an apportionment plan, which was vetoed by the Governor. To resolve the deadlock, the State Supreme Court ruled that the Congressional Districts be used for the 1972 election, despite a gubernatorial veto, but that the Assembly and the Senate elections be based on previously existing boundaries. In addition, the Court appointed a Special Masters Committee on Reapportionment to do the task which the Governor and the Legislature had failed to accomplish.

This body ignored the usual practice in reapportionment of preserving the seats of incumbents, often by gerrymandering. Instead, the Masters used computers to scientifically arrange districts with a maximum of 2 per cent variance in population. The Masters stressed that districts should be contiguous and compact, following county and city lines where practical; the community interests of the population of an area were considered; state senate districts were formed by combining adjacent assembly districts; and, where possible, assembly district boundaries were used as congressional district boundaries. The Masters' recommendations were accepted by the State Supreme Court in November, 1973, and the new districts were in effect for 1974. Despite the innovative character of the plan, most politicians accepted it.

REFERENCES

In the compilation of this *Historical Atlas of California* certain works have been consulted extensively. Foremost of these has been Hubert H. Bancroft, *History of California* (7 vols., San Fancisco, 1886–90). The standard single volume histories of the state frequently used were Walton Bean, *California: An Interpretive History* (New York, 1968); John W. Caughey, *California* (New York, 1970); Andrew F. Rolle, *California: A History* (New York, 1969); Ralph J. Roske, *Everyman's Eden: A History of California* (New York, 1968). For obvious reasons, the single volume work most often utilized was Warren A. Beck and David A. Williams, *California: A History of the Golden State* (New York, 1972). Also widely used were Charles E. Chapman, *A History of California: The Spanish Period* (New York, 1921); Irving B. Richman, *California Under Spain and Mexico, 1535–1857* (Boston, 1911); Robert Glass Cleland, *A History of California: The American Period* (New York, 1922) and *California in Our Time, 1900–1940* (New York, 1947).

Among the general geographies of value have been David N. Hartman, *California and Man* (Dubuque, Iowa, 1964, 1968); Paul F. Griffin and Robert N. Young, *California the New Empire State* (San Francisco, 1957); David W. Lantis, Rodney Steiner, and Arthur E. Karinen, *California: Land of Contrast* (Belmont, Calif., 1963, 1970); and Robert W. Durrenberger, *Patterns on the Land* (Palo Alto, 1965, 1968), which is basically a geography atlas.

Many specialized studies have likewise been of great assistance to the authors. Prominent among these have been Harry Hansen, Ed., *California: A Guide to the Golden State* (New York, 1939, 1954, 1967); Erwin G. Gudde, *California Place Names* (Berkeley, 1949, 1960, 1965); Alfred Stone, Ed., *California Information Almanac* (Lakewood, Calif., 1963); *California Statistical Abstract* (Sacramento, 1970).

The base maps often used were the United States Geological Survey (USGS), *State of California* (1:1,000,-000, 1949); (USGS), *State of California* (1:500,000, 1949); Army Map Service (AMS), many different maps and various dates (1:250,000 series).

References for individual maps are listed below. Publication information is given in the first listing of each book and is not repeated in subsequent references.

Map 1. A Goodly Islande

Baker, Elna, *An Island Called California* (Berkeley, 1971).

Chapman, *History of California.*

Cutter, Donald C., "Sources of the Name California," *Arizona and the West*, Vol. III, No. 3 (Autumn, 1961), 233–43.

Hutchinson, W. H., *California: Two Centuries of Man, Land, and Growth in the Golden State* (Palo Alto, 1969).

Leighly, John, *California as an Island* (San Francisco, 1972).

Map 2. Relief

"Mineral Resources of California," Bulletin 191, California Division of Mines and Geology (San Francisco, 1969).

Hansen, *California Guide.*

Raisz, Erwin, *Landforms of California and Nevada* (map).

Map 3. Geomorphic Provinces

"Mineral Resources of California," Bulletin 191.

Lantis, Steiner, and Karinen, *California: Land of Contrast.*

Map 4. Major Faults and Earthquakes

Clark, William B., and Carl J. Hauge, "The Earthquakes.... You Can Reduce the Danger," *California Geology* (Nov., 1971), 203–17.

Hill, Robert T., *Southern California Geology and Los Angeles Earthquakes* (Los Angeles, 1928).

Holden, Edward S., *A Catalogue of Earthquakes on the Pacific Coast 1769–1897. Smithsonian Miscellaneous Collection* (Washington, 1898).

Iacopi, Robert, *Earthquake Country. How, Why, and Where Earthquakes Strike in California* (Menlo Park, 1964).

Rapoport, Robert, "Earthquake Do's and Dont's," *Los Angeles Times West Magazine* (June 27, 1971).

The San Andreas Fault, United States Department of the Interior, Geological Survey (Washington, 1965).

Map 5. Mean Annual Rainfall

Dale, Robert F., "Climate of California," in U.S. Weather Bureau, *Climatography of the United States No. 60-4, Climates of the States, California* (Washington, 1959).

Elford, C. Robert, "Climate of California," in U.S. Weather Bureau, *Climatography of the United States No. 60–4, Climates of the States, California* (Washington, 1970).

Map 6. Mean Minimum Temperature, January

Bailey, Harry P., *The Climate of Southern California* (Berkeley, 1966).

Dale, "Climate of California."

Elford, "Climate of California."

Gilliam, Harold, *Weather of the San Francisco Bay Region* (Berkeley, 1970).

Map 7. Mean Maximum Temperature, July

Same as Map 6.

Map 8. Native Vegetation

Burcham, L. T., *California Range Land: An Historic-Ecological Study of the Range Resources of California*. Division of Forestry, Department of Natural Resources (Sacramento, 1957).

Map 9. Fauna—I

Dasmann, William P., *Big Game of California* (Sacramento, 1968).

Kozlik, Frank, "Waterfowl of California," *Outdoor California*, Vol. 35, No. 5 (Sept., Nov., 1970).

Longhurst, William M., A. Starker Leopold, and Raymond F. Dasmann, *A Survey of California Deer Herds*, Game Bulletin No. 6 (California Department of Fish and Game, Sacramento, 1952).

McLean, Donald D., *The Quail of California*, Game Bulletin No. 2 (California Division of Fish and Game, Sacramento, 1930).

Mallette, Robert D., *Upland Game of California* (California Department of Fish and Game, Sacramento, 1969).

Seymour, George, *Furbearers of California* (Sacramento, 1960).

Species and Varieties of Deer in California, Bulletin No. 1 (California Fish and Game Commission, Sacramento, 1913).

Taber, Donald T., and Raymond F. Dasmann, *The Black-Tailed Deer of the Chaparral*, Game Bulletin No. 3 (California Division of Fish and Game, Sacramento, 1942).

Map 10. Fauna—II

Dasmann, *Big Game of California*.

Jones, F. L., *A Survey of the Sierra Nevada Bighorn* (Berkeley, 1950).

O'Connor, Jack, *Big Game Animals of North America* (New York, 1961).

Sampson, Arthur W., and Beryl S. Jespersen, *California Range Bushlands and Browse Plants*, Manual 33 (University of California Division of Agriculture Sciences, Berkeley, 1963).

Sheeham, Joe, "A New Policy for the Tule Elk," *Outdoor California*, Vol. 32, Nos. 1 and 2 (Jan., Feb., Mar., April, 1971).

University of California Museum of Vertebrate Zoology, Distribution Map, "Original Distribution of Elk in California" (Berkeley, 1942).

Map 11. Native Groups, 1770

Caughey, John Walton, Ed., *The Indians of Southern California in 1852, The B. D. Wilson Report and a Selection of Contemporary Comment* (San Marino, 1952).

Forbes, Jack D., *Native Americans of California and Nevada: A Handbook* (Healdsburg, Calif., 1969).

Heizer, Robert F., and Alan F. Almquist, *The Other Californians: Prejudice and Discrimination Under Spain, Mexico, and the United States to 1920* (Berkeley, 1971).

Heizer, Robert F., and M. A. Whipple, Eds., *The California Indians: A Source Book* (Berkeley, 1951, 1971).

"Indians: The California Tribes," U.S. Department of Interior, Bureau of Indian Affairs (Sacramento, 1966).

Kroeber, Alfred L., *Handbook of the Indians of California* (Berkeley, 1925, 1953).

Kroeber, Theodora, *Ishi in Two Worlds: A Biography of the Last Wild Indian in North America* (Berkeley, 1961).

Merriam, C. Hart, Ed., *Studies of California Indians* (Berkeley, 1955).

Map 12. Early Spanish Explorations

Bannon, John Francis, *The Spanish Borderlands Frontier 1513–1821* (New York, 1970).

Bolton, Herbert Eugene, *Rim of Christendom: A Biography of Eusebio Francisco Kino* (New York, 1936).

Bolton, Herbert Eugene, "The Mission as Frontier Institution in the Spanish-American Colonies," *American Historical Review*, Vol. XXIII, No. 3 (Oct., 1917), 42–61.

Bolton, Herbert Eugene, "The West Coast Corridor," in John Francis Bannon, *Bolton and the Spanish Borderlands* (Norman, 1964).

Chapman, Charles Edward, *The Founding of Spanish California* (New York, 1916).

Holmes, Maurice G., *From New Spain by Sea to the Californias 1519–1668* (Glendale, 1963).

Richman, *California Under Spain and Mexico*.

REFERENCES

Wagner, Henry R., *Spanish Voyages to the Northwest Coast of America in the Sixteenth Century* (San Francisco, 1928).

Map 13. Sea Explorations—Sixteenth Century

Chapman, *Founding of Spanish California.*

Cutter, Donald C., *The California Coast* (Norman, 1969).

Holmes, *From New Spain by Sea to the Californias.*

Richman, *California Under Spain and Mexico.*

Wagner, *Spanish Voyages to the Northwest Coast of America.*

Map 14. Sea Explorations—Seventeenth Century

Bancroft, *History of California.*

Chapman, *History of California.*

Holmes, *From New Spain by Sea to the Californias.*

Mathes, W. Michael, *Vizcaíno and Spanish Expansion in the Pacific Ocean, 1580–1630* (San Francisco, 1968).

Richman, *California Under Spain and Mexico.*

Wagner, *Spanish Voyages to the Northwest Coast of America.*

Map 15. First Spanish Explorations—South

Bancroft, *History of California*, Vol. I.

Bolton, Herbert Eugene, *Anza's California Expeditions* (5 vols., New York, 1966).

Bolton, Herbert Eugene, "In the South San Joaquin Ahead of Garces," *California Historical Society Quarterly*, Vol. X, No. 3 (Sept., 1931), 210–19.

Chapman, *Founding of Spanish California.*

Chapman, *History of California.*

Diary of Miguel Costanso: The Portola Expedition of 1769–1770. Edited by Frederick J. Teggart (Berkeley, 1911).

Diary of Pedro Font: The Anza Expedition of 1775–1776. Edited by Frederick J. Teggart (Berkeley, 1913).

Priestley, Herbert Ingram, *Franciscan Explorations in California* (Glendale, 1946).

Diary of Vicente Vila: The Portola Expedition of 1769–1770. Edited by Robert Selden Rose (Berkeley, 1911).

Map 16. First Spanish Explorations—Central

Bolton, "In the South San Joaquin."

Chapman, *Founding of Spanish California.*

Chapman, *History of California.*

Gifford, E. W. and W. Egbert Schenck, "Archaeology of the Southern San Joaquin Valley, California," in *American Archeology and Ethnology.* Vol. XXIII (1926–28), 1–122.

Diary of Miguel Costanso.

Priestley, *Franciscan Explorations.*

Diary of Vicente Vila.

Map 17. First Spanish Expeditions—The Bay

Bancroft, *History of California*, Vol. I.

Bolton, *Anza's California Expeditions.*

Bolton, Herbert Eugene, *Outpost of Empire: The Story of the Founding of San Francisco* (New York, 1939).

Cook, Sherburne F., "The Aboriginal Population of Alameda and Contra Costa Counties, California," in *Anthropological Records*, Vol. 16, No. 4 (Berkeley, 1957).

Diary of Pedro Fages: Expedition to San Francisco Bay in 1770. Edited by Herbert Eugene Bolton (Berkeley, 1911).

Diary of Pedro Font.

Priestley, *Franciscan Explorations.*

"Rivera at San Francisco: A Journal of Exploration," Tr. by Alan K. Brown, *California Historical Society Quarterly*, Vol. 41, No. 4 (Dec., 1962), 325–41.

Treutlein, Theodore E., *San Francisco Bay: Discovery and Colonization 1769–1776* (San Francisco, 1968).

Map 18. First Spanish Expeditions—North

Bancroft, *History of California*, Vol. II.

Chapman, *History of California.*

Cutter, Donald, "Moraga of the Military: His California Services, 1784–1810" (M.A. thesis, University of California, Berkeley, 1947).

Cutter, Donald, "Spanish Explorations of California's Central Valley" (Ph.D. dissertation, University of California, Berkeley, 1950).

The Diary of Ensign Gabriel Moraga's Expedition of Discovery in the Sacramento Valley, 1808. Translated and edited by Donald C. Cutter (Los Angeles, 1957).

Priestley, *Franciscan Explorations.*

Map 19. Missions, Forts, and Towns During the Spanish Period 1769–1822

Bancroft, *History of California*, Vols. I & II.

Chapman, *History of California.*

Richman, *California Under Spain and Mexico.*

Map 20. Spanish Expeditions into the Interior, 1800 to 1810

Bancroft, *History of California*, Vol. II.

Chapman, *History of California.*

Cook, Sherburne F., "Colonial Expeditions to the Interior of California: Central Valley, 1800–1820," in *Anthropological Records*, Vol. 16, No. 6 (Berkeley, 1960).

Cutter, "Spanish Exploration."

Moraga, Diary of.

Priestley, *Franciscan Explorations.*

*Map 21. Spanish Expeditions into the Interior,
1810 to 1820*

Same as map 20.

*Map 22. Mexican Expeditions into the Interior,
1820–30*

Bancroft, *History of California*, Vol. III.

Cook, Sherburne F., "Expeditions to the Interior of California: Central Valley, 1820–1840," in *Anthropological Records*, Vol. 20, No. 5 (Berkeley, 1962).

Cook, Sherburne F., to Ynez D. Haase, December 17, 1969, personal correspondence.

Kroeber, *Handbook of the Indians of California.*

Priestley, *Franciscan Explorations.*

*Map 23. Miwok-Yokut Raids into Mexican Territory,
1830–40*

Cook, "Expeditions to the Interior of California, 1820–1840."

Cook, Sherburne F., *The Conflict Between the California Indian and White Civilization*, 2 vols. (Berkeley, 1943).

Frakes, George E. and Curtis B. Solberg, Editors, *Minorities in California History* (New York, 1971).

Heizer and Almquist, *The Other Californians.*

Map 24. Mexican Land Grants

Avina, Rose Hollenbaugh, "Spanish and Mexican Land Grants in California" (M.A. thesis, University of California, Berkeley, 1934).

Becker, Robert H., *Designs on the Land: Diseños of California Ranchos* (San Francisco, 1969).

Becker, Robert H., *Diseños of California Ranchos: Maps of 37 Land Grants* (San Francisco, 1964).

Bowman, Jacob N., "Index of the Spanish-Mexican Private Land Grant Records and Cases of California" (unpublished manuscript, Bancroft Library, 1958).

Bowman, Jacob N., "Index to Maps of Private Land Grant Cases of California" (unpublished manuscript, Bancroft Library, 1943).

California, State of, General Land Office Maps, 1885, 1944.

Corbett, Francis James, "The Public Domain and Mexican Land Grants in California" (M.A. thesis, University of California, Berkeley, 1959).

Cowan, Robert G., *Ranchos of California* (Fresno, 1956).

Gates, Paul W., *California Ranchos and Farms 1846–1862* (Madison, 1967).

Gates, Paul W., "The California Land Act of 1851," *California Historical Society Quarterly*, Vol. L. No. 4 (Dec., 1971), 395–430.

Hutchison, Claude B., Ed., *California Agriculture* (Berkeley, 1946).

Ross, Ivy Belle, "The Confirmation of Spanish and Mexican Land Grants in California" (M.A. thesis. University of California, Berkeley, 1928).

Shumway, Burgess, Mck, "Ranchos of California: Patented Private Land Grants Listed by Counties" (Works Progress Administration, Los Angeles, 1940–41).

Tays, George, "How Lands Were Granted in Hispanic California" (M.A. thesis, University of California, Berkeley, 1942).

Weststeyn, Lela Margaret, "The Expansion of the Land Grant System Under the Last Two Mexican Governors—Manuel Micheltorena and Don de Jesus Pico" (M.A. thesis, University of Southern California, 1936).

(The above bibliography was also consulted for the maps of the individual counties).

Map 25. Mexican Land Grants—Shasta and Tehama

Army Map Service, 1:250,000 series, Redding (NK 10–11), 1964 revision; Ukiah (NJ 10–2) 1965 revision; Chico (NJ 10–3), 1966 revision.

*Map 26. Mexican Land Grants—Butte, Colusa, Glenn,
Yolo, Yuba, and Sutter.*

Army Map Service, 1:250,000 series, Santa Rosa (NJ 10–5), 1964; Ukiah (NJ 10–2), 1965 revision, Chico (NJ 10–3), 1966 revision; Sacramento (NJ 10–6), 1964 revision.

Map 27. Mexican Land Grants—Mendocino, Lake

Same as Map 26.

*Map 28. Mexican Land Grants—
Sacramento, San Joaquin and Amador*

Army Map Service, 1:250,000 series, Sacramento (NJ 10–6), 1964 revision; San Jose (NJ 10–9), 1956, 1966 revision.

*Map 29. Mexican Land Grants—Marin,
Napa, Solano, Sonoma*

Army Map Service, Santa Rosa (NJ 10–5), 1957, 1964; San Francisco, 1964.

*Map 30. Mexican Land Grants—
Alameda, Contra Costa, Santa Clara, San Francisco,
San Mateo, Santa Cruz*

Army Map Service, 1:250,000 series, San Francisco, 1964; Santa Cruz, 1965.

Arbuckle, Clyde, and Ralph Rambo, *Map of Santa Clara Co. Ranchos* (no scale, 1968).

Map 21. Mexican Land Grants—Monterey, San Benito

Army Map Service, 1:250,000 series, Santa Cruz, 1965. Engineering Department, County of Monterey, *Land Grants of Monterey* (1″ = 4 miles, n.d.).

Map 32. Mexican Land Grants—Stanislaus, Merced, Mariposa

Army Map Service, 1:250,000 series, Santa Cruz (NJ 10–12), 1965; San Jose (NJ 10–9), 1956, 1966 revision, Mariposa (NJ 11–7), 1964 revision.

Map 33. Mexican Land Grants—Fresno, Kings

Army Map Service, 1:250,000 series, Fresno.

Map 34. Mexican Land Grants—Kern

Army Map Service, 1:250,000 series, Los Angeles (NI 11–4), 1968 revision. Bakersfield (NI 11–1), 1966.

Map 35. Mexican Land Grants—San Luis Obispo

Army Map Service, 1:250,000 series, San Luis Obispo (NI 10–3), 1963 revision; Santa Maria (NI 10–6, 9); Los Angeles (NI 11–4), 1968 revision.

Map 36. Mexican Land Grants— Ventura, Santa Barbara

Army Map Service, 1:250,000 series, Los Angeles (NI 11–4), 1968 revision: Santa Maria (NI 10–6, 9).

Map 37. Mexican Land Grants—Los Angeles, Orange

Army Map Service, 1:250,000 series, Los Angeles, 1959; San Bernardino, 1966; Santa Ana, 1960, 1965.

Title Insurance and Trust Co., *The Old Spanish and Mexican Ranchos of Los Angeles County* (1″ = 5 miles, Los Angeles, c1937).

Title Insurance and Trust Co., *The Old Spanish and Mexican Ranchos of Orange County*, California (no scale, Los Angeles, n.d.).

Map 38. Mexican Land Grants— Riverside, San Bernardino

Army Map Service, 1:250,000 series, San Bernardino, 1966; Santa Ana, 1960, 1965.

Map 39. Mexican Land Grants—San Diego

Army Map Service, 1:250,000 series, San Diego (NI 11–11), 1964 revision; Santa (NI 11–8), 1965.

Map 40. Russian-American Company Settlement, 1812–41

Haase, Ynez D., "The Russian-American Company in California," (M.A. thesis, University of California, Berkeley, 1952).

Ogden, Adele, *The California Sea Otter Trade* (Berkeley, 1941).

Map 41. Trade During the Spanish-Mexican Period.

Arnaz, Jose, "Memoirs of a Merchant," tr. and ed. by Nellie Van de Grift Sanchez, *Touring Topics* (Sept., Oct., 1928).

Buell, Robert Kingery, and Charlotte Northcote Skladal, *Sea Otters and the China Trade* (New York, 1968).

Cleland, Robert Glass, *The Cattle on a Thousand Hills* (San Marino, 1951).

Dana, Richard Henry, *Two Years Before the Mast* (New York, 1840).

Hafen, LeRoy R., and Ann W., *Old Spanish Trail: Santa Fe to Los Angeles* (Glendale, 1954).

Lawrence, Eleanor, "Mexican Trade Between Santa Fe and Los Angeles, 1830–1848," *California Historical Society Quarterly*, Vol. X, No. 2 (May, 1931), 27–39.

Ogden, *California Sea Otter Trade.*

Map 42. Mountain Passes

Baxter, Don Jr., *Gateways to California* (San Francisco, 1968).

"Mountain Passes Issue" *Noticias: Santa Barbara Historical Society*, Vol. X, No. 2 (Spring, 1964).

Map 43. The Mountain Men

Cleland, Robert Glass, *This Reckless Breed of Men: The Trappers and Fur Traders of the Southwest* (New York, 1952).

Dale, Harrison Clifford, *The Ashley-Smith Explorations and the Discovery of a Central Route to the Pacific 1822–1829* (Glendale, 1941).

Farquhar, Francis P., "Walker's Discovery of Yosemite," *Sierra Club Bulletin* Vol. XXVII, No. 4 (Aug., 1942), 35–49.

Hill, Joseph J., "Ewing Young in the Fur Trade of the American Southwest," *Oregon Historical Quarterly*, Vol. XXIV, No. 1 (March, 1923), 1–35.

Morgan, Dale, *Jedediah Smith and the Opening of the West* (Indianapolis, 1953).

Pattie, James Ohio, *Personal Narrative* (Philadelphia, 1831, 1962).

Map 44. Anglo-American Immigrant Trails Before the Conquest

Cleland, *History of California.*

Moody, Ralph, *The Old Trails West* (New York, 1963).

Map 45. Fremont and the Bear Flag Revolt

Hawgood, John A., "John C. Fremont and the Bear Flag Revolution: A Reappraisal," *Southern California Quarterly*, Vol. XLIX, No. 2 (June, 1962), 67–96.

Hussey, John A., "The United States and the Bear Flag

Revolt" (Ph. D. dissertation, University of California, Berkeley, 1941).

Marti, Werner H., *Messenger of Destiny* (San Francisco, 1960).

Ide, William B., *Who Conquered California* (Claremont, 1880).

Nevins, Allan, *Fremont: Pathmaker of the West* (New York, 1939).

Rogers, Fred B., *Bear Flag Lieutenant: The Life Story of Henry L. Ford* (San Francisco, 1951).

Tays, George, "Fremont Had No Secret Instructions," *Pacific Historical Review*, Vol. IX, No. 2 (June, 1940), 159–71.

Map 46. The Donner Tragedy

McGlashan, Charles Fayette, *History of the Donner Party* (Stanford, 1879, 1947).

Stewart, George R., *Ordeal by Hunger: The Story of the Donner Party* (New York, 1936).

Map 47. Anglo-American Conquest, Phase I

Connor, Seymour V., and Odie B. Faulk, *North America Divided: The Mexican War, 1846–1848* (New York, 1971).

Marti, *Messenger of Destiny*.

Price, Glenn W., *Origins of the War with Mexico: The Polk-Stockton Intrigue* (Austin, 1967).

Smith, Justin H., *The War with Mexico* (2 vols., New York, 1919).

Map 48. Anglo-American Conquest, Phase II

Clarke, Dwight L., *Stephen Watts Kearney, Soldier of the West* (Norman, 1961).

Connor and Faulk, *North America Divided*.

Cooke, Philip St. George, *The Conquest of New Mexico and California* (New York, 1878).

Coy, Owen C., *The Battle of San Pasqual* (Sacramento, 1921).

Nevins, *Fremont*.

Smith, *The War with Mexico*.

Woodward, Arthur, *Lances at San Pasqual* (San Francisco, 1948).

(The authors have omitted a map of the battle of San Pasqual because there is no adequate material available in either primary or secondary sources from which to accurately draw such a map).

Map 49. Routes to the Gold Fields

Bieber, Ralph P., *Southern Trails to California in 1849* (Glendale, 1937).

Caughey, John Walton, *Gold is the Cornerstone* (Berkeley, 1948).

Egan, Ferol, *The El Dorado Trail: The Story of the Gold Rush Routes Across Mexico* (New York, 1970).

Evans, George W. B., *Mexican Gold Trail* (San Marino, 1945).

Kemble, John H., *The Panama Route, 1848–1869* (Berkeley, 1943).

Paul, Rodman W., *California Gold: The Beginning of Mining in the Far West* (Cambridge, 1947).

Powell, H. M. T., *The Santa Fe Trail to California, 1849–1852* (San Francisco, 1931).

Read, Isaac, "The Chagres River Route to California," *California Historical Society Quarterly*, VIII (1929), 3–16.

Rydell, Raymond A., "The Cape Horn Route to California, 1849," *Pacific Historical Review*, XVII (1948), 149–63.

Map 50. The Gold Rush Period, 1849–1869

Caughey, *Gold is the Cornerstone*.

Clappe, Louise, *The Shirley Letters From the California Mines 1851–1852* (New York, 1949).

"Mineral Resources of California," Bulletin 191.

Paul, *California Gold*.

Paul, Rodman, *Mining Frontiers of the Far West: 1848–1880* (New York, 1963).

Map 51. Main Stage Coach Roads and Wells Fargo Offices, 1860–1880

Banning, William and George H., *Six Horses* (New York, 1930).

Hungerford, Edward, *Wells Fargo: Advancing the American Frontier* (New York, 1949).

Jackson, W. Turrentine, *Wagon Roads West* (Berkeley, 1952).

Shumate, Albert, *The Life of George Henry Goddard* (Bancroft Library, Berkeley, 1969). *Map titled Britton & Rey's Map of the State of California George H. Goddard, 1857* (end leaf).

Wells, Fargo & Co's Express, *List of Offices, Agents and Correspondents* (corrected July 1, 1880, n.p.).

Winther, Oscar, *Via Western Express and Stagecoach* (Stanford, 1945).

Map 52. The Butterfield Overland Mail Route

Conkling, Roscoe P. and Margaret B., *The Butterfield Overland Mail, 1857–1869* (3 vols., Glendale, 1947).

Hafen, Le Roy R., *The Overland Mail, 1849–1869* (Cleveland, 1926).

Root, Frank A., and William Elsey Connelley, *The Overland State to California* (Topeka, 1901).

Waterman, L., Ormsby, *The Butterfield Overland*

Mail, ed. by Lyle H. Wright and Josephine M. Bynum (San Marino, 1962).

Map 53. The Pony Express

Bradley, Glenn D., *The Story of the Pony Express* (Chicago, 1913).

Chapman, Arthur, *The Pony Express* (New York, 1932).

Hanson, Robert A., "Notes on the Trail of the Pony Express" (mim. copy, Berkeley, n.d.); also map, *The Trail of the Pony Express San Francisco, Calif. to St. Joseph, Mo. April 1860 to Nov. 1861* (scale 1″ = 30 miles).

Howard, Robert West, *Hoofbeats of Destiny: The Story of the Pony Express* (New York, 1960).

Jackson, W. Turrentine, "A New Look at Wells Fargo, Stagecoaches and the Pony Express," *California Historical Society Quarterly*, Vol. XLV, No. 4 (Dec., 1966), 291–324.

Settle, Raymond W., and Mary Lund, *Empire on Wheels* (Stanford, 1949).

Settle, Raymond W., and Mary Lund, *Saddles and Spurs* (Harrisburg, Pa., 1955).

Smith, Waddell F., Ed., *The Story of the Pony Express* (San Rafael, 1964).

Map 54. United States Military Posts

Frazer, Robert W., *Forts of the West* (Norman, 1965).

Heitman, Francis B., *Historical Register and Dictionary of the United States Army, from Its Organization, September 29, 1789 to March 2, 1903* (2 vols., Washington, 1903).

Outline Description of U.S. Military Posts and Stations in the Year 1871 (Washington, 1872).

Prucha, Francis Paul, *A Guide to the Military Posts of the United States 1789–1895* (Madison, 1964).

Whiting, J. S., and Richard J., *Forts of the State of California* (Seattle, 1960).

Map 55. Mariposa Indian War, 1850–1851

Bunnell, Lafayette H., "The Date of the Discovery of the Yosemite," *The Century Magazine*, Vol. XL, No. 5 (Sept., 1890), 795–97.

Bunnell, Lafayette H., *Discovery of the Yosemite and the Indian War of 1851* (Los Angeles, 1911).

Eccleston, Robert, *The Mariposa Indian War, 1850–1851. Diaries of Robert Eccleston: California Gold Rush, Yosemite, and the High Sierra.* Introduced and edited by C. Gregory Crampton (Salt Lake City, 1957).

Kuykendall, Ralph S., "History of the Yosemite Region," in Ansel F. Hall, Ed., *Handbook of Yosemite National Park* (New York, 1921).

Mitchell, Annie R., *Jim Savage and the Tulareño Indians* (Los Angeles, 1957).

Russell, Carl Parcher, *One Hundred Years in Yosemite* (Stanford, 1931).

Russell, Carl Parcher, "The Geography of the Mariposa Indian War," *Yosemite Nature Notes*, Vol. XXX, Nos. 3, 4, 6, 7, (Mar., Apr., June, July, 1951).

"The Great Yo-Semite Valley," Hutchings California Magazine, Vol. IV, No. 4 (Oct., 1859), in Robert R. Olmstead, Ed., *Scenes of Wonder & Curiosity: Hutchings California Magazine 1856 Through 1861*, (San Francisco, 1962).

Map 56. The Modoc War, 1872–73

Bancroft, Hubert H., *History of Oregon*, Vol. II (San Francisco, 1888).

Brown, Dee, *Bury My Heart at Wounded Knee*, (New York, 1970).

Brown, William S., *California Northeast: The Bloody Ground* (Oakland, 1951).

Dillon, Richard H., *Burnt Out Fires: California's Modoc Indian Wars* (New York, 1973).

Dillon, Richard H., "Costs of the Modoc War," *California Historical Society Quarterly*, Vol. XXVIII, No. 2 (June, 1949), 161–64.

Du Bois, Cora, "The 1870 Ghost Dance," in *Anthropological Records*, Vol. 3, No. 1 (Berkeley, 1930).

Dunn, J. P. Jr., *Massacres of the Mountains: A History of the Indian Wars of the Far West* (New York, 1886, 1969).

Murray, Keith A., *The Modocs and their War* (Norman, 1959).

Map 57. Indian Lands

Bureau of American Ethnology, *Indian Land Cessions in the United States.* Compiled by C. C. Royce, Annual Report 1896–7, pt. 2 (Washington, 1899).

Reports of the Department of the Interior from Sacramento, Riverside and Phoenix offices, "Lands Under Jurisdiction of the Bureau of Indian Affairs as of June 30, 1971."

Map 58. Mission Indian Lands

Department of the Interior Office of Indian Affairs, map entitled *Mission Indian Reservations, California* (1938).

Reports of the Department of Interior, June 30, 1971.

Sutton, Imre, "Land Tenure and Changing Occupance on Indian Reservations in Southern California" (Ph.D. dissertation, University of California, Los Angeles, 1964).

Sutton, Imre, "Private Property in Land Among Reservation Indians in Southern California," *Yearbook of the Association of Pacific Coast Geographers*, Vol. 29 (1967), 69–89.

Map 59. State Boundaries

Elliott, Janet, "The History of the Seat of Government of California," (Unpublished M.A. thesis, College of the Pacific, 1942))

Ellison, William Henry, *A Self Governing Dominion California, 1849–1860* (Berkeley, 1950).

Foote, Francis Seeley, "The Boundary Line Between California and Oregon," *California Historical Society Quarterly*, Vol. XIX, No. 4 (Dec., 1940), 368–72.

Hendry, Geo W., "Francisco Palou's Boundary Marker," *California Historical Society Quarterly*, Vol. V, No. 4 (Dec., 1926), 321–27.

Landrum, Francis S., "A Major Monument: Oregon-California Boundary," *Oregon Historical Quarterly*, Vol. LXXII, No. 1 (Mar., 1971), 5–53.

Leslie, Lewis B., "The International Boundary Survey From San Diego to the Gila River," *California Historical Society Quarterly*, Vol. IX, No. 1 (Mar., 1930), 3–15.

McDow, Roberta Blakely, "A Study of the Proposals to Divide the State of California from 1860 to 1952" (M.A. thesis, College of the Pacific, 1952).

State of California, *Interstate Compact Defining the Boundary Between the States of Arizona and California* (Sacramento, 1965).

Van Zandt, Franklin K., *Boundaries of the United States and the Several States*, Geological Survey Bulletin 1212 (Washington, GPO, 1966).

Map 60. Principal Meridians and Base Lines

Billington, Ray Allen, *Westward Expansion* (New York, 1949).

Brown, Gertrude L., "Initial Monuments for California's Base and Meridian Lines," *California Historical Society Quarterly*, Vol. XXXIV, No. 1 (Mar., 1955), 1–18.

Manuel of Instructions for the Survey of the Public Lands of the United States 1947 (Washington, 1947).

USGS, *State of California, Base Map* 1:1,000,000 (1949, edition 1954).

Maps 61–64. County Boundary Changes

The basic source for the county structure of California is Owen C. Coy, *California County Boundaries* (Berkeley, 1923).

Map 65. 1970 County Structure

Bureau of the Census, Department of Commerce, "1970 Census of Population, Advance Report, California" (Washington, 1971).

Map 66. County Seats

Hyink, Bernard L., Seyom Brown, and Ernest W. Thacker, *Government in California* (New York, 1959, 1971).

Turner, Henry A., and John A. Vieg, *The Government and Politics of California* (New York, 1960).

Map 67. Railroad Grant Lands

Brown, James L., *The Mussel Slough Tragedy* (n.p., 1958).

Daggett, Stuart, *Chapters on the History of the Southern Pacific* (New York, 1922).

Dana, Samuel Trask, and Myron Krueger, *California Lands: Ownership, Use, and Management* (Washington, 1958).

Evans, Cerinda W., *Collis Potter Huntington* (2 vols., Newport News, Va., 1954).

Lands Granted to the Southern Pacific Railroad in California, Map of (San Francisco, 1918).

Lavender, David, *The Great Persuader* (New York, 1969).

Lewis, Oscar, *The Big Four* (New York, 1938, 1971).

Myrick, David F., "Land Grants: Aids and Benefits to the Government and Railroads and to the Southern Pacific Company" (mim. of the Southern Pacific Co., 1969).

Taylor, Paul, "Water, Land, and People in the Great Valley," *The American West*, Vol. V, No. 2 (March, 1968), 24–29; 68–71.

Tutorow, Norman E., *Leland Stanford: Man of Many Careers* (Menlo Park, 1971).

Map 68. Railroads

California, 1926 Edition of the Official Railroad, Map of (scale, 1″ = 15 miles).

Hanft, Robert M., *Pine Across the Mountain: California's McCloud River Railroad* (San Marino, 1971).

Johnson, Hank, *Railroads of the Yosemite Valley* (Long Beach, 1963).

Kneiss, Gilbert H., *Bonanza Railroads* (Stanford, 1941).

Kneiss, Gilbert H., *Redwood Railways* (Berkeley, 1956).

Lavender, *The Great Persuader*.

McAfee, Ward, "Communities in Conflict: California's Railroad Development and Regulation, 1850–1911" (unpublished manuscript used by courtesy of Golden West Books, San Marino).

Poor's Manual of Railroads (New York, 1870–1930).

Thompson, Rolland C., "The Railroad Boom in the

Los Angeles Area, 1886–1890" (M.A. thesis, Claremont College, 1942).

Wagner, Jack R., *Short Line Junction: A Collection of California-Nevada Railroads* (Fresno, 1956).

Map 69. Great Sheep and Cattle Ranches, circa 1900

Cameron, K., Engineer, files of, (Miller & Lux Engineering Office, Los Banos):
Gilroy File 1913–34.
Rancho San Lorenzo (Peachtree) file 1920–30.
Santa Clara and San Benito Counties file 1925–26.

Miller & Lux Inc., *Map of San Joaquin Valley Lands in Stanislaus, Merced, Madera & Fresno Counties* (n.p. 1935?).

Outcalt, John, *History of Merced County* (Los Angeles, 1925).

Radcliffe, Corwin, *History of Merced County* (Merced, 1940).

Documents in Granville L. Rogers private library, Dos Palos, California:
Report on title of property of the Lux Divided Lands Incorporated, A Corporation in Monterey County (n.d., 17 pp.)
Deed, Henry Miller to Charles Lux and Charles Lux to Henry Miller, dated May 19, 1883. Peachtree Ranch. (4 pp.)
Miller and Lux, lands adjoining San Lorenzo Rancho (Peachtree, n.d., 1 p.)
Deed, Charles Kerr to Henry Miller and Charles Lux, dated Sept. 3, 1875. (Recorded at the request of Wells Fargo and Co., Sept. 4, A.D. 1875 at 15 minutes past 3:00 P.M. in Book 5 of conveyances page 4144 followings Monterey County Records, Peachtree Ranch, 61 pp.)
Plats, Monterey Co. Lands, Mar. 6, 1888 (21 pp.).

San Benito County, Official Map of, (1891).

Santa Clara County, Official Map of, (1903).

Treadwell, Edward F., *The Cattle King* (Fresno, 1931, 1950). .

Winchell, Lilbourne Alsip, *History of Fresno County and the San Joaquin County Valley* (Fresno, 1933).

Map 70. Great Sheep and Cattle Ranches, circa 1900

Ballis, George, "Profile of Power Structure in San Joaquin Valley" (12 p. mim., Piedmont, n.d.).

Bonsal, Stephen, *Edward Fitzgerald Beale* (New York, 1912).

Buffington, M. W., Official Map of Kern County, 1910. (manuscript in Kern Co. Surveyor's office, Bakersfield).

Cameron, Engineer K. "El Chicote Rancho File, 1933–1934" (M/L Engineering Office).

Crow, Earle, *Men of El Tejon: Empire in the Tehachapis* (Los Angeles, 1957).

Kern County Land Company, Annual Reports 1892–1966.

Kern County Land Company, Descriptive Brochures of Rosedale and other Colonies, 1892, in Huntington Library, San Marino.

Kern County, Official Map of, (1892).

McIntire, Frank C., *Official Map of Kings County* (1908).

McCarthy, Dennis (Vice President and General Counsel, Tejon Ranch Co.) letters and map to Ynez D. Haase, Sept. 4, 1970, May 16, 1972.

Magruder, Genevieve Kratka, *The Upper San Joaquin Valley, 1772–1870* (Bakersfield, 1950).

Means, Thomas, "Report on Farming Lands, Miller and Lux Inc., Southern Division Kern and Kings Counties, California" (n.p., 1919).

Miller and Lux, Inc., Map of Lands in Kings, Tulare, Kern and San Luis Obispo Counties, California (n.d., 1935?).

Morgan, Wallace M., *History of Kern County California* (Los Angeles, 1914).

Robinson, W. W., *The Story of Kern County* (Bakersfield, 1956).

Taylor, "Water, Land, and People in the Great Valley."

Tejon Ranch Company Annual Reports, especially 1971.

Treadwell, *The Cattle King.*

Map 71. Great Sheep: and Cattle Ranches, circa 1900

Bixby-Smith, Sarah, *Adobe Days* (Cedar Rapids, Iowa, 1926).

Cleland, Robert Glass, *The Cattle on a Thousand Hills.*

Cleland, Robert Glass, *The Irvine Ranch of Orange County* (San Marino, 1952).

Hotchkis, Katharine Bixby, "Rancho Los Alamitos," Balboa, 1964 (manuscript in Huntington Library, San Marino).

Hough, John Cushing, "Abel Stearns" (Ph. D. dissertation, University of California, Los Angeles, 1961).

"Inventory of the Bixby Records Collection in the Palos Verdes Library and Art Gallery," Los Angeles, 1940 (Works Progress Administration Project).

Robinson, W. W., *Ranchos Become Cities* (Pasadena, 1939).

Map 72. Great Sheep and Cattle Ranches, circa 1900

Acquisition Map, Piedmont Department, Properties, Monterey, San Luis Obispo Counties, Dec. 1937. Hearst Sunical Land and Packing Corp.

Carlson, Oliver, and Ernest Sutherland Bates, *Hearst: Lord of San Simeon* (New York, 1936).

Lamb, Frank W. and Gertrude, *San Simeon: A Brief History* (Fullerton, 1971).

Letters dated May 31, 1972, and June 9, 1972, from A. J. Cooke, Sunical Division, The Hearst Corporation, to Y. D. Haase.

Lewis, Oscar, *Fabulous San Simeon: A History of the Hearst Castle* (San Francisco, n.d.).

Older, Fremont, *George Hearst, California Pioneer* (Los Angeles, 1933, 1966).

Personal Conversation between Doris Lemuel Ingles of Ventura, Ca. and Y. D. Haase.

Map 73. Transhumance Sheep Trails, 1865–1905

Austin, Mary, *The Flock* (Boston, 1906).

Los Angeles Times (June 22, 1966).

Wentworth, Edward Norris, *America's Sheep Trails* (Ames, Iowa, 1948).

Map 74. Population Distribution

Bureau of the Census, State of California, 1860, 1900, 1940, 1960.

Durrenberger, Robert, *California: The Last Frontier* (New York, 1969).

Gordon, Margaret S., "Population," in R. W. Durrenberger, *The Geography of California in Essays and Readings* (Los Angeles, 1959).

Map 75. Population 1970

"1970 Census of Population, California: Advance Report," Bureau of the Census, United States Department of Commerce, 1971.

"Is California's People Boom Over?" *U.S. News and World Report*, Vol. 70 (June 21, 1971), 37–8.

"Population Forecasters Foresee a Drop in Public School Enrollment; Advisory Council Calls for Population Controls," *California Journal*, Vol. III, (Feb., 1972), 56–7.

"The Golden State Loses Its Glow," *Newsweek*, Vol. 78 (Aug. 2, 1971), 52.

Map 76. Major Irrigation Systems in the San Joaquin Valley

Cooper, *Aqueduct Empire*.

Harding, *Water in California*.

Morgan, *History of Kern County*.

Outcalt, *History of Merced County*.

USGS, *State of California* (1:1,000,000, shade relief) 1949.

Radcliffe, *History of Merced County*.

Rogers, Granville L., "A History of the Canal System of the Central California Irrigation District Prior to 1940," (6 p. mim., Dos Palos, 1970).

Treadwell, *Cattle King*.

Winchell, *History of Fresno County and the San Joaquin Valley*.

Map 77. Major Man-Made Water Systems

"California State Water Project: 1970," State of California, The Resources Agency, Department of Water Resources, Sacramento.

Cooper, *Aqueduct Empire*.

Seckler, David, Ed., *California Water: A Study in Resource Management* (Berkeley, 1971).

"The California State Water Project Summary: Nineteen-Seventy," Bulletin No. 132–71, State of California, The Resources Agency, Department of Water Resources, Sacramento.

Map 78. Los Angeles Owens River Aqueduct

Chalfont, W. A., *The Story of Inyo* (Bishop, 1922, 1933).

Cooper, *Aqueduct Empire*.

Dasmann, Raymond F., *The Destruction of California* (New York, 1965).

Kinsey, Don J., *The Water Trail: The Story of Owens Valley and the Controversy Surrounding the Efforts of a Great City to Secure the Water Required to Meet the Needs of an Ever-growing Population* (Los Angeles, 1928).

Mayo, Morrow, *Los Angeles* (New York, 1933).

Nadeau, Remi A., *The Water Seekers* (Garden City, 1950).

State of California, *Ownership of Lands in Mono and Owens Basin*, Map (1960) Los Angeles Department of Water and Power, *Water and Power* (1968).

Map 79. Imperial Valley, 1901–1907

Cooper *Aqueduct Empire*.

Force, Edwin T., "The Use of the Colorado River in the United States, 1850–1933" (Ph.D. dissertation, University of California, Berkeley, 1936).

Harding, Sidney T., *Water in California* (Palo Alto, 1960).

Hosmer, Helen, "Imperial Valley," *The American West*, Vol. III, No. 1 (Winter, 1966), 34–49.

Hundley, Jr., Norris, *Dividing the Waters* (Berkeley, 1966).

Imperial Irrigation District, "Historic Salton Sea; Power for Imperial and Coachella Valleys; Imperial Valley Salt Balance" (3 booklets, El Centro, n.d.).

Sykes, Godfrey, *The Colorado Delta* (Washington, 1937).

Waters, Frank, *The Colorado* (New York, 1946).

REFERENCES

Map 80. San Francisco Earthquake and Fire, 1906

Bronson, William, *The Earth Shook, The Sky Burned* (New York, 1959, 1971).

The California Promotion Committee, *Map of Part of San Francisco, California Showing Buildings Constructed and Buildings Under Construction During the Year After the Fire of April 18, 1906* (no scale, San Francisco, 1907).

Thomas, Gordon and Max Morgan Witts, *The San Francisco Earthquake* (New York, 1971).

Wells Fargo Bank History Room, Map of Part of San Francisco, California Showing Buildings Constructed, and Building Under Construction During the Year After Fire of April 18, 1906 (Map No. 7879).

Map 81. Wild Land Fires, 1960–70

"A Week of Wildfire in Southern California," State of California, Division of Forestry (Sacramento, 1967).

Clar, C. Raymond, *Evolution of California's Wildland Fire Protection System.* State of California, Division of Forestry (Sacramento, 1969).

Forest Fire Report, 1955. State of California, Division of Forestry (Sacramento, 1955).

Haase, Ynez D., Letters from State Forest Ranger, Division of Forestry, Sacramento; Fire Control Officer, United States Forest Headquarters at, San Francisco and Angeles, National Forest, Cleveland National Forest, San Bernardino, Los Padres, Tahoe, and Klamath.

Lillard, Richard G., *Eden in Jeopardy* (New York, 1966).

Los Angeles Times, various dates.

The State Forester's Report. State of California, Division of Forestry, (Sacramento, 1960, 1964, 1965, 1966, 1967, 1968, 1970).

Map 82. St. Francis Dam Disaster

Outland, Charles F., *Man-Made Disaster: The Story of St. Francis Dam* (Glendale, 1963).

Teague, Charles C., *Fifty Years a Rancher* (n.p., 1941).

Map 83. 100-Year Floods

California High Water 1968–1969. State of California, Department of Water Resources, Bulletin No. 69–69 (Sacramento, June, 1970).

Flood! State of California, Department of Water Resources, Bulletin No. 161 (Sacramento, Jan., 1965).

Floods of December 1955 in California. Division of Water Resources (Sacramento, Jan., 1956).

Lillard, *Eden in Jeopardy.*

Thompson, Kenneth, "Historic Flooding in the Sacramento Valley," *Pacific Historical Review,* Vol. XXIX, No. 4 (Nov., 1960), 349–360.

Map 84. Santa Barbara Oil Spill

"California: The Great Blob," *Newsweek,* Vol. 73 (Feb. 17, 1969), 31–32.

"California: Another Oil Slick," *Newsweek,* Vol. 73 (Feb. 24, 1969), 37.

Dye, Lee, *Blowout at Platform A,* (Garden City, N.Y., 1971).

Easton, Robert, *Black Tide* (New York, 1972).

"Environment: Tragedy in Oil," *Time,* Vol. 93 (Feb. 14, 1969) 23–25.

"Environment: The Dead Channel," *Time,* Vol. 93 (Feb. 21, 1969), 21.

"Goo Fishes In," *Newsweek,* Vol. 74 (Dec. 8, 1969), 100.

"Oil on Troubled Waters," *Time,* Vol. 95 (Feb. 9, 1970), 46.

Molotch, Harvey, "Santa Barbara Oil Slick," *Ramparts,* Vol. 8 (Nov., 1969), 43–51.

National Science Foundation, Division of Graduate Education in Science and Marine Science Institute, University of California, Santa Barbara, *Santa Barbara Oil Symposium, Offshore Petroleum Production, An Environmental Inquiry* (Santa Barbara, 1970).

"Oil's Aftermath," *Time,* Vol. 97 (Mar. 1, 1971), 37.

Snell, David, "Iridescent Gift of Death," *Life,* Vol. 66 (June 13, 1969), 22–27.

Map 85. National Forests

Bureau of Land Management Map, *Resources and Recreation, Public Lands, California* (n.d.).

Establishment and Modification of National Forest Boundaries: A Chronological Record 1891–1962 (Washington, 1962).

Forests of California, State of California, Division of Natural Resources (Sacramento, 1955).

Freeman, Orville L., and Michael Krome, *The National Forests of America* (New York, 1968).

Natural Resources of California, United States Department of Interior (Washington, 1951).

Our National Forests, United States Department of Agriculture Information Bulletin #49 (Washington, 1951).

National Forests in California, United States Forest Service (n.p., n.d.).

Map 86. Major Army Installations During World War II

"Military Installations in the State of California During World War II," in a letter from Albert V. Blair,

Acting Chief, Reference Service Branch, National Archives and Records Center, to Warren A. Beck, July 27, 1970.

Scanlon, Tom, Ed., *Army Times: Guide to Army Posts* (Harrisburg, Pa., 1963).

Sullivan, Charles J., *Army Posts and Towns* (Los Angeles, 1942).

Map 87. Major Army Air Force Installations During World War II

"Air Corps Station List," Aug. 25, 1941 (Air Force Museum, Dayton).

Craven, Wesley Frank, and James Lea Cate, *The Army Air Forces in World War II: Men and Planes*, Vol. VI (Chicago, 1955).

Harley, R. Bruce, "The Beginnings of March Field 1917–1918," *Southern California Quarterly*, Vol. LIII, no. 2 (June, 1971), 147–58).

MacCloskey, Monro, *The United States Air Force* (New York, 1967).

"Military Installations in the State of California During World War II."

"U.S. Army and Navy Directory of Airfields," Feb. 1, 1944 (Air Force Museum, Dayton).

Map 88. Major Navy and Marine Installation During World War II

Brochure, Eleventh Naval District, Jan. 1, 1945 (Port Hueneme Naval Center).

"List of Marine Corps Installation in California During World War II," in letter from Colonel F. C. Caldwell, Director of Marine Corps History to Warren A. Beck, Aug. 3, 1970.

"Locations of Naval Shore Establishments as of 15 February, 1944," Navy Department, Bureau of Yards and Docks.

"Shore Establishment Operating Plan," 11th and 12th Naval Districts (Aug. 1, 1944).

Various Maps showing Marine, Navy, and Coast Guard Installations in Bureau of Yards and Docks In Port Hueneme Naval Center.

Building the Navy's Bases in World War II, United States Navy Department, Bureau of Yards and Docks (2 vols., Washington, 1947).

"U.S. Army and Navy Directory of Airfields."

Map 89. Petroleum Fuels

California Oil and Gas Fields: Supplemental Maps and Data Sheet, State of California, Department of Conservation, Division of Oil and Gas (Sacramento, 1969).

"Mineral Resources of California," Bulletin 191.

Map 90. Gold and Mercury

Caughey, *Gold is the Cornerstone*.

"Mineral Resources of California," Bulletin 191.

Map 91. Minerals

"Mineral Resources of California," Bulletin 191.

Map 92. Borax Mines and Roads of the Late 1800's

Letter, Carla M. Block, Death Valley National Monument, National Park Service, to Ynez D. Haase, Jan. 21, 1971.

"100 Years of U.S. Borax," *Pioneer* (Mar.–Apr., 1972), 4–12.

The Story of Borax (Los Angeles, 1969).

Weight, Harold W., *20 Mule Team Days in Death Valley* (Twentynine Palms, 1955).

Map 93. Major Agricultural Areas

Braun, Elmer W., *Agriculture in the Economy of California* (Sacramento, 1967).

California Crop and Livestock Reporting Service, "California Field Crops Statistics, 1866–1946" (Sacramento, 1947).

Fite, Gilbert C., *The Farmers' Frontier 1865–1900* (New York, 1966).

Hartman, *California and Man*.

Hutchison, *California Agriculture*.

Map 94. Agriculture—Livestock

California Crop and Livestock Reporting Service, "California Agriculture 1970" (Sacramento, 1971).

Map 95. Agriculture—Citrus

"California Agriculture 1970."

California Crop and Livestock Reporting Service, "California Fruit and Nut Crops 1909–1955," (Sacramento, 1956).

California Crop and Livestock Reporting Service, "1970 California Fruit & Nut Acreage," (Sacramento, 1971).

Map 96. Agriculture—Other Fruits and Vegetables

"California Agriculture," 1970.

"California Fruit and Nut Crops 1909–1955."

"1970 California Fruit & Nut Acreage."

Map 97. Agriculture—Major Field Crops

"California Agriculture 1970."

"California Field Crops Statistics, 1866–1946."

Map 98. Lumber

Adams, Kramer, "Earliest Use of Redwood," (Oct., 1969, n.p.), Staff Report furnished by Mr. Adams.

Adams, Kramer, *The Redwoods*. New York: Popular Library, n.d.

Baker, Harold L., *California's Timber Industries: Some Facts and Figures*. Forest Service U.S. Department of Agriculture, Pacific Southwest Forest and Range Experiment Station, Misc. Paper No. 38, Sept., 1959.

Barrette, B. R., D. R. Gedney, and D. D. Oswald, *California Timber Industries 1968—Mill Characteristics and Wood Supply*. State of California, Division of Forestry, Sacramento.

Brown, Alan K. *Sawpits in the Spanish Redwoods* (San Mateo, 1966).

Bunje, Emil, "History of the California Lumber Industry" (unpublished WPA manuscript in Huntington Library, San Marino, 1936).

Burgess, Sherwood D., "Lumbering in Hispanic California," *California Historical Society Quarterly*, Vol. XLI, No. 3 (Sept., 1962), 237–48.

Burgess, Sherwood D., "References Made to Early Logging in Southern Redwood Empire," Seminar Report, (n.p., n.d.).

Burgess, Sherwood D., "The Forgotten Redwoods of the East Bay," *California Historical Society Quarterly*, Vol. XXX, No. 1 (Mar., 1951), 1–14.

Clar, C. Raymond, *California Government and Forestry: From Spanish Days–1927*. Sacramento State Printing Office, 1959.

Clar, C. Raymond, "Harvesting and Use of Lumber in Hispanic California," *Sacramento Corral of Westerners* (1971), 1–12.

Lamm, W. E., *Lumbering in Klamath* (n.p., n.d.).

May, Richard H., *A Century of Lumber Production in California and Nevada*. Forest Service, U.S. Department of Agriculture, California Forest and Range Experiment Station, Forest Survey Release No. 20, June, 1953.

Oswald, Daniel D., California's Forest Industries—Prospects for the Future, Forest Service U.S. Department of Agriculture, Pacific Northwest Forest and Range Experiment Station, USDA Forest Service Resource, Bulletin PNW-35.

Stanger, Frank M., *Sawmills in the Redwoods: Logging in the San Francisco Peninsula 1849–1967* (San Mateo, 1967).

Map 99. Fisheries

California Ocean Fisheries Resources to the Year 1960 State of California, Department of Fish and Game (Sacramento, 1961).

Godsil, H. C., *The High Seas Tuna Fishery of California*, State of California, Division of Fish and Game (Sacramento, 1938).

Hermann, Richard F. G., and John G. Carlisle, Jr., *The*

California Marine Fish Catch for 1968 and Historical Review 1916–1968, State of California, Department of Fish and Game (Sacramento, 1970).

Lyles, Charles H., *Fishing Statistics of the United States 1966* (Washington: 1968).

Map 100. Conservation Corps Camps

Harper, Charles Price, *The Administration of the Civilian Conservation Corps* (Clarksburg, W. Va., 1939).

Leuchtenberg, William E., *Franklin D. Roosevelt and the New Deal 1932–1940* (New York, 1963).

Salmond, John A., *The Civilian Conservation Corps, 1933–1942: A New Deal Case Study* (Durham, 1967).

State of California, Map of Emergency Conservation Corps Camps (Washington, Base Map 1928, scale 1″ = 12 miles).

Swain, Donald C., "The National Park Service and the New Deal, 1933–1940," *Pacific Historical Review*, Vol. XLI, No. 3 (Aug., 1972), 312–32.

Summary Reports of the Director of Emergency Conservation Work (Washington, 1933–43).

Map 101. Political Districts

Bemis, George W., "Sectionalism and Representation in the California State Legislature, 1910–1931" (Ph.D. dissertation, University of California, Berkeley, 1935).

"Does Apportionment Have to be This Way," *California Journal*, Vol. III, 2 (Feb., 1972), 58–63.

"Easy Congressional Reapportionment Gets Crunched Between Rival Demands of Republicans and Democrats in the Legislature," *California Journal*, Vol. II, 10 (Nov., 1971), 302–303.

Hardy, Leroy C., "The California Reapportionment of 1951" (Ph.D. dissertation University of California, Los Angeles, 1955).

"Legislative Struggles with Reapportionment Problems Behind the Scenes," *California Journal*, Vol. II, 6 (June, 1971), 168–74.

Los Angeles *Times*, Nov. 29, 1973.

Pitt, Leonard, *California Controversies: Major Issues in the History of the State* (New York, 1968).

"Reapportionment Decision of the California Supreme Court," filed Nov. 28, 1973. The Legislature of the State of California et. al v. Ed Reinecke, as Lieutenant Governor of the State etc, et, al; *California Reports*, 1973.

"Reapportionment Reels Toward the Court as Republicans Deadlock Democrats," *California Journal*, Vol. II. 11 (Dec., 1971), 328–9.

"Reports and Recommendations of Special Masters on Reapportionment," California State Supreme Court, Aug. 31, 1973. (Also Appendix A and Appendices B and C).

"Senators and Assemblymen Remain Divided on Re-apportionment as Time Runs Out," *California Journal*, Vol. II, 9 (Oct., 1971), 264–65, 268.

"Supreme Court Rules Against Reapportionment Plans, Reapportionment Commission," *California Journal*, Vol. III, 1 (Jan., 1972), 7–9.

REFERENCES

INDEX

Numbers in this index refer to map numbers; there are no page numbers. Numbers in italics mean that the item will be found on the map.